CONGRESS

CONGRESS

A Performance Appraisal

Andrew J. Taylor

North Carolina State University

WESTVIEW PRESS

A MEMBER OF THE PERSEUS BOOKS GROUP

Westview Press was founded in 1975 in Boulder, Colorado, by notable publisher and intellectual Fred Praeger. Westview Press continues to publish scholarly titles and high-quality undergraduate- and graduate-level textbooks in core social science disciplines. With books developed, written, and edited with the needs of serious nonfiction readers, professors, and students in mind, Westview Press honors its long history of publishing books that matter.

Copyright © 2013 by Westview Press

Published by Westview Press,
A Member of the Perseus Books Group

All rights reserved. Printed in the United States of America. No part of this book may be reproduced in any manner whatsoever without written permission except in the case of brief quotations embodied in critical articles and reviews. For information, address Westview Press, 2465 Central Avenue, Boulder, CO 80301.

Find us on the World Wide Web at www.westviewpress.com.

Every effort has been made to secure required permissions for all text, images, maps, and other art reprinted in this volume.

Westview Press books are available at special discounts for bulk purchases in the United States by corporations, institutions, and other organizations. For more information, please contact the Special Markets Department at the Perseus Books Group, 2300 Chestnut Street, Suite 200, Philadelphia, PA 19103, or call (800) 810-4145, ext. 5000, or e-mail special.markets@perseusbooks.com.

Library of Congress Cataloging-in-Publication Data

Taylor, Andrew J., 1966–
  Congress : a performance appraisal / Andrew J. Taylor.
    pages cm
  Includes bibliographical references and index.
  ISBN 978-0-8133-4572-7 (pbk. : alk. paper)—ISBN 978-0-8133-4573-4 (e-book) (print) 1. United States. Congress. 2. United States. Congress—Evaluation. I. Title.
  JK1041.T395 2013
  328.73–dc23
                            2012035826

10 9 8 7 6 5 4 3 2 1

CONTENTS

PREFACE

To say Congress is unloved is an obvious understatement. It is loathed and the attitude is pervasive; it is not just conveyed by a few populist politicians and influential talking heads in Washington. As a scholar of Congress, I have recognized its faults for many years, but I always thought such a trenchant assessment was unfair. A couple of years ago I finally decided to stop contemplating and actually test the proposition by writing this book. In it, I establish basic aspirations for Congress informed by contemporary theorists and the country's Founders. These are then fashioned into more specific targets—I call them benchmarks—by examining what peer legislatures and the House and Senate of the past have done. I evaluate performance by applying the benchmarks to the Congress of today.

Readers are unlikely to interpret the appraisal as a withering assault. A few, however, might view it as an apology, an excuse for an ossified and corrupt body with an uncaring and self-obsessed membership. They would be wrong. It is a comprehensive, accessible, and, I believe, evenhanded evaluation of our national legislature. It is an effort to set the record straight, or at least straighter, for a broad audience—students, scholars, practitioners, and, indeed, anyone with more than a passing interest in the governmental institution the Framers did, after all, decide to make the subject of Article I of the Constitution.

Because this book is essentially the culmination of more than two decades' worth of thinking about Congress, it would be impossible for me to thank everyone who has contributed to it. I need to make space, however, to mention some particularly important people and experiences. My wife, Jennifer, and children, Matthew and Lindsay, have been a constant source of encouragement and support. So have my parents, John and Ronnie Taylor. My editors at Westview, Toby Wahl and Ada Fung, were always efficient, always helpful. A number of anonymous reviewers spent many valuable hours reading versions of the manuscript. I am very grateful to them. More than a decade ago I was the American Political Science Association's (APSA) William A. Steiger Congressional Fellow. It was a formative year and helped shape not only my knowledge of Congress but my respect for it too. The School of Public and International Affairs at North Carolina State University provided financial assistance through a summer grant and its faculty—my colleagues—a stimulating environment in which to undertake this project. Anyone who reads the book can quite quickly tell I have stood on the shoulders of scholars in the APSA's legislative studies section. They make a great community of which I am proud to be a part. I also want to recognize two professors, both very dear to me, who passed on during the duration of this project. My graduate adviser Howard Reiter made me a political scientist; my good friend Walter Lackey made me a better one.

Because this is a book motivated by reason, a seemingly rare commodity in the political world these days, I dedicate it to my brother Simon, a man both open in heart and level in head.

1

THE MUCH-MALIGNED LEGISLATIVE BRANCH

Congress is extremely unpopular. In the months leading up to the 2010 midterm elections, only about 20 percent of Americans approved of the job the institution was doing. Several polls that spring had the figure as low as 15. This put Congress well behind the other branches of government—President Obama's job approval was around 45 percent, the Supreme Court's somewhere in the mid-50s. Gallup reported consistently during the summer and fall of 2010 that about 60 percent of Americans—the highest proportion on record—believed most members did not deserve re-election. A March 2010 poll undertaken by the Pew Research Center for the People and the Press asked 749 Americans to provide one word that best described their current impressions of Congress. Eighty-six percent offered something negative; "dysfunctional," "corrupt," and "self-serving" were the top three responses.[1] The opprobrium did not distinguish by party. A September 2010 Gallup poll revealed 33 percent of Americans approved of the job congressional Democrats were doing, 32 percent that of congressional Republicans. A grassroots Internet-based movement led by groups like Get Out of Our House called on voters to defeat all incumbents who were running for re-election.

If anything, matters worsened after the election. During the busy lame-duck session in December, Congress had reached its lowest level of public support since Gallup had begun surveying Americans on the topic in 1974.[2] Although the House came under Republican control after the party, in the words of President Obama, "shellacked" the Democrats and picked up sixty-three seats, the general dissatisfaction continued at historic levels during the early months of the 112th Congress. When the Obama administration and congressional Republican leaders warred over an extension to the nation's borrowing authority in the summer of 2011, 77 percent of respondents to a CNN/Opinion Research Center (ORC) poll described the principals' behavior as being like that of "spoiled children"; only 17 percent felt they had acted as "responsible adults."[3] In September 2011 only 12 percent of respondents to a CBS News/*New York Times* poll said they approved of the job the institution was doing; with the economy still extremely sluggish the figure reached a miserable 9 percent in October. According to Gallup's poll the rating recovered only slightly in the spring of 2012, by which time a political action committee (PAC) called the Campaign for Primary Accountability was diligently raising money to purge the House of its incumbents.[4]

It has not always been this way. As Figure 1.1 demonstrates, approval ratings were similarly low for a short while in the late 1970s and early 1990s, but at that time the public lacked confidence in just about all public officials—Jimmy Carter's and Bill Clinton's approval ratings were about fifteen percentage points lower than Barack Obama's scores—and the intensity of the hostility to Congress was short lived.[5] In the aftermath of 9/11, moreover, there was some hope the federal legislature would again be seen as a body fit for the world's greatest democracy. Whether the result of Congress's defiant response to its selection as an Al Qaeda target or its swift action on a variety of proposals to put the country back together again and send it off on the trail of terrorists, the institution's public approval rating climbed as high as 84 percent in a Gallup poll of late 2001. That seems such a long time ago now. By contrast, the public's current mood is especially dark. It does not much like its political leadership and clearly Congress is a particular object of its anger.

It is also not like this elsewhere. Although citizens across the world tend to hold their parliaments in lower esteem than they do their civil services and military institutions, support for the work of legislative bodies is higher abroad than it is in the United States. Since 2006 the World Economic Forum has reported that business executives in Canada, Germany, and the United Kingdom all rank their parliaments as more "effective" than do their counterparts in this country. The World Values Survey taken in the middle part of the last decade revealed approximately 30–40 percent of respondents in western European countries had a "great deal" or "quite a lot" of confidence in their national legislature. This was about double the figure for Americans and Congress (Griffin 2010, 362).

Why Americans Dislike Congress
Scandal and More Scandal

For most of us, it is not difficult to understand why Congress generates these feelings. It seems perpetually mired in scandal. Every time we open a newspaper or turn on cable news there is evidence to confirm Mark Twain's aphorism that "there is no distinctly native criminal class except Congress."[6]

In 2008, for example, Rick Renzi (R-AZ) was charged with thirty-five counts of violating federal law. He had sold real estate to a business associate and then introduced legislation to increase its value dramatically by making it the subject of a federal land

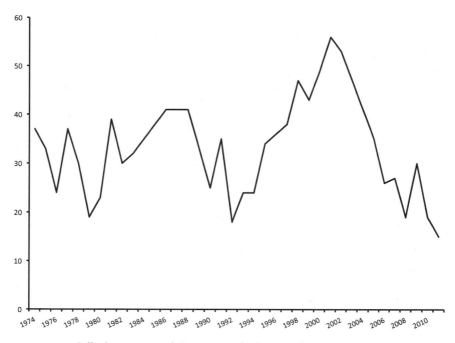

FIGURE I.I Gallup's mean annual Congressional job approval scores, 1974–2011

swap. He also diverted insurance premium money into his campaign treasury. Reporters then suspected Renzi of working the Bush Justice Department to have the US district attorney investigating his case fired. In 2005, Rep. Randy "Duke" Cunningham (R-CA) resigned after admitting to receiving gifts from the head of a defense company in return for his efforts to secure tens of millions of dollars in government contracts. The next March he was sentenced to over eight years in prison. The Cunningham story unfolded at the same time a number of Republican House members were caught up in a scandal involving the brash and influential lobbyist Jack Abramoff. Rep. Bob Ney (R-OH) resigned in 2006 and was later sentenced to thirty months for granting Abramoff, his associates, and often unwitting clients favors such as introducing legislation, inserting statements into the *Congressional Record*, and generating government business. In return Ney received such luxuries as foreign trips and the use of boxes at sporting events. Rep. John Doolittle (R-CA) resigned in 2009 after it was discovered his wife and chief of staff had been on Abramoff's payroll and the congressman had received gifts and campaign contributions from the lobbyist. Doolittle personally promoted the interests of the lobbyist's biggest clients, the Northern Mariana Islands and several Indian tribes. Five congressional staffers were directly connected to Abramoff's schemes and pled guilty to charges.[7]

Democrats have peddled influence for personal gain just as assiduously. In 2002 Rep. James Traficant (D-OH) became the first member expelled from the House in more than twenty years after he was convicted on ten counts of bribery, tax evasion, and racketeering for taking campaign funds for personal use. He served seven years in prison. Sen. Roland Burris (D-IL) was suspected of striking a deal with Gov. Rod Blagojevich (D-IL) so that he could be named to the seat vacated by Barack Obama when he left for the White House. Blagojevich was sentenced to fourteen years and Rep. Jesse L. Jackson, Jr., (D-IL) was caught up in the scandal. In 2011 the former chair of the Ways and Means Committee Rep. Charlie Rangel (D-NY) was tried and then convicted and censured by the full House for tax evasion, inappropriate use of member privileges, and wrongful leasing of property. Rep. William Jefferson (D-LA) received gifts for himself and family members in exchange for assisting a company in its dealings in Africa and the United States. Several aides were indicted, and Jefferson was stripped of committee membership by fellow Democrats after he was re-elected in 2006. He then went on to lose his very safe Democratic district in 2008 and was later sentenced to thirteen years in prison. The episode is perhaps best known for the discovery of $90,000 in the congressman's freezer and a controversial FBI search of his congressional office.

The biggest fish to be found guilty of political corruption in recent years, however, was former House majority leader Tom DeLay (R-TX). DeLay was first elected to the House from the Houston suburbs in 1984 and quickly rose through the Republican ranks. He was Speaker Newt Gingrich's (R-GA) whip immediately after the party captured control of the House for the first time in forty years in the 1994 elections. Known as the Hammer for his aggressive tactics and fierce partisanship—he co-led the K Street Project, an effort to pressure interest groups into hiring only Republicans—DeLay orchestrated Rep. Dennis Hastert's (R-IL) rise to the Speakership after Gingrich resigned in 1998. In 2003, after his predecessor Rep. Dick Armey (R-TX) retired, DeLay took his seat as the number two member of the House.

DeLay was accused of numerous abuses. He was closely connected to Jack Abramoff, having been on an infamous golfing trip to Scotland with the lobbyist. Indeed, DeLay's deputy chief of staff Tony Rudy left to work with Abramoff at his company Greenberg Traurig. A chief of staff, Ed Buckham, remains under investigation for close links with Abramoff. But it was for his fundraising in Texas state legislative races that DeLay was convicted. In an ultimately successful effort to secure a Republican majority in Austin willing to conduct a controversial and unscheduled congressional redistricting, DeLay directed corporate cash through his PAC to seven candidates for state legislature so as to hide the funds' source. He was found guilty of felony money laundering by a state court in November 2010.

Of course, there have been sex scandals as well. Rep. Mark Foley (R-FL) resigned from Congress just before the 2006 elections after it was discovered he had sent sexually suggestive electronic messages to teenage male pages. House Republican leaders were roundly criticized for being unresponsive to earlier warnings about Foley's conduct. Sen. Larry Craig (R-ID) was arrested for lewd conduct in a Minneapolis airport men's restroom in the summer of 2007. Sen. David Vitter's (R-LA) phone number was discovered during part of the investigation into "DC Madam" Deborah Jeane Palfrey's escort service. Vitter quickly came out and admitted marital infidelity and a connection with the operation. He stayed in the Senate. Palfrey was convicted and later killed herself. Rep. Vito Fossella (R-NY) declined to run for re-election in 2008 after it became public knowledge that he had fathered a child with a woman who was not his wife. Fossella's problems were compounded by a DUI arrest at the time the affair hit the news. Rep. Eric Massa (D-NY) resigned in March 2010 after a House investigation of claims that he groped male staff was revealed. Sen. John Ensign (R-NV) resigned in 2011 following press reports that his parents paid money to a former top aide whose wife had had an affair with the senator. The Senate's ethics committee later found substantial evidence Ensign had violated federal law. Rep. Christopher Lee (R-NY) resigned suddenly in February 2011 after it was discovered he had essentially solicited sex on Craigslist. In May, Rep. Anthony Weiner (D-NY) used the Internet to send a lewd photo of himself to an unsuspecting Seattle woman. It was later revealed he had used social networks to make advances to women on a regular basis. When a porn star claimed she had received inappropriate messages from him, Weiner could no longer deflect the concerted push for his resignation within the Democratic Party, and he stepped down. Then in July Rep. David Wu (D-OR), who, according to staff, had been behaving erratically for some months, was accused of an aggressive and unwanted sexual encounter with a teenage girl. When added to previous allegations about sexual misconduct from his college days, the charge effectively forced the congressman's resignation.

These episodes have merely built upon a foundation of disillusionment dug largely by scandals since the 1960s. It was then that Congress first aggressively and systematically investigated and prosecuted ethics violations—both bodies created select committees on standards of official conduct in the wake of incidents involving Bobby Baker, Sen. Lyndon B. Johnson's (D-TX) chief of staff from his days as majority leader, and Rep. Adam Clayton Powell (D-NY). Four scandals were particularly harmful, largely because they involved so many members. The Koreagate investigation of the mid-1970s centered upon the South Korean government's efforts to prevent a US military withdrawal from its peninsula. Through a businessman called Tongsun Park, the South Koreans channeled bribes and favors to as many as ten Democratic House members, of whom three were censured or reprimanded and one was convicted and sentenced to prison. In the Abscam scandal of the late 1970s and early 1980s, the FBI used a fictional sheikh to offer money in return for political favors. Six lawmakers were convicted of bribery. Five senators were investigated for their improper efforts to protect Charles Keating's savings and loan from federal investigators in the late 1980s, of whom one, Alan Cranston (D-CA), was rebuked formally by the Senate's ethics committee. In the early 1990s a series of investigations into the operations of the House Bank and Post Office discovered many members had overdrawn their accounts for a prolonged period and others had laundered money using postage stamps and postal vouchers. Four former members were convicted or pled guilty on charges related to the banking scandal, two, including Rep. Dan Rostenkowski (D-IL), the chair of the Ways and Means Committee, went to prison for their roles in the post office affair. In fact the 1976–1990 period was particularly bad for Congress. For these and other indiscretions, a total of four House members were censured and seven formally reprimanded. Two senators—Herman Talmadge (D-GA) in 1979 and David Durenberger (R-MN) in 1990—were censured.

Scandal even surrounded two House Speakers at the end of the twentieth century. Rep. Jim Wright (D-TX) resigned in 1989 after the House's ethics committee issued a report criticizing his acceptance of honoraria and royalties for a book he had written as well as efforts to use his official position to secure a job for his wife.[8] In 1997 Newt Gingrich was fined $300,000 by the body's ethics committee for misleading its investigation into possible misuse of funds generated by a college course the speaker taught.[9]

It is certainly true that Congress has attempted to clean up its act. When the Republicans took power in 1995, both bodies increased registration requirements for lobbyists. They also instituted a gift ban that prohibited privately paid recreational travel and greatly reduced the value of meals and presents members and their staff could receive from official representatives of organized interests. When the Democrats vaulted into House and Senate majorities after the 2006 elections, they secured passage of the Honest Leadership and Open Government Act. The legislation restricted the ability of departing members to lobby their former colleagues, placed significant limits on the kind of travel members could undertake, and established a comprehensive ban on gifts. In 2008, the House established the Office of Congressional Ethics—a body made up of outsiders granted the authority to initiate investigations against members suspected of unethical behavior. All this had little effect on Americans' views of legislators' integrity, however. According to an April 2011 Rasmussen poll, 43 percent of respondents believed most members of Congress were corrupt. A Gallup November 2009 poll revealed 55 percent of Americans believed members of Congress had "low" or "very low" "honesty and ethical standards." This was the highest level of distrust reported for lawmakers since Gallup began the survey in the late 1970s—greater than that of both stockbrokers and car salespeople.[10]

Self-Obsession

Many Americans have a theory about this behavior. Senators and representatives are believed to be, in the famous words of political scientist David Mayhew (1974a), "single-minded seekers of reelection." Everything they do is interpreted by the press and public alike as a way of enhancing their chances of being returned to Washington—whether to accumulate further power or feather their own nests. This would not be so bad if it came with an energetic commitment to constituent needs and the broader public interest. But the citizenry has a seemingly unshakeable belief that members are intensely self-interested and care little for anyone or anything but themselves and their own political careers. A June 2010 Gallup poll revealed that, among those who felt most members did not deserve to be re-elected that fall, about a third came to their opinion because they saw legislators as self-absorbed and unconcerned with the everyday problems Americans faced. The other two-thirds split on their reasons—many cited members were doing a bad job, focusing on the wrong issues, or had just been in Congress too long.[11]

Intensive efforts to secure re-election and a fundamental neglect of the public's interests are not inconsistent, at least in the minds of many citizens. Members exploit their time in Washington to extract campaign contributions from lobbyists. Every night Congress is in town, fundraisers are held all across the city. Legislation provides an opportunity to bolster campaign coffers too—as recently as 2010 the Office of Congressional Ethics recommended, but the House Ethics Committee refused, an investigation of the scheduling of fundraisers with Wall Street executives by seven representatives during the House's deliberation on the financial regulatory system overhaul bill.[12] A Center on Congress survey conducted by Indiana University in October 2008 reported 51 percent of respondents believed members listen most to lobbyists; only 11 percent the "voters back home." Roll-call votes, committee assignments, and floor speeches are all seen as ways to advance political careers, not serve the populace. That the system provides tremendous incentives for legislators to form such "unremitting electoral preoccupations" seems beside the point (King 1997). Primary elections, a fully private campaign finance system, short terms (at least for the House), and weak political party organizations have all conspired to create a "permanent campaign" in which issues of governance and any desire to make good public policy are pushed to the side.[13] A March 2010 Pew Research poll reported 52 percent of respondents believed "the political system can work fine, the members are the problem," compared to 38 percent who held the opinion "most members have good intentions it is the political system that is broken."

Partisanship and Polarization

Americans, particularly those who consider themselves political independents or moderates, are also upset by what they see as extreme partisanship on Capitol Hill (Harbridge and Malhotra 2011; Ramirez 2009). Throughout the 2000s the Pew Research Center tracked the public's views on partisanship in Congress and asked whether citizens believed Democrats and Republicans there were "bickering more than usual." Just about all of the time a comfortable majority replied in the affirmative.[14] In a December 2011 United Technologies/*National Journal* poll, 80 percent of respondents believed this to be the case.[15] Prominent middle-of-the-roader Sen. Olympia Snowe (R-ME) cited this as the reason for her retirement from the upper body in February 2012. "The center," *Politico*'s Jonathan Allen (2012) wrote in reaction to Snowe's announcement, is "fleeing" Congress.

These views make sense given congressional behavior. Sometimes the interparty spats seem quite petty and personal. In the summer of 2011, President Obama and House Speaker John Boehner (R-OH) squabbled publicly and apparently unprecedentedly over the timing of a presidential speech to a joint session of Congress. Sometimes rancorous arguments break out when members of both parties agree on the underlying issue. Americans witnessed many such examples in the spring of 2012. Despite some considerable bipartisan consensus on the measures, Congress passed long-term authorizations of the Violence Against Women Act, highway projects, and the Export-Import Bank only after protracted wrangling. Enactment of such legislation is usually routine and banal. In March, Rep. Barney Frank (D-MA) had his words stricken from the record in a dispute over which party should get the credit for a jobs bill that passed with overwhelming support. In April, Democrats and Republicans agreed action should be taken immediately to prevent a doubling of the interest rate paid on student loans but still contrived to stall a bill that would do precisely that.

More often, however, the conflict is truly substantive. Deep partisan clashes over fiscal policy were a hallmark of 2011. Republicans focused on significant spending cuts and reforms to Medicare and Medicaid; Democrats more on increasing taxes for the wealthiest Americans and protecting spending on research and infrastructure. Absent a dramatic last-minute agreement late into a Friday night, the government would have shut down in April. The same thing would have happened in December without another "midnight" deal. Christmas was "celebrated" with a rancorous partisan argument over how to extend a temporary two percentage point payroll tax cut for tens of millions of workers. The disputes were particularly intense during the summer over what historically had been a rather mundane task of increasing the "debt ceiling," or borrowing authority of the Treasury. A divided Washington only came together on a pact to do so less than two days before a predicted and possibly devastating government default in August.[16] Part of the solution was the Joint Select Committee on Deficit Reduction, or "supercommittee." Consisting of six Democrats and six Republicans, it was designed specifically to overcome partisanship and yet failed spectacularly, unable to come up with a proposal prior to its deadline of late November.

Figure 1.2 reveals these divisions more systematically. It reports the proportion of all recorded votes in both the House and Senate on which a majority of Democrats opposed a majority of Republicans. These are called party unity votes. There are still a significant number of bipartisan votes but the chart makes it clear that in both bodies partisanship on roll calls has been increasing since the late 1960s.

The most direct cause of this partisanship is increased ideological polarization. Congressional Democrats are becoming more liberal; congressional Republicans more

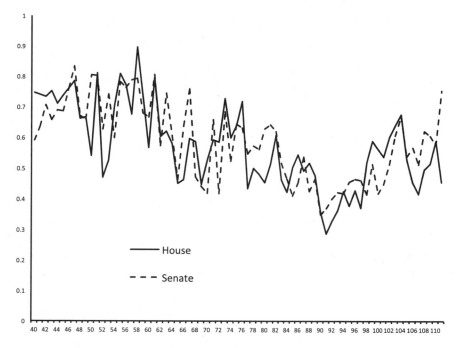

FIGURE 1.2 Party unity votes in Congress, 1869–2010

conservative. In addition, both parties in both houses are becoming more ideologically cohesive. Figures 1.3 and 1.4 display the parties' median first-dimension DW-NOMINATE scores in the Congresses since World War II. These scores have been calculated by political scientists from roll-call data and essentially place each member in each Congress on a single liberal-to-conservative dimension with a value of +1 denoting the conservative pole and −1 the liberal pole (McCarty, Poole, and Rosenthal 2006; Poole and Rosenthal 1997).[17] Polarization is on vivid display in both the House and Senate. The solid lines represent the median scores of all members of the party in the chamber. The spaces between the dashed lines represent the size of one standard deviation in the scores of all members of the party in the chamber. Universally, although at slightly different rates, the solid lines diverge and the dashed ones for each party come together. Figure 1.3 corroborates Thomas Mann and Norman Ornstein's (2012, 51–58) assertion that the polarization is "asymmetric" and Republicans, especially in the House, have become more conservative than the Democrats have become liberal.

Congress watchers have attributed the polarization to many causes. Journalists, particularly, blame the gerrymandering of congressional districts into safe seats.[18] The lack of competition has encouraged members to become more extreme. In the South it has had a particularly profound effect as conservative white voters and liberal black voters

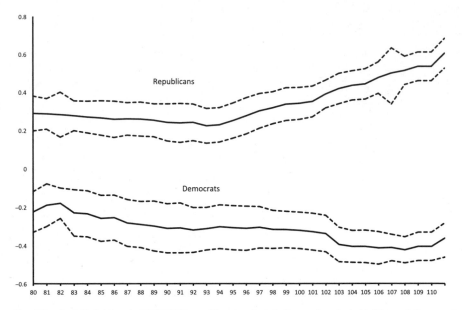

The solid lines denote the first-dimension DW-NOMINATE score of the party median in the Congress. A one-standard deviation span in these scores is revealed by the distance between the dashed lines.

FIGURE 1.3 House party DW-NOMINATE scores, 1947–2010

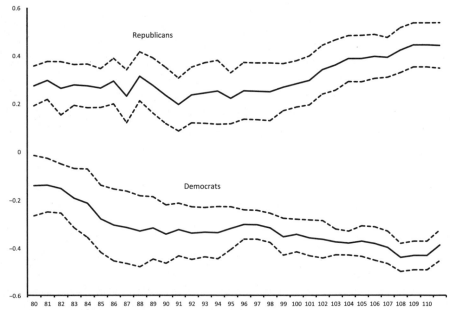

The solid lines denote the first-dimension DW-NOMINATE score of the party median in the Congress. A one-standard deviation span in these scores is revealed by the distance between the dashed lines.

FIGURE 1.4 Senate party DW-NOMINATE scores, 1947–2010

have been segregated by a combination of legislative scheming and federal law—amendments to the Voting Rights Act in 1982 called on many states to draw some districts so that a majority of constituents were from a racial minority. Georgia's delegation on either side of the 1990s redistricting is the most spectacular example. In the 102nd Congress (1991–1993), the last with House districts constructed using 1980 census data, Georgia was represented by one Republican, one African American Democrat, and eight white Democrats. The round of redistricting that followed altered matters dramatically. By the 105th Congress (1997–1999), the state was represented in the house by eight Republicans—including Speaker Newt Gingrich—and three Democrats, all of them black and all of them quite liberal. In fact there was just one white Democrat from the Deep South states of Alabama, Georgia, Louisiana, Mississippi, and South Carolina in the House of the 112th Congress (2011–2013).

More academic types have pushed back against the gerrymander claim, not least because polarization is almost as great in the Senate as it is in the House.[19] They cite other causes of polarization. One is a "sorting" of the population. Bill Bishop (2008), for instance, has written that the coasts and industrial Midwest are increasingly liberal and the South and plains states increasingly conservative because individuals migrate to regions where the majority of the indigenous population shares their values. This has accelerated the decline of the old southern conservative Democrat and liberal northern Republican, or Boll Weevils and Gypsy Moths as they used to be called. The result is uncompetitive elections and further encouragement for ideological extremism. Others view the sorting to be something more than geographical. Mann and Ornstein (2012, 58–67) posit Americans have divided themselves into two separated ideological and partisan communities based upon the sources within the new media—cable television news, talk radio, and the Internet—from which they get their political information. By refusing to expose themselves to alternative viewpoints, citizens allow the media they do consume to strengthen existing attitudes. Matthew Levendusky (2009) argues the electorate has essentially mimicked the polarization of the nation's political leadership as it categorizes itself into two quite distinct political camps.

The recent interparty polarization and intraparty homogenization within Congress has been labeled "conditional party government" by political scientists John Aldrich and David W. Rohde (Aldrich 1995; Aldrich, Berger, and Rohde 2002; Rohde 1991). It not only signifies greater partisanship but contributes to it. A basic tenet of the conditional party government model is that in polarized and homogenous parties rank-and-file members are willing, for the purposes of furthering both their policy and electoral interests, to delegate power over the legislative agenda and floor proceedings to a small group of leaders with policy preferences that reflect theirs. The expectation is that the leaders act in a dogmatic and assertive manner and employ procedures to the benefit of partisan colleagues and the detriment of the opposition (Theriault 2008 134–142). With regards to their control of the legislative agenda, they ensure that bills their party opposes do not come to the floor and those that it supports do (Cox and McCubbins 2005). This is especially the case in the House. Some have demonstrated, however, that leaders of the Senate majority use procedural powers to realize their party's policy goals as well (Den Hartog and Monroe 2008, 2011; Gailmard and Jenkins 2007).

Scholars point to other causes of polarization. Alan Abramowitz (2010) has written recently that it is not the fault of elite strategy and political rules. Voters have just become more partisan and polarized. Nolan McCarty, Keith Poole, and Howard Rosenthal (2006) attribute the polarization to increased income inequality and immigration. It is certainly the case that wealthier Americans have become richer as average incomes have stagnated. For example, in constant dollars the mean household income for the top 5 percent of the population was $295,000 in 2009 compared to $184,000 in 1984; these figures for the middle fifth of the population are $49,500 and $44,100. The previous two decades also witnessed the largest influx of foreigners looking to make a home in the United States since the turn of the twentieth century. About fifteen million individuals have obtained permanent resident status here since 1995.

Regardless of its sources, a "disappearing center," to use Abramowitz's (2010) words, is problematic for two reasons. First, many suggest it contributes to gridlock and a decline in legislative productivity (Harbridge and Malhotra 2011; Jones 2001, 2010). Without moderates to bring their more extreme colleagues together, it is difficult to produce coalitions big enough to push bills through Congress. This, in turn, naturally frustrates Americans desiring a public response to societal problems. It can also weaken their basic trust in government (King 1997; Hetherington 2005).[20] Second, polarization discourages the kind of behavior in members of Congress that the public wants to see. Throughout the summer of 2011 as legislators worked on fiscal problems, significant majorities of Americans called on them to compromise.[21] John Hibbing and Elizabeth Theiss-Morse (2002) demonstrate from analyses of opinion surveys and focus groups that, although sometimes quite partisan themselves, citizens want members of Congress to focus pragmatically on solving problems rather than fighting each other.

The Problems with Process and Policy

The work of Hibbing and his colleagues has identified additional reasons why we do not like Congress. It claims the federal legislature is designed to disappoint. Along with Theiss-Morse, Hibbing argues Americans want their governmental institutions to execute a form of "stealth democracy" in which elected officials listen to public concerns but do not bother the citizenry with details about policy and the political process (Hibbing and Theiss-Morse 2002). In their earlier work the authors had shown that Congress was disliked because it was consultative, inclusive, and slow to act (Hibbing and Theiss-Morse 1995). Americans want its decision-making processes to more closely resemble those of corporations. They just want it to produce. According to a December

2011 United Technologies/*National Journal* poll, more than half of Americans believed the current Congress had "accomplished less" than recent ones. This was by some distance the biggest number since the question was first asked in 1998.[22] President Obama tapped into the feeling by effectively running against a "do-nothing" Congress in his re-election campaign.

The public also does not like certain policy outcomes. In 2010, for instance, there was a widespread belief Congress was spending too much. The federal budget had reached about $3.5 trillion, creating an annual deficit of approximately $1.4 trillion and an accumulated debt that was roughly the size of the entire American economy. An important result was the emergence of the Tea Party, a disparate coalition of organized groups and grassroots activists that held a variety of conservative views but was held together by a belief that the federal government's reach was too great and its fiscal health alarmingly poor (Skocpol and Williamson 2012; Zernike 2010).[23] Its central argument resonated tremendously—a 2009 Gallup poll revealed Americans believed the federal government wasted fifty cents of every dollar.[24] Constituting a very small proportion of spending, earmarks—the directing of federal money for specific programs in particular states and congressional districts—became a special target of wrath. They emerged as a symbol of waste and an indicator of the tight control special interests had over policy making. A November 2010 Rasmussen poll found 48 percent of respondents wanted a ban on the practice and 75 percent felt that the rewards they brought were unfairly distributed.

The Tea Party and Republicans more generally were also assisted during the 2010 campaigns by a deep opposition to the health care reform law passed in March. Forty-eight percent of subjects in the exit polls of that year called for the law to be overturned.[25] Numerous town hall–style meetings held by Democratic House members to discuss the legislation with constituents, particularly during the summer of 2009, turned into raucous protests against "Obamacare." Some representatives were subject to verbal abuse and physical threats. Several of those who voted for the legislation were defeated at the polls (Nyhan et al. 2012).

Everyone's a Critic

It does not help that many members do not think much of Congress themselves. During the 2012 elections, legislators rarely mentioned their Washington experience in campaign ads. A sizeable number of Republican candidates in 2010, particularly those with ties to the Tea Party, ran explicitly against the institution. They excoriated Congress, its members, and the way it works whenever the opportunity to do so arose. The strategy at least partially capitalized on Democratic control: as David Jones and Monika McDermott (2009) explain, voters generally hold the majority party accountable for the legislature's performance. But there was also an innate antipathy to Congress as a whole. Many conservative candidates felt the modern institution was horribly distant from the one built by the country's revered Founders and completely incapable of listening to the concerns of people like themselves. The approach, not surprisingly, paid off. As Daniel Lipinski, William Bianco, and Ryan Work (2003) show, "running with Congress" and demonstrating institutional loyalty is not a good electoral tactic—particularly in a year when voters' views of the federal legislature are as poor as they were in 2010 and 2012.

Even before the 112th Congress, with its Tea Party adherents, was sworn in, there had recently been few members whom Donald Matthews (1960) would have considered "institutional patriots." The promotion of Congress's interests has rarely been rewarded by party leaders or the voters. There are obvious exceptions: a very partial bipartisan list of late twentieth-century institution builders might include senators like Robert Byrd (D-WV), Joseph Clark (D-PA), Robert M. LaFollette (R-WI), and Charles McCurdy Mathias (R-MD) and House members such as Richard Bolling (D-MO), Phillip Burton (D-CA), Barber Conable (R-NY), Bill Frenzel (R-MN), and Mike Monroney (D-OK). But congressional careers like these are rare.

With such little public support and so few members concerned with the health of the institution, Congress cowers, particularly in the face of executive aggrandizement. The dramatic expansion of presidential power has been exhaustively detailed as it accelerated through the twentieth century. It seemed to reach a critical level in the 1970s when Arthur Schlesinger Jr. (1973) penned his influential book *The Imperial Presidency* just as Watergate was unfolding and the Vietnam War coming to a close. As observers like Andrew Rudalevige (2005) and Charlie Savage (2007) have noted, it might have grown further during the administration of President George W. Bush. Bush justified much of the War on Terror with a theory of a robust "unitary executive" (Calabresi and Yoo 2003). President Barack Obama's creation of executive agencies to implement both the 2010 health care legislation and Dodd-Frank financial regulatory overhaul suggests the trend has continued. In the time since Franklin D. Roosevelt established what scholars call the modern presidency, presidents have routinely committed troops into action without a formal declaration of war, crafted American diplomatic policy alone, aggressively employed the veto, taken it upon themselves to issue signing statements to mitigate the effects of congressional action, invoked executive privilege to protect internal communication from legislative scrutiny, appointed policy advisers without requesting Senate confirmation, constructed the principal components of the annual policy agenda, and promulgated rules and executive orders that essentially constitute unilateral legislating.[26] Congress has, on occasion, pushed back. It impeached President Bill Clinton in 1998 and has conducted a series of other investigations of administration behavior that may have clipped the executive's wings for a brief moment. But more frequently it has acquiesced in presidential predominance. Such timidity has hardly earned respect from either the public or the White House.

The low esteem in which the public holds Congress is not shared by all students of the institution. The prominent scholar of Congress and the Constitution Louis Fisher

(2010) has written an eloquent defense of the legislative branch. He is part of a very small minority, however. His tone is reminiscent of the late 1950s and early 1960s when political scientists resolutely protected the institution's interests (Burnham 1959; Kendall 1960). Today it seems discordant. A large number of books and articles have been published over the past few years declaring Congress to be, as the title of Mann and Ornstein's (2006) book puts it, *The Broken Branch*. In late 2008, Boston University Law School held a symposium titled "The Most Disparaged Branch." Several of the papers presented and that made up a subsequent issue of the school's law journal are critical of congressional behavior and operations.[27] Kenneth R. Mayer and David T. Canon (1999) wrote around a decade ago about a "collective dilemma" in which the individual self-interest of members clashed directly and destructively with the needs of Congress. They offered some reforms but largely shrugged their shoulders and suggested we live with the problem. A book by a former Republican staffer, Joseph Gibson (2010), aims its anger at Congress's arcane, complicated, and opaque rules. Former Republican representative Joseph DioGuardi (2010) has written in an updated edition of a book first penned nearly twenty years ago that the institution's problems stem primarily from its irresponsible fiscal policy. The liberal good government group Fix Congress Now sees campaign finance practices as the source of the public's distrust. A disparate group of reform types and academics has suggested the public sees Congress as out of touch because House members represent too many constituents.[28] They propose increasing the size of the body. Mann and Ornstein (2012), perhaps the two most influential Congress watchers of the present era, have followed up their 2006 effort with a book that has an equally damning title, *It's Even Worse Than It Looks*. In 2006 they viewed Congress's most serious problems to include "a loss of institutional identity, an abdication of institutional responsibility vis-à-vis the executive, the demise of regular order (in committee, on the floor, and in conference), and the consequent deterioration of the deliberative process" (Mann and Ornstein 2006, 215). Today it is a legislature horribly unequipped to deal with two "ideologically-polarized, internally-unified, vehemently-oppositional, and politically-strategic" parties (Mann and Ornstein 2012, 102). By their reckoning, congressional Republicans are a particular problem.

THE ESSENCE OF THE BOOK

Quite clearly, Congress is maligned. No one very much likes it these days. Is this pervasive belief fair? The goal here is to answer that basic question, a question that has rarely occurred to the institution's detractors. My book is not an unapologetic and vigorous defense of Congress. Our national legislature is far from perfect. But I believe the book presents a judicious and comprehensive performance appraisal of the institution that examines all aspects of its life—its representation function, procedures, organizational design, relationship with other branches, and policy outputs. As such, the book is designed to temper the anger directed at Congress. I think it asks us to be a little more reasonable. By way of conclusion, it echoes Mayhew's (2009, 357) assessment that, "Congress, if considered in perspective, is not all that bad."

The assessment is undertaken by comparing the character and behavior of today's Congress against a variety of standards, or what I like to call benchmarks. "Benchmarking" is undertaken by public and private organizations all the time. For some reason or another Congress has been overlooked. Surely, however, an institution of its importance should be subject to a fair and comprehensive appraisal of what it does.

My evaluation instrument is first fashioned from a set of somewhat abstract aspirations we should have for congressional performance. The aspirations are generated from canonical Western and modern political thought on issues like democracy and representation, constitutional principles, and the views of the country's Founders. From them I craft the benchmarks: specific, measurable, and reasonable targets for congressional performance. These are informed by a survey of congressional history and the records of legislative bodies in advanced industrialized democracies and the American states. In their creation, I am sensitive to the many exogenous constraints to which members and the institution are subject. I do not attempt to compare congressional performance against some idealized behavior, such as pure forms of democracy that political theorists discuss, or legislative bodies in places or times very different from the United States of today.

I will reveal that in some areas the contemporary Congress meets these benchmarks; in others it falls short. The aggregate effect, however, is to provide a more measured and nuanced evaluation of congressional performance. Where the institution could do better, I offer meaningful and attainable reforms. Where it does well, I acknowledge the fact.

THE PLAN OF THE BOOK

The next chapter presents the fundamental aspirations that undergird the analysis. They are generated from a survey of the literature in a variety of the discipline's fields, particularly political theory and American political history. The goal, as stated, is to fuse normative concerns with common practices in legislative bodies and come up with some justifiable expectations that the American people should have of Congress in the early part of the twenty-first century. The exercise, of course, compels me to engage in value judgments of my own. Still, I will assiduously justify each benchmark by explaining its connection to its related aspiration, measuring it against past and current legislative behavior, and placing it in the context of contemporary American public life.

The remainder of these chapters is devoted to an application of the benchmarks. Throughout each of the chapters from 3 through 8, the aspirations outlined in Chapter

2 are fashioned into specific benchmarks. In Chapter 3 I examine how Congress represents Americans. The subject is addressed in two principal ways. The first is what Nadia Urbinati (2006) calls "political representation" and Hanna Pitkin (1967, 209) describes as "acting in the interests of the represented, in a manner responsive to them." Here I look at Congress's capacity to represent both national and local interests. Congress is an institution of the federal government charged primarily with providing solutions to the country's problems. It should therefore take into account the interests and reflect the will of the American public. But it also consists of what Andrew Rehfeld (2005) calls "territorial constituencies." House districts and states vary tremendously in composition and, given the country's enormous size and complexity, Congress ought to be sensitive to local and regional concerns as well.

Second, I tackle the issue of what Pitkin (1967) labels descriptive, rather than substantive, representation. Assuming that descriptive representation is generally beneficial, I am interested here in how well Congress's membership reflects the country's diverse demography.

Chapter 4 essentially examines how well integrated into civil society Congress is. This involves several quite disparate investigations. I look at the stability of membership and the height of barriers to entry. The argument is that at least a moderate amount of turnover and reasonable standards for admission are good, although I am cognizant of the advantages brought by a professional political class.

I evaluate another kind of openness as well. I examine the transparency of congressional proceedings and how amenable members and their staff are to the world outside Capitol Hill. Both contribute greatly to a healthy representative democracy.

Chapter 4 concludes with an assessment of members' actions, specifically their responsibility to constitutional principles and to conduct themselves in a manner that maintains the public's trust in Congress. In a healthy representative democracy, elected officials model good citizenship.

Chapter 5 analyzes how the House and Senate are structured. It is difficult to make normative assessments of legislative organization, but I recognize explicitly both the efficiency and productivity benefits of centralization and the informational and political legitimacy gains to be made by decentralization. There should exist, in other words, some kind of balance. I look at a broad variety of congressional procedures and analyze how they recognize and exploit the advantages of an appropriate balance of legislative centralization and decentralization.

Chapter 6 examines what members do during the legislative process. I present two characteristics that I argue are critical to superlative legislating: debate and deliberation. I show how both the House and Senate exhibit reasonably high levels of each of these, especially when compared with other national bodies and American state legislatures. I also demonstrate distinct intercameral differences and, somewhat regretfully, a decline in deliberative qualities over time. Still, the overall result is a lawmaking process that is broadly participatory and inquisitive.

Whereas Chapter 6 looks at process, Chapter 7 is focused exclusively on outcomes. An effective Congress must be capable of creating policy, particularly when the American public is actively seeking solutions to societal problems. I examine policy outputs in two basic ways. First, I present a quantitative analysis of the rather large literature on laws passed by Congress. Second, I assess the quality of legislation produced. I look to see whether policy created by Congress has generally promoted the national interest. I look at the ideological consistency or programmatic qualities of the body of laws passed in any one Congress or period. Consistency is considered desirable so that the public can engage in behavior that has predictable consequences and so that governmental action is not dissonant or self-defeating. Toward the end of the chapter, I examine whether policy is evenly applied or allows for exceptions. I argue laws should be simple and general. Finally, I look at congressional efforts to meet the nation's long-term challenges.

Chapter 8 focuses on Congress's obligation within the system of separation of powers to stand up to and oversee the other branches of government. When Congress is weak, Fisher (2010, 143) has written, so are legislators' attention to societal interests and public trust in government. I am particularly interested in how Congress has pushed back against executive power. I evaluate congressional efforts to monitor, investigate, and circumscribe the exercise of executive power, particularly when it impinges on the legislature's prerogatives. The basic story is clearly one of executive aggrandizement, but Congress has worked hard at times to assert itself in the interbranch relationship.

In the last part of the chapter, there is a brief analysis of Congress's relationship with the courts. I talk about the various armaments Congress has in its battle with the judiciary and show how Congress uses this arsenal.

All in all, Congress's performance does not warrant the tremendous disdain in which it is currently held. Using reasonable benchmarks—and not fanciful thinking—I show that a thorough appraisal of Congress reveals a legislature in pretty good health, particularly when compared to other bodies at the state level or from around the world. It clearly represents parochial interests sufficiently, but Congress is also sensitive to national concerns and mass opinion and is tuned into debates about public policy. The lawmaking process is good at leveraging information, largely transparent, and generally facilitates broad participation, especially in the Senate. It can also be productive when it needs to be and generate programmatic and temporally stable policy. Oversight of the other branches of government can be vigorous and effective.

In a final chapter I present some reforms. There are legitimate reasons to be critical of Congress: entry into it can be difficult and there is little turnover, debate and deliberation are not what they could be, policy outputs are sometimes problematic, and congressional oversight has on occasion been lacking. With these issues in mind, and with the belief that Congress can always improve on what it already does well, I conclude by offering and discussing a series of reforms. Some of them are modest; some a little more ambitious. Some are original, but most have been suggested by members, journalists, public interest groups, and scholars before. A first set would make congressional elections more competitive. A second focuses on congressional procedures in an effort, among other things, to make them more transparent. Others address the quality of the legislative process, policy outcomes, and oversight of the executive.

Before we think about reform, however, we need to know where we stand. A just and systematic appraisal of Congress's performance is in order. I begin, then, with the aspirations. What should we really want of our national legislature?

2

WHAT WE SHOULD
WANT OF CONGRESS

Americans have judged Congress and the verdict is, quite clearly, guilty—guilty of corruption, self-obsession, ignorance of the public's interests, abuse of the public's trust, and causing many of the policy problems the country currently faces, either by passing bad laws or being incapable of doing anything at all. This is reflected dramatically in survey after survey of public attitudes about our federal legislature.

Evaluating whether this judgment is fair is the central task of this book. There are two reasons why we might believe the public has treated Congress unjustly. The first concerns the basic expectations it has of congressional behavior. These might be unrealistically high or so variable, incoherent, or inappropriate that they defy proper application. For example, it seems as though each individual American holds Congress to her own individual standards. Those with greater knowledge of Congress undertake strict performance-based evaluations (Mondak et al. 2007). Jones and McDermott (2009) discover a healthy relationship between public evaluation and congressional performance by finding that citizens, particularly engaged ones, tend to be more critical of Congress and its accomplishments the more distant they find themselves from its majority party. This is the kind of assessment we want. But those with less information tend to base their evaluation on other matters—including the general state of the economy, over which Congress exercises limited control, and even personal feelings about the president (Lebo 2008; Kimball 2005; Mondak et al. 2007; Ramirez 2009). It does not help generally uninformed individuals that the nation lacks a clear universal understanding of what Congress is supposed to do.

On the occasions they use policy-based assessments, Americans tend to be self-centered. Individuals want Congress to focus on parochial economic interests, to cut taxes and increase spending for their personal needs and desires (Rudolph 2002). They also send Congress contradictory signals. Throughout 2011, polls revealed Americans wanted it to tackle the national debt. A September CNN/ORC poll reported 95 percent of respondents felt that some spending cuts were necessary in order to achieve that goal. Yet, when asked what kinds of programs Americans want spending reduced for, they demurred. A Harris poll of February 2011 showed that a majority of respondents wanted to cut spending for only six of nineteen policy areas, preferring to maintain or increase current spending levels for the remaining thirteen, which included programs like pollution control, food stamps, defense spending, and mass transit.[1] The public does not always seem to want Congress to make coherent, and therefore often responsible, national fiscal policy.

In a series of fascinating and comprehensive studies, Hibbing and his colleagues have shown Americans' aspirations for the internal workings of the House and Senate are entirely inappropriate (Hibbing and Larimer 2008; Hibbing and Theiss-Morse 1995, 2002). In the tradition of best American political practices, both bodies have incentives that motivate members to run for re-election. Both make themselves permeable to the views of outsiders. Both have procedures consistent with deliberation and debate. Yet citizens continue to dislike ambitious politicians and "special" interest groups. They seem to think that deep down Americans can quite easily agree on solutions to the country's problems and that therefore policy conflicts and the weighing of alternatives are unnecessary and cause harmful delays. As Hibbing and Christopher Larimer (2008, 11) put it, "the more Congress is doing its job, the more unpopular it is with the public." To Barbara Sinclair (2009), the public criticizes Congress precisely because it is such a democratic institution.

The second reason to question Americans' negative views of Congress is that they might be derived from false or incomplete information about legislative performance. Although their role is vital, the media's coverage of Congress has deteriorated.[2] Newspapers, the outlets that have traditionally given Congress its most intensive and serious treatment, have seen their readers flee—national circulation declined 10 percent between 2009 and 2010 alone. Now much of the public views Congress through the eyes of cable news stations and the opinionated hosts of their evening shows—at the height of his popularity in 2010, Glenn Beck's program on Fox News attracted an audience more than three times larger than that of the country's purported newspaper of record, the *New York Times*. According to the Pew Research Center's Project for Excellence in Journalism, as of 2010 more people got their daily news from the Internet than from newspapers.[3] When they cover Congress in an outwardly objective manner, the media focus on elections and powerful or colorful members, rather than on legislative activity and policy outputs (Cook 1986; Fogarty 2008). The image conveyed is distorted and partial. Television coverage has generally presented a rosy picture of incumbents and their activities, for example (Prior 2006).

Regardless of the source of their information, people's knowledge of Congress is poor. Mayhew (2009) observes the public has little understanding of the complex system of separation of powers and believes Congress assumes functions that are assigned by the Constitution to the other branches of government. Such inaccuracies inevitably elevate expectations about performance to levels that cannot plausibly be met. Even basic facts evade many Americans. Generally about three in four know which party is in the majority in the House, but when asked about individual members and pieces of legislation, it becomes clear citizens' knowledge diminishes. In a Pew Research Center poll undertaken in April 2007, only 15 percent could name Harry Reid (D-NV) as the Senate's majority leader—this had improved a bit to 39 percent by the time Pew did its January 2010 survey. Just 24 percent in the 2007 poll knew Congress had recently passed an increase in the minimum wage, and only 29 percent in the October 2009 version knew cap-and-trade legislation was related to energy and the environment. Levels of knowledge are as bad when it comes to procedures.[4] Only 26 percent in the January 2010 survey knew that sixty votes were necessary to break a Senate filibuster.[5]

So perhaps the public needs some help creating standards that it can apply fairly and effectively. It is, to some considerable extent, using suspect and insufficient information to judge Congress on impracticable and unreasonable criteria. In any representative democracy the public's views of legislative behavior and performance should be given proper deference. But we should recognize that a systematic and just evaluation requires standards constructed from other sources as well. The people are not always right.

To get an accurate handle on congressional performance, these standards, or benchmarks as I call them, must be applied to all areas of legislative life. I identify these areas as the representation of the American public; the accessibility, openness, and trustworthiness of the institution; congressional organization; the consideration of legislation; policy outcomes; and checking and balancing the other branches. Each is discussed in its own chapter.

The benchmarks must first be constructed, however. They must be realistic and reasonable. As Mayhew (2009, 369) argues, evaluators of Congress "should consult real-world standards, not fanciful counterfactuals." They must allow for broad application across legislative bodies and time. This is a tricky proposition. To build the benchmarks, I start with a set of simple and somewhat abstract ideas taken from normative political theory and American public life, with particular emphasis on the Founders and other influential thinkers about politics and government. These values constitute signposts pointing Congress in a particular direction. They are basic aspirations, one for each area of legislative life. They may not be particularly precise, but they constitute fundamental behaviors, procedures, practices, and policies worth emulating.

FOUNDATIONAL ASPIRATIONS

So what makes a good legislature? Scholars have not done as much work directly exploring normative issues like this as one might expect, but there exists a great deal of theoretical work to guide us. It hardly constitutes a cohesive body of thought found in an easily identifiable small number of sources, but I think it is fair to say there is broad, if latent, somewhat nebulous, and not particularly intense, agreement among those who have attempted serious answers to the question. The public, political scientists, historians, journalists, influential men and women of America's past, and members from today and yesterday have all ruminated on the kinds of values Congress should reflect.[6] What follows is an exploration of the most prominent. I consider them aspirations.

1. A Robust Representative Democracy

The Framers made it clear that a representative democracy was preferable to the pure or direct ones practiced in ancient Athens and the town halls of New England. Elected bodies facilitated union because it was impossible to bring citizens directly into the policy-making process in a country as large as the new United States. Moreover, and as James Madison wrote in *Federalist 10*, assemblies "refine and enlarge the public views, by passing them through the medium of a chosen body of citizens, whose wisdom may best discern the true interest of their country, and whose patriotism and love of justice will be least likely to sacrifice it to temporary or partial considerations" (Hamilton, Madison, and Jay 1982, 55). In direct democracies, however, "a common passion or interest will, in almost every case, be felt by a majority of the whole; a communication and concert result from the form of government itself; and there is nothing to check the inducements to sacrifice the weaker party or an obnoxious individual" (55).

Still, this did not diminish the importance of the public's will in the making of policy. The Framers thought institutions of the new federal government, particularly the elected ones, needed to reflect what Americans wanted. A delegate or agent model of representation should also direct legislators' actions. "A dependence on the people," according to Madison, "is no doubt the primary control on the government" (Hamilton, Madison, and Jay 1982, 316). To John Adams, a legislature "should be in miniature an exact portrait of the people at large," and as such "it should think, feel, reason and act like them" (Adams 1776, 6).

Americans are not, of course, a monolithic bunch. They have a diverse array of positions, however derived, on just about any issue in public life. They are often split quite evenly. That congressional action should reflect the public will therefore requires the institution's collective decisions to be consistent with the policy preferences of a subset of citizens. Democratic theory asserts a special status to the views of a majority. Aristotle (1981) talked of a democracy as "rule by the many," even if he was not a particularly energetic endorser of the concept. The seventeenth-century English thinker John Locke, a man who was revered by the Founders, saw majority rule and the consent of the governed as central tenets of democracy. Much later, economist Kenneth May asserted that majority rule was a superior voting system because it uniquely demonstrated critical characteristics like neutrality and the equal treatment of participants. As political scientist Robert Dahl (1956) pointed out, this is the case even if we take a utilitarian approach and consider that members of the minority might hold more intense preferences.[7] If policy positions can be ordered along a single dimension, then political scientists frequently elevate the choice of the middle one because a majority will always prefer it to any alternative (Black 1948; Downs 1957). A legislature that produces laws that are frequently inconsistent with majority opinion, therefore, cannot be healthy for the greater society.

Basic democratic theory also suggests legislatures are more than mere reflections of the broader society they represent. As Pitkin suggests, government should be "responsive to popular wishes when there are some" but also "promote the public interest" (Pitkin 1967, 233). Edmund Burke (1997) said in his famous 1774 Bristol speech that because it consists of trustees rather than agents, "Parliament is a deliberative assembly of one nation, with *one* interest, that of the whole; where, not local purposes, not local prejudices, ought to guide, but the general good, resulting from the general reason of the whole." The public interest or what we might call the national good is not just the arithmetical sum of the individual desires of all of a society's members. For the Founders it transcended self-interest and brought together a community of individuals into a collective. With this logic, Congress is not a giant logroll in which members or groups of members representing regions, industries, or occupational sectors secure policies their constituents desire.

Although they embrace it, Americans have never really understood exactly what is meant by their common good or national interest. To the progressives and communitarians of today, it is a call on people to realize they have a stake in and should contribute to an enterprise that is much larger than themselves (Etzioni 2004; Tomasky 2006). To those on the right-hand side of the ideological spectrum, it has a different appeal. American conservatives in the mold of Russell Kirk (1953) defer to tradition and place an emphasis on service to country and the moral imperatives of a religious society. Libertarians, like former presidential candidate Rep. Ron Paul (R-TX), want a minimalist government that is respectful of the rights of individuals. Indeed, they tend to agree with John Stuart Mill's (1982) classic argument in *On Liberty* that majorities can be tyrannical and that government should frequently act to check them. Libertarians might not think of the common good in the way others do (Hudson 2008), but they can list a great many public policies that they believe are best for us. Reflexive lawmaking that, with tremendous sensitivity to constituent opinion, faithfully promotes parochial interests and neglects basic national objectives and values is therefore unlikely to provide policy, at least in the aggregate, that pleases most Americans. Such policy will not have the consistency, discipline, and foresight necessary to promote national peace and prosperity, convey moral principles, and protect the rights of numerical minorities and individual citizens.

Members of Congress must therefore protect the championless common American good from individual concerns frequently animated by human passion. They must balance what we might consider parochial and national interests, the needs and wants of their constituents with the needs and wants of the country. They should, in Rehfeld's (2009) words, work for both the good of the whole, as well as the good of the part. The Framers of the Constitution recognized this quite explicitly. The House's direct and frequent elections, larger membership, and generally smaller constituencies made its members behave like agents and focus more on local concerns. The two-year terms, according to Madison in *Federalist 57*, forced upon House members "a habitual recollection of their dependence on the people." As he noted in *Federalist 39*, the body derived "its powers from the people of America." The Senate, in contrast, reflected federal principles and represented the states, whose legislators handpicked its members. Senators were to have six-year terms. This resulted in a more composed, studious, and judicious body. It was to be a kind of American House of Lords (Swift 1996). "The use of the Senate," wrote Madison (Farrand 1966, 151) as he observed the debates at the Constitutional Convention, "is to consist in its proceedings with more coolness, with more system and with more wisdom, than the popular branch." The metaphor was reshaped by George Washington when he compared lawmaking to coffee drinking. "We pour," Washington told Thomas Jefferson, "legislation into the senatorial saucer to cool it."[8] The Senate was uniquely capable of distancing itself from public feelings and could consequently mitigate their effects on policy. One of its principal responsibilities was to protect the common good and more national interests.

Congress should therefore provide substantive representation by promoting the interests of American society and its most populous constituent parts. Many who think deeply about democracy suggest descriptive representation has merits as well (Mansbridge 1999; Dovi 2002; Phillips 1995; Williams 1998). As John Adams noted, Congress should resemble the people it represents in addition to giving them the policy they want. In a country as diverse as the United States, a legislature that looks like its citizenry will be capable of tapping a tremendous diversity of opinion, knowledge, and experience. High levels of descriptive representation are also said to enthuse and empower minority citizens and women, bringing about greater trust in government and increasing participation in politics (Bobo and Gilliam 1990; Banducci, Donovan, and Karp 2004; Mansbridge 1999). Congressional scholars have shown that black members are more likely to address African American interests than their white colleagues (Canon 1999; Grose 2011), and female members are more likely to address issues of greater concern to women than men (Kittilson 2008).

It is one thing to say Congress should look like America. It is another to hold it accountable for doing so. Electoral rules determining candidate and voter eligibility are mostly found in the Constitution and state law. Candidate recruitment is not a responsibility of Congress, and it can hardly control what the public thinks. Still if at least a modicum of descriptive representation is salubrious, we can legitimately judge Congress on this score. An institution seemingly welcoming of diverse individuals is likely to encourage many types of Americans to try to become its members.

The standards of substantive and descriptive representation are to be applied to the institution's performance, not those of any one or group of individual members. I appraise the collective. Many individual members might not do these things particularly well but the dyadic form of representation—"the connection between individual members of Congress and their constituents" (Ansolabehere and Jones 2011, 293)—is largely irrelevant to my analysis. I take Pitkin's (1967, 221–222) more macro view of representation as a "public, institutionalized arrangement" where representation emerges not from "any single action by any one participant, but [from] the over-all structure and functioning of the system."

2. A Transparent, Accessible, and Trustworthy Legislature

Americans cannot expect Congress to reflect these basic understandings of representation unless they can hold its members accountable. At the very least, therefore, a healthy representative democracy requires a legislature that is transparent, that can be observed from outside. Congress must allow the public to see what it is doing. As Jeremy Waldron (2009, 337–340) argues, transparency is the "first virtue" of legislatures.

Today such openness essentially means facilitating media coverage of Congress's daily workings, particularly the important business of considering and disposing of legislation in committee and on the floor. It also means establishing clear, simple, and logical procedures that permit the public to understand members' individual and collective behavior and connect it to policy positions and legislative outcomes. In fact, it may be that a failure to do much of this has contributed to Congress's low approval ratings. As Mayhew (2006, 225–226) notes, Americans are experiencing increasing difficulty understanding congressional life as laws get thicker and procedures more complex.

Congress must also be susceptible to input from citizens and the entities that represent groups of them. It needs, in other words, to be sensitive to the public's wishes. To do this, members and their staffs must be committed to seek public views on issues and willing and able to meet with constituents and the agents of organized interests, whether in Washington or at home. They must be given the resources to absorb and process the tremendous amount of information they receive about public wants and needs.

Accessibility means being permeable as well. So as to enhance Congress's democratic legitimacy, its membership must not stagnate—there should be "circulation of the elite," in the words of Italian philosopher Vilfredo Pareto (1966, 108–111). Ordinary citizens must feel they could become members if they so desire. Barriers to entry must be low. When this is the case, social mobility and political competition increase as talented individuals with alternative viewpoints detect opportunities for advancement and undertake serious bids for elected office. Potential and capable challengers are numerous and incumbents presumably work hard to secure re-election. This, in turn, enhances their sensitivity to public demands.

Finally, members must not betray the public trust. "Trust" is a slippery concept for political scientists and has been given many meanings. Rather like Francis Fukuyama (1995), I argue it rests on shared moral values among members of a community. In a democracy, representing public views is surely one of these.[9] But there are many others. At the beginning of the book, I listed a series of scandals that have contributed to the view Americans have of their Congress. In each there was an explicit violation of a sort of code of ethics, a set of requirements about how those in positions of authority should behave that generates elemental public trust in government. The kind of Congress we want should minimize such violations by its membership.

3. Desirable Principles of Organization

Legislative bodies are organizations, a distinguishable collection of individuals purposively brought together in a formal bounded setting and whose behavior and relationships are regulated by rules and norms. For instance, Congress's principal responsibility is to make laws. Its members work in the Capitol complex in Washington, DC, and their professional behavior is directed by requirements described in the Constitution, statute, the House and Senate rulebooks, and conventions and precedents.

To function well and therefore achieve their objectives, organizations need to be structured in particular ways. Scholars of organizational effectiveness generally believe that hierarchical and highly formalized arrangements are productive. This was the view of Frederick Winslow Taylor (1998) and others who transformed the understanding of business practices at the turn of the twentieth century. It was also the view of their contemporaries who studied society and administration. The founders of sociology, Max Weber (1947) and Emile Durkheim (1947), saw modern public life as a rationalized arrangement in which labor was neatly divided and roles clearly defined. To Weber, especially, this made it productive, at least in a material sense. Knowledge and wealth grew dramatically, even though individual freedom was curtailed, behavior formulaic, and the world an impersonal place.

Scholars of legislatures see virtue in many of these kinds of structures too. Nelson Polsby (1968) argued the House of Representatives had developed "universalistic and automated decision making." Among the practices that brought about its "institutionalization" were the seniority system, which rewarded members who served long tenures with important appointments (Epstein et al. 1997; Polsby, Gallaher, and Rundquist 1969) and the "property rights norm" in the committee assignment process—the no-

tion that arose on Henry Clay's (Rep.-KY) watch that members can retain their committee seats indefinitely (Jenkins 1998).[10] Advancements such as these constituted an
effort to order and hierachicalize a growing body in which individual members increasingly looked to national politics as a career. They were also a response to the intensified demands of constituents and the increasingly complex policy world in which
the House operated. Mechanistically-applied and highly-routinized procedures coupled
with centralized leadership helped divert energy from conflicts over legislative process
into efforts to generate legislative output.

Most of the work on the variation of policy outputs across time suggests that partisanship and members' policy preferences do most to explain whether a Congress will
get a lot of legislating done or be gridlocked (Binder 2003; Chiou and Rothenberg
2003; Krehbiel 1998; Schickler 2000). Organization matters only in that it is shaped
by lawmakers interested in having it advantage particular outcomes. But there is an
argument that institutional arrangements are exogenous of members' views of issues
and can therefore have an independent and direct effect on legislative fertility (Taylor
2012a). As a result of its larger size and workload (Taylor 2012a), the House established
procedures that centralize the body and provide majority parties with significant control of the agenda (Cox and McCubbins 2005). The House tends to approve more
legislation than the Senate, most of which the majority wants to become law.

Centralized and formalized arrangements may enhance effectiveness, but they inevitably idle much of an organization's capacity. By granting individuals in the broader
membership authority, leaders can motivate the rank and file to deliver important benefits. In a legislative setting, this has generally been done by a committee system—a
fact understood and then forcefully articulated by Keith Krehbiel (1991).[11] In return
for jurisdiction over policy areas or important parts of the parent body's responsibilities,
committees generate valuable information—information that can be used to develop
legislative solutions to complex societal problems. At the individual level, members'
dedication to committee work promotes policy specialization and is frequently rewarded with advancement on the committee.

It is also important to note that legislatures are not just any type of organization.
They are public entities. Congress serves 310 million masters. It has 310 million shareholders, if you will. It exists in what we would like to think is a robust representative
democracy. Centralization is problematic because members represent distinct and
bounded constituencies—congressional districts in the House and states in the Senate.
If some House members' involvement in policy making is restricted more than others',
the interests of those they represent are neglected, and important democratic principles
violated. The problem is perhaps mitigated a bit in the other body of Congress because
all Americans have two senators who represent them. Still, unequal participation and
hierarchical procedures there are likely to have the same troubling effect.

Many agree with the influential French social scientist Robert Michels (1949)
who noted that all political organizations, no matter what their mission, turn in-

eluctably into oligarchies. Protecting members' rights to broad and equal participation is not easy. But that does not mean they should not be goals. We should desire a Congress that balances these conflicting principles. We should want an informed legislature that reflects democracy in that it facilitates all members' involvement in important decision making but realizes the need for hierarchical and entrenched organizational arrangements that promote efficiency and allow the body to perform its core responsibilities.

Before we leave this topic, it is important to note that holding Congress accountable for the way it is structured is perfectly legitimate. The Constitution did not mandate any organizational principles. In fact it is largely silent on these matters. Only three leadership positions are mentioned in the document, the Speaker of the House and the president and president pro tempore of the Senate. Article II, Section 5, states that a majority shall constitute a quorum in both bodies and that, by the request of one-fifth of those present, a vote on any question must be recorded. Really, apart from that, the House and Senate were free to arrange themselves as they wished. Indeed, the language of Article II, Section 5, states this quite explicitly: "Each House may determine the Rules of its Proceedings."

4. A Healthy Legislative Process

Legislatures make public policy in the form of laws—instruments used to solve societal problems and meet the challenges their members' constituents face. The process by which they do this should exhibit certain characteristics. For the most part these characteristics are essential to meeting other basic goals of congressional performance I have outlined above, such as broad participation, productivity, transparency, public education, and promotion of the common good.

The two characteristics that occupy the lion's share of scholars' attention are what Joseph Bessette (1982) calls debate and deliberation. Debate is the vigorous exposition and championing of an informed and developed point of view and its defense in the face of an opposing argument. It involves the competition of positions or ideas and an effort to generate support for them.

Deliberation is somewhat different. Congressional scholar Steve Smith (1989, 238–239) describes it as "reasoning together about the nature of a problem and solutions to it." Edward Lascher (1996, 506) defines it as "the extent to which legislators engage each other's arguments." In other words, deliberation is a process of collective policy making in which legislators work through alternatives in an informed and rational manner. It forces them to learn about policy problems and proposals and is said to nurture sensitivity to the public good (Bessette 1994; Lascher 1996). According to the famous political theorist John Rawls (1997, 772), deliberation in legislative bodies is so important that it is one of the "three essential elements of deliberative democracy"— the other two being the public's reason and its ability to act upon it.

What might provide tangible evidence of the presence of these rather abstract principles? Alone, absent or silent members cannot be debating or deliberating. Congress must be in session and as many members as possible engaged in the consideration of legislation. As the vocal advocate of deliberative democracy, James Fishkin (1995) notes this participation ought also to be even across members.

Content is critical too. Members must interact and engage each other's arguments. Give and take is inherent to debate and deliberation. Members must reason as well— that is, they should explain instead of merely state. Jürg Steiner and his colleagues (2004, 20–21) argue that a "logical justification" of an argument is central to deliberation. Finally, recognition of the public, rather than a narrow or parochial, interest is important. As Steiner and others (2004, 21) put it, deliberation constitutes "a sense of empathy or solidarity that allows the participants to consider the well-being of others and of the community at large."

Debate and deliberation can occur at many stages of the legislative process. Although members might engage in both with constituents and journalists, it is their use of them in making law that we should care about most.

5. Effective Policy

Effective public policy must be a central goal of all legislatures. It seems to me that, in the aggregate, a body of laws should have four main qualities.

The first is the potential for quantity. I say potential because many political observers believe that by legislating Congress cannot help but do harm. This is generally the view of contemporary constitutional conservatives who embrace the system of checks and balances constructed by the Framers to make policy making so difficult— the fealty of many professed members of the Tea Party to the Constitution is based largely on a belief that government, particularly at the federal level, can do nothing right (Foley 2012, 20–75; Lepore 2010; Skocpol and Williamson 2012). There is even evidence the broader public appreciates congressional inactivity. Robert Durr, John Gilmour, and Christina Wolbrecht (1997) report approval of Congress is inversely related to legislative productivity.

But Congress should be capable of making policy when it believes it needs to. When societal problems present themselves, we should want it to produce solutions. It is possible conditions could improve without government intervention. Frequently, however, without corrective action economic downturns can turn quickly into harmful recessions—as the 2008 financial crisis demonstrated. This argument is not inconsistent with the Founders' thinking. Although early Americans' fondness for incrementalism is obvious, many of them realized the large number of veto points in the federal policy-making system could actually grease the wheels by forcing participants to cooperate. An unproductive process would inevitably raise questions about the reasons for legislators' presence in Washington (Amar 2005, 61–62).

The argument is also not ideological. If the status quo is liberal, conservatives will hope for legislation to move policy in a rightward direction. This is what drove the effort to reverse what many call Obamacare. It is what motivated the new Republican congressional majorities after they had taken control of both chambers for the first time in forty years following the 1994 elections. As the presumed Speaker and ostensible leader of the party's election success, Rep. Newt Gingrich (R-GA) said, on the night of the victory, "We want to replace the whole current structure of the welfare state with something new" (Wolf, 1994).[12] The House Republicans' "Contract with America"—that acted as a kind of platform for candidates during the campaign—was chock-full of ambitious ideas to fundamentally change the direction of American public policy. Ultimately, the contract's fortunes were mixed, but there was no denying its forceful intent (Bader 1996; Gimpel 1996).

The remaining characteristics of effective public policy all have to do with quality, or substance, as opposed to quantity, or amount. As noted earlier, the Founders believed deeply in the existence of a common good that cannot be understood as the sum of the preferences of all of a society's individual members. This commonweal amounted to some basic conditions the collective should enjoy. The Founders were not particularly forthcoming as to what these should be, although the preamble to the Constitution provides some obvious hints: "We the People of the United States, in Order to form a more perfect Union, establish Justice, insure domestic Tranquility, provide for the common defence [sic], promote the general Welfare, and secure the Blessings of Liberty to ourselves and our Posterity, do ordain and establish this Constitution for the United States of America." So too does Article I, Section 8, of the document that calls on Congress to, "provide for the common Defence [sic] and general Welfare of the United States." I think it is therefore reasonable to suggest certain policies are, on balance, good for the whole. Today policy goals are inevitably caught up in ideological and partisan disputes, but conservatives and liberals can agree on objectives such as elevating the general standard of living, keeping the nation secure, and improving the process of government.

Mayhew (2005, 184–191) is helpful in further exploration of the quality of policy outputs. He talks of the value of "programmatic coherence," or ideological consistency, in a body of statutes. Such a collection of policies ensures the country and its citizenry are not working at cross-purposes in different issue areas. It provides some clarity as individuals, groups, and firms make plans for the future. It assists voters as they make connections between a candidate's views, the philosophies of the parties, and general policy outcomes. The thinking, according to Mayhew (2005, 184), is that ideologically consistent policy outcomes "provide a graspable politics to sectors of the public who might be interested in such change."[13]

Mayhew (2005, 184–191) also mentions "budgetary coherence." The problems of inconsistency are perhaps most dramatically apparent in fiscal policy. Spending increases coupled with tax cuts is likely to result in budget deficits that, at least if significant or persistent, can do considerable harm to the country's economic health.

The great French Enlightenment philosopher Jean-Jacques Rousseau explains the next quality we should seek in a legislature's lawmaking. Rousseau's (1968) particular understanding of the social contract is most frequently remembered for concepts like the general will or phrases such as, "Man is born free, and everywhere he is in chains." Overlooked is his argument that laws should be applied to all equally; they should be general. There should be no exceptions or carve outs for individuals, and public policies should "consider subjects en masse and actions in the abstract, and never a particular person or action." Locke (1988) had introduced the idea about a century earlier in his famous *Second Treatise*.

Others have picked up Rousseau and Locke's point. In the late 1960s, Theodore Lowi (1979) began to advocate what he called juridical democracy. According to Lowi, among its many virtues, this type of governance would reverse the post–New Deal tendency to make policy in a discretionary fashion that essentially reflected interest-group politics. Such policy is inherently inconsistent, unpredictable, and ad hoc. It creates resentment among "losers" who see the process as capricious. Universal, transparent, and simple principles should be transformed into law to provide outcomes with legitimacy. When policies are, in the words of Robert C. Grady (1984, 409), "generalizable to anyone, not limited to someone," individuals are reminded of their place in broader society and feel as if they are treated justly.[14]

Finally, we should want policy to be forward looking. It is all very well for a body to be capable of producing laws and solving crises quickly. But effective policy making should help society meet its long-term and possibly much greater challenges. A concerted and continual effort to deal with huge problems that loom in the future is clearly admirable. As a strategy, it is also certainly preferable to the much more costly and socially disruptive task of averting disaster when it is upon you.

The challenge presented by Social Security furnishes a classic example. For several decades now, the country has known that it cannot continue to run the program the way it has. Beneficiaries rely on payments from the payroll taxes of current workers and a trust fund made up of government debt obligations. Benefits are already exceeding revenues, meaning administrators are tapping the trust fund to pay seniors. Without policy intervention, the trust fund itself is likely to dry up sometime in the 2030s.

When judging Congress on what it produces, it would be wise to remember that public policy in this country is shaped tremendously by other institutions. Economic policy, for instance, is also made by the president, executive agencies like the Treasury, and independent bodies like the Federal Reserve. Court decisions frequently matter too. The effects of policy can be so obfuscated by the actions of foreign countries, multinational corporations, and the American consumer that it is difficult to know whether Congress was really advancing or undermining the national interest when it passed a particular law. Still, I think it is fair to say Congress is largely responsible for important shifts in policy. If legislation is essentially an instrument designed to solve societal problems, then it is right to hold Congress accountable for the general health of the country.

6. Vigorous Checking and Balancing

It seems almost quaint now when we realize many of the Framers believed the stability within the system of separation of powers would be most threatened by congressional assertiveness and not that of either of the other branches. Hamilton wrote that the judiciary constituted the "least dangerous" branch. It had "no influence over either the sword or the purse; no direction either of the strength or of the wealth of the society; and can take no active resolution whatever" (Hamilton, Madison, and Jay 1982, 472). Madison devoted the whole of *Federalist 48* to the explanation of how the Constitution had done a more effective job circumscribing executive and judicial power and that the legislature's authority to determine salaries would permit it significant influence over the decisions made by the president and the courts. If history was a guide, this would be problematic. Across the states, Madison wrote, "the legislative department is everywhere extending the sphere of its activity, and drawing all power into its impetuous vortex" (Hamilton, Madison, and Jay 1982, 301).

Federalist 48 was not an argument for the suppression of Congress, though. The Framers were democrats in the context of their day and were influenced deeply by Locke, who had promoted the primacy of legislative power on many occasions.[15] This is demonstrated by Congress's constitutional right to impeach and remove presidents and judges and to establish and abolish components of the other two branches. Madison, it has been argued, advocated for equilibrium among the branches, a stable relationship, not necessarily an equal one (Wills 1999, 84–88). Regardless, to guard against "a gradual concentration of the several powers in the same department" he wrote later in *Federalist 51*, officials in each branch needed to be given "the necessary constitutional means and personal motives to resist encroachments of the others." These would include the presidential veto and the Senate's authority to ratify treaties and confirm appointments to executive and judicial offices. Power would not accumulate dangerously, Madison suggested, as long as "the provision for defense" was "made commensurate to the danger of attack" (Hamilton, Madison, and Jay 1982, 315–316).

If power has accumulated since that time, it has done so in the hands of the president and federal judges. Woodrow Wilson's (1901) "congressional government"—one in which presidents faithfully execute the will of the legislature—is an artifact of the eighteenth and nineteenth centuries. Today the president heads an organization of about 1.8 million civilian and about 1.4 million active-duty military employees. It costs roughly $1.4 trillion a year to run. Since the New Deal the departments and agencies he leads have been delegated authority by Congress to make rules that have the force of law. This practice is now so commonplace that these promulgations occupy about 140,000 pages of the Code of Federal Regulations annually. The president also routinely issues executive orders that constitute unilateral lawmaking, albeit in narrowly construed policy areas.[16] Since Ronald Reagan's time, we have seen about forty of these a year. Presidents Bill Clinton and George W. Bush were particularly taken with a device called a signing statement, something they used to impose a particular and personal interpretation of the law on the personnel charged with administering it (Savage 2007, 228–249). The modern Supreme Court thinks nothing of declaring federal statutes unconstitutional, a power, called judicial review, it has enjoyed since *Marbury v. Madison* was decided in 1803. About 150 of the nation's laws have been voided by its top court, the vast majority of them since 1950.

So it is appropriate Congress fight back and, to paraphrase Madison in *Federalist 51*, make its ambition counteract that of its competitors. Sometimes it has done this quite vigorously. There were clusters of investigations of executive activity after the Civil War, during the Grant administration, in the 1920s, after Franklin Roosevelt's presidency, and on national security policy during the Cold War.[17] The Nixon presidency was ultimately killed by Watergate, Reagan's crippled by Iran-Contra, and Clinton's wounded by a variety of congressional investigations during his second term—investigations that culminated in his impeachment by the House of Representatives.[18] These periods of activity have usually been accompanied by laws designed to arrest executive aggrandizement. Watergate and Vietnam, for example, were followed by the War Powers Resolution that was supposed to restrict the president's use of military forces abroad, the Budget and Impoundment Control Act that was designed to compel the president to spend money appropriated by Congress, and the Ethics in Government Act that established an independent counsel that could be employed to look into presidential malfeasance.

For the most part, however, Congress has not behaved this way. The executive branch has been particularly adept at exploiting crises and using them to add permanently to its power. The Great Depression and World War II were utilized by Franklin Roosevelt to expand the presidency's reach tremendously. Congress delegated legislative authority to executive agencies, and in 1939 the Executive Office of the President was created—a whole new component to the branch that provided presidents with political and policy advice and support.[19] More recently, President George W. Bush's War on Terror spawned policies in which the executive branch eavesdropped on communications between Americans and foreigners, grabbed and indefinitely detained terrorist suspects, and engaged in controversial and, many believe, illegal interrogation techniques. It did this unilaterally and without consulting Congress or reverting to the criminal justice system.[20] The actions were reminiscent of Lyndon Johnson and Richard Nixon. Both of these presidents conducted the Vietnam conflict without any formal declaration of war from Congress, and Nixon's hubris during the Watergate affair demonstrated that the country's chief executive now saw few limits to his power. As Nixon famously observed during an interview with the British journalist David Frost, "If the president does it that means it's not illegal."[21]

Not only would the Framers want Congress engaged assiduously in checking and balancing, the public tends to think it is a good idea as well. A 2004 survey by the Annenberg Institutions of American Democracy Project reported that when it comes to important decisions 59 percent of Americans preferred Congress to make them, only 21 percent the president.[22] Fourteen percent advocated a joint decision-making model. The same survey revealed 70 percent of respondents believed legislative checks on the executive were "a good thing."

Whether pushing back against the courts is important to Americans is a different issue. In recent years, the job approval ratings of the Supreme Court have generally been about thirty percentage points higher than Congress's. I think it is fair to say, however, that the judiciary should not be given free rein. As William Howard Taft wrote before his days as president and then chief justice of the United States, the right to question judicial decisions is "of vastly more importance to the body politic than the immunity of courts and judges from unjust aspirations and attack" (Taft 1895).

But we should not want Congress to dominate the executive branch or judiciary. It should know its place in the American political order and demonstrate a certain constitutional sensibility. This is a fuzzy concept, to be sure. It most definitely involves a respect for the autonomy of the other two branches of government. Congress may not owe the president "deferential loyalty," but it has some obligation to provide "independent and informed judgment" (Fisher 2009, 147). As for the courts, Congress should recognize the important and cherished principle of judicial independence in our system of separation of powers—or in any kind of democratic system for that matter. An appropriate role for Congress therefore also incorporates an explicit recognition of the rights of states, individuals, and other governmental institutions that are enshrined in the Constitution.

CONCLUSION

The six principles discussed above are aspirational. They provide unambiguous signposts. The next step is to have them guide the construction of specific objectives. These are built from observations of contemporaneous peer institutions, namely national legislatures and parliaments in advanced industrialized democracies and bodies in the American states.[23] They are also informed by congressional history. The resulting benchmarks can be applied to legislative performance in general so that we might analyze, with some precision and objectivity, how well the Congress of today is doing. There are thirty-seven of them. They are necessarily of tremendously varying degrees of importance, utility, and exactitude but collectively outline in some detail what a good legislature should be.

Each of the next six chapters deals with a single aspiration. I present the derived benchmarks, justifying, and providing an appraisal of congressional performance against each. If recent trends suggest Congress is meeting the benchmarks or at least moving in the direction of them, we have evidence that the institution is performing at a level we should want it to and that popular assessments of what it does are inaccurate and unfair.

3

DO WE HAVE A ROBUST
REPRESENTATIVE DEMOCRACY?

The aspiration that guides the benchmarks appraised in this chapter is a robust representative democracy. Congress must be sensitive and responsive to public opinion as it attempts to solve societal problems and designs policy to promote the national interest. This is not always easy, as the public does not always agree with itself or congressional majorities on what is best. As Democrats, led by President Obama, forged ahead with their health care reform legislation in 2010 for instance, a plurality of Americans continually expressed their opposition to the legislation.[1]

Congress should also mirror the general population's demographic composition. Open and free societies ought to have legislative bodies reflective of the citizenry.

BENCHMARK #1
To reflect the will of the American people, Congress should track
alterations in the policy preferences of the general public quite closely.

Justification
Congress is criticized continually for being out of step with the American public. According to a Program on International Policy Attitudes (PIPA) poll of March 2008, when asked how much the United States was governed by the "will of the people," respondents gave an average score of four, with zero denoting "not at all" and ten "completely."[2] That is quite surprising when you consider the terms of members of the House of Representatives are very short. At two years, their duration is less than those of any other comparable national body in the world. Although senators have relatively lengthy six-year terms, one-third of the body is up in each two-year federal election cycle. The finding is also surprising when you consider Britons, whose House of Commons

generally serves a five-year term and whose House of Lords is unelected, gave their parliament a 4.9 on the PIPA poll.[3]

It should not be too difficult to judge how well Congress actually reflects the sentiment of the nation. To gauge congressional responsiveness to public opinion on important issues, we can track changes in policy outputs and the preferences of legislators to see whether they match those in the positions of voters and the broader public. If the electorate tacks to the right, then so should the House and Senate's membership. The legislation Congress produces should become more conservative. The magnitude of these changes should also reflect those in the public's views.

The effort to create such a benchmark faces two significant challenges, however. First, it is hard to measure the sensitivity of many national legislative bodies to changes in public opinion. Disciplined commitment to previously announced policy platforms is a hallmark of most parliamentary parties. They are not designed to alter their positions between elections.[4]

The second problem is that we do not really have systematic and reliable public opinion data from before World War II. This makes comparing the responsiveness of modern Congresses to those of the past just about impossible. Scholars like Mayhew (2008) argue legislation has matched public moods at other times in American history. Progressive Era reforms enacted in response to public concerns about unfettered capitalism, political corruption, and moral decay in the early 1900s furnish a good example.[5] But we have little rigorous evidence to this effect.

Fortunately, some recent impressive work has gauged the responsiveness of legislatures and their policy outputs in the modern period. Shin-Goo Kang and G. Bingham Powell (2010) show that alterations in the median voter's position bring about commensurate changes in a country's social welfare spending. This is the case across advanced Western democracies regardless of electoral system. Political scientists have used opinion polls and legislative roll-call voting to place the public and lawmakers in the American states within the same policy space (Shor and McCarty 2011). This allows for accurate and sophisticated comparisons of the two. Work by Jeffrey Lax and Justin Phillips (2012), for instance, reveals that state policies mirror public opinion quite well, although legislative majorities often generate outcomes that are more extreme than residents seem to want. The public generally gets what it wants on salient policies like abortion, health care, and education, even if legislatures tend to "overshoot" a little as the median resident moves to the left or right.

This research helps construct a baseline for our judgment of congressional responsiveness. The standard is legitimately high. Congress should track alterations in the policy preferences of the American public quite closely. Empirical work reveals a strong relationship between public opinion and legislative behavior. Changes in the direction of the former are replicated faithfully by the latter, even if the magnitude of the response is sometimes exaggerated.

Appraisal
Responsiveness to Electoral Outcomes

Our evaluation should begin with the recognition that members of Congress are elected using a simple-plurality, first-past-the-post system that is known for its winner-take-all properties. Candidates need only win one more vote than their nearest rival to be elected to the body for which they are running. Citizens who supported losing candidates effectively see their votes wasted. This method of choosing legislators therefore does not provide a particularly faithful reflection of public sentiment—at least as it is expressed at election time. The proportion of seats won by a party is frequently quite different from the proportion of votes it attracts across the country. In 2010, for instance, the Republicans secured 55.6 percent (or 242) of the House's 435 seats but only 51.6 percent of the votes cast nationally. This did not betray an innate Republican bias in the system, just one that generally favors the party that wins control of the body. In 2008, the Democrats had won 59.1 percent of the seats with 53.2 percent of the vote.[6]

It would be unfair to fault Congress for this. Not everyone participates in congressional elections, particularly in midterms when there is no presidential race and when turnout often amounts to only about 40 percent of eligible voters—in 2010 the figure was 41 percent. Moreover, the electoral system used to translate public preferences into members of Congress has been largely constructed from an amalgam of constitutional edicts, court rulings, and state laws. Legislators cannot really be held responsible for the rules they are elected under. The Constitution grants each state two senators and distributes House seats among them based upon their relative population. To be sure, the mandate that House members be elected in single-member districts emanates from federal statute originally passed in 1842 and iterated for a final time in 1967, but critical electoral rules like the simple plurality voting system and the timing of elections are essentially beyond the control of Congress. The drawing of House district lines, a practice undertaken every decade after the census, is the charge of state legislatures.[7] The frequent gerrymandering members might either benefit from or be hurt by is formally out of their hands.[8] Voter qualifications are protected by the Constitution in the Fifteenth, Nineteenth, Twenty-Fourth, and Twenty-Sixth Amendments, which prevent Americans from being denied the vote on the basis of race, gender, inability to pay a poll tax, and, unless they are under eighteen, age. They are more precisely defined by state law. The 1965 Voting Rights Act and its four subsequent updates demonstrate Congress's authority and willingness to affect voting practices, although enforcement authority lies with the US Department of Justice. Recent efforts to bolster the integrity of elections by compelling voters to show identification as well as to make participation easier by liberalizing absentee requirements and allowing people to register and vote in a single transaction came from by the states.[9]

As such, members of Congress can really influence electoral rules only at the margins, and then only on certain circumscribed issues. They have the ultimate authority to seat colleagues, although today this occurs rarely and only for extremely close and contested races. The system of campaign finance is probably the principal way Congress affects election administration, but even here it has not operated unfettered. Complex and comprehensive restrictions on money in congressional elections have been set in a variety of federal laws. Most recently the Bipartisan Campaign Reform Act (BCRA) of 2002 banned unlimited and lightly regulated soft money donations to parties, increased individual contribution ceilings to candidates, and prohibited advertising that named a federal candidate in the thirty days before a primary and sixty days before a general election (Malbin 2006). Court decisions then repealed or amended many of these rules. In *Buckley v. Valeo* (1976), the Supreme Court declared statutory limits on how much congressional candidates could spend an unconstitutional violation of the First Amendment. In *Citizens United v. Federal Election Commission* (2010), the court issued a blanket prohibition against legal restrictions on independent federal election expenditures by interest groups. The decision essentially paved the way for what are now called Super PACs, entities not formally associated with a candidate that can spend unlimited amounts from unconstrained sources to influence voters.

Despite all this, the outcomes of modern House elections have still traditionally captured the fundamental public mood of the time, and they have shaped the policy agenda and actions of the subsequent Congress by altering the behavior of returning incumbents or electing significant numbers of freshmen shaped by the political conditions that propelled them to victory. For example, in 2010 a poor economy, concerns about the country's fiscal health, and discontent with policies crafted by President Barack Obama and the Democratic majorities in Congress allowed Republicans to pick up six seats in the Senate and a net of sixty-three in the House, delivering control of the lower chamber to them in the biggest defeat for a presidential party in terms of House seats lost since 1938. Eighty-four Republican freshmen were elected to the House. An amorphous but extremely energetic collection of conservative activist groups, frequently labeled the Tea Party, endorsed, campaigned for, and contributed money to Republican candidates who shared their deep animosity toward the Obama administration and its policies (Jacobson 2011) and zeal for the country's founding principles and reduced federal spending (Foley 2012; Skocpol and Williamson 2012). Although the Tea Party's impact on the election is sometimes overstated— endorsements seemed to matter only in primaries (Karpowitz et al. 2011) and most of its candidates were interested mainly in airing the movement's issues in quixotic, and ultimately fruitless, efforts to defeat powerful Democratic incumbents (Cho, Gimpel, and Shaw 2011)—there is little doubt constituent groups like Americans for Prosperity, Freedom Works, and Tea Party Patriots and associated figures like former Republican vice presidential nominee Sarah Palin and Fox News commentator Glenn Beck tapped into a deep discontent felt across the country. Exit polls reported that 73 percent of respondents were either dissatisfied or angry with the federal government and a majority explicitly supported the Tea Party movement.

The new House pushed in a markedly conservative direction. It immediately voted to repeal Obama's signature legislative accomplishment, the historic health care reform legislation, and later passed bills to reverse the administration's policy on the housing crisis and reduce regulatory burdens on businesses. In the summer of 2011, under intense pressure from his rank and file, Speaker John Boehner (R-OH), by threatening to withhold the House's required approval of a debt-limit extension, forced President Obama and the Democratic Senate to accept significant long-term cuts to government spending (Draper 2012, 222–280; Mann and Ornstein 2012, 10–30).[10] No previous Congress had so aggressively used the renewal of the federal government's borrowing authority as leverage before.

The same kinds of effects were felt in the House after the 1994 and 2006 elections. In the first of these, Republicans picked up fifty-four seats without losing a single one. They also secured a majority in the body for the first time in forty years. In a highly unusual strategy for a congressional party, House Republican leaders constructed a platform for their candidates to run on. Their Contract with America did not resonate especially with the electorate—of the approximately 30 percent of voters who had even heard of the document, only one-sixth said that it made them more likely to vote Republican (Jacobson 1996). But it did provide an agenda that matched the acrimony of the time, much of which was aimed at President Bill Clinton and a Democratic Congress that had not appreciably improved the economy or solved crucial problems like rising crime. The contract also provided coherence to Republicans as they set about moving policy rightward. It listed ten measures on subjects ranging from congressional reform to overhauls of the welfare and criminal justice systems (Gimpel 1996).[11] With the exception of a constitutional amendment mandating term limits for members of Congress, the House passed all of them within one hundred days, although not all made it into law.

Voters were upset again in 2006 but this time with Republicans, particularly President George W. Bush. The economy was in relatively good shape, but there was considerable frustration with the wars in Afghanistan and Iraq and a belief that, chiefly because of its handling of Hurricane Katrina the previous year, the administration was incapable of governing effectively. The proportion of the electorate that reported casting a protest vote against the president was, at 36 percent, about the same as in 2010 (Jacobson 2007). The Democrats secured a net gain of thirty-one seats and by doing so regained control of the House for the first time since 1994. The party's "Six for '06" platform could not make it past President Bush, but its chief elements—including a minimum wage increase, the implementation of the 9/11 Commission's recommendations, stem-cell research funding, and cutting student loan rates—all sailed through the House. Democratic leaders and committee chairs also worked hard to alter the administration's policies in Afghanistan and, particularly, Iraq. On more than one occasion, Speaker Nancy Pelosi (D-CA) called the administration's efforts in Iraq a "failure."[12] To be sure, Democrats enjoyed mixed success on this front—in early 2007, for example, Bush embarked on the "surge" in Iraq and added twenty thousand troops to US forces in the country—but there is no doubting the president was constrained. By September 2007, General David Petraeus, commander general of the multinational force in Iraq, was talking about a significant drawdown of US troops there. By 2009 spending on the Iraq war was coming down precipitously.

Other post–World War II midterms have brought large losses for the president's party and a change in the direction of American public policy. In 1974, just two months after President Gerald Ford had unconditionally pardoned his predecessor Richard Nixon for any crimes he might have committed during the Watergate scandal, congressional Republicans were routed. After losing a net forty-eight seats, they occupied only one-third of the House in the following Ninety-Fourth Congress, a nadir reminiscent of Lyndon Johnson's landslide in 1964 and surpassed only during the party's dark days of the Depression and New Deal. Ford was largely irrelevant and often invisible as congressional Democrats overhauled unemployment compensation, invigorated environmental regulations, approved major energy price controls, and enacted two significant tax reforms (Greene 1995).

Sometimes the effects of a significant electoral victory are mitigated. In 1958, a severe recession on the watch of President Dwight Eisenhower caused the Republicans to lose forty-eight seats. The result underscored the president's lame-duck status and intensified a leadership vacuum in Washington caused by ideological divisions among congressional Democrats. An influx of new more liberal Democratic members in the House—the important Democratic Study Group was formed in 1959 (Stevens, Miller, and Mann 1974)—battled with conservative southerners like Wilbur Mills (D-AR) and Howard W. Smith (D-VA) who still chaired crucial committees such as Ways and Means and Rules. Little got done, although the Landrum-Griffin Act, one of the most important pieces of modern labor legislation, was passed.

During presidential election years, congressional candidates occasionally ride into office on the coattails of the winning ticket. The result is a forceful push of public policy in the ideological direction of the incoming president. In 1964, Lyndon Johnson crushed his Republican opponent, Sen. Barry Goldwater (R-AZ), in the biggest popular vote victory since Franklin Roosevelt lost only Maine and Vermont to Alf Landon in 1936. House Democrats dramatically enlarged their majority by gaining thirty-seven seats. In the following Eighty-Ninth Congress, Johnson and the Democrats on the Hill set about enacting the Great Society. Medicare and Medicaid were established, the federal government first began to fund schools meaningfully, the Voting Rights Act was approved, and an array of environmental and regulatory legislation was enacted (Dallek 1999). Forty-four years later, Barack Obama's election to the White House extended new Democratic majorities in Congress—in the House by twenty-one seats. Although with perhaps not quite as far-reaching an agenda as Johnson, Obama and his legislative allies worked to convert the clear repudiation of the Bush years into changes in policy. After Congress had approved legislation arguably necessitated by economic crisis, such as the approximately $787 billion stimulus bill and measures to prop up the housing sector and assist individuals subject to foreclosure, Democrats in the House set about overhauling health care, regulating credit card companies, extending Food and Drug Administration (FDA) oversight to include tobacco, revamping the financial services industry, repealing Don't Ask, Don't Tell (DADT), and passing cap-and-trade rules. All but the last became law.

In 1980, it was Republicans who acted upon electoral vindication. The party narrowed the Democratic House majority by thirty-four seats, making it the slimmest advantage since the late 1950s. With a new Republican president, Ronald Reagan, and control of the Senate, Republicans set about enacting an ambitious conservative agenda. Tax and spending cuts were the prime goals and, with the assistance of conservative Democrats, House Republicans were able to radically reduce individual income and corporate taxes and to slash domestic spending by $35 billion for 1982 alone, an 8 percent reduction from the previous fiscal year.[13]

Sometimes elections generate reform impulses Congress turns into laws. The 1974 election, for example, gave birth to the "Watergate babies," a collection of seventy-five freshmen House Democrats that included Tom Harkin (D-IA), George Miller (D-CA), and Henry Waxman (D-CA) among their number. Along with many disgruntled returning liberals and some minority Republicans, the class set about overhauling House rules and procedures. Seniority was no longer sacrosanct, and the selection of committee chairs was essentially turned over to the Democratic caucus. As a result, three sitting chairs, F. Edward Hébert (D-LA) of armed services, Wright Patman (D-TX) of banking and currency, and W. R. Poage (D-TX) of agriculture, were cast aside. Committee proceedings were also opened up as the reformers brought increased transparency to the House's business (Deering and Smith 1997, 33–42; Rieselbach 1994, 45–93).

In 1992, the relative positions of the House parties were not changed particularly; the Republicans gained just nine seats. But a wave of retirements, many a result of the House Bank scandal touched on in Chapter 1, created room for 110 newcomers, the largest freshman class since 1948. Eighteen of the 63 Democratic rookies were women, some motivated by the Senate confirmation proceedings surrounding Clarence Thomas's nomination to the Supreme Court and the belief that Washington was rife with sexism and insensitive to women's interests.[14] Others, including many of the Republicans, arrived outraged over the previous Congress's scandals. This energy, which created impetus for the liberal component of incoming president Bill Clinton's policy agenda—health care reform, family and medical leave, Americorps, gun control, and

DADT—therefore also pushed for political change.[15] Reform efforts undertaken by an alliance of members on the Joint Committee on the Organization of Congress, energetic freshmen, and outside good-government groups such as the Renewing Congress Project were, however, largely unsuccessful. Campaign finance reform, a revamp of the committee system, and a concerted attempt to force members of Congress to live under the same laws as the rest of the country were blocked by a combination of obstructionist Republicans and reluctant senior Democrats, most notably the listless Speaker Tom Foley (D-WA) (Mann and Ornstein 2006, 85–95). It would not be until the following Congress, with new Republican majorities in both chambers and fresh reform-minded leadership, that real change would take place. The Congressional Accountability Act, subjecting legislators to federal laws from which they had previously been exempt, became law at the very beginning of 1995.[16] The House also cut committees and staff, established term limits for the Speaker and committee chairs, banned proxy voting in committees, ordered greater transparency for formal meetings, and started a thorough audit of the institution's books.

To provide more systematic and comprehensive data consistent with the basic argument that Congress responds to election results, I present Figure 3.1. The graph plots the votes cast for individuals of the two major parties that was won by Republicans against the chamber membership's median DW-NOMINATE score for the following Congress. The data points are labeled by year of the election and include all contests from the end of World War II through 2008. As can plainly be seen, electoral support for Republicans is transformed quite faithfully into a commensurate move rightward of the House median: high values of DW-NOMINATE denote a relatively conservative body. It moves back when Americans vote for Democrats. There are some exceptions, however. The first two elections, in 1946 and 1948, were good for Democrats but did not result in particularly liberal Houses, largely because back then the parties were not quite so ideologically distinct. Many conservative southerners populated the Democratic caucus. The big differences in DW-NOMINATE scores between 2004 and 2006 demonstrate the polarization I mentioned in Chapter 1. When the parties are as ideologically different as they are today, a change in the majority party can result in large and often exaggerated shifts in the position of the chamber median. These particular findings are consistent with Bafumi and Herron's (2010) work that shows members to be more extreme than their constituents, even when their seats have just changed hands between the parties.

The connection between election results and the ideological composition of the Senate is attenuated somewhat because only one-third of the body is up each cycle. There are, however, numerous examples of elections that have profound effects on behavior. The 1980 Senate elections were historic in that Republican gains of twelve seats brought the party majority status. Liberal Democratic stalwarts such as Birch Bayh (D-IN), Frank Church (D-ID), John Culver (D-IA), George McGovern (D-SD), Warren Magnuson (D-WA), and Gaylord Nelson (D-WI) were defeated. Some

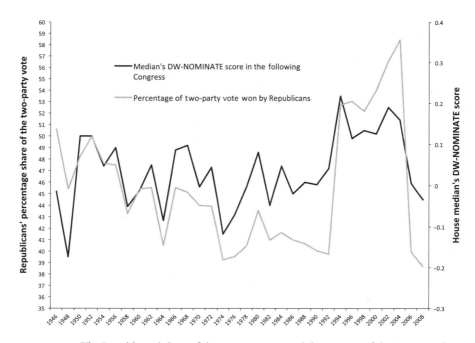

FIGURE 3.1 The Republicans' share of the two-party vote and the position of the House median in the following Congress

of the new Republicans, like Paula Hawkins (R-FL), Don Nickles (R-OK), Dan Quayle (R-IN), and Steve Symms (R-ID), provided significant support to conservative causes. In 1986, the tide turned and Republicans lost seven of the seats they had gained six years earlier.[17] This enabled the Democrats to seize back control of the Senate and essentially release any hold the Reagan administration had over domestic policy matters—forcing through, for example, significant deficit-reduction measures including tax increases and, over Reagan's vetoes, important transportation, water quality, and civil rights legislation. As noted earlier, 1994 witnessed a further reversal when the Republicans again captured the majority. The election of conservatives like Spencer Abraham (R-MI), John Ashcroft (R-MO), Bill Frist (R-TN), Rod Grams (R-MN), James Inhofe (R-OK), Jon Kyl (R-AZ), Rick Santorum (R-PA), and Fred Thompson (R-TN) provided significant momentum to a Republican policy revolution that had clearly begun in the House.

Because the Senate is so much smaller than the House, membership change brought about outside of the regular election process can have substantial impact on the body. In May 2001, James Jeffords, a Republican from Vermont, decided to bolt from his party and become an independent willing to support the Democrats. At the time the chamber had fifty senators from each party and was led by the Republicans only because Vice President Dick Cheney had the authority to break tie votes on organizational matters.

Jeffords's defection therefore formally placed the body in Democratic hands, and Tom Daschle (D-SD) became majority leader.[18] The consequences for policy outcomes were probably minimal because that September Al Qaeda attacked the United States: 9/11 dominated politics and the next year was devoted to bipartisan efforts to prosecute the war on terrorism, strengthen internal security, and mitigate a recession. A second example comes from the Eighty-Third Congress. Republicans held the presidency and a one-seat advantage over the Democrats as the Senate convened. But during 1953 and 1954 nine Senators died and one resigned. This tilted the balance in favor of the Democrats on two occasions, and they could have taken control for much of 1954. Instead they accepted Republican stewardship; possibly because Minority Leader Lyndon B. Johnson understood how difficult management of the ongoing investigation of Senator Joseph McCarthy (R-WI) might be for his party. Again policy remained largely unaffected.

Responsiveness to Public Opinion

As noted, responsiveness to election results perhaps does not provide the best or fairest way to judge Congress's sensitivity to the public's will. We should therefore also explore whether the legislature tracks the views of Americans as they are expressed in a less formal but more frequent manner outside elections. In other words, we ought to investigate whether congressional behavior reflects public opinion. One way to do this is to compare the DW-NOMINATE score of the median House member and senator with a measure of the public's position on the same liberal-to-conservative dimension. Left- or rightward moves in mass attitudes should be matched by those in the same direction and of approximately the same magnitude undertaken by the median legislators. Fortunately James Stimson (Erikson, MacKuen, and Stimson 2002; Stimson 1991, 2004) has constructed a basic measure of the country's "policy mood" from a bevy of public opinion surveys administered from the early 1950s to the present. The public's mood is placed on a single ideological scale with higher values indicating greater liberalism.

Figure 3.2 tracks Stimson's measure against the DW-NOMINATE score of the median House member and Senator for every Congress since the Eighty-Third, which opened in 1953. Because mood scores are annual, I provide the average score of the two years of each Congress. I have inverted the axis for the DW-NOMINATE scores to make them directionally consistent with the mood data.

The figure tells an interesting story. The public mood indicator reveals increasing liberalism through the 1950s and 1960s, a quite dramatic turn to the right as we move through the 1970s, a snap back leftward in the 1980s through the early 1990s, ten years of moderate conservatism divided by the turn of the millennium, and a recent but hardly dramatic liberal turn in the past handful of years. The story of the 1950s and 1960s is well known. To social commentators like Lionel Trilling (1950), the early part of the period was marked by a liberal hegemony in which business and labor came

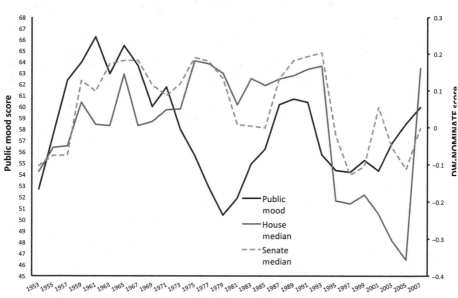

FIGURE 3.2 Public opinion and the ideological placement of median House and Senate member, 1953–2008

to a consensus forged by economic prosperity and a fear of communism. This liberal creed took on a sharper tone in the 1960s as the civil rights, students', women's, and environmental movements compounded the New Deal belief that government could solve problems like social inequality and poverty (Milkis and Mileur 2005). The 1970s saw a strong reaction to this as traditional conservatives lamented a dramatic decline in respect for authority and moral values, and economic conservatives worked to reduce taxes and the reach of government (Berman 1994; Edsall 1991).

By comparison to the tumultuous years from 1960 to the mid-1980s, the past quarter century has seen public views moderate. At first glance this is difficult to believe. After all, we have witnessed terrorist attacks, wrenching wars in Iraq and Afghanistan, economic and fiscal crises, and polarizing cultural debates. But throughout the 1990s Gallup reported that a plurality of Americans considered themselves moderates rather than liberal or conservative.[19] Only in 2009 did that change, when 40 percent self-identified as conservative. In 2010, a historic year for Republicans at the polls, the figure was still only 42 percent. It dropped to 35 percent in 2012 when 44 percent considered themselves moderates. Moreover, as Morris Fiorina, Samuel Abrams, and Jeremy Pope (2010) have written, Americans are not quite as divided on issues like abortion and homosexual rights as the media and the behavior of political elites would lead us to believe. Those with megaphones—such as talk-show hosts, political pundits, and, of course, members of Congress—may be shrill, but today the rest of America seems to be a fairly middle-of-the-road place.

During only one of these episodes are both bodies of Congress discernibly out of step with public opinion. Democrats were able to maintain control of Congress in the 1970s and, although they lost the Senate between 1981 and 1986, the House as well through the late 1980s. There may have been some conservative movement on high-profile policy outcomes—the Carter Congresses enacted airline and trucking deregulation, for example—but on roll calls the House and Senate remained quite far to the left of the public. This was a period of elevated inflation and unemployment and a period of concomitant decline in confidence in government and the policies made largely by the Democrats who controlled it. It was also a period when greater ideological cohesion among congressional Democrats encouraged their leaders to take control of both legislative procedures and their rank and file, in turn greatly reducing the willingness and opportunity for their more conservative colleagues to buck the party (Rohde 1991).

You also get a sense that the House was markedly more conservative than the public and the Senate in the late 1990s through 2005. The ambitious and forceful agenda of Speaker Newt Gingrich (R-GA), based on the Contract with America that many new Republican members believed had won them majority status in the 1994 elections, energized a cohort of conservative Republicans who were discernibly to the right of their more senior colleagues. They continued with this agenda, motivated initially by deep animosity to the Clinton administration—best exemplified by the House's impeachment of the president in late 1998—and then by support for President George W. Bush's neoconservative foreign policy and tax-cutting philosophy. Throughout these years House Republicans clung to majorities that were among the smallest in history, and, as Bush's slim victories in 2000 and 2004 demonstrate, the Republican grip on national power was far from tight.

Apart from these two examples, however, the bodies do a reasonable job of tracking public opinion, an observation consistent with the work of Stimson and his colleagues, who quite crucially demonstrate that it is Congress tracking the public and not the other way around (Stimson, MacKuen, and Erikson 1995; Erikson, MacKuen, and Stimson 2002). At least on domestic policy, Congress followed the public to the left in the 1960s. It followed the public to the right through the first half of the 1990s. Whether the public's views are translated into congressional behavior through elections and member replacement rather than an alteration of the positions of sitting legislators is really secondary to this basic finding, although it is worth noting that Figure 3.2 does provide evidence for the first of these propositions. The House only moved to match the public's conservatism in the 1990s when the Republicans won a majority in the 1994 elections and to pull close to the public's liberalism when Democrats took the reins after the 2006 contests.

Some of the incongruity might be because as individuals members vote mainly to satisfy the electoral coalition they need to put together to win their next election—one that is made up largely of people who identify with their party and therefore have preferences discernibly to the left or right of the district median (Bishin 2000). This is reinforced by the need to win primaries, contests for the party's nomination dominated by activists who tend to be considerably more extreme than other voters (Fiorina and Levendusky 2006). Research demonstrates House Republicans are particularly receptive to the policy demands of district partisans (Clinton 2006). Moreover, some argue legislators' roll-call behavior is a response to the interests of their most affluent and politically active constituents, a group not fully representative of the public as a whole (Bartels 2008). Others, such as Bill Bishop (2008), suggest congressional districts are gerrymandered into homogenous units where one party can dominate and the views of its followers are accentuated and unchallenged on the campaign trail. The result is a House of Representatives full of entrenched ideologues. Still, even this skeptical literature is not totally inconsistent with the observation that members are in tune with large numbers of the people they serve.

Additional evidence suggests Congress meets, or at least approaches, this first benchmark. Tracy Sulkin (2011) demonstrates that in recent congressional elections members generally keep the promises they make on the stump. They do so because voters hold them accountable for what they have said during the campaign.

The public also holds members accountable for their roll-call records (Ansolabehere and Jones 2010). Those who vote most obstinately with their parties and against their constituents' wishes are most likely to lose the upcoming election (Canes-Wrone, Brady, and Cogan 2002; Carson et al. 2010). Members respond to their constituents' opinions at the individual issue level as well (Canes-Wrone, Minozzi, and Reveley 2011; Nicholson-Crotty, Peterson, and Ramirez 2009). This is particularly the case for matters, such as welfare, health care, and education, that are important to the public (Wlezien 2004). Many House Democrats are believed to have lost their seats in the 2010 midterms because of their support for items on the Obama agenda, particularly health care reform (Nyhan et al. 2012).[20] Among the influential and previously popular Democrats who voted for the Patient Protection and Affordable Care Act (PPACA) and lost were Jim Oberstar (D-MN), Ike Skelton (D-MO), and John Spratt (D-SC), all of them chairs of standing committees. Both collectively and individually, therefore, members of Congress track public opinion fairly well because they face punishment at the ballot box if they do otherwise. This, quite clearly, is a description of a pretty healthy representative democracy.

BENCHMARK #2
To promote local interests, about half of members' overall effort and resources should be devoted to district and state concerns.

Justification
As with their endeavors to represent national opinion, members of Congress are shaped greatly by rules imposed on them as they work to promote more local concerns. In

many ways, the Constitution and state and federal law assist them in this task. Although numerous states used the general ticket system until the Apportionment Act of 1842—Connecticut, Georgia, New Hampshire, and New Jersey were the most prominent examples—since 1900 House members have nearly always come from single-member districts. Legislation passed in 1967 mandated that they do.[21] Each represents roughly seven hundred thousand people who live in contiguous areas fully contained within a single state and that are often dominated by a single or very small number of industries. The population is frequently racially and religiously homogenous, and policy preferences can be quite uniform too. Legislators selected by this kind of system from districts where there is little diversity of ideology and opinion on national issues seem to be chosen by many voters on the basis of the "personal vote," or what Bruce Cain, John Ferejohn, and Morris Fiorina (1987, 9) understood as electoral support that emanates from the candidate's "personal qualities, qualifications, activities, and record." A central part of congressional elections since the 1950s, voters look particularly to how the incumbent has represented the district's concerns and their own immediate interests (Herrera and Yawn 1999). This is done largely by securing federal resources for local businesses, nonprofits, and governments and by assisting constituents in their dealings with the federal government—casework such as locating lost Social Security checks, deciphering eligibility requirements for veterans' benefits, and expediting passport requests.

The Senate is more naturally predisposed to divining national opinion because of its larger, more heterogeneous constituencies and the constitutional imperatives that it ratify treaties and confirm presidential appointments. That the body is viewed as a springboard to the presidency adds to this (Burden 2002). Senate campaigns tend to focus on the "bigger" issues (Abramowitz and Segal 1992). This has not prevented senators from promoting parochial interests, however. Research on the content of senators' press releases reveals their authors to be tremendously interested in securing federal resources for their states (Grimmer 2010). Attentiveness to local needs is particularly acute among senators from small states (Atlas, Hendershott, and Zupan 1997; Lee and Oppenheimer 1999).

Such localism is evident in bodies across the globe. It is the case in Latin America, where electoral rules provide incentives for legislators to cultivate a personal vote (Crisp, Kanthak, and Leijonhufvud 2004), something that is exacerbated in the open-list or primary systems of candidate nomination most typical in the Western Hemisphere (Carey and Shugart 1995). In Argentina (Eaton 2002), Brazil (Ames 1995; Desposato and Scheiner 2009; Mainwaring 1999), and Mexico (Langston 2010), legislators work continually to secure for their constituents programs funded by the central government. These can be in the form of roads, sewers, and law enforcement resources.

It is also surprisingly the case in parliamentary and unitary systems like the United Kingdom, however, where incentives to secure particularized benefits are not supposed to be strong and legislators presumably focus on national policy and the elements of the governing party's platform. A number of scholars have shown that members of these bodies focus quite intently on pork-barrel politics and the personal requests of constituents who are having trouble navigating local and national bureaucracies (Heitshusen, Young, and Wood 2005; Gaines 1998). In the British case, the parochialism is largely attributable to single-member and quite small constituencies—roughly seventy thousand eligible voters in the 2010 election.

It makes sense to create a benchmark for Congress from observations of legislatures in which lawmakers are elected from single-member districts in simple-plurality contests. These legislators do not share representational responsibilities with colleagues, and the number of constituents they serve is generally quite small. Of course, with its two-member districts and large constituencies—forty-three states today have a population of at least one million—senators should find it harder to meet any benchmark. Regardless, I think a high bar constitutes an appropriate standard for us to apply to congressional performance in the aggregate. Excessive localism should be avoided, not least because an unhealthy focus on parochial concerns would lead to uneven and incoherent policy riddled with exceptions. But surveys have suggested a plurality of Americans prefer their representatives work on local issues rather than national ones (Grant and Rudolph 2004). This has probably been the case since French aristocrat and astute political observer Alexis de Tocqueville toured the country during the Jacksonian era. Tocqueville observed that Americans saw their representative not only as a legislator for the state but "as the proxy of each of his supporters, and they flatter themselves that he will not be less zealous in defense of their private interests than of those of the country" (Tocqueville 1945, 2:91).

Appraisal

Unfortunately, we do not have comprehensive data on longitudinal changes in members' attention to the kind of local and even quite personal matters constituents evidently would like addressed. The literature on casework shows members' attentiveness to the matter shapes public views of them (McAdams and Johannes 1988; Parker 1980; Parker and Goodman 2009; Serra and Moon 1994). It does not speak to fluctuations across time and how valuable casework is to institutional performance, however. What we might call "local issues" are really addressed in political science by studies of distributive or pork-barrel spending patterns—where federal grants and contracts go. Again, however, individual members, and not the legislature as a whole, provide the unit of analysis. The scholarship has focused largely on whose constituents get the lion's share of this federal spending (Bickers and Stein 2000, 2004; Lee 2003; Lowry and Potoski 2004; Primo and Snyder 2010; Rundquist and Carsey 2002; Stein and Bickers 1995). It is frequently members with important institutional positions or from competitive districts.

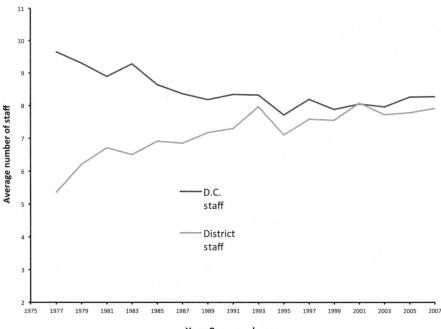

FIGURE 3.3 The average number of staff per House member assigned to Washington and the district, 1977–2008

Still, even if we cannot directly and systematically observe members reflecting and acting upon local concerns, we can examine the time and resources they commit to such issues. Attention to constituency needs, after all, is a necessary condition for Congress to perform this valuable function. Figure 3.3 displays data from a Congressional Research Service report on the number of staff House members have placed in both their Washington and district offices since 1977 (Petersen 2010, Reynolds, and Wilhelm 2010). It demonstrates quite dramatically that members have assigned an increasingly larger proportion of their staff closer to their constituents. The trend escalated particularly quickly in the 1980s so that by today House members' personal staff is split almost evenly between Capitol Hill and the district.

Casework is the prime responsibility of district and state staff. The greater investment of staff resources back home is therefore an obvious indicator of members' increased attention to the more personal needs of the public. Even a perfunctory glance at legislators' professional websites confirms this. Members tend to advertise their willingness to help constituents with private concerns as much as they do their legislative accomplishments on the national stage (Adler, Gent, and Overmeyer 1998).

Members also seem to be spending more time at home. Figure 3.4 displays the number of days per Congress the House and Senate were in session from the end of

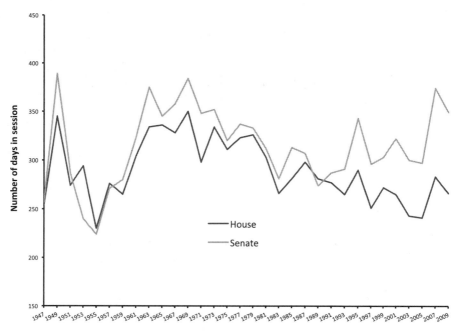

FIGURE 3.4 The number of days the House and Senate were in session per Congress, 1947–2010

World War II until today. The general trend since the late 1970s has been for both bodies to give their members increased opportunities to visit with their constituents. It accelerated on the House side in the 1990s as many legislators felt increased pressure to attend closely to voters and Republican leaders were keen to contrast their members' openness and sensitivity to mass opinion with the previous professionalized, aloof, and elite Democratic Congresses. It has been facilitated in both the House and Senate as leaders have adjusted legislative schedules to allow career-minded members more time to attend to their constituents. There are frequent recesses—recently relabeled "district work periods" in the House—and floor votes and committee business are generally squeezed in during the middle of the work week. Observers frequently refer to the House as a "Tuesday–Thursday" club (Nokken and Sala 2002). Rules provide members with generous travel allowances that increase the further the member's home is from Washington. Since 1995 the House, as part of a general office or Member's Representational Allowance (MRA), has also permitted members to spend on travel at the expense of other overhead.

When it took control at the beginning of 2007, the new Democratic majority vowed to spend more time in Washington making policy (Taylor 2012a, 184). The recent increase in session time has been short lived, at least for the lower chamber.

Under Speaker John Boehner (R-OH) and Majority Leader Eric Cantor (R-VA), the new Republican majority leadership pledged at the beginning of the 112th Congress in January 2011 to adhere to a "two-weeks-on-one-week-off" schedule so as to save tax-payers money and provide members with greater certainty as they planned their professional lives. In the formal announcement Cantor seemed not to realize that perhaps the policy's most important effect would be to allow members lengthier stays at home.

Overall, the Senate is in formal session for approximately half of the time. The House's sessions are a bit shorter for just about every observation in the time series, perhaps highlighting its more parochial inclinations or the Senate's tradition of unlimited debate, a procedural distinction we shall discuss later. Regardless, I think it is fair to say the House has provided constituents with ample opportunity to communicate their views on local and personal matters directly to their representatives. The second benchmark is met.

One last point on provincialism is in order. We cannot satisfactorily analyze how much of Congress's legislative activity is concerned with local or state issues and how much is more national in scope. It is prohibitively difficult to determine whether a bill introduced or passed in Congress has primarily local effects or is designed to solve more collective problems—think, for example, of defense and transportation authorization and appropriations bills that essentially set broad federal policies in these areas but are often considered full of pork-barrel spending for members.

But we can identify some activities that are probably indicative of the kind of excessive localism and unhealthy policy process we should want to avoid. According to data from the Congressional Bills Project, commemorative legislation, in which Congress names public buildings, issues honorific titles and medals, and recognizes achievements and causes, has increased twofold as a proportion of all House bills introduced since the 1980s.[22] In absolute terms, however, it still only accounts for about 3 percent of the measures the House considers each Congress. Private bills introduced by members to provide relief and exceptional treatment for an individual, most often on immigration matters, have decreased in number precipitously (Boylan 2002; Hill and Williams 1993). Only 116 of these bills were introduced in the House and Senate in the 111th Congress of 2009–2010, about one-tenth of those introduced in the 93rd Congress thirty-six years earlier.

Congressional attitudes toward earmarks have improved as well. An earmark is funding that is directed by law to geographically specific projects. These might include support for highways, ports, fire houses, academic centers, mass transit, and cultural amenities. Members generally request them at the subcommittee or full committee stage, and they are most often inserted into appropriations bills then (Crespin, Finocchiaro, and Wanless 2009; Lazarus 2010). According to CRS, there were 15,877 earmarks worth $47.4 billion inserted into bills for the 2005 fiscal year. By 2010 these numbers were 9,499 and $15.9 billion respectively. The decline is explained by greater public criticism of earmarks. Groups such as Taxpayers for Common Sense and Ending

Spending have worked assiduously to get media coverage of the issue, and it was central part of the Tea Party's "campaign" in the 2010 elections. In turn, this opprobrium has brought about both formal and informal reforms. The new Democratic majority altered House and Senate rules early in 2007 to list the proposers of earmarks and narrowly targeted tax cuts in committee and conference reports. Members were also permitted to bring against an earmark a point of order that made its provisions debatable. President George W. Bush directed executive departments and bureaus to ignore earmarks contained in endnotes or appendixes of the formal legislative record. In 2010 House Democratic leaders announced a ban on earmarks to for-profit entities, and Republicans imposed an outright prohibition on earmarks originating from their members.

BENCHMARK #3
To further descriptive representation, at least one in every four members of Congress should be a woman.

Justification

Many legislative bodies in advanced industrialized Western democracies are between 35 and 45 percent female—particularly those in northern Europe like Sweden (45 percent in 2011), Finland (40 percent), Belgium (39 percent), and the Netherlands (39 percent). Rich countries in the Anglophone world have smaller proportions of women legislators and for cultural reasons provide more reasonable targets. In 2011 Australia's lower body was 25 percent female, Canada's and the United Kingdom's 22 percent. With the exception of the British House of Lords, the upper bodies had greater proportions of women. Toward the low end of Western democracies were Catholic countries like France and Ireland, the latter having around 18 percent women in the lower house, 21 percent in the upper house.[23] Closer to home the National Conference of State Legislatures (NCSL) reported in 2009 that 24 percent of legislators in the American states were women.[24] States in New England and the southwest had particularly large proportions of female legislators.

Countries like Argentina, Finland, and South Africa have "gender-based quotas" where positions on party lists or actual seats in parliament are reserved for women (Hughes 2011; Jones 2009).[25] The United States does not and arguably should not.[26] But, given that about 51 percent of the general population is female and some Western countries reach levels much higher, a benchmark of 25 percent is certainly not unduly demanding. The United Nations set the goal that 30 percent of all national legislators be women back in 1995.

Appraisal

As Figure 3.5 shows, even though the first women were elected to Congress in the early twentieth century—Jeannette Rankin (R-MN) to the House in 1916, Hattie

Wyatt Caraway (D-AR) to the Senate in 1932—the institution is still quite some way short of this benchmark.[27] It was not until the 1970s that women regularly won sizable numbers of seats without the help of familial association—before then many succeeded their late husbands. Mae Ella Nolan (R-CA) became the first woman to chair a House committee in 1923 but, because the committee had the rather unimportant jurisdiction of post office expenditures, it was not until Mary T. Norton (D-NJ) headed the Committee on Labor in the Seventy-Fifth Congress, begun in 1937, that a woman really occupied a position of some formal power in the House. A comparable breakthrough in the Senate was not seen until Nancy Landon Kassebaum (R-KS) became chair of Labor and Human Resources in 1995.[28] It also took a long time for women to be selected for formal leadership positions within the congressional parties. Chase Going Woodhouse (D-CT) was appointed Democratic caucus chair in the House in 1945 and Margaret Chase Smith (R-ME) became Republican conference chair in the Senate four years later. Of the 270-odd women who have served in Congress, only one has been a body's leader. After Democrats took control of the House in the 2006 elections, they elected Nancy Pelosi (D-CA) to be its Speaker the following January.

The figure demonstrates a slow but nevertheless discernible and presumably irreversible increase in the number of women serving per Congress since Rankin was first elected. The House and Senate are at least traveling in the right direction. The movement is essentially linear, although there have been a couple of periods of acceleration. A year after the controversial and, for the Senate at least, embarrassing confirmation process for Supreme Court nominee Clarence Thomas, observers declared 1992 "The Year of the Woman" as forty-seven women won election to the House (forty-eight if you include the delegate from the District of Columbia, Eleanor Holmes Norton) and four to the Senate, Barbara Boxer (D-CA), Dianne Feinstein (D-CA), Carol Moseley-Braun (D-IL) and Patty Murray (D-WA). Some female candidates that year—including Murray allegedly—were motivated to run by the sexism they believed the all-male Senate Judiciary Committee demonstrated in its treatment of Anita Hill, a law professor who accused Thomas of sexual harassment when he was her superior at the Equal Employment Opportunity Commission. As members, they had appreciable influence on the legislative process, and many aggressively pursued passage of bills on issues important to women (Swers 2002). For no other apparent reason than pure coincidence, the 107th Congress saw a greater than 50 percent increase in the number of female senators. Joining nine colleagues were Maria Cantwell (D-WA), Hillary Rodham Clinton (D-NY), and Debbie Stabenow (D-MI) all elected in 2000. Jean Carnahan (D-MO) and Lisa Murkowski (R-AK) were appointed to the Senate later in that Congress—Carnahan replaced her husband who was posthumously elected in 2000, and Murkowski was selected by her father to succeed him on his swearing in as Alaska's governor. The 2012 elections brought five new women to the Senate—Tammy Baldwin (D-WI), Heidi Heitkamp (D-ND), Mazie Hirono (D-HI), and Elizabeth Warren (D-MA)—bringing the body's total of female members to a record twenty.

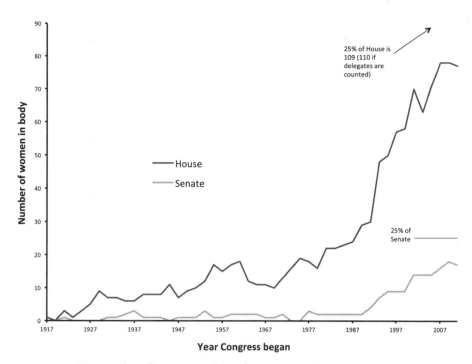

FIGURE 3.5 The number of women members of Congress, 1917–2011

Why does Congress have so few female members? Among the reasons offered are voters' prejudices (Fox and Smith 1998; Lawless and Fox 2005), more intense competition for their seats than that experienced by men (Milyo and Schosberg 2000; Lawless and Pearson 2008), and a greater reluctance on the part of women to run for office because of the tremendous strains campaigns place on a candidate's family life (Lawless and Fox 2005). In their study of Pelosi's career, Ronald Peters and Cindy Simon Rosenthal (2010, 193–226) also suggest the existence of an innate sexism in Congress.

BENCHMARK #4
To further descriptive representation, at least 9 percent
of members of Congress should be African American
and 3 percent should be Hispanic.

Justification

It is similarly tricky to set ethnic, racial, and religious targets. Definitions of minority peoples differ across the globe. Moreover, in some places the representation of racial, ethnic, national, or religious minorities in government is inflated because the group traditionally holds a great deal of political and economic power. So perhaps it is best to stick to the American context. In 2009, the NCSL found that 9 percent of seats in state legislatures were held by African Americans, 3 percent by Hispanics, and 1 percent by Asian Americans—a figure inflated by the high proportion of native Hawaiians in elected office there. The numbers varied tremendously by state. Not unsurprisingly blacks were represented in larger proportions in southern states, where they make up a greater percentage of the general population. The same logic applies to Latinos and Latinas, who made up more than one-fifth of the legislators in the southwestern states of California, New Mexico, and Texas. At the very least, proportions similar to these seem a reasonable benchmark for Congress.

Appraisal

The application of the race and ethnicity of membership benchmark reveals a mixed performance. Figure 3.6 shows the number of African Americans who have served in Congress since 1929. It tells two distinct stories. Whereas the House has met the benchmark for the size of its black membership, the Senate is woefully short of it. The first black senator was Hiram Rhodes Revels, a Republican who was appointed to a vacant seat to represent Mississippi for just two years, 1870 and 1871, during Reconstruction. Blanche Kelso Bruce, another Republican from Mississippi, became the first African American selected to a full term in the Senate in 1874. When he left after giving up on pursuit of a second term, it took eighty-five years until another black man became a member of the body, Edward W. Brooke (R-MA). Brooke was the first African American popularly elected to the Senate. The first black woman and Democrat were not elected until 1992 when Carol Moseley-Braun won her contest in Illinois. Two of the other three African-American senators have also been Illinois Democrats—Barack Obama, who was elected in 2004, and the man who was controversially selected to succeed him when he entered the White House, Roland Burris. The third is Tim Scott (R-SC) who was appointed to fill a vacancy in late 2012. Possible reasons for the dearth of black senators are that states with larger proportions of African Americans tend to have more racially conservative white populations (Avery and Fine 2012) and that black House members running for the higher office tend to have roll-call records well to the left of median voters in Senate elections (Johnson, Oppenheimer, and Selin 2012).

The story of African American House members has five distinct parts. The first is set during Reconstruction when, free and granted citizenship and voting rights, black southerners teamed up with pro-Union whites to elect Republicans to Congress. Several of these men were black, reflecting the burgeoning influence and fundamental size of the African American population in the South. In 1870 Joseph Rainey of South Carolina—a state with a majority black population—was elected to the House. Between then and the end of Reconstruction in the late 1870s, thirteen other African Americans, all from the South, served in the body. A smattering of others did so in the 1880s and

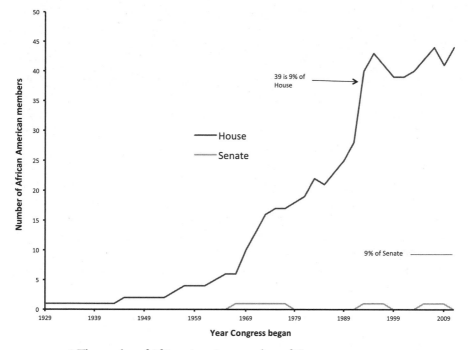

FIGURE 3.6 The number of African American members of Congress, 1929–2011

1890s. Between 1901 and 1929, however, there were no African American members. Black voting rights were rescinded by white Democratic state legislatures intent on seg-regating southern society when the federal government abandoned Reconstruction. Opportunities for African American political candidates were not much better in the North.

Although Oscar De Priest (R-IL) was elected in 1928, the third period is essentially barren too. It is not until the late 1960s, several years after the Civil Rights and Voting Rights Acts, that we witness a meaningful augmentation of black representation in the House. Benefitting from an influx of black migrants into northern cities and the ac-tivism and political organization of the broader civil rights movement, ten blacks were either elected or re-elected in 1968, including Shirley Chisholm (D-NY), John Conyers (D-MI), Gus Hawkins (D-CA), Adam Clayton Powell Jr. (D-NY), Louis Stokes (D-OH), and the path-breaking William L. Dawson (D-IL), the first African American to chair a standing committee when he was picked to head the Executive Departments panel in 1949.

In 1982, Congress extended the Voting Rights Act so as to, among other things, increase the number of African Americans in Congress by instructing states on how to draw House districts. The thinking was that, unless blacks could select a "candidate of choice," their votes were diluted, and their capacity to influence the policy process reduced commensurately. Following the next census in 1990, there was consequently a significant increase in the number of districts, particularly in the South, in which a majority of voters were black (Grose 2011, 38–44). This starts the fifth period. Thirteen new black members were elected from southern districts like these in 1992, including Rep. Jim Clyburn (D-SC), who would become majority whip in 2007, contributing to a 40 percent increase in African American representation in the House overall. Some of these states had not had a black member of Congress since Reconstruction. Even though the courts have whittled away at the constitutional justification for majority-minority districts, black representation in the House has not receded, and many African American members now represent districts that are majority white (Grose 2011).[29]

Congress does better on Hispanic representation. In the nineteenth century, Latino and Latina members tended to be delegates from territories or Puerto Rico and therefore did not have floor voting rights. The first fully recognized Hispanic member of Congress, Romualdo Pacheco, a Republican and former governor of California, was elected in 1876. Until recently, there have been relatively few Hispanic members, most of whom represented western states with large Spanish-speaking populations. In fact only seven Hispanics have ever served in the Senate and just forty-nine in the House. The vast majority of them have been Democrats. Eight Hispanics won election to the lower chamber for the first time in 1992 alone. They benefitted, like many black candidates, from the creation of majority-minority districts—although in these instances the constituencies were in places like California, New York, and Texas. In 2010 five Republican Hispanics won House seats, almost doubling the number of Hispanic Republicans who have ever served in the body.

During the 113th Congress of 2013–2015, twenty-eight Hispanics will serve in the House, three in the Senate—Bob Menendez (D-NJ), Marco Rubio (R-FL), and Ted Cruz (R-TX). In the case of the Senate, where Hispanics, like blacks, do not form a majority of constituents for any member, this is at the benchmark of 3 percent. The House also passes its test. Over one in twenty House members in the 113th Congress will be a Latino or Latina. The figures are also clearly rising. As the Hispanic population grows and becomes more organized and engaged in politics, its numbers are likely to increase even more (Casellas 2011).

Mainly because they make up quite small proportions of the general population, I do not analyze other racial and ethnic groups in quite the same way I do African Americans and Hispanics. It is worth noting, however, that the number of Asian Americans, native Hawaiians, or Pacific Islanders elected to Congress is beginning to rise quite dramatically. Of the twenty-one members that have been of Asian heritage, nine served in the 112th Congress. Native Americans, however, are as marginalized in Congress as they are broader society. Only one sitting federal legislator is Native American, Rep. Tom Cole (R-OK), who is a registered member of the Chickasaw Nation.

BENCHMARK # 5
To further descriptive representation, Congress's membership should reflect proportions of religious affiliation in the general population.

Justification
Americans are of many faiths. So are their state legislators. Although they often refuse to specify a religious affiliation when asked, according to the NCSL's 2009 figures, about 60 percent of lawmakers are Protestant, 28 percent Catholic, and 3 percent Jewish. This closely resembles the general population and seems a fair benchmark for Congress.

Appraisal
Congress clears the benchmark for religious heterogeneity. In the 112th Congress of 2011–2013, about 57 percent of members were Protestant, 29 percent Catholic, and 7 percent Jewish (Manning 2011). Baptists and Methodists made up the largest subgroups among the Protestants. The distribution essentially mirrors the general population with the qualifier that the proportion of Jewish members is quite a lot greater than in the country as a whole. There is also a smattering of Mormons, Greek Orthodox, Buddhists, and Muslims—Rep. Keith Ellison (D-MN) became the first Muslim elected to Congress in 2006. It is hard to argue Congress is not diverse when it comes to religious affiliation. What is more, the diversity has had some demonstrated policy effects. Research suggests members' religion has influenced their votes on issues like religious freedom and human cloning (Burden 2007, 112–136).

BENCHMARK #6
To further descriptive representation, Congress's membership should reflect the proportion of the general population that has served in the military.

Justification
Descriptive representation is a concept that extends to life experience and occupations as well. We do not have figures from the American states, but about 22 percent of the general adult population has served in the military. Given the foreign policy and national security responsibilities of Congress, it is not unreasonable to expect a similar proportion of the House and Senate membership to have been in uniform.

Appraisal

There were 118 veterans in the 112th Congress (Manning 2011). This constitutes a marked reduction in the number over time—there were 167 in the 107th Congress and 398 in the 91st Congress of 1969–1971 (Manning 2011). Undoubtedly a principal reason is that the generations that experienced the draft, particularly during World War II, Korea, and Vietnam, are dying or retiring from work (Bianco 2005). However, the current figures show Congress to be an almost exact microcosm of the general population and, therefore, to meet the benchmark. Twenty-two percent of members have served in the military. Moreover, the strong call to political service felt by veterans of recent conflicts like those in Iraq and Afghanistan means military personnel are likely to continue to win congressional elections in the future (Kurtz 2010). In 2010, twenty-seven Iraq and Afghanistan veterans were general election candidates for House or Senate seats.

BENCHMARK # 7

To further descriptive representation, Congress's membership should reflect the occupational types of the general population.

Justification

Congress could realize significant informational gains if its membership reflected the occupational diversity of broader society. According to the NCSL the approximately 85 percent of state legislators who did not count themselves as legislative professionals in 2007 reported a whole array of occupations. At about 15 and 12 percent of all legislators respectively, lawyers and the retired made up much of the group. In states like Florida, Massachusetts, Ohio, New Jersey, New York, and Texas, the NCSL's 2009 figures show more than one-quarter of members had JDs. But there were sizeable numbers of business owners, executives, educators, farmers, realtors, and medical professionals. Perhaps the only occupations appreciably underrepresented were the science and technology fields and the traditional trades. These omissions are not trivial, particularly given the complex nature of public policy. They should not, however, detract from the fundamental observation that this is an impressive diversity. Congress ought to be held to the same high standard.

Appraisal

Members certainly have diverse occupations and professional experiences. There is naturally a large representation of career politicians. For example, 263 members of the 112th Congress had been state legislators, 39 of them mayors, and over 100 of them congressional staffers. Eleven senators had been governors and 49 of them House members. Although there are only about two-thirds of the lawyers there were twenty-five years ago, the legal profession was also overrepresented and recent Congresses have had about 200 JDs. What is more, there tend to be very few members who could be considered laborers (Carnes 2012). Still, the 112th Congress counted numerous journalists, accountants, farmers, social workers, educators, doctors, psychologists, and ordained ministers among its members (Manning 2011). This is a performance that, in the very least, closely approaches the benchmark.

Two Quick Notes on Descriptive Representation

I have omitted any real mention of class or socioeconomic status in this analysis of descriptive representation in Congress. The logic applied to gender, race, religion, military service, and occupation can also be used on wealth. Carnes (2012) demonstrates that working-class and poorer Americans are grossly underrepresented in Congress—he also shows members' class affiliations have an independent effect on their voting records. The institution evidently fails to meet any plausible target we could set for it. I do not establish a benchmark here because I discuss questions of members' wealth in some detail in the next chapter.

It is also worth briefly mentioning sexual orientation. We do not really have a good handle on how many Americans are lesbian, gay, bisexual, or transgender (LGBT). There has also been very little research done on the importance of descriptive representation for the LGBT community, although Donald Haider-Markel (2007) found the more homosexual legislators there are, the more that community's interests are furthered. We do know there have been very few openly gay and lesbian members. The number in recent Congresses is two or three, including Rep. Barney Frank (D-MA), who chaired the Financial Services Committee for four years. The 2012 elections saw the first successful openly gay candidate sent to the Senate—Tammy Baldwin who had been serving in the House—and openly bisexual candidate elected to the House—Kyrsten Sinema (D-AZ).

Conclusion

Congress generally meets or exceeds the benchmarks we have set for it on matters of substantive representation. It is quite responsive to the public's policy demands on a continual basis, and it more often than not reacts as we would like to election outcomes. It is sensitive to local concerns. The record is a little more mixed when it comes to descriptive representation. With the curious exception of African Americans in the Senate, targets for levels of racial and ethnic representation are currently met. Members of Congress have a rich variety of occupational backgrounds, life experiences, and religious

BENCHMARK FOR CONGRESSIONAL PERFORMANCE	APPRAISAL
1. To reflect the will of the American people, Congress should track alterations in the policy preferences of the general public quite closely.	Largely met
2. About half of members' time and resources should be committed to local issues and concerns.	Met
3. At least 25% of members should be women.	Not met
4. At least 9% of members should be African American and 3% Hispanic.	House met, Senate not met
5. Membership should reflect patterns of military service in the general population.	Met
6. Membership should reflect patterns of religious affiliation in the general population.	Met
7. Membership should reflect patterns of occupational diversity in the general population.	Met

TABLE 3.1 Appraising congressional performance on benchmarks related to representation

affiliations. The institution still lags terribly behind peers in the proportion of female members, however. Table 3.1 provides a succinct summary of the chapter's findings.

They are important. As noted earlier, much of the discontent with Congress focuses on the notion that it is significantly out of step with the policy preferences and fundamental values of most Americans. It appears this assessment is unfair.

4

IS CONGRESS A
TRANSPARENT, ACCESSIBLE,
AND TRUSTWORTHY
LEGISLATURE?

The aspirations that mold the benchmarks in this chapter relate to Congress's role in American public life. Without transparency, citizens are uninformed about the activities of their elected officials. Representative democracy does not work as it should. Members of Congress must also be accessible so that people can express their views to them. Barriers to entry must be low so individuals can have realistic aspirations to membership and can relate to lawmakers in a way that legitimizes legislative action and policy outcomes. Finally, the institution must encourage behavior becoming representatives of the people. When members act unethically, they lose the public's trust.

BENCHMARK #8
Congress's daily business should be visible to the public.

Justification

Transparency in government is a key characteristic of the democratic process. An open government allows its operations to be observed and evaluated by the public and media. Citizens can make connections between elected officials' formal actions and their own and the country's general condition. They can then make informed decisions as to the quality of their representation, hence holding policy makers accountable and ensuring that outcomes are consistent with public preferences. Transparency also minimizes corruption (Adsera, Boix, and Payne 2003), to use former Supreme Court justice

Louis Brandeis's words, "sunshine is the best disinfectant."[1] Government is obligated to serve the public's interests, and only by knowing what it is truly doing can people force it to perform its duty.

Appraisal

By most international measures, the United States has a transparent national government (Kopits and Craig 1998). But its legislature has not always been as visible as it is today. In fact, in replicating the Continental Congress, the Senate initially met behind closed doors. The decision to convene out of the public eye does not seem to have been conscious; indeed, there is no record of any discussion of the matter (Kerr 1895, 39). It was nevertheless met with significant opposition by state legislators who, presumably wanting to hold their appointees accountable, called for sessions to be held in public. Republicans were particularly supportive of transparency. By December 1795, Federalist opposition had withered, and the Senate, like the House, started to conduct its business in the open (Wirls and Wirls 2004, 166–170).

The public galleries in Congress were frequently crowded during the nineteenth century. This was particularly the case for important debates or when people suspected a charismatic orator would be speaking—the "Great Triumvirate" of Senators John C. Calhoun (D-SC), Henry Clay (Whig-KY), and Daniel Webster (Whig-MA) were especially popular (Peterson 1987). If a citizen could not attend House or Senate sessions in person, she could always read accounts of them. Article I, Section 5, of the Constitution compels each body to "keep a Journal of its Proceedings," and from the very beginning they have done so either individually, in the *House Journal* and *Senate Journal*, or together, in the *Debates and Proceedings in the Congress of the United States*, the *Register of Debates*, the *Congressional Globe*, and the *Congressional Record*.[2] It was not until 1851, however, that the *Congressional Globe* provided something close to a verbatim transcript. The *Congressional Record*, a complete and faithful representation of Congress's plenary proceedings, was first published in 1873.

Press coverage of Congress grew as the institution made it increasingly easy for reporters to cover it. Both the House and Senate admitted stenographers in 1802. In 1827, the House put reporters on the floor so as to avoid errors in their coverage, and the Senate followed suit eight years later. In the late 1850s, when both bodies moved into their new chambers, permanent press galleries were constructed. This ushered in an era of greater access for the media. By World War I both chambers had allowed the press to effectively police itself. In 1939 both invited radio reporters in; two years later both accepted magazine reporters. Live gavel-to-gavel television coverage—brought to the public today via C-SPAN and C-SPAN 2—was established in the House in 1979 and the Senate seven years later.

As the news industry grew, so did the amount of attention paid to Congress. There are surprisingly few systematic longitudinal studies of the quantity of media coverage of Congress, but those that exist generally show a linear upward trend. There is evidence that television news stories about the institution was minimal between Watergate and the 1994 elections. The public seemed much more interested in stories about the president (Lichter and Amundson 1994, 133–135). However, Timothy Cook's (1989, 59–62) study of the number of House members mentioned on the network television nightly news shows a steady increase from 1969 through 1986: in the early years about one in four members was mentioned; by the early 1980s the figure was nearly one in two. Michael Robinson (1981) demonstrates an increase in the use of House radio and television studios by members and a rise in the number of journalists credentialed for the press galleries from the late 1950s to late 1970s. Douglas Harris (1998) and Gary Lee Malecha and Daniel Reagan (2004) reveal dramatic recent increases in the coverage of House leaders. As if to heighten public cynicism in Congress, research shows that the media focus more on those members whose policy preferences seem different from their constituents than those who march in lockstep (Fogarty 2008).

Although we do not have reliable data on their impact, cable news, talk radio, and the Internet also clearly inform the public about the workings of Congress. To generate audiences, many of these outlets often appeal to emotions rather than reason and convey information concisely but simplistically. They are watched, listened to, and read by people who agree with their point of view—for example, Fox News Channel's audience is overwhelmingly Republican; MSNBC's Democratic.[3] Nevertheless, they do transmit information. The Internet also gives members the opportunity to communicate directly with their constituents and the press. They have exploited it assiduously, and today their websites are sophisticated and distinctly personal, varying significantly depending upon the owner's chamber, seniority, race, and gender (Gulati 2004; Niven and Zilber 2001). Facebook and YouTube are now extremely popular among members. Twitter adoption on the Hill has been quick and dramatic as well (Chi and Yang 2010; Glassman, Straus, and Shogan 2010; Lawless 2011). The benchmark is surely met.

BENCHMARK #9
Congress should have many formally recorded plenary votes.

Justification

Congress is transparent in a fundamental way. But can the public access information that will help it form a meaningful evaluation of the institution? It should be familiar, for example, with legislators' most important business. This is probably voting on the floor. Without these votes, bills cannot become law, the country cannot legally go to war, programs cannot be funded, presidential vetoes cannot be overridden, and the executive and judicial branches cannot be fully staffed. Each member has the right to a vote and only one vote on each measure.[4] As a central part of members' collective and individual record, citizens must know what actions their representatives have taken on policy matters.

But to what degree? As Thomas Saalfeld (1995) noticed in the early 1990s, many national parliaments in western Europe frequently do not record votes in the plenary—among these are the bodies in Germany, Italy, and the Netherlands. Historically, American state legislatures have used recorded votes much more. In all but five states, constitutions or legislative rules require a recorded vote on the final passage of bills. In the five without requirements, South Carolina has the highest threshold for putting members on the record—although by international standards it might be considered low—only 5 of 46 senators and 10 of 124 House members need to request a recorded vote to make it happen.[5] On this issue at least, we should want Congress to be closer to the American rather than European tradition.

Appraisal

There is no constitutional obligation that the House and Senate make public the floor votes of their members. Indeed, both the House and Senate still allow members to vote viva voce or by voice. Although under Article I, Section 5, of the Constitution, "the Yeas and Nays of the Members of either House on any question shall, at the Desire of one fifth of those Present, be entered on the Journal," until about the early 1950s they relied greatly on voice votes for bills and amendments on important and contentious measures. Research shows that around the turn of the twentieth century more than half of the bills that might be considered "landmark" were not subject to a recorded vote; today it is closer to 10 percent (Madonna and Lynch 2012).[6]

Since 1972, recorded votes in the House have been taken by electronic device. This helped reduce the number of voice and teller votes by making the recording of members' selections quicker and easier.[7] House members can now place identifying cards into slots on the back of benches on the House floor and press the appropriate button to record their choice as "yea," "nay," or "present."[8] When it wishes to record votes, the smaller Senate still uses a roll call and members respond as their names are read. This differs from a traditional voice vote in that members do not all call out simultaneously and then allow the presiding officer to determine the victorious side. Senators' votes are published in the *Congressional Record* and are as transparent as those of their colleagues in the House.

Figure 4.1 shows the number of recorded votes taken by the House and Senate in each Congress since 1789. It demonstrates a quite dramatic increase, particularly in the House, where there have been many more recorded votes than in the Senate over the past twenty years. In addition to the introduction of electronic voting, this can be explained by an explosion in the number of amendments offered on the House floor (Smith 1989).

In one sense we do not know if this is a lot because we are unsure precisely how many times the House and Senate have used voice votes over the years.[9] Remember, however, that the benchmark just asks that there be many, demonstrating the importance

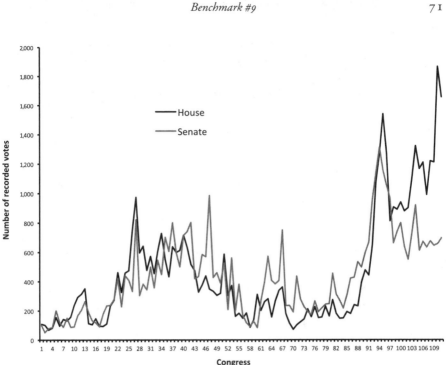

FIGURE 4.1   The number of recorded votes in the House and Senate, 1789–2009

of having members on the formal record about a great deal of legislation on numerous issues.

It would be fair to say therefore that the benchmark regarding recorded plenary votes is met. Yet Congress goes further. Members' positions on bills are publicized prior to floor vote as well. The *Congressional Record* makes known, and then the media and websites like the Library of Congress's *Thomas* disseminate, the names of members who have sponsored and cosponsored bills. Sponsorship and cosponsorship—the latter being the expression of one's formal support for a bill after it has been introduced or sponsored by a colleague—demonstrate members' legislative priorities and policy preferences. Prior to 1969, cosponsorship was restricted: each House bill could have only one cosponsor. Between then and 1979 there was a twenty-five-member-per-bill cap. The rules' effect on restricting the public's capacity to know where legislators stood on legislation was mitigated somewhat by members' tendency to introduce duplicate bills. But today there is no such restriction. Members can sponsor or cosponsor any bill on any subject at any time, and they frequently do. The median number of bills cosponsored by a House member in the 111th Congress (2009–2011) was 317; in the Senate it was 192. That is a significant amount of information about members' preferences for the public to digest.

It also raises the question: Why such transparency? Congressional scholars have suggested members provide it for electoral reasons in a purposive effort to demonstrate meaningful concern about their constituents' policy needs and desires. In April 2012, for example, the Senate debated legislation known as the Buffett Rule—a bill that would establish a minimum tax rate for millionaires named after the investor Warren Buffett—despite the Democratic leadership knowing it was unlikely to be approved by the chamber and had no chance of being considered in the House and therefore passed into law. The goal was simply to get a recorded vote—in this case on a motion to end an obstructionist filibuster—with which candidates, either Democratic members themselves or Democrats challenging Republicans up for re-election, could campaign. Symbolic legislative action is presumably even more prevalent in sponsorship and cosponsorship behavior, because members are effectively free to take any position they would like on any issue of their choosing (Garand and Burke 2006; Koger 2003).

BENCHMARK #10
Congress should have open committee proceedings.

Justification

The work of committees is crucial. It involves the formulation and revision of bills and their preparation for floor disposition—without committee assent, bills cannot generally get to the floor. It should therefore occur in the open so that the public and legislators who do not sit on these panels can understand what has been done.

Although plenary proceedings and member floor votes are largely transparent in all American state legislatures these days, committees still often work in the dark. According to a 2004 report of the NCSL, well over half of the bodies did not report roll calls on a committee's final approval of a bill, and forty chambers did not even require their committees to take minutes.[10] It is fair to expect Congress to do better.

Appraisal

Historically, congressional committee proceedings have not been as transparent as those on the floor. After the passage of the Legislative Reorganization Act in 1946, House and Senate standing committees became more powerful. They were given codified jurisdictions, permanent staff, and oversight responsibilities (Deering and Smith 1997, 30–32). In addition to this authority and prestige, the principles of seniority, where the member of the majority with the longest service automatically becomes chair, and property rights, where legislators who were on a panel in the previous Congress have a right to continue to sit on it in the current one, provided committees with autonomy. They responded by keeping many of their proceedings secret even as Congress generally became more open.

The Legislative Reorganization Act of 1970, however, forced transparency upon committees. (Deering and Smith 1997, 35). They were compelled to make individual members' votes public. Previously only vote totals had been reported. By 1973, the House ruled that all committee meetings—including hearings and markups where members debate and amend legislation—should be public unless a majority of members voted in an open session to the contrary. The Senate essentially duplicated these sunshine provisions in 1975. In 1995, on the first day Republicans controlled the body in forty years, the House adopted a rule mandating committee meetings be open to the public.

Traditionally the most consequential work of conference committees, the panels consisting of both House and Senate members that are convened to reconcile intercameral differences in bills passed by both bodies, has taken place behind the scenes in private negotiations between the principal legislators. The committees fulfilled their legal obligations by meeting once in public view for a short and not particularly substantive session. Sometimes even conferees themselves have not known what is going on. In a famous story from 2006, Rep. Charlie Rangel (D-NY), the ranking member on the House Ways and Means Committee at the time, ran around the Capitol looking for his elusive conference committee. Having found it, he knocked on the door of the room where the meeting was being held. The chair of both Ways and Means and the conference, Rep. Bill Thomas (R-CA), appeared and told Rangel, "This meeting is only open to the coalition of the willing" (Taibbi 2006).

In 2010, however, Congress opened the entire conference proceedings on the financial regulatory overhaul bill known as Dodd-Frank to television cameras. This was quite revolutionary. In January and February 2012 it did the same for the conference committee on a payroll tax holiday extension bill.

Congress meets the benchmark for transparency in committee as well, therefore. Still, committee proceedings are not always as open as they could be. In the fall of 2011, the critically important work of the Joint Select Committee on Deficit Reduction or "supercommittee" was allowed to take place outside of the public eye, much to the chagrin of lobbyists and legislators not on the panel.

Although formal and authoritative actions may be taken publicly in committees and on the House and Senate floors, much of the crafting of legislation and many important commitments of support happen more informally and in private. The House's decision to reject a budget deal including tax increases during the standoff over the debt ceiling in the summer of 2011 was effectively made in closed-door Republican conference meetings. The bill that the House and Senate eventually passed and President Obama ended up signing was really negotiated in private meetings and phone calls between the president and Vice President Joe Biden on the Democratic side and Senate Minority Leader Mitch McConnell (R-KY) and Speaker John Boehner on the Republican side. So was the legislation to prevent a federal government shutdown in April 2011 and the work to avert the "fiscal cliff" of debilitating spending cuts and tax increases done in late 2012. This kind of high-level executive-legislative "summitry" has been happening for many years (Sinclair 2012, 157–158). The important budget agreements of the 1980s and 1990s—the so-called Gramm-Rudman-Hollings deficit reduction legislation, the 1990 deal in which President George H. W. Bush famously broke his "no new taxes" pledge, and the 1997 balanced budget bills—are perhaps the best examples (Gilmour 1995; Palazzolo 1999). It is in private party meetings and face-to-face leadership get-togethers that the legislative heavy lifting gets done.

BENCHMARK #11
Congress should have rules that are simple, clear, and few in number.

Justification

Transparency also implies a kind of simplicity of procedures. Complicated rules make it difficult for citizens to connect legislative behavior with policy outcomes. They effectively allow members to hide their decisions and shirk their responsibilities. Public confidence in legislative practices is likely to erode. One way to measure procedural convolution might be to look at the size of a body's rulebook. Many long rules suggest obfuscation and likely constitute a lawmaking process the public cannot understand and consequently distrusts. Lack of codification may increase leaders' discretionary powers, but at least members and voters can readily understand simpler arrangements.

No one has really looked at rule books in a systematic manner. But greater transparency means that American state legislatures have made theirs readily available. To some, these rule books might be considered short—perhaps because the institutions see the benefits of strong and discretionary leadership and because state constitutions often enumerate procedures for them.[11] Regardless of their relative length, however, I think it is fair to say most contain between about sixty and one hundred separate rules. These rules tend to be fairly short and, on the surface at least, uncomplicated. We should want House and Senate rules to emulate them.

Appraisal

At first glance, the House and Senate to have clear and easily understood legislative processes. Lawmaking seems to follow a fairly simple model, a distinctly American blueprint described in civics classes and the popular old *Schoolhouse Rock* song, "I'm Just a Bill." For a bill that becomes law the sequence goes like this: a member introduces it, the bill goes to committee, it is reported to the floor, it is debated and voted on by members, the process is repeated in the other body, the House and Senate reconcile different versions if necessary, the bill is reported to the president. Then if he likes it he signs it, and it becomes law; if not, he vetoes it, and Congress tries to override him. As if to confirm this impression, the House and Senate rule books are quite short. In the 112th Congress (2011–2013) the House had thirty-eight rules, although at nearly sixty-six thousand words they do not make quick and easy reading. The Senate had forty-four rules of fewer than half that number of words.[12]

But the public remains confused about congressional procedures. This perturbation stems at least somewhat from significant bicameral differences. The House, for example, has a Rules Committee whose principal responsibility since the 1880s has been to promulgate "special rules" that describe the terms of debate for most bills that go to the floor (Roberts 2010). A crucial part of each special rule determines how the bill can be amended. Most are fairly simple. A closed rule prohibits floor amendments completely—this kind of rule is traditionally given bills reported from the Ways and Means Committee, which has jurisdiction over taxes, Social Security, Medicare, and trade. An open rule allows amendments to the entire bill; a modified open or modified closed rule restricts amendments to certain sections of it. Structured rules specify particular amendments are in order and frequently limit the amount of time their debate should consume (Oleszek 2011a, 156–157).

Over the past few decades, however, the House has devised more complicated special rules for reasons that can only conceivably be viewed as political (Sinclair 2012, 31–38). Its Rules Committee has come up with the tortuous "King-of-the Hill" and "Queen-of-the-Hill" rules, for example (Oleszek 2011a, 158–160). The former permits votes on a series of substitute amendments—complete other versions of the bill—but makes only the vote on the final one meaningful. Regardless of what happens to all of the other substitutes, if the final substitute is defeated, the original bill survives. The Queen of the Hill provides greater options to the general membership in that it is the substitute with the most votes that, so long as it garners the support of a majority, replaces the original legislative vehicle. Both rules allow members to take floor votes on popular proposals that have no formal legislative consequences. Instead, these votes can provide helpful talking points on the campaign trail.

Two of the most closely watched bills of recent years demonstrate how complex and deceiving special rules can be. Democrats argued repeatedly during 2011 that debt limit extensions had traditionally been granted with minimal fuss. But that description glossed over what many considered the leadership's shenanigans. Using the so-called Gephardt rule (named for former House majority leader Richard Gephardt [D-MO]), the House regularly permitted special rules that bundled debt limit raises with the much larger resolutions setting spending and revenue targets in the budget. This was done to prevent a separate vote on the former and allow members to avoid appearing fiscally irresponsible. The Treasury could go on borrowing, even though it was hard to ascertain whether the House had taken a vote on the matter. During the passage of the PPACA in 2010, the House Democratic leadership seriously contemplated a maneuver that would have essentially allowed the body to approve the Senate version of the legislation without a direct vote on the floor: instead the special "self-executing" rule for a different bill correcting unpopular parts of the Senate legislation would have included a provision simply asserting the main bill had been approved by the House. According to Republicans, the Democrats just wanted to wave a magic wand and have the president's controversial health care bill approved—"deem and pass," many seethed, was the way the majority conducted the legislative process.

Some House bills do not need a special rule—or even to be reported by a standing committee.[13] They are disposed of under the "suspension of the rules." Bills called up this way go to the floor for an evenly divided forty minutes of debate. No amendments are in order, but the bill requires the support of two-thirds of members present and voting to pass. Both Democrats and Republicans have guidelines designed to constrain the use of the procedure. Typically it is confined to the beginning of the week—Monday and Tuesday only, although Wednesday as well sometimes—and for uncontroversial or ceremonial bills (Oleszek 2011a, 135–140).[14] Among the bills passed this way in early 2012 were the Mark Twain Commemorative Coin Act and the World War II Memorial Prayer Act. However, the procedure can be deployed at the Speaker's discretion and has been used to expedite the passage of important legislation on occasion. In 2009, for example, the House considered a bill greatly expanding the FDA's capacity to regulate the nation's food supply under suspension. Although Democratic leaders could muster 280 votes, they were 7 shy of the two-thirds needed for passage. The bill was eventually approved through the regular process. In 2011, Republican leaders brought a bill repealing the ban of incandescent light bulbs to the floor under suspension. With 233 members voting in favor, it fell 52 votes short of the required amount.

Although its rule book is considerably shorter, the Senate's procedures are, if anything, more complicated. This is because the upper body is regulated greatly by precedents, conventions, and more informal norms—or what political scientist Donald Matthews (1960) called "unwritten rules of the game." It has a tradition of obstruction, which will be a focus of the next chapter. It is altogether less enamored with codification than the House and tends to move legislative measures along using unanimous consent more frequently.

Instead of special rules, for example, Senate leaders try to craft unanimous consent agreements (UCAs). UCAs, often the product of extensive negotiations because they must be agreed to by all senators, regulate floor proceedings on a measure by imposing time limits on debate and enumerating amendments that are in order. The former is important because standing Senate rules essentially allow for unlimited floor debate. The latter is crucial because, unlike the House, the Senate does not have a germaneness rule—a regulation prohibiting members from offering amendments that are not considered relevant to the underlying bill. Absent a UCA, therefore, any amendment could be offered to any bill.

So as to strike the requisite balance between an individual senator's demands and the necessity to move legislation through the process, some UCAs have become quite complex (Oleszek 2011a, 232–242; Smith and Flathman 1989). They list numerous amendments and explain in detail how debate will unfold. Often, a bill will be on the floor as a UCA while it is still being crafted. Some have multiple UCAs that describe a lengthy and complicated process and the treatment of other pieces of legislation. The UCA for the bill that prevented a government shutdown in April 2011 was only agreed to by Senate Republicans if it included provisions allowing for separate floor votes on measures to prohibit federal funds being spent on Planned Parenthood and the controversial health care reform legislation passed the previous year.

Perhaps no other practice explains the complexity, uniqueness, and, indeed, mystery of Senate operations than the hold. To be found nowhere in written rules, holds are an informal custom that leaders tend to, although are not compelled to, respect. Holds occur when senators request floor consideration of a measure be prevented or at least postponed until a demand or set of demands is met. Holders used to remain anonymous. In March 1999, Majority Leader Trent Lott (R-MS) and Minority Leader Tom Daschle (D-SD) wrote to colleagues explaining their intention not to recognize holds that were unaccompanied by a signed letter of explanation to the measure's sponsor and committee of jurisdiction (Oleszek 2007, 201–202). The Lott-Daschle directive had little tangible effect. A section of the Honest Leadership and Open Government Act passed in 2007, however, contained provisions forcing notice of holds to be placed in the *Congressional Record* and, six days after that, mandating leaders to recognize publicly who is blocking the legislation. At the beginning of the 112th Congress in 2011, the Senate agreed to reduce the time until the holder's identity is disclosed to two days.[15]

Holds can be individual or collective. They might be extortionate, an effort to extract concessions from leaders on other matters. Sen. Jesse Helms (R-NC) frequently employed holds on Clinton administration nominees to ambassadorial positions when he was chair of the Foreign Relations Committee so as to win reforms of the State Department and United Nations. They might be what Helen Dewar (2003) calls "Mae West" holds, essentially an attempt to attract attention in the hope that a senator will "stop by and work something out." With a deal consummated, the hold is withdrawn. Sometimes a hold seems nothing more than the snarl of a cantankerous member. In March 2010, Sen. Jim Bunning (R-KY) single-handedly prevented disposition of legislation extending unemployment benefits until he was granted a floor vote on a measure that would pay for them. Bunning, who was retiring and had become somewhat of a pariah even in Republican circles, relented under considerable pressure from senators of both parties.[16] The original measure ultimately passed 78 to 19.

I think it is fair to say, therefore, that Congress falls somewhat short of the benchmark about the simplicity, number, and transparency of its rules. Many proceedings are not so much governed by rules as by arcane and complex traditions and conventions. The codification that exists does not preclude ad hoc arrangements and a significant amount of leadership discretion in the use of practices. There is inconsistency across chambers and even individual pieces of legislation as members attempt to pass or block measures in differing strategic environments. The rules may be relatively few, but they have created extremely complicated procedures that even attentive watchers of Congress can find very difficult to understand (Sinclair 2012). Indeed, political scientists suggest that the public's frustration with Congress is at least somewhat attributable to a legislative process that is difficult to understand (Hibbing and Theiss-Morse 2002; Mayhew 2006, 225–226).

So as to make this general point more forcefully, let us briefly examine the "crown jewel" of the 111th Congress's (2009–2011) legislative accomplishments, health care reform. Following that through to enactment is enough to make anyone's head spin.

The Legislative Passage of the PPACA

By the fall of 2009, numerous committees had considered a health care bill. One was approved by Sen. Tom Harkin's (D-IA) Health, Education, Labor, and Pensions (HELP) Committee after the Senate's Finance panel dithered a little, skittish about a provision called the public option that would create a federal government-run insurance exchange. Finance passed a version of the legislation without the public option in October. On the House side, three different committees had passed iterations of the same health care bill, HR 3200, by mid-July. Education and Labor, Energy and Commerce, and Ways and Means, all reported the measure under a complex process called multiple referral in which the Speaker—here Rep. Nancy Pelosi (D-CA)—can assign legislation to any number of committees with shared jurisdiction over items of broad scope (Sinclair 2012, 142–144).

With bills ready for the floor, the House decided to go first. Instead of sending HR 3200 forward, however, Speaker Pelosi put up another bill, HR 3962, that had been reported by John Dingell's (D-MI) Energy and Commerce Committee. With its defeat in the Senate's Finance Committee, Democratic leaders realized a public option was dead, and Dingell's new bill excluded the provision. Floor consideration took place in a rare Saturday session on November 7, 2009.

Before HR 3962 could go to the floor, however, it required a special rule from the Rules Committee. The one reported essentially defied categorization. It called for four hours of debate on the nearly two-thousand-page bill and recognized two amendments to be in order. The rule also had a self-executing quality. It allowed for consideration of HR 3961, a bill that reduced Medicare payments so as to allow HR 3962 to meet certain cost estimates assigned it by the Congressional Budget Office (CBO), and, if HR 3961 passed, it automatically attached HR 2920 as new matter to it. HR 2920 had passed the House earlier in the year and iterated Democrats' commitment to budget neutrality—that is, new spending programs would be accompanied by policy changes designed to generate offsetting revenues. At one level, therefore, HR 3961 and HR 2920 constituted political cover for Democrats who worried that health care reform would be seen as too costly.

After the House had approved the rule and HR 3962—the bill on a 220–215 vote—it was the Senate's turn. Majority Leader Harry Reid (D-NV) was not really sure he had sixty votes, or a filibuster-proof majority, for a health care bill that the House would like and the president would sign. Still, he forged ahead, trying to merge the HELP- and Finance-passed legislation. In late October Reid announced the Senate bill would contain a public option that states could exclude themselves from. Reid would utilize an uncontroversial House bill providing home-buyer tax credits to service personnel and other federal employees, HR 3950, as his vehicle. It had recently passed the lower chamber under suspension of the rules. The strategy provided an important procedural advantage. Rule XIV permits the Senate to report House-passed bills straight to the calendar and hence bypass committee. HR 3950 would therefore become merely a placeholder, a means by which Reid could offer his health care bill as a substitute in the form of an amendment.

The Senate began its consideration of Reid's substitute—senators cared little for the content of HR 3950—the week before Thanksgiving. Reid's first course of action was to call for what is widely known as pre-emptive cloture on the necessary initial motion to proceed. Senate majority leaders can do this because they have the right to be recognized by the presiding officer first as a debate commences. Understanding that Senate Republican opponents would filibuster, Reid invoked the mechanism to begin to bring debate to a close on the motion before it had even started. In a critical vote, he got exactly the minimum sixty votes needed to move ahead.

On December 19, 2009, Reid was forced to announce an amendment to his substitute after he realized there were not enough votes to get a bill containing a public option approved. The procedural effect was to generate additional hurdles. Now there would have to be three votes, one each on the new amendment, the original substitute amendment, and the underlying bill. Each motion to bring these about would obviously be filibustered and therefore three more cloture votes would also be needed.

To overcome these obstacles, Reid used his parliamentary advantages. He invoked pre-emptive cloture on the three motions and then "filled the amendment tree," a strategy that prevents other members from being able to offer amendments. In a series of nail-biting votes, all three cloture motions received the minimum sixty votes. The process was long and excruciating for Democrats. Under Rule XXII cloture motions only ripen two days and one hour after they have been filed. Even if invoked, they allow for thirty hours of additional debate. It was the morning of Christmas Eve before the Senate got through the three measures and eventually passed its health care bill 60–39.

The Senate's consideration of health care reform was managed by a large number of complex UCAs drawn up by Reid and Senate Minority Leader Mitch McConnell (R-KY). The UCAs tended to extend debate for a number of hours and arrange, at the end of that time, for votes on certain amendments. Republicans naturally did not negotiate away their procedural prerogatives in these deals. Throughout the six weeks health care reform was on the Senate floor, they used all the obstructionist techniques they could. They insisted on the reading of the entire bill and amendments. They called for votes on constitutional points of order, motions on the compliance of amendments with budget rules, and appeals to rulings by the presiding officer. They forced debates on motions to proceed. Ultimately, there were votes on six motions to commit the bill to committee and roll calls on 16 amendments of the 510 that were offered.

The bill was still not law. Legislation must be passed in identical form by both bodies, a constitutional principle known as bicameralism that is contained in Article I, Section 7, and that has been interpreted by the Supreme Court to mean that both the House and Senate pass bills with the exact same text.[17] Frequently with bills of the scope and importance of health care reform, the House and Senate use a conference committee to reconcile differences. Conference committees contain members from both bodies who negotiate with one another in an effort to come up with a single version of the bill. Sometimes the final product or conference report looks more like the House-passed version; sometimes it looks more like the Senate-passed version. In recent years there have been numerous complaints that conference committees are essentially rewriting bills and largely ignoring the iterations approved by the two chambers of Congress. Regardless, once reported, this singular bill goes back to the House and Senate for final approval. Amendments are not allowed on the floor, although a filibuster could happen in the Senate.

On health care reform, however, the House and Senate leadership chose a different path. In mid-January 2010, Majority Leader Reid and Speaker Pelosi announced they had come to an agreement. Because Senate support for health care reform was so fragile, the House had agreed to move in what most commentators considered a rightward direction to adopt the Senate's version. The pressure to do so was escalated when, in a special election for the seat of the recently deceased Sen. Ted Kennedy (D-MA), Republican Scott Brown was sent to Washington on what was essentially an anti–health care reform platform. In a frank admission that the coalition was no longer capable of quelling a filibuster, Reid informed Minority Leader McConnell in March that, if necessary, he would proceed with health care reform using a procedure called budget reconciliation. Congress had made that possible in its budget resolution of April 2009. Under Senate rules, debate on bills considered this way can be brought to an end by a simple majority vote.

House Democrats from all parts of the ideological spectrum took issue with provisions of the Senate bill, complicating matters further.[18] Reid and Pelosi therefore made the decision to have the House pass the Senate bill and then offer a new bill with some "fixes" that the Senate could accept. The Senate would have to pass this second and revisionary bill so as to amend the underlying legislation and bring it into line with the wishes of House Democrats. Reid could promise it would do this because the fixing legislation, HR 4872, was a budget reconciliation bill. The bill also included a broad restructuring of student loan programs that was popular among Democrats. It was at this stage—and for the Senate bill—that Pelosi suggested the House employ the special rule Republicans criticized as "deem and pass." After significant resistance even among her own caucus, she backed away from the proposal, however, and, along with Rules Committee chair, Louise Slaughter (D-NY), came up with a single closed rule to have HR 3590 and HR 4872 dealt with sequentially in what amounted to the same debate. On March 21, the House passed the main Senate bill in a dramatic 219–212 vote and the "fix" 220–211.[19] The Senate took up the fix bill on March 23. Predictably, it was met by Republican opposition. There were dozens of proposed amendments and motions to commit the bill back to committee or to challenge the legislation on budgetary grounds but, assisted most crucially by the reconciliation procedure, it was approved by the body on a 56–43 vote within two days.

The saga was not over. During the Senate debate on the fix, Republicans offered amendments on several minor flaws in the legislation that Democrats helped them approve. This necessitated that the House once again approve a special rule that would allow for consideration of the now Senate-revised fix or reconciliation bill. In a single day, March 25, this rule was approved, and the amended fix bill adopted 220–207. Having already signed HR 3590 a week earlier, President Barack Obama did the same to HR 4872 on March 30. What were formally titled the Patient Protection and Affordable Care Act and the Health Care and Education Reconciliation Act, together known as health care reform, or "Obamacare," were the law of the land.[20]

BENCHMARK #12
Congress should have member disclosure requirements
that exceed those of most of the American states.

Justification

Public knowledge of members' financial interests and professional activities facilitates accountability and is an important deterrent to corruption. The Center for Public Integrity has undertaken broad and systematic evaluations of American state legislatures' disclosure rules—regulations that mandate reports of matters such as members' personal finances and contacts with lobbyists, as well as mechanisms available to enforce them.[21] In its studies, western states have tended to demonstrate the strongest requirements—the top five in 2006 were Washington, Hawaii, Texas, Alaska, and Arizona, all of which called for considerable personal and professional revelatory data from legislators. Given the staff and budgetary resources at its disposal and the significant consequences of its authoritative decisions and the policy it makes, we should expect Congress to perform at this level too.

Appraisal

Congress can force members to disclose their personal and campaign finances and professional contacts. It has done so with increasing vigor. Since the 1970s, federal law has restricted campaign fundraising and spending by congressional candidates. Part of the regulatory regime calls upon office seekers to disclose contributors and how they spend their resources. Today the law states that candidates must identify any PAC or party organization that gives them money, any individual who gives them more than $200, and all expenditures in excess of $200 to any individual or vendor.[22]

Whereas members provide the Federal Election Commission with reports of campaign activities, the House and Senate ethics committees police personal financial matters. These rules—the most recent of which are contained in the 2012 STOCK (Stop Trading on Congressional Knowledge) Act—are robust enough to force even candidates' spouses and dependents to file. Covered individuals must report income; assets such as stocks, bonds, and real estate; liabilities; and all transactions involving investment vehicles that are in excess of $1,000.[23] Violations are punishable by law and offenders can go to prison.

Rules on contacts between lobbyists on one side and members and their staff on the other have become increasingly strict as well. The Republican-controlled Congress passed the Lobby Disclosure Act in 1995 and expanded the types of individuals considered lobbyists, increased the number of activities considered lobbying, and strengthened lobby registration requirements. Later in that Congress, the House approved a ban on gifts over fifty dollars to members and staff from outside sources. It also prohibited meals with lobbyists unless they were broadly attended affairs or the food was of nominal value.

Many legislators and observers soon determined these rules were insufficient to prevent the appearance of and potential for corruption, however. The scandal involving the lobbyist Jack Abramoff was particularly important in this regard.[24] Abramoff's infamous 2002 golf trip to Scotland on which he took several congressional staffers and Rep. Bob Ney, illustrated how policy makers could travel with lobbyists under the thin guise that the visit had educational value and was taken in an official capacity. Abramoff's connection to Republican leader Rep. Tom DeLay shone light on the K Street Project, an effort by those high up in the Republican congressional majority to have interest groups with issues in front of the federal legislature hire lobbyists of whom they approved—generally as a result of an ongoing or previous professional relationship. When Democrats took control of Congress again after the 2006 elections, they passed the Honest Leadership and Open Government Act. The legislation was wide-

sweeping and included provisions to restrict the capacity of members to lobby immediately after leaving office, prohibit members and their staff from influencing hiring
decisions by private organizations (a clear reference to the K Street Project), expand
the ban on outside gifts, greatly limit travel with lobbyists, and increase the reporting
requirements placed on individuals who wish to lobby. I think it is fair to say that
Congress meets the benchmark for public disclosure of members' activities.

BENCHMARK #13
Members should have adequate staff—about ten to fifteen each.

Justification

For a legislature to be fully integrated into public life, it needs to be more than heard
and understood. It needs to listen and understand. Citizens of an effective representative democracy must have the capacity to communicate their policy preferences and
general concerns about public issues to elected officials. At a certain level all legislatures
in advanced democracies make their members accessible to citizens. The public can
write letters to, phone, and e-mail their representatives. The media frequently report
on public feeling about policy and government performance.

Still, it is presumably the case that members of some bodies are discernibly more
accessible than others. There are several indicators we can use to understand the sus-
ceptibility of Congress to external influences. One is staff. At any time, there are only
a maximum of 535 members of Congress. Today there are about 310 million Americans. Legislators therefore need fairly large and competent staffs to act as agents if they
are to have meaningful contact with constituents and be able to hear what they have
to say. Staff size is, of course, an indirect measure, not least because it is related to a
body's formal workload (Grossback and Peterson 2004). But legislators with larger
staffs are capable of having some form of meaningful contact with greater numbers of
their constituents. Staff are a conduit between the representative and the people she
represents and can communicate their views to one another.

Staffing in Congress's peer legislatures is patchy. At most, members of parliaments
in western Europe, Australia, Canada, and Japan have about three or four personal
staff assigned to them (Harfst and Schnapp 2003). Members of only thirteen American
state senates and twelve lower chambers have year-round district staff (*Book of States*
2010). According to NCSL, members in the most professional of state bodies—
California, Michigan, New York, and Pennsylvania particularly—have about nine staff.
Of course, the vast majority of state legislators and members of national parliaments
have thousands fewer constituents than their congressional counterparts. At least when
it comes to contact with the public, therefore, they have less need for a comprehensive
staff. It is therefore reasonable to set this benchmark higher.

Appraisal

In the last chapter, I discussed how members divide their staff between the district or state and Washington. Here I am interested in the size of staff in the aggregate. There are essentially four types of staff on the Hill: personal staff who work for individual members, committee staff, leadership staff, and institutional staff who operate support entities such as the Congressional Research Service (CRS) and Government Accountability Office (GAO). Unsurprisingly, all have increased in size over the past century. Before 1893, members were prohibited from paying for staff assistance. After the law was changed, legislators were initially allowed just one staffer. By the late 1970s rules permitted House members to have eighteen permanent and four part-time staff. Today, excluding those assigned to positions that are not directly related to Congress's core functions—police, janitors, Government Printing Office employees, and the like—the legislative branch has about twenty-two thousand staff in all. A bit over half of these are personal. Some conservatives have criticized the growing staffs as emblematic and perhaps even related to the growth in government more generally,[25] but the size of the legislative branch's staff pales in comparison to that of the executive branch—where there are nearly two million civilian employees alone. Congress's portion of the federal budget is very small; at $4.5 billion it consumes about 0.12 percent of annual government spending. What is more, on the House side there is about one personal staffer to every thirty-nine thousand Americans, a figure that has not really risen since 1960 when members had half the personal staff but the country had only about 50 percent of its current population.

Today House members enjoy the support of approximately sixteen to twenty individuals, a figure they can adjust because staff salaries are included in an overall budget they are given each year—this is the MRA described in Chapter 3. Because of the tremendous variety in the population of the states, Senators today can have about eighty staffers, with the average being around thirty-five. This surely means Congress exceeds the benchmark. Staff of these amounts ought to provide constituents with some meaningful connection to their representation and members with access to the kind of knowledge about public views required to make informed decisions.

BENCHMARK #14
Members should spend about half of their time in the district or state.

Justification

Members themselves are more accessible to the public when they spend time away from Washington and at home among their constituents. They can get a direct feel for the public's mood and listen to concerns and policy recommendations. Being back in the district also educates them on issues of local concern. Members have significant responsibilities in the legislature itself, but we should want them to spend time at home. How much, exactly, is difficult to say with any real confidence. In the 2009–2010 biennium, state legislatures were in session anywhere from Wyoming's 42 days to Michigan's 348—the median was 110 days. Comprehensive and comparable figures for national parliaments are difficult to compile, but these bodies tend to be in session for a little longer. In the single year 2008, for instance, the United Kingdom's House of Commons sat for 149 days, the German Bundestag 100, the Irish Dáil 96, the Canadian House of Commons 93, the Australian House of Representatives 69, and the New Zealand House of Representatives 61. As I suggested above, when creating an appropriate division of legislators' attention between national and local issues, perhaps a roughly even split between time spent in session and that with constituents is desirable. This would put Congress at the top end of the time-in-session standings—a target that is probably appropriate given the complex and broad policy matters for which it is responsible.

Appraisal

As we saw in the previous chapter, members do spend about half of their time in their districts or states. Over the past few decades Congress was formally in session for about 300 to 350 days per Congress.

It is important to recognize there are other indicators of members' commitment to an ongoing dialogue with their constituents. Legislators have press secretaries whose job it is to communicate with journalists to explain their thinking on issues. Many write regular columns in local newspapers and appear frequently on radio and television in their districts and states (Davidson, Oleszek, and Lee 2012, 135–136). Some members, particularly party leaders and committee chairs, receive significant coverage in the national media. They are regular guests on the Sunday morning political talk shows and cable news. With the explosion of national media outlets, even junior members now get opportunities to speak to a broader audience. In 2011, for example, freshman Rep. Renee Ellmers (R-NC) was a regular guest on cable news and the subject of a *New York Times* profile (Steinhauer 2011a). She even gave the Republican response to the president's weekly radio address. Ellmers received the attention because she was viewed as a bridge between the House Republican leadership and Tea Party caucus.

We have noted members' increased utilization of the Internet and social media to convey information to constituents. They also have less technological means of doing so. Since the very first Congress, members have enjoyed the franking privilege, the permission to send mail to constituents under their signature without postage (Glassman

2007).[26] Today congressional offices send out, free of charge, thousands of letters informing constituents of what their member of Congress is doing. There are limits on the numbers sent—franking costs diminish House members' capacity to pay other operating expenses, and senators' allowances are capped—but, given how readily lawmakers take advantage of the opportunity, old-fashioned correspondence sent via the US Postal Service is still an effective means of communication.

Members spend their time at home connecting directly with constituents as well. This is what political scientist Richard Fenno Jr. (1978) famously called "home style": the presentation of self and explanation of Washington activity in forums as diverse as supermarket check-out lines, the member's district office, a Rotary Club meeting, or Independence Day parade. Lawmakers are also increasingly relying upon "town hall" meetings to speak with constituents. These events take place in facilities like high school gyms or local municipal government buildings and can be structured discussions about particular issues or free-wheeling debates about anything that interests the audience. Over the past couple of years, they have become increasingly raucous affairs, as Congress has dealt with controversial legislation and the public's mood has soured. As activists and extremists have targeted the events, some have become very heated and often violent—this was especially the case over the summers of 2009 and 2011 when the conversation at town halls focused on health care reform and fiscal policy.

BENCHMARK #15
Congress should have meaningful turnover, and approximately
20 percent of the House should turn over each Congress;
about 50 percent of the Senate each six years.

Justification

At the heart of representative democracy is the belief that just about any adult citizen should be eligible for, and indeed quite plausibly capable of securing, a seat in the legislature. Writing in *Federalist 10*, Madison demonstrated the Founders' penchant for a certain refined class of elected official but qualifications for congressional office holders were not particularly onerous. The principal requirements set by the Constitution were that Senators be thirty years old and residents of their states. House members need to be twenty-five and residents of the state, although not necessarily the district, they are elected to represent.

Although today the House and Senate are the ultimate judges of an aspiring member's credentials, the Constitution's remain the basic qualifications for office and are therefore largely beyond the reach of lawmakers. What is more, members use their discretionary seating power only in instances when election outcomes are hotly disputed. This is not as rare as you might think. Jeffrey Jenkins (2004) found 601 contested elections from 1789 to 2002, the majority of which admittedly occurred between the end of the Civil War and 1900. The most recent example was in 2008 when the House finally seated Vern Buchanan (R-FL) fifteen months after the people of Florida's Thirteenth Congressional District voted in his contest against Democrat Christine Jennings. Florida's Elections Canvassing Commission had originally declared Buchanan the winner by 369 votes, but Jennings took her case to state court and was able to prevail on the House Democratic majority to have the Committee on House Administration at least investigate voting irregularities (Lisk 2008, 1213–1217).

We must therefore look elsewhere to determine how high the contemporary Congress sets barriers to entry. Turnover is an obvious subject. A certain amount of change in the membership is important because it circulates elites, encourages candidates with diverse political interests, and can bring about changes in policy (Matland and Studlar 2004; Schlesinger 1966). It mitigates what political scientist Keith Jackson (1994, 270) calls the three As, "arrogance, apathy, and atrophy." Like formal qualifications, member turnover is not entirely controlled by the legislature. Elections and voting are regulated greatly by the Constitution and state law, and, as we have noted, Americans often vote for congressional candidates using heuristics that have little to do with legislative performance, particularly partisanship (Bartels 2000; Brown and Woods 1991; Lau and Redlawsk 2006; Lockerbie 1991) and presidential popularity (Abramowitz 1985; Campbell 1991; Ferejohn and Calvert 1984; Kernell 1977a).

A legislature can create conditions favorable for turnover, though. It can establish rules that encourage competition and the candidacies of nonmembers—in the area of campaign finance, for example. It can be the kind of body that those with political ambitions aspire to join. Turnover is, in short, a useful proxy for accessibility.

Fortunately, there has been quite a bit of comparative work on legislator turnover. Richard Matland and Donley Studlar (2004) looked at annualized turnover rates in lower bodies of twenty-five advanced industrialized democracies from 1979 to 1994 and found an average of about 9.5 percent of members per year. Turnover was particularly high in Greece and Portugal and quite low in Germany and the United Kingdom. In the American states turnover is a little higher, largely because many bodies are considered "part time" or impose limits on the number of terms their members can serve (Moncrief, Niemi, and Powell 2004). Over the past twenty years, about one in four state legislators has been replaced at the end of each term—a rate that was decreasing quite markedly until the term limits movement took hold in the 1990s (Moncrief 1999).[27] Even in 2010, a year in which Republicans made historic gains, just 1,765 of the roughly 7,400 seats up for election went to someone new.[28] It seems quite justifiable then to ask for the House to turn over about 20 percent of its membership after each election. A legitimate target for the Senate, with its six-year terms, is much harder to identify. Perhaps about half of the Senate every six years is a reasonable expectation.

Appraisal

Figures 4.2 and 4.3 demonstrate how turnover in Congress has developed over the course of American history. Figure 4.2 provides the percentage of House members and senators in their first Congress. Figure 4.3 displays the average number of years served by members in a Congress. The differences in House and Senate term lengths make direct comparison very difficult, but both figures show how indicators of turnover have declined across time.

More specifically, the figures reveal three distinct periods.[29] In the first, from roughly the Fifteenth to Fortieth Congress (1817–1869), turnover is high, and length of service relatively short. Note also that there is a great deal of difference between the House and Senate. Relative to the rest of American history, senators served much longer than House members, and their turnover was discernibly less—most of this being is explained by the longer term in the upper body. Legislators during the first forty years of the United States were influenced greatly by classical republican ideas about the national benefits of frequent rotation in office (Struble 1979; Young 1966).

In the second and third periods—from about the Forty-Second to Seventy-First Congresses (1871–1931) and from about the Seventy-Fifth to One Hundredth Congresses (1937–1989)—the two bodies moved together and turnover declined greatly as the number of years members served increased. According to John Gilmour and Paul Rothstein (1996), the second period can be explained by declining retirements and the desire of legislators to stay in office, itself a product of the increased power of the federal government, the demise of the norm of rotation in office, and the widespread recognition that in the age of capitalism a man could not simultaneously practice public- and private-sector careers (Kernell 1977b). Internal organizational changes also played a role. The emergence of seniority as a means of distributing power and assigning formal positions was particularly crucial in this regard (Polsby 1968).

The third period is a function of declining electoral competitiveness and the rise of incumbency advantage. The innate benefit of already holding office is the product of many things, including access to the media, large campaign war chests, and privileges of office that help burnish members' reputations with their constituents. Two books written in the 1970s helped political scientists understand this phenomenon particularly well. Mayhew (1974a) argues that, with large staffs, significant office budgets, accommodating leaders, and procedures constructed to make its members look influential, Congress was designed perfectly for incumbents who wished to serve for many years. Morris Fiorina (1977) writes that the large byzantine federal bureaucracy furnished members with opportunities to assist constituents who were lost within it.

The benchmark for turnover seeks membership change in Congress of greater magnitude than Americans are currently experiencing. Of course, one reason might be be-

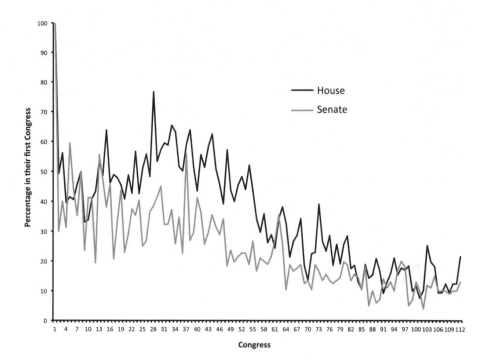

FIGURE 4.2 The percentage of members who were in their first Congress, 1789–2011

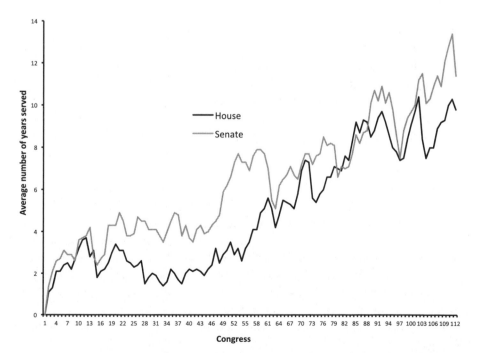

FIGURE 4.3 Average number of years served by members in the House and Senate, 1789–2011

cause the public wants it that way. It tends to like its own representation a great deal more than it does Congress as a whole (Davidson, Oleszek, and Lee 2012, 488–490), and we have already noted the institution's general responsiveness to mass opinion. Recent elections, moreover, particularly those of 1992, 1994, 2006, and 2010 have shaken the House up a bit.

But there are suggestions that the lack of turnover should be of concern. Congressional scholars have noted that competitive races—marginals as they are sometimes called—have diminished appreciably over the past half century (Ansolabehere, Brady, Fiorina 1992; Mayhew 1974b). In seats that are truly uncompetitive at the general election stage, members move to the ideological extremes more than the public seems to want (Griffin 2006; Ladewig 2010). A perceived lack of competition also discourages smart and experienced potential challengers who could bring fresh energy and perspective to Congress but, understanding the significant opportunity costs of a congressional campaign and the damage defeat can inflict on long-term political aspirations, decide to defer (Gaddie 2004; Maestas et al. 2006). The decision to run for office is a complicated one that frequently depends on the potential candidate's personal circumstances (Fox and Lawless 2011), but the strategic political environment is clearly a crucial component (Kazee 1994; Stone and Maisel 2003). As re-election rates frequently topping 90 percent demonstrate, incumbents become increasingly secure, challengers increasingly reluctant, and House membership, increasingly stagnant.[30]

BENCHMARK #16
Congress must have sizeable proportions of members
who take at least several distinct paths to office.

Justification
Career paths can shed light on how permeable a legislature is. If new entrants tend to follow similar journeys into the body, we might argue that barriers are relatively high and prospective candidates who must take alternative routes disadvantaged. Systematic data on pretenure careers from abroad is just not available, although work on western European legislatures suggests an increased uniformity there (Best and Cotta 2000; Patzelt 1999). The backgrounds of British MPs, for example, are quite clearly becoming more homogenous. In both major parties, more members today are trained in the professions, particularly law and journalism (Cairney 2007).

Establishing a fair and precise goal for variation in the pretenure career paths of members of Congress is therefore impossible. Political careers seem to have become universally more professional and uniform, but in the absolute sense heterogeneity still exists. I think it is still reasonable and important to ask for variance in members of Congress's professional experiences prior to their arrival in Washington. Marked diversity would demonstrate a legislature open to individuals from many walks of life.

Appraisal

Little systematic study has been made of the pre-Congress careers of members, but data we do have suggest patterns are emerging and variation is diminishing, in turn confirming Joseph A. Schlesinger's (1966) observation in his seminal study of political ambition. Scott MacKenzie (2009, 2011) demonstrates that, in the period between the Civil War and World War II, paths to congressional office streamlined considerably as prospective members increasingly embarked on professional lives in politics. An important reason seems to be the emergence of the Australian ballot and the primary election as the means of nominating candidates.[31] Ambitious individuals had to invest time building personal coalitions of voters, something best done by campaigning for and holding office.

Today House members are increasingly running for Senate. Around one-half of all sitting senators have served in the House. For some, the development has contributed to polarization in the upper chamber, as members used to serving homogenous constituencies and in a combative and majoritarian body increasingly populate the upper chamber (Theriault and Rohde 2011). Others see effects on the behavior of members when they are still in the House. The lower body has encouraged policy specialization by creating strong autonomous committees with fixed jurisdictions. To demonstrate proficiency to voters, members have taken advantage of this to become experts. But members running for the Senate and therefore wishing to represent a broader constituency tend to present themselves as generalists (Victor 2011).

State legislatures have also become a kind of staging post for those desiring legislative careers in Washington (Canon 1990)—at least until recently, particularly Democrats (Berkman 1994). The consequences have been interesting. For example, the establishment of state legislative term limits has increased the supply of politically experienced congressional candidates, and elections have become more competitive (Birkhead, Uriati, and Bianco 2010; Steen 2006a). Still, on balance, the increasing professionalism of politics means it is reasonable to claim there are disappointingly few distinct routes to Capitol Hill these days. On this score, Congress is not discernibly superior to peer institutions. The benchmark is largely unmet.

BENCHMARK #17
Congressional membership should not just be for the rich;
the mean wealth of members should put them somewhere close
to halfway between the average and richest Americans.

Justification

The wealth of members might also tell us much about the height of entry barriers. Wealth does not really mean the salaries paid to legislators—individuals receive these after they are sworn in. Indeed, if salaries were indicators of members' wealth, then US House members and senators would be just about the richest in the world (Squire

2008). In advanced industrialized countries, only Japanese lawmakers get paid more and then by only about 5 percent. Members' salaries of $174,000 are considerably higher than those of legislators in other Anglophone countries like Australia, Canada, New Zealand, South Africa, and the United Kingdom.

Instead we should be interested in a broader understanding of members' financial circumstances. Rich legislators are emblematic of an institution that is insular and difficult to enter unless you are of considerable means. Russia's Duma has arguably the wealthiest membership these days; it included twelve billionaires in 2008. Unfortunately we do not have a tremendous understanding of how wealthy legislators generally are. This should not preclude us setting a target. Accepting that members of Congress are likely to be successful and educated individuals before they enter office, perhaps having wealth that puts them, on average, discernibly above the median American but below the country's richest citizens, is a desirable and reasonable goal.

Appraisal

A 2010 Center for Responsive Politics study revealed Congress to have 237 millionaires and the median wealth of a House member to be just over $750,000, that of a senator $2.38 million.[32] Legislators are clearly much better off than the general population, where only 1 percent can be considered millionaires and the median household income is about $50,000 a year. In fact, as a class, members of Congress are in the top 1 to 3 percent of all Americans when ranked by economic means.[33] The gap is also growing. Whereas in the quarter century between 1984 and 2009 the median total income of a House member grew by over 150 percent, it barely moved for the general public.

That this benchmark is not met is problematic whether members acquire their wealth before or after their arrival in Washington. The former suggests high barriers to entry, the latter self-imposed high barriers to exit—a matter equally inimical to turnover. Some members are clearly rich before they run for Congress. Among the self-made millionaires on the Hill is Rep. Darrell Issa (R-CA), who is worth about $450 million, money made largely from his personal car alarm business. Among those who were born rich is Sen. John Kerry (D-MA), whose mother was a member of the Forbes family that made its fortune in the nineteenth century. Kerry also married money. His current wife, Teresa Heinz Kerry, has income from the Heinz food company—her previous husband, and Kerry friend, Sen. John Heinz (R-PA) was an heir to the fortune when he died in 1991. Others seem to acquire much of their wealth in office. The amount of money members make outside of their congressional salaries has increased quite dramatically over the past few years.

Recent research has also shown that the investment portfolios of senators perform better than we should expect (Ziobrowski et al. 2004). Late in 2011, books by disgraced lobbyist Jack Abramoff (2011) and the Hoover Institution's Peter Schweizer (2011) caused quite a stir by explaining the observation. Schweizer's thesis was that members from both bodies have traded stocks and bonds after receiving what amounts to inside information. These actions were particularly egregious and profitable during the financial crisis of late 2008, when many Americans saw their investments nosedive. The uproar compelled Congress to pass the aforementioned STOCK Act in early 2012.

BENCHMARK #18
Members of Congress should generally be educated, and a large majority of them have college degrees.

Justification

It should be noted that not all barriers to membership are necessarily bad. Notwithstanding Sen. Roman Hruska's (R-NE) famous claim, used in his defense of Nixon Supreme Court nominee G. Harrold Carswell, that the mediocre are entitled to a little representation, we might want members of Congress to have some relevant credentials and qualifications. Having a formal education is not a sufficient condition for competent legislating. It may not even be a necessary one. But education implies knowledge of policy and societal problems and some level of skill that may translate into the practice of governing. Educational qualifications are also conveniently transparent and highly correlated with general cognitive ability.

Appraisal

The membership of recent Congresses has been well educated. In the 112th Congress (2011–2013), for example, 92 percent of House members and all but one Senator had a bachelor's degree. Over half had postgraduate degrees—mainly in law and medicine. The benchmark is met.

BENCHMARK #19
Unethical and illegal behavior of members of Congress should be very rare.

Justification

Members of Congress should not only listen and relate to us, they need to maintain our trust. This entails acting with moral authority. Only by meeting the highest standards for ethical conduct can they hope their collective and authoritative decisions will be accepted by the public. Moreover, whether they like or not, members have been elevated to positions of public leadership, and therefore they model behavior for their fellow citizens. After the shooting of Rep. Gabrielle Giffords (D-AZ) in January 2011, Congress undertook a tremendous amount of soul-searching. Legislators and observers alike made persuasive arguments that a vitriolic political rhetoric and deep incivility in Washington had, in some way, spilled over into the general populace and made the institution a target.

Determining whether any one legislative body has members who are more trustworthy, ethical, or less corrupt than another's is effectively impossible. Moral and legal standards differ across the world, and so presumably do the official and informal codes of conduct for political figures that are derived from them. The Italians' historical tolerance of corruption in their Chamber of Deputies is testament to that (Chang, Golden, and Hill 2010). Their tolerance for the antics of former Prime Minister Silvio Berlusconi perhaps revealed a different view of sexual behavior in public life too. At least before International Monetary Fund chief and prospective Socialist Party presidential candidate Dominique Strauss-Kahn was very publicly arrested on rape charges in 2011, the French also seemed to think politicians' sexual escapades were their own business. President Nicolas Sarkozy's cabinet at that time included Frederic Mitterrand, a nephew of the former president who had had numerous extramarital affairs and had written about his sexual encounters with small boys during a trip to Thailand. It is hard to imagine an American winning a seat in Congress after publicizing these details about his past.

Counting the number of expulsions from a legislative body is therefore meaningless. Rules and the willingness to apply them will differ tremendously. In American history, only twenty members have been expelled from Congress—fifteen senators and five House members, the most recent being Rep. Jim Traficant (D-OH) in 2002 after he was convicted of bribery, racketeering, and tax evasion. Only three members of the British House of Commons have been expelled since 1900.[34] Ten members of India's Lok Sabha, its lower house, were expelled in December 2005 alone, essentially for selling their right to ask questions in parliament. Even if we could engage in meaningful comparison, it would be hard to determine how much of its members' improper behavior was caused by a legislature's rules and values. Broader cultural norms and personal faults clearly play a substantial role in the dishonorable actions of lawmakers. So do entrenched institutions like electoral systems, some of which seem predisposed to corruption (Chang 2005; Gingerich 2009).[35]

So what are reasonable expectations for the behavior of members of Congress? In some regards that is an easy question to answer. On ethical and moral matters we should have zero tolerance for offenders. We should hold our federal elected officials to the highest standards possible.[36]

Of course this might be a little unrealistic. Members of Congress are naturally susceptible to the temptations of power, money, and sex. Just like others, they might be falsely accused too—many recent investigations are alleged by critics to have been partisan, unjust, and based upon misleading and incomplete information. Perhaps it would be fairer to suggest these incidents should be extremely rare. We would like to see at most only a very small number of members engaged in practices that are unambiguously unethical or immoral.

Appraisal

Earlier we noted numerous examples where members of Congress have betrayed the public trust and acted in immoral and illegal ways, both in the performance of their public duties and the conduct of their private lives. Unfortunately, it does not seem to be particularly rare, and we probably should recognize that Congress does not meet the benchmark we have set for it. However, it would be inaccurate for us to suggest the decline in ethical standards in Congress is a recent phenomenon. It is very difficult to undertake systematic temporal analyses of member behavior, but what measures we do have do not suggest the current era is one of particularly acute ethical decline.

Incidents of incivility provide a good example. Many individuals might not consider uncivil behavior to be unethical—even though civility is essentially a form of respect and tolerance of others.[37] But it is certainly a kind of behavior we aspire to and therefore should want our elected officials to exhibit. Polls continually find that about half of Americans believe politics are more uncivil today than they were a decade ago, and certainly heightened partisanship and ideological polarization bring about the kind of deep conflicts in public life that could easily become coarse.[38] Eric Uslaner (1993, 40–41), however, argues incivility "reached a fever pitch in the antebellum period." Forty percent of all instances of what he calls "breaches in comity" during the 1790–1956 period occurred in the thirty years leading up to the civil war.[39] Other studies come to similar conclusions. A 2011 report by the Annenberg Public Policy Center revealed demands that words be ruled out of order and rulings when words were deemed out of order were no more frequent in the House than at any previous time in American history.[40] In fact, by those measures, the House of the 1940s was more uncivil than today's. Lawrence Dodd and Scot Schraufnagel (2007) gauge incivility by examining media coverage of Congress. They report that levels of incivility are marginally higher today than they were a half century ago but appreciably lower than they were in the last thirty years of the nineteenth century.

Data on more serious offenses and unequivocally unethical behavior lead to similar, if unavoidably tentative, conclusions. Article I, Section 5, of the Constitution allows each body to expel members by a two-thirds vote. The House and Senate can also choose to use a lesser punishment and censure members. Of the forty-nine censures or expulsions in American history, ten have occurred in the past half century. This sounds bad when we realize that nineteen of the remaining cases were during the Civil War and involved violators' support for the Confederacy. But perhaps it is not quite so disconcerting if we consider the tremendous resources congressional investigators now have to root out misconduct. It may be that incidents of unethical behavior are no more frequent these days; Congress just has the means to discover and prosecute them.

For example, a pervasive and aggressive media is assisted by new technology, transparency laws such as the Freedom of Information Act (FOIA), and a greater willingness of the public to scrutinize public officials. In 2012 numerous House members caught up in a publicized ethics scandal lost reelection efforts, including Reps. Silvestre Reys

(D-TX), Laura Richardson (D-CA), David Rivera (R-FL), and Cliff Stearns (R-FL).[41] Congress also has new institutions capable of following up on information uncovered by reporters. The Senate Select Committee on Standards and Conduct was established in 1964. One of the committee's first actions was to establish official rules of behavior for members and staff. The House's panel was formed as a select committee in 1966 and acquired standing status the next year. Reforms in 1989 and 1997 made it easier to initiate investigations, professionalized and increased the size of the staff, and gave minority members more power. In 2008 the House created the Office of Congressional Ethics (OCE) to report cases to the committee. Even in its short existence, the establishment of the OCE is widely believed to have helped the House enforce ethics regulations.[42]

The codification of stricter standards of behavior and the formation of institutions dedicated to enforcing them are, in and of themselves, important developments. Congress may seem to be nurturing corruption and other kinds of moral turpitude, unethical conduct, and generally undesirable behavior, but it has also taken concrete steps to stamp them out. Its success has been mixed, and for that reason we ought to recognize it has not met the benchmark set for it. But we do need to give it credit for at the very least recognizing these issues and undertaking a genuine attempt to address them and to compel lawmakers to behave in a manner becoming membership in our federal legislature.

CONCLUSION

As a legislative body at the center of an advanced and vibrant democracy, Congress behaves almost schizophrenically. We saw in Chapter 3 that it is very responsive to public opinion on national, state, and local matters. This is not surprising, given how transparent it is and how willing its members are to listen to their constituents. But at the same time Congress seems inaccessible and remote. Its members sometimes behave in a way that suggests they do not believe general codes of ethical conduct apply to them. Many of its procedures are undeniably complex. Observers experience considerable difficulty linking the individual and collective behavior of legislators with policy outcomes. In a purportedly classless society with a strong populist heritage and little tolerance for individuals who consider themselves above the masses, Congress is extremely difficult to get into. The Senate is widely known as "the world's most exclusive club."[43] Those who have not previously held important political office are increasingly less likely to get elected. The public dislikes Congress yet returns most of the same people election after election, people who are much wealthier than the average American.

As Table 4.1 demonstrates, however, Congress meets or exceeds many of the benchmarks set for it as we gauge its transparency, accessibility, and trustworthiness—essentially the extent to which it is integrated into American public life. The general assessment that Congress is out of touch with the country's mainstream is rather unfair.

BENCHMARK FOR CONGRESSIONAL PERFORMANCE	APPRAISAL
8. Congress's daily business should be visible to the public.	Met
9. Congress should have many formally recorded plenary votes.	Met
10. Congress should have open committee proceedings.	Met
11. Congress should have rules that are simple, clear, and few in number.	Not met
12. Congress should have member disclosure requirements that exceed those of most of the American states.	Met
13. Members should have adequate staff—about ten to fifteen each.	Met
14. Members should spend about half of their time in the district or state.	Met
15. Congress should have meaningful turnover: approximately 20 percent of the House should turn over each Congress, about 50 percent of the Senate each six years.	Not met
16. Congress should have sizeable proportions of members who take at least several distinct paths to office.	Largely not met
17. Congressional membership should not just be for the rich. The mean wealth of members should put them somewhere close to halfway between the average and richest Americans.	Not met
18. Members of Congress should generally be educated, and a large majority of them have college degrees.	Met
19. Unethical and illegal behavior of members of Congress should be very rare.	Not met

TABLE 4.1 Appraising congressional performance on benchmarks related to transparency, accessibility, and trustworthiness

5

DOES CONGRESS HAVE
DESIRABLE PRINCIPLES OF
ORGANIZATION?

The aspiration shaping the benchmarks in this chapter is to have a legislature organized in an optimal manner. What, exactly, this constitutes is difficult to say with great precision. But the design needs to be sensitive to Congress's many responsibilities—from lawmaking to representing local concerns to checking the executive and judicial branches. These often place conflicting demands on the institution and, because outcomes are shaped by structure, call for very different and often contradictory rules and procedures. Spending on transportation needs provides a good example. Congress must approve reasonable appropriations bills in a timely manner so that projects can move forward effectively but at minimal cost. At the same time, however, the procedures used to commit transportation dollars must be fairly distributed to the hundreds of jurisdictions requesting support for highways, bridges, and mass transit.

THE PRINCIPLES OF CENTRALIZATION
AND DECENTRALIZATION

To some institutions, outputs are more important than processes, and the needs of members secondary to other concerns. Businesses are like this. They must provide a product to customers in a timely manner and at minimal cost. They are therefore centralized, structured in a vertical manner with decisions made by a relatively small number of leaders at the top and then carried out by much larger numbers of workers further down.

The Constitution may guarantee Congress's existence but, if the branch is to be effective and serve the public interest, it has to produce. In this way it is like a corporation that is in the business of making laws. Congress probably does not have to generate massive amounts of legislation every year. However, significant societal problems often arise, and the federal government is the only entity with the authority, will, and resources to solve many of them. Under these circumstances Congress is expected to do something. Sometimes for better, sometimes for worse, Congress has moved over the past half century to alleviate recessions, provide a significant amount of funding for elementary and secondary education, extend civil rights, protect the environment, expand health care and public pension programs, assist in recovery from natural disaster, and regulate hiring policies, working conditions, and business practices in the private sector. It has built highways, supercomputers, and spacecraft—or at least paid contractors to do so on its behalf. It has funded our armed forces and with the president sent them abroad to protect our interests and fight our enemies. Quite simply, Congress does produce, and frequently it does because it needs to and the public wants it to. Centralization facilitates this productivity.

Congress is also very different from a business, however. Legislators represent citizens and their interests in the policy process, and therefore the institution ought to be somewhat more horizontal in design, with members having roughly equal powers and influence over decisions that are made after careful consideration and with broad participation. Congress should demonstrate characteristics of decentralization.

Americans value this second organizational principle. The public continually complains about gridlock but finds checking and balancing appealing—it often prefers a Congress that will counter a president over one that will facilitate his agenda.[1] It sometimes believes Congress acts too hastily as well. In an October 2010 survey, the Center on Congress at Indiana University reported that 86 percent of respondents believed it better for Congress to "take the time to consider issues thoroughly" than "pass legislation quickly and efficiently."

Congress must therefore try to combine centralization and decentralization. This is no easy task. The two are opposing forces, and at any particular time competing groups of members are at work pushing the House and Senate in procedural directions that best suit their interests. Both bodies have, over time, granted certain members formal positions of power—the Speaker, floor leaders, and committee chairs are the most obvious examples. These individuals, who since the end of the Civil War have been members of the majority party, have an interest in accumulating greater power and furthering centralization so as to advance their own policy preferences. Rank-and-file members, particularly those in the minority party, will tend to push for greater decentralization.[2] When House and Senate rules give them influence in the legislative process, they are better situated to shape law. Congressional scholars have written that the outcome of this procedural conflict depends upon a number of things, the relative strength of the political parties and changes in the size and workloads of the bodies being the most important (Binder 1997; Dion 1997; Schickler 2001; Taylor 2012a).

Regardless of how congressional organization changes, however, the main point is that this is a continual struggle. There is no conscious permanent design for the way Congress must operate. The Constitution says very little on the subject.[3]

BENCHMARK # 20
The floor agenda should be set by entities that constitute a representative and fairly large but manageable subgroup of the membership—perhaps 10 to 20 percent of the body.

Justification

A fundamental virtue of legislative centralization is that it assumes procedures exist to induce a form of equilibrium. Without formal rules and widely accepted norms and practices, we have what Gary Cox (2005, 141) calls "the legislative state of nature" and what Richard McKelvey (1986) labels "institution-free" legislatures. It is likely nothing would get done because any member could introduce any bill onto the floor at any time and any individual member could prevent any bill from coming to a vote. Any conceivable amendment could be offered. Put succinctly, there would be chaos, particularly because most legislative bodies have large numbers of members and consider multidimensional and complex issues (McKelvey 1976).

A particularly important procedure that necessarily has the effect of privileging certain members and therefore centralizing a body is control of the floor agenda. In most legislatures around the world, the floor agenda—that is the flow of bills to the plenary—is orchestrated by a single member or a subgroup of members usually from the majority party or governing coalition. These actors often have positive and negative agenda power, that is, the power to shape proposals and determine their fate by moving them to the floor or killing them. Agenda setters tend to promote proposals they like and push them on to the floor. If the agenda setter and general membership have very different policy preferences, many bills are unlikely to be approved. The agenda setter will not want to send forward a bill a floor majority embraces, while a bill the agenda setter supports will find it difficult to summon the number of votes needed to pass. However, even with a modicum of agreement, an agenda-setting model is, for the purposes of productivity anyway, preferable to what might be considered a free-for-all, where there is no widely agreed-upon member or group of members who can determine what proposals the plenary will consider.

I think it is fair to say we accept that agenda-setting procedures have merit. But which are best? There certainly is a great deal to choose from. Herbert Döring (2001) explains that government control of the floor agenda varies across western European countries. In places like Greece, Ireland, and the United Kingdom, control is particularly tight—all of these governments essentially control the plenary agenda and restrict what are generally called private members' bills from coming to the floor. Even within the confines of the American context, the variety of procedures is dizzying. Some committees in state legislatures must hear bills, others do not have to. Some must report bills, others can block them (Anzia and Cohn 2011; Martorano 2006).

Without a real guide, any target for Congress might seem a little arbitrary. I suggest the floor agenda should be set by a group of members who together constitute a minority of the body. This group ought to be quite exclusive, so as to allow those who both care and know quite a bit about the legislation to examine it first. It makes sense to permit those with information and intense preferences to take the lead in policy formation and initial review. Remember, the full membership still gets to debate and vote on a bill should it proceed to the floor. As for the precise size of these groups, we should not want every member to be on every one of them; that would undermine the information-gathering and efficiency, or division-of-labor, benefits of such a system. Perhaps somewhere around one-tenth to one-fifth of the membership makes sense and allows the body to exploit the gains that can be generated by agenda-setting institutions.

Appraisal

In both chambers of Congress, committees emerged to set the floor agenda. Until about 1820, the House and Senate relied largely on select committees. These were very small groups of members—often as few as three—charged with generating a single bill suitable for floor consideration. As a result, hundreds of these ad hoc panels were appointed in many of the early Congresses. Members were appointed to them not so much for their partisan affiliation or policy preferences but for their expertise and interest in the issue (Canon and Stewart 2001, 178). The committees were temporary, in that they disbanded after their responsibilities had been discharged. As a practical matter, their agenda-setting powers were limited. At the time rather inchoate legislative proposals were initially debated on and approved by the floor before the select committee was appointed and assigned with generating language suitable for dispositive floor consideration (Cooper and Young 1989).

Very quickly, in fact almost overnight in the Senate, a system of standing committees emerged to replace select committees (Gamm and Shepsle 1989; Jenkins and Stewart 2002). These committees had more anchored jurisdictions and, although their membership turned over quite rapidly at first, were permanent in the sense that they received all bills on a particular topic and survived over multiple Congresses. By the 1850s, individual House members were introducing bills themselves, and committees began to acquire the authority to report them to the floor (Cooper and Young 1989). By 1900, the current textbook legislative process was largely in place. Congressional committees had significant proposal powers in that they could amend and ratify bills assigned to them. They had important veto powers, and it was very difficult for the floor to receive bills when a majority of the committee of jurisdiction did not approve. This was especially the case in the House. The body's discharge procedure, first established in 1910, today allows a simple majority of members to force a committee to report a bill by signing a petition to that effect. But it has never been a particularly practical way of sidestepping obstinate committees, even at the lower thresholds of 145 or 150 members, where it was from 1924 to 1925 and 1931 to 1935 respectively. Members are often reluctant to sign these petitions, largely because the procedure might generate retaliatory challenges to the authority of the committees to which they belong (Burden 2003; Miller and Overby 2010). At most, only one or two are successful per Congress.

If anything, committees became even more powerful in the first three-quarters of the twentieth century. Since the 1800s, the House had operated under a property rights norm by which lawmakers who wished to be reappointed to a committee they had served on in the previous Congress were as a matter of course (Jenkins 1998). The practice was formalized in the early 1900s (Deering and Smith 1997, 26–27). At the same time both bodies built a seniority system in which the longest-serving majority party member of the committee became its chair (Goodwin 1959). The practices conspired to make committee assignments automatic and members practically immune from forced removal. Moreover, extended service on a committee allowed members to acquire important information about issues within its jurisdiction. For many in Congress, this specialization was a public good that deserved deference (Asher 1974). By the 1960s, then, committees had both procedural power and significant autonomy. At least until the early 1970s, chairs also had almost complete control over committee operations, hired staff, scheduled hearings and meetings, recruited witnesses, and made budgetary decisions (Bolling 1965; Galloway 1953; Fenno 1973).[4] Standing committees and their leaders exerted great control over the floor agenda, and there was little others could, or wanted to, do about it.

Some have argued committees' agenda powers are used benignly. Krehbiel (1991), for example, forwards an information theory of congressional organization in which committees serve at the pleasure of the full body. Committees are created because they have efficiency properties, largely demonstrated by how they divide labor within a chamber. The legislature maintains control over individual committees by threatening to shrink their jurisdictions or abolish them entirely and by ensuring that they are composed of lawmakers whose policy preferences reflect those of the general membership.

By contrast, other congressional scholars argue that it is really the majority party that controls the agenda. This is true in the Senate where the majority leader formally introduces bills onto the floor and has skillfully exploited other procedural privileges. He can invoke Rule XIV, which places items directly onto the legislative calendar, bypassing committee. This is typically done to House-passed measures (Koempel 2005; Oleszek 2011a, 285–287).[5] The Senate majority leadership has also proven quite capable of galvanizing its rank and file so as to defeat minority amendments, frequently by employing tabling motions and issuing points of order (Den Hartog and Monroe 2011, 112–145).

It is truer in the House. Gary Cox and Mathew McCubbins (2005) produced what they call the "procedural cartel theory." They argue the House majority party exploits the Speaker's powers to regulate tightly the flow of legislation to the floor, ensuring that bills the party does not like stay off it and that bills the party does like meet with its approval. For the most part, recent Speakers have followed Dennis Hastert's informal rule that a majority of the majority party should support a bill for it to be sent to the floor—although John Boehner ignored the principle when putting a tax bill before the House during the "fiscal cliff" crisis of December 2012. Since the mid-1970s, House Speakers have also used their discretionary power to refer bills of broad scope and potentially significant impact to multiple committees in an effort to manipulate the floor agenda (Sinclair 2012, 142–144). The important 2009 cap-and-trade energy bill was initially referred to nine committees: Energy and Commerce, Foreign Affairs, Financial Services, Education and Labor, Science and Technology, Transportation and Infrastructure, Natural Resources, Agriculture, and Ways and Means. Even after bills are reported from committee, most need a special rule from the Rules Committee, of which nine of its thirteen members are handpicked from the majority party caucus by the Speaker. Designated as a privileged matter, this special rule can be debated and voted on promptly with passage meaning immediate consideration of the bill itself. Moreover, in all cases the Speaker, leader of the majority party as well as the House's presiding officer, must schedule bills for floor debate.

Cox and McCubbins (2005) demonstrate that these procedures have profound effects. For example, the majority party is hardly ever "rolled"—that is, it is very rare that a majority of majority party members are on the losing side of a vote (93–99)—although this did happen quite spectacularly over the "fiscal cliff" legislation brought to the floor by Speaker John Boehner on New Year's Day 2013. They show that bills that pass the House tend to move policy much further in the ideological direction desired by the majority party than the floor median should want. In other words, outcomes seem more consistent with the preference of the median member of the majority (Cox and McCubbins 2005, 171–197).

Party control of committees is also secured because, although they usually honor members' requests, leaders have tremendous influence over assignments. They dominate the panels each party in each chamber uses to determine who will fill their slots on standing committees (Democrats call them Steering and Outreach; Republicans, Committees on Committees).[6] Their latitude in these decisions increased as the property rights and, particularly, seniority principles eroded. The three-term limits for chairs used by both House parties since the mid-1990s have only expanded leaders' influence over committees and the individuals who sit on them.[7]

Members have found themselves particularly vulnerable to the retaliatory use of the assignment process if they are under investigation and, therefore, hurting the party's reputation—Rep. William Jefferson (D-LA), he of money-in-the-freezer fame, was expelled from Ways and Means in 2006. But policy disputes have been important catalysts as well. In 1982 House Democrats threw Phil Gramm (D-TX) off the Budget Committee after he sided with minority Republicans to push through President Reagan's tax cuts. Gramm quit the party and the House and regained his seat after a special election in which he ran as a Republican. Republican leaders evicted a small number of Tea Party dissidents from committees for the 113th Congress. The first time in the modern era the seniority principle was violated came in 1975 when newly elected, liberal northern and western Democrats forced their leadership to remove three southern conservative Democratic chairs, F. Edward Hébert (D-LA) of Armed Services, Wright Patman (D-TX) of Banking, and W. R. Poage (D-TX) of Agriculture, with whom they had fundamental ideological disagreements. Melvin Price (D-IL) lost his position as chair of Armed Services in 1985, and John Dingell had control of his beloved Energy Committee taken away from him in 2007. Republican leaders overlooked Joe McDade (R-PA) as chair of Appropriations in 1995 and Marge Roukema (R-NJ) as chair of Financial Services in 2001. In both instances many rank-and-file members believed they were too moderate to be trusted at the helm of such important panels. In 2004 Republican leaders removed the chair of Veterans' Affairs, Rep. Chris Smith (R-NJ), from the committee entirely for publicly contradicting Speaker Dennis Hastert's (R-IL) position on spending increases for veterans' benefits. In the 112th Congress (2011–2013), fewer than one-third of chairs were the longest-serving committee members from the majority Republican conference.

Committees are largely window dressing in this partisan model of lawmaking. The majority party and its leadership are the House's real agenda setter; the committees merely serve them. This is especially the case at a time like the present when the party caucuses are ideologically polarized and homogenous. John Aldrich and David W. Rohde (2000, 2001; Rohde 1991) call the current period of great partisanship, which essentially began in the late 1970s, one of "conditional party government." With the parties distinct and cohesive, the majority rank and file is particularly supportive of leadership and permits it to employ procedures and practices assertively in an effort to push through the party's legislative proposals. Congress, and particularly the House, is extremely centralized, and committees have lost autonomy and influence—that is, their capacity to decentralize. With a full agenda that it promised to rush through the House, the Republican leadership in 1995 controlled and streamlined the committee process so as to send items in the Contract with America quickly to the floor (Gimpel 1996, 42–114). Speaker Nancy Pelosi did much the same with the Democratic "100 hour" package of proposals in 2007.

Regardless, vibrant standing committees still constitute a critical and signature organizational feature of both the House and Senate. Standing committees craft bills and, admittedly with considerable assistance from the Speaker and Rules Committee in the House and majority leader in the Senate, are gatekeepers to the floor. These are important tasks. So as to realize efficiency gains but also ensure a significant proportion of the general membership can influence the floor agenda, the benchmark for committees is to consist of somewhere between one-tenth and one-fifth of the body of which they are a part. In the Senate this means committees should have somewhere in the neighborhood of ten to twenty members. For committees with narrower and perhaps less important jurisdictions, this does seem to be the case. In the 112th Congress (2011–2013), for example, the Committee on Small Business and Entrepreneurship had nineteen members, the Committee on Rules and Administration eighteen, and the Committee on Veterans' Affairs fifteen. Even Foreign Relations, a committee that is hardly unimportant, had nineteen members. But other committees were quite large. Armed Services had twenty-six members, Finance and Commerce, Science, and Transportation twenty-five each. Because these are panels with broad jurisdictions that cover issues vital to the country, it is perhaps not surprising that so many senators should wish to be on them. Moreover, the Senate can afford to do more of its business on the floor. It has only one hundred members, and standing rules certainly provide its committees with fewer agenda powers than their counterparts in the lower chamber. Senators can sometimes offer bills directly to the floor by motion, the germaneness rule permits them to offer bills as floor amendments to other bills, and, as we noted earlier, Rule XIV provides a way to sidestep committee consideration of bills, especially those first passed by the House.[8] Still it is true that Senate committees might be too large to deliver many benefits of centralization. With each senator often a member of five or six committees, opportunities to specialize are diminished as well.

By this reckoning, House committees are more optimally sized. In the 112th Congress most were between about forty and fifty members. The largest committees, Armed Services and Financial Services, had sixty-one members each, perhaps reflecting the great attention paid to issues in their jurisdictions over the past several years. The numbers reflect reductions in the sizes of committees from the previous Congress, when Democrats were in control. Then the largest committee was Transportation and Infrastructure, with seventy-four members.

In sum, it seems fair to say that committees, the institutions Congress has established to filter legislation before it reaches the floor, provide adequate representation. The average rank-and-file member in both bodies plays a meaningful role in agenda setting, at least within the handful of policy areas that match the jurisdictions of the committees she belongs to. Because of the property rights norm and the assignment process, members do this largely on issues of their, and presumably their constituents', choosing. Committees are not, on the whole, overly large. They are therefore capable of delivering the efficiency gains provided by specialization and the division of labor. Despite the intense partisanship of the day, motivated and often knowledgeable members work in small groups to prepare legislation and build and "road test" arguments for and against it in an expeditious manner. Colleagues can divert their efforts and attention to other matters and be assured that when a bill comes to the floor it has usually already gone through a quite rigorous process and has a reasonable chance of passage.

BENCHMARK #21
A majority should be able to bring floor debate on a bill to a close.

Justification

Debate termination is an important procedure because without it floor proceedings can, theoretically at least, last indefinitely. A member or group of members should be able to bring debate on a bill to a close so that the body can vote. Under extreme decentralizing rules, small numbers of opponents of legislation can obstruct, and majorities, regardless of how large, might be incapable of pushing through measures they support.

Legislative bodies use numerous methods to terminate floor debate. Internationally, some parliaments in established democracies, particularly those in Scandinavia and the Low Countries, have quite open-ended proceedings. Others, such as those of Anglophone countries, allow a simple majority of members or, as in the cases of eastern Europe and Latin America, individual leaders to bring about an end to debate (Taylor 2006). In the American states most chambers allow a simple majority of members present to invoke what is called the previous question, although there are several bodies with higher thresholds such as a simple majority of those elected or two-thirds of members present. By contrast, in the same way the Belgians, Danes, and Swedes have no formal way to bring floor debate to an end, the Delaware and Vermont Senates are absent a previous question procedure altogether (Taylor 2012a, 18).

Again, settling on a preferred procedure is a rather difficult task. The great value of centralization is legislative efficiency and policy productivity. Requiring greater than a simple majority of members to terminate debate clearly invites obstructionism. But permitting leaders or select legislators to do so chafes against our democratic sensibilities. The power is likely to be used prematurely to truncate proceedings and undermine the kind of debate and deliberation that are central to a healthy legislative process. It seems best to have a procedure built around majoritarian principles. Allowing a simple majority of those present or elected to bring proceedings on a measure to a close balances the virtues of centralization with those of decentralization. It is also consistent with Americans' basic views of legitimate political practices.[9]

Appraisal

The House

The House terminates floor debate through the previous question. This procedural device is a nondebatable motion that brings consideration of a measure to an immediate halt and moves it directly to a vote. The motion must be approved by a simple majority. The House formally adopted the previous question as it is used today in late 1811 when a large and energetic group of freshmen eager for war with Britain—including the newly elected Henry Clay (KY) who was made Speaker—decided, along with senior Republicans, to overcome the Federalist minority's resistance to military confrontation with procedural reform (Binder 1997, 43–67). Before that time the meaning of the previous question had been ambiguous. In 1807 Speaker Joseph Varnum (Rep-MA) determined it ended debate, but he was overruled by a significant majority of members after a move to appeal the decision. When, in February 1811 as a divided country moved closer to war, Varnum upheld this alternative interpretation and announced approval of a previous question motion did not stop debate, the House changed its mind, and in a partisan vote the Republican majority forced the more restrictive understanding of the procedure upon the body. This meaning was then written into House rules the following December.

The previous question soon emerged as an effective tool. A simple majority could now terminate debate, and the floor dispose of measures more expeditiously. Today it is more often than not invoked pre-emptively. The special rules given bills generally include language stating that the previous question is ordered after the time allotted for debate has expired. In these instances, the previous question is adopted when a simple majority of members present and voting passes the special rule immediately prior to consideration of the underlying bill.

The previous question did not quickly eliminate floor obstruction, however. Although initially rare, as the House membership and workload grew and policy disputes deepened, members engaged in filibusters, speaking on the floor for hours on end so as to prevent a vote on a bill (Koger 2010, 39–77). When the number of filibusters spiked in the late 1880s and early 1890s, the House responded with additional reforms to centralize floor procedures (Koger 2010, 53–56). The House Rules Committee first began to promulgate special rules in an effort to limit floor amendments and debate time in 1883. Then, in 1890 under the leadership of Speaker Thomas Brackett Reed (R-ME), the House adopted what came to be known as Reed's rules. First, the Speaker ended the practice of the "disappearing quorum" in which members on the floor could avoid being counted as present by refusing to answer a call of the roll. Article I, Section 5, of the Constitution compels each body to use a simple majority as a quorum, and House rules allow its Committee of the Whole, where much legislative business is undertaken, to operate when at least one hundred members are present.[10] Reed instituted the change as the House debated a disputed election case from West Virginia, an issue that tended to be highly partisan and that would therefore galvanize the Republican majority. As Democrats dived under desks and ran for the exits so that the Speaker could not see and count them, many shouted "Czar, Czar." Their efforts were in vain, at least in the immediate term. The ruling was codified two weeks later on a strict party-line vote.

Reed's second act was to end the practice of members offering motions purely for the purpose of delaying consideration of a measure. The very day after he had ruled against the disappearing quorum, the Speaker announced he would no longer entertain motions he believed to be dilatory. The prohibition on motions of this type was enumerated into House rules with the disappearing quorum ban.

Democrats rescinded these rules after winning a large majority in the 1890 elections. However, nearly two Congresses of Republican obstructionism, crowned by a massive filibuster on procedural matters, compelled them to abandon their quixotic embrace of minority rights and accept the benefits of Reed's decisions (Koger 2010, 55; Schickler 2001, 46–50). In 1894 both the disappearing quorum and dilatory motion bans were permanently incorporated into House rules. The power to manage floor proceedings was consequently centralized further, here quite clearly into the hands of the majority party's leadership.

These days, bills that reach the House floor can be assured of timely disposition. The most important are debated under a process described by the special rule and need only the approval of a floor majority. The number of amendments that can be offered is regularly limited to a few. Dilatory motions and other efforts to impede the bill's progress are not in order. When the time for debate expires, the previous question is called as a matter of course. The minority is granted the right to offer a motion to recommit—essentially an effort to have the bill sent back to committee and, therefore, killed.[11] This nearly always fails. The House then moves to a vote. The House floor is majoritarian. In the context of legislative institutions, its debate termination procedure is therefore quite centralized, and the benchmark is met.

The Senate

The Senate operates very differently. Largely because it was rarely used, the body dropped a previous question provision from its rules in 1806 (Binder 1997, 43). The procedure has never been resurrected. Together with the tradition that the senator who holds the floor has the power of recognition—a right of the presiding officer in the House—this means consideration or measures may be unlimited in the Senate and members can undertake filibusters to prevent any debatable motion on the floor from coming to a vote.

Senate filibusters were not a particularly regular occurrence until the late nineteenth century (Koger 2010, 51–53; Wawro and Schickler 2006, 182–187). When members obstructed efforts to dispose of legislation, they could generally be overcome by a majority of their colleagues (Wawro and Schickler 2006, 127–157). The accelerated growth of the Senate's membership and workload together with greater partisanship and heterogeneity of policy preferences, however, dramatically increased filibustering in the thirty years that straddled 1900 (Wawro and Schickler 2006, 186–193). The outbreak of obstructionism threatened to bring the Senate to a halt. When, in the words of President Woodrow Wilson, "a little group of willful men representing no opinion but their own" prevented the government from arming merchant ships as it prepared for war with Germany in the spring of 1917, the body wrote Rule XXII and established the procedure of cloture. From then on, any effort by a member or group of members to prevent the Senate from voting on a matter could be ended by a super-majority of colleagues. The 1917 iteration of the rule put this figure at two-thirds of members present and voting.

Interestingly, Rule XXII did very little to affect the incidence of filibustering. Until the mid-1960s, only a small handful of motions to invoke cloture were filed each year. Even at the time of the great filibusters over civil rights legislation in 1957 and 1964—the first of which motivated the longest individual filibuster in American history, Sen. Strom Thurmond's (D-SC) twenty-four-hour-and-eighteen-minute monologue—the Senate generally ran smoothly, and members employed obstruction only under extraordinary circumstances and when they believed it was fully justified. In the 1970s, however, something changed. There was a considerable escalation in filibustering so that by the end of the first decade of the 2000s, senators were filing in excess of 130 cloture motions a Congress.[12]

Today a resourceful and motivated Senate minority can tie the body in knots—sometimes, as was the case in the 111th Congress (2009–2011), filibustering seemingly uncontroversial bills that eventually passed by eighty or more votes (Mann and Ornstein 2012, 89–91). It is no wonder that party leaders consider sixty members as more important a target than the simple majority of fifty-one needed to control committees and occupy leadership positions.[13] The intense partisanship and polarization of today's Senate makes this even more apparent. Democrats were appropriately disconsolate when Sen. Scott Brown (R-MA) won Ted Kennedy's old seat in January 2010. Their majority had slipped to fifty-nine, and the future of President Obama's agenda, particularly health care reform, was under considerable threat.[14] The nearly $800 billion economic stimulus plan the Obama administration proposed in early 2009 to alleviate the deep recession scraped through with sixty votes after three Republican moderates—Sens. Susan Collins (R-ME), Olympia Snowe (R-ME), and Arlen Specter (R-PA)—were persuaded to vote for it and overcome their partisan colleagues' filibuster. This was in the early months of a popular president's first term, a period when the White House is supposed to be at its most powerful. Normally sixty is harder to get. The last Congress in which the majority was as large as in 2009 was the Ninety-Fifth (1977–1979). There were sixty-one Democrats in the Senate then.

Julia Azari and Jennifer Smith (2012) argue the proliferation of filibustering and cloture motions is largely a result of them becoming acceptable practice. Others have suggested that reforms made since World War II have encouraged filibustering by reducing the cost of obstruction for both opponents and supporters of a bill. The first of these changes occurred in 1949. It raised the bar for cloture and permitted it invoked only by two-thirds of the entire membership but had compensatory centralizing effects, particularly by broadening its possible application to procedural matters and nominations and treaties (Binder 1997, 191–193; Koger 2010, 164–165). Crafted by Majority Leader Lyndon Johnson (D-TX) in 1959, a further alteration lowered cloture back to two-thirds present and voting and permitted it invoked on motions to proceed to rules changes. Probably the most impactful reform was adopted in 1975 when the threshold was brought down to its current level of three-fifths of the body, or sixty votes. As a reaction to the blocking of civil rights legislation, this change had been sought by a bipartisan liberal coalition for about a decade (Gold and Gupta 2004). Revisions in 1979 and 1986 were designed to weaken the capacity of senators to engage in postcloture filibusters, a practice perfected by individuals such as Sen. James Allen (D-AL) (Koger 2010, 176–179). The 1979 change placed a 100-hour limit on postcloture debate. The 1986 one reduced it further, to 30 hours.

There was one other important reform, although it was announced by the leadership rather than added to the formal rules. During the 1970s, when he was majority whip, Sen. Robert Byrd (D-WV) established the track system. Under this practice the consequences of obstruction were minimized. Whereas a filibuster had effectively blocked not only the measure under consideration but all other legislation awaiting floor debate, Byrd and Majority Leader Mike Mansfield (D-MT) began to pull stymied measures to make way for others, hence establishing different "tracks" for floor proceedings. No longer would members have to engage in Mr. Smith filibusters—so named because they involve a constant presence on the floor, just like the Jimmy Stewart character's exhausting effort in Frank Capra's famous movie, *Mr. Smith Goes to Washington*. The majority leadership quickly began to exploit the new practice and, as a result, opponents of bills understood their filibusters would not harm the prospects of legislation they did support. Floor obstruction naturally increased.

The Senate majority leadership has fought back against the filibuster using a variety of strategies. Two—both of which were demonstrated during the consideration of the health care reform bill discussed in the previous chapter—are made possible by the majority leader's right to initial recognition. This practice stems from 1937 when President of the Senate and Vice President of the United States John Nance Garner (D-TX) decided that under the standing rule compelling the presiding officer to recognize the first senator to address him, he would allow the majority leader, if that individual so desired, to begin floor debate. The minority leader would then be granted the courtesy before the traditional "first-come-first-served" practice took effect (Gamm and Smith 2002).

Because cloture motions take two days to ripen, the majority leader might expedite proceedings by filing for it as he begins floor debate on a bill. This is called pre-emptive cloture. The majority leader can also immediately "fill the amendment tree." Because

Senate precedents limit the number of amendments that are in order at any one time, he can effectively prevent anyone else from offering them until his have been disposed of. The tree is filled by a series of substitute and perfecting amendments. The practice is increasingly utilized. Harry Reid apparently exploited it forty-three times in the 111th Congress (2009–2011). It is particularly helpful when invoking cloture pre-emptively because it protects the underlying measure from alteration as the required debate before final vote unfolds.[15]

The motion to table is another useful tool (Den Hartog and Monroe 2011, 130–139). Here a senator moves to kill an amendment. Because the motion is not debatable, it cannot be filibustered. The procedure therefore provides a quick way to beat back minority efforts to change legislation. Its usage increased greatly after the 1970s. Around 80 percent of these motions are approved.[16]

Moreover, not all measures can be filibustered in the Senate. Since 1974, the body's rules have made budget bills and reconciliation—a legislative vehicle frequently used for changes in tax law and entitlement programs like Social Security—immune from the filibuster. Congress has also imposed statutory restrictions on the use of the device. The Defense Base Realignment and Closure Act of 1990 set up a series of "rounds" in which bipartisan commissions would select military installations from across the country for downsizing or termination and then, if the president approved, offer these lists to Congress for its consideration. The goal was to cut waste from the Department of Defense's budget and move the military beyond the Cold War.[17] Because members fight tenaciously for federal resources and their constituents' interests, lawmakers understood that the regular legislative process would be obstructed by affected senators. The legislation therefore allowed only an up-or-down vote on the proposal and prohibited a filibuster. The deal elevating the debt ceiling and creating a process to produce significant deficit reduction that was approved in the summer of 2011 protected the recommendations of the "supercommittee" appointed to examine federal fiscal policy from a filibuster on the Senate floor. The safeguard proved unnecessary because, as noted earlier, the committee failed to issue a report.

Whereas the House meets the benchmark that a majority of members can bring floor debate to an end, the Senate most clearly does not. Only twenty of ninety-nine state legislative bodies have procedures that make debate termination more difficult (Taylor 2012a, 18).[18] Most bodies in advanced industrialized democracies have rules that permit leaders or a simple majority to close plenary proceedings (Taylor 2006). The Senate floor could be more centralized and efficient, and possibly without losing much in the way of benefits generated from broad participation and serious deliberation.

Over the last several years, there have been numerous efforts to reform the Senate's Rule XXII. All of them have been to reduce the number of members needed to invoke cloture. The recent attention to the matter was initiated by Republicans. In early 2005, Majority Leader Bill Frist (R-TN) made it clear that he was considering the "nuclear option" to force Senate consideration of the blocked nominations of several federal judges. Using this strategy, the Republican leadership was willing to move that the Senate should allow a simple majority to approve judicial nominations because disposition in this way is implied by the Constitution. The statement would require a finding from the chair who, the scenario goes, would uphold it. Supporters of the filibuster would then be backed into a corner. To overturn the ruling, they would have to offer an appeal. An appeal is debatable and therefore could be subject to a filibuster that would unlikely muster enough opposition to break it. If this were to happen, the ruling would stand. Moreover, supporters of the ruling could offer a motion to table the appeal that is not debatable and would probably be upheld on a strict majority vote. Either way this would constitute the full Senate's ratification of a ruling from the chair, providing it even greater weight and effectively making it part of the Senate's precedents.[19] The process is called the nuclear option because its invocation would presumably so incense the minority that it would use any and all available parliamentary tactics to bring the Senate to a complete halt.

The nuclear option was effectively taken off the table in May 2005 when a bipartisan group of senators, called the Gang of Fourteen, agreed that they would neither support such a ruling nor, except under extraordinary circumstances, a filibuster of any future judicial nominees.[20] Attacks on the filibuster continued, however, and reached new heights in the 110th Congress (2007–2009) when the Republican minority repeatedly used the tactic to block the Democrats' agenda. Democratic senators and Congress watchers offered an array of reform proposals. So far none have come close to fruition.

BENCHMARK #22
All members should have approximately the same number of committee assignments.

Justification

Work on legislative organization suggests committee systems can deliver the benefits of decentralization, in addition to centralization. Informational theories, for example, state that bodies can overcome deficiencies in knowledge by encouraging all members to specialize in particular issue areas on committees enhanced with procedural advantages (Krehbiel 1991). Gains-from-trade theories note certain policy benefits can be derived from an inclusive committee system with strong powers, and assignment processes based upon self-selection (Weingast and Marshall 1988).

A healthy committee system should therefore exhibit a kind of duality. The centralizing benefits of preplenary review demand that subgroups of legislators are given power to set, or at minimum significantly shape, the floor agenda. At least on the legislation that comes under their review, these lawmakers ought to have some expertise and relatively intense preferences about it. Decentralization, however, calls on bodies to have these groups, at least in the aggregate, represent the general membership and facilitate broad participation. Rank-and-file legislators should be invited to join them, and their work should be respected.

Attaching some kind of quantifiable target to the decentralizing character of congressional committees is difficult, but I think it is fair to say that all individual members of the House and Senate should have a significant role in preplenary review. To promote broad and equal participation, a body's members should have roughly an equal number of committee assignments.

Appraisal

Members of Congress do indeed have roughly the same number of committee assignments. Today Senators sit on between five and six committees. They initially request positions and then are appointed by partisan panels dominated by the leadership utilizing a complex process in which assignments are made to tiers of committees that are categorized on the basis of the importance of their jurisdictions. The top (Super A) tier consists of Appropriations, Armed Services, Commerce, Finance, and Foreign Relations, and nearly every senator is assigned to at least one of these committees. On the House side, members tend to have just one or two committee assignments but may be on quite a few subcommittees. The parties' appointing panels grant members either one exclusive or two nonexclusive committees. Appropriations, Energy and Commerce, Rules, and Ways and Means have been the chief, and frequently only, exclusive committees for both parties over the past few Congresses. The remaining are considered nonexclusive, although both parties allow members to serve on Intelligence or Ethics (officially Standards of Official Conduct) without the assignments counting against them. The parties' full membership then ratifies the appointments.

The assignment panels consider informal factors like geographic, racial, and gender balance when making their decisions (Frisch and Kelly 2006). They also endeavor to match committees to members' expertise. Assignments to important House committees like Appropriations and Ways and Means frequently go to members who consistently support the leadership's legislative agenda and find themselves in potentially tough re-election races (Hasecke and Mycoff 2007; Kanthak 2004). At the beginning of the 112th Congress, Republican leaders placed an unusually large number of freshmen on the Energy and Commerce and Financial Services Committees. Much of the logic seems to be that, in anticipation of a vigorous challenge in 2012, these members would be well positioned to raise money from the deep-pocketed groups and corporations interested in matters within the committees' jurisdictions.

BENCHMARK #23
The House and Senate should have an appropriate number of committees—perhaps around fifteen to twenty.

Justification

In Congress the jurisdictions of standing committees cover a clearly delineated area of public policy and therefore a limited proportion of the legislation introduced into their parent bodies. If there are too few committees and jurisdictions are commensurately large, the informational and efficiency gains made by specialization and the division of labor are lost. Decentralization is also undermined because a subset of members has significant influence over a broad set of issues. If there are too many committees, the policy space is fractured and coherent policy making is made more difficult. Specialization gains can also be limited because members might have to take on many assignments.

In recent years state legislative bodies have quite consistently averaged around seventeen to nineteen committees each (*Book of States* 2010). They view this as a sensible way to divide public policy. As such it seems a reasonable target for Congress. The states have greater responsibilities for policies like education and law enforcement, but Congress deals exclusively with matters like foreign affairs.

Appraisal

Figure 5.1 shows the number of standing committees both the House and Senate have operated since the First Congress. It reveals a steady rise in both bodies until 1920 when there was a major restructuring in the Senate, as the body abolished forty-two obsolete panels. Further reductions were made with the 1946 Legislative Reorganization Act. This time the House experienced the greater change, having its committees cut from forty-eight to nineteen. Since then, however, there has been remarkable stability. The last time the number of committees in a body was changed in any meaningful way occurred in 1995 when the incoming House Republican majority abolished three committees to demonstrate its commitment to efficient governance—the panels killed were District of Columbia, Merchant Marine and Fisheries, and Post Office and Civil Service. In 2005, the House created the Committee on Homeland Security and carved out a jurisdiction for it from those of existing panels. Although there are always turf battles over the scope of legislative authority (King 1997), with these exceptions

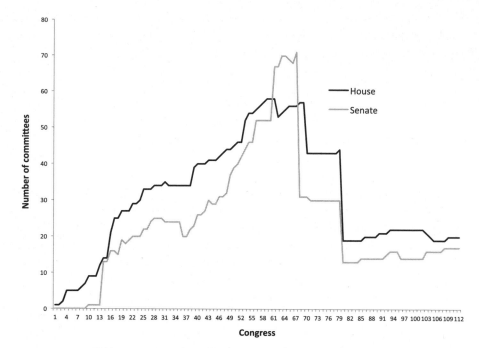

FIGURE 5.1   The number of standing committees in Congress, 1789–2011

formal jurisdictions have remained quite firm. Most changes in the past decade or so have been cosmetic. The House's Banking and Financial Affairs Committee became Financial Services in 2001. Foreign Affairs was known as International Relations between 1995 and 2007.

The House had twenty standing committees and the Senate seventeen in the 112th Congress (2011–2013). This included the Ethics and Rules committees in the House, neither of which is conventional.[21] It excluded all other types of committees, such as the Senate's Ethics Committee because, although it essentially does the same thing as the House's and investigates member conduct, it is officially a select committee. The Senate Aging Committee is a special panel that is really a debating chamber for issues like Social Security and Medicare. The bodies' Intelligence committees are considered special—or permanent select in the rather contradictory language of the House—because their jurisdictions are considerably limited and memberships much more evenly divided among the parties than standing committees. The Joint Committees on Printing, Taxation, and the Library, and Joint Economic Committee are different in that they consist of lawmakers from both bodies and do not have the authority to report legislation but instead provide analysis in an advisory capacity.

Conference committees are excluded too. Made up of members from the House and Senate, these report legislation back to the bodies. Assignments are made by presiding officers and each house gets a single vote.[22] Conferees do not act as individuals. Moreover, conference committees are temporary in that they are created for the sole purpose of dispensing with one bill, and, when their work is done, they disband. Recent evidence suggests they are being used less and less. In the 110th Congress (2007–2009), about 58 percent of major bills went to conference compared to 95 percent in the 109th (2005–2007). Instead, the House and Senate have been increasingly playing "ping pong," trading amendments until they have each passed the same identical version of the bill. This is essentially what happened on health care reform in 2010.

Conference committees are nevertheless powerful. They determine the substance of legislation by working out whether to adopt the House version of a provision, the Senate version, something in between, or, although rules are supposed to preclude such efforts, language the conference committee itself has written.[23] They also have what political scientists refer to as *ex post veto* power and can kill bills by not reporting them (Shepsle and Weingast 1987).[24] In many ways, these important agenda powers still belong to the standing committees. House and Senate leaders generally populate conferences with members of the standing committees that reported the bill to the floor in the first place (Lazarus and Monroe 2007; Vander Wielen and Smith 2011).[25]

The width of the terrain covered by standing committees varies tremendously. The House sends tax, trade, Social Security, and Medicare legislation to its Ways and Means Committee. The House Small Business Committee essentially deals with issues related only to small businesses, and even then it shares jurisdiction over regulatory matters with Energy and Commerce and over federal aid with Appropriations. The Senate's HELP Committee receives legislation related to most critical domestic policy issues. Its Rules and Administration Committee is responsible for the workings of the parent body and matters like presidential succession and the Capitol's artwork. But the number of committees each body has is very close to the benchmark set for them. There are enough committees to ensure individual members have some meaningful influence over the floor agenda.

BENCHMARK #24
Bill introduction procedures should be open.

Justification

Through their representation, all Americans should have the capacity to influence the policy matters Congress addresses. Bill introduction should be permissive so that members are free to ask Congress to consider measures on a broad range of issues. Many national parliaments have significant restrictions on what legislation can be proposed, when it can be proposed, and who can propose it (Mattson 1995). In the United Kingdom's House of Commons, for example, private members' bills or legislation sponsored by lawmakers outside of government can only be introduced or read first under certain conditions—generally if its patron is lucky enough to win a lottery—and at reserved times. In the German Bundestag bills must be sponsored by 5 percent of members before they can be considered. Some American state legislative bodies constrain bill sponsorship practices as well, particularly by preventing the introduction after certain dates. This contributes to the tremendous variation in the number of bills across chambers (Squire and Hamm 2005, 116–118).

Appraisal

Prior to the Civil War, most House bills were introduced by committee (Cooper and Young 1989). Members could petition committees to produce bills, but the only ways they could introduce them directly were on the one or two days a week set aside for private members' bills or through approval of a "motion to leave" for the purposes of introducing a bill. Since the 1880s, however, any member has been able to introduce any bill on any issue whenever the House and Senate are in session. On occasion nominal requirements must be met. At the beginning of the 112th Congress (2009–2011), and largely in response to pressure from its influential Tea Party caucus, the Republican majority established a rule that all measures introduced needed to be accompanied by an explicit statement in the *Congressional Record* demonstrating its authorization by the Constitution. But no formal permission was required.

As Figure 5.2 shows, House members introduce roughly 6,000 to 7,000 bills per Congress, senators around 3,500 to 4,000. These numbers are down significantly from the 1970s, especially in the House, when between 15,000 and 20,000 bills were introduced per Congress. The relaxation of cosponsorship restrictions discussed in Chapter 4 meant that members no longer had to introduce duplicate bills to demonstrate their support for legislation. But that is still about 15 bills per House member and 35 bills per senator per Congress. Committees, of course, are not compelled to report or even consider bills, but at least the act of introduction is extremely open. This benchmark is met.

BENCHMARK #25
Restrictions on members' floor amendments should be minimal.

Justification

The last procedure discussed in this chapter governs floor amendments. Legislative bodies tend to have standing rules that enumerate the rights of members to offer revisions to bills in plenary. Across the world, these rights vary substantially. Approximately three-fourths of American state legislatures and the vast majority of national parliaments prohibit amendments that are not germane to the underlying bill (National Conference of State Legislatures 1996; Taylor 2006). Others, particularly those in Latin

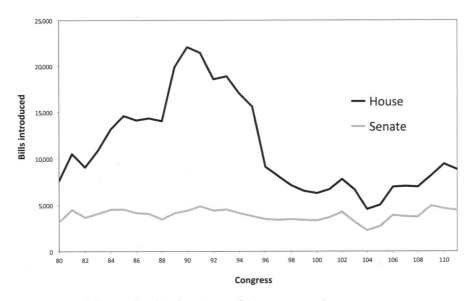

FIGURE 5.2 Bills introduced in the House and Senate, 1947–2011

and Germanic countries, have additional restrictions, such as precluding amendments that have not been offered previously in committee or do not have the support of party leaders (Taylor 2006). Obviously floor amendments need to be regulated to some extent, if only to reduce the temptation for members to deploy them for purposes of delay and obstruction. But we want to encourage broad participation in the lawmaking process. The standard in many bodies across the world is that beyond germaneness, restrictions on floor amendments are light. This should be the goal for Congress as well.

Appraisal

The House floor process is quite tightly controlled by the presiding officer—known as the Speaker when the House is in formal session or the chair when it is operating as the Committee of the Whole. The person who occupies the position of chair has the authority to recognize members who wish to participate in proceedings and is usually a majority party designate and not the official Speaker whose responsibilities are generally performed off the floor and include setting the policy agenda, meeting with members, organizing the floor schedule, fielding calls from the president and Senate leadership, and campaign fundraising and appearances. The precise mixture is a function of the Speaker's personality; some recent ones, like Newt Gingrich and Nancy Pelosi have enjoyed publicity and exercising strict control, others, like Dennis Hastert

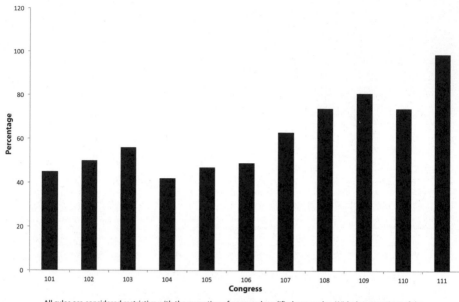

All rules are considered restrictive with the exception of open and modified-open rules. With the exceptions of the 110th and 111th Congresses for which data were calculated by the author from the House Rules Committee's "Survey of Activities" reports, data are from Wolfensberger (2002, 2007).

FIGURE 5.3 The percentage of House special rules that were restrictive, 1989–2010

(R-IL), have preferred to work behind the scenes on strategy.[26] This seemed to be the philosophy of the Speaker in the 112th Congress, John Boehner.

The presiding officer enforces the special rule, itself debated for one hour evenly divided between the sides and subject to a simple majority vote. It used to be the case that special rules were much more permissive. In addition to the very complicated rules described earlier, the last twenty years have witnessed a dramatic increase in those that limit floor amendments. Figure 5.3 demonstrates this trend by showing the percentage of special rules governing amendments granted in a Congress that were restrictive in nature—that is neither open nor modified open (most of the bill is open to amendment). It reveals quite clearly that majorities have come to understand the benefits of restrictive rules (Roberts 2010; Owens and Wrighton 2008). This was even the case for the Republicans in the mid-to-late 1990s who had promised during their victorious 1994 election campaign to use more inclusive and open special rules whenever possible (Owens and Wrighton 2008). Nathan Monroe and Gregory Robinson (2008) have argued the leadership employs restrictive rules to ensure approved bills are closer to the position of the majority party median than that of the chamber median.

Moreover, House standing rules require floor amendments be germane. Six specific tests of germaneness cumulatively circumscribe the authority of members to offer floor amendments; they include relevance to the bill's general purpose, the reporting committee's jurisdiction, and the topic, breadth, and temporal nature of the provision subject to the potential amendment.[27] Their practical effect, particularly when compounded by a restrictive special rule, is to greatly limit floor amendments. Floor amendments were numerous in the 1970s and 1980s, especially on issues that divided southern conservative Democrats and their more liberal northern colleagues (Smith 1989). Significantly fewer of them are proposed today. There were 786 floor amendments offered in the House during the 111th Congress (2009–2011) compared to 1,006 in the 97th Congress (1981–1983).

It is easier to offer amendments to bills in the Senate—although, because of the filibuster, it is not always simple to bring them to a vote. There is no comprehensive standing germaneness rule, and only general appropriations bills and bills on which cloture has been invoked are protected from amendments that are not related to the underlying measure. The rules that regulate debate must, in theory at least, be approved by all senators, not just a simple majority. As noted earlier, the Senate restricts the nature and number of floor amendments through unanimous consent agreements. The result is that many more floor amendments are offered in the Senate. When the body debated the financial regulatory overhaul legislation, or Dodd-Frank bill, in the spring of 2010, 434 amendments were proposed for consideration. The House's version, in what amounted to an unusual demonstration of openness for the lower body, was subject to a mere 24.

It is quite clear that the Senate meets and probably exceeds the benchmark regarding the restrictions on floor amendments. In fact, it has perhaps the most open process of all national legislative bodies in the industrialized world (Taylor 2006). It is a little more difficult to evaluate the House. However, with the exception of the germaneness rule—one that is almost universal across the globe—floor amendments can only be restricted by a majority of legislators. If members want a bill to be susceptible to amendment, they can quite easily make it so.

CONCLUSION

Americans should want a legislature that practices good politics and governance. This is easier said than done. In a democratic system with a great diversity of interests such as ours, there ought to be broad participation in the policy process. This requires institutions with decentralized procedures that allow all members to have some kind of influence over process and outcomes and that facilitate intelligent, judicious, and extended consideration of the problems facing society. But we also value efficiency and

BENCHMARK FOR CONGRESSIONAL PERFORMANCE	APPRAISAL
20. The floor agenda should be set by entities that constitute a representative and fairly large but manageable subgroup of the membership—perhaps 10 to 20 percent of the body.	Met
21. A majority should be able to bring floor debate on a bill to a close.	House met, Senate unmet
22. All members should have approximately the same number of committee assignments.	Met
23. The House and Senate should have an appropriate number of committees—perhaps around fifteen to twenty.	Met
24. Bill introduction procedures should be open.	Met
25. Restrictions on members' floor amendments should be minimal.	Met

TABLE 5.1 Appraising congressional performance on benchmarks related to organizational design

a government that is capable of meeting challenges in a timely manner. Organizational features that emphasize hierarchy, expedite decision making, and limit contributions from members help achieve these particular aims.

As Table 5.1 demonstrates, Congress seems to pull off this organizational balancing act well. Just about all of the benchmarks set for it in this chapter are met. Its committee system permits broad participation in setting the floor's aggregate agenda while rewarding specialization, exploiting expertise, and efficiently sorting through the thousands of bills members are free to introduce every year. The House floor process better demonstrates principles of centralization in that debate length and amendments are generally limited and the presiding officer exerts tight control. A majority of members can terminate proceedings. The Senate floor process exhibits many more features of decentralization, particularly because debate is theoretically unlimited and amendments largely unrestricted. Given that to become law legislative proposals must pass through both bodies, perhaps it is appropriate to consider the organizational characteristics of the House and Senate together. If that is the case, they complement each other quite nicely.

6

DOES CONGRESS HAVE A
HEALTHY LEGISLATIVE
PROCESS?

Facilitative rules and procedures are a necessary but not sufficient condition for the kind of decision making we should want from Congress. Organization and outcomes are not everything. If the process is uninformed, policy is misguided. If it lacks participation, authoritative decisions may be viewed as illegitimate. Members must therefore be crafters, not just passers, of laws. They must be willing to exploit procedural opportunities in a positive way, a way that will benefit both Congress and the nation. Congress should encourage a process that forces legislators to vigorously defend and promote their positions in a contemplative and interactive manner. The aspiration motivating the benchmarks in this chapter is what I term a healthy legislative process.

THE PRINCIPLES OF DEBATE AND DELIBERATION

In Chapter 2, I suggested two aspirational features of a healthy legislative process. Debate, the competition of developed, cogent, and expressed ideas, forces legislators to defend their positions and permits their constituents to learn about policy options and their advocates in Congress. Deliberation requires members to engage one another actively. Legislators must justify arguments in empirical, logical, and broadly appealing terms. They should rebut opposing claims directly. They ought to revise their original positions when challenged by compelling counterpoints. The enterprise is obviously collective and sensitizes members to others' interests and views.

Generating reasonable and evidence-based expectations for the amount and type of debate and deliberation we should witness from Congress is very difficult. There is no real consensus as to appropriate indicators of these qualities. Steiner and his colleagues have created a discourse quality index to measure levels of deliberation in legislatures (Steiner et al. 2004). Its main components include the capacity to participate in proceedings uninterrupted, respect for opponents and their demands, rational justifications rooted in the public good, and the willingness to compromise. Gary Mucciaroni and Paul Quirk (2006) focus on the capacity of the legislative process to allow Congress to make decisions in an informed and rational way. They essentially fact check the comments made by participants to see how informed the process is. Measurement challenges remain, however, and it is not surprising little systematic work has been done on debate and deliberation in national and American legislative bodies, including the Congresses of the past.[1]

The nature of formal congressional proceedings—committee work and floor consideration of measures—are too important not to be done well. Their thorough evaluation may be difficult, but we should still attempt its undertaking. In that spirit, I present and apply three benchmarks designed to detect the presence of debate and deliberation in Congress's official business.

BENCHMARK #26
Formal congressional proceedings should have significant
influence on members' preferences and actions.

Justification

In an analysis of twenty-nine case studies of bills on domestic issues dealt with by Congress from 1946 to 1970, Bessette (1994) found limited amounts of debate and deliberation. Although members were sometimes persuaded to take specific courses of action by their colleagues, Bessette argues they came into dispositive proceedings—whether in committee or on the floor—with quite intense pre-existing preferences. He suggests these preferences tended to be anchored in ideologies and partisanship.

Bessette's work provides an important, if indirect, indicator of the extent to which debate and deliberation have occurred in Congress. If, during formal proceedings, members do not seem to change their policy preferences and act in a manner affected by their colleagues' arguments, it is hard to make a case that debate and deliberation of the quality and quantity we should desire have taken place.

Appraisal

Party

Members are influenced by a variety of different pressures. We saw in Chapter 1, for example, that the House and Senate parties are becoming increasingly polarized and internally homogenous as Democrats move together to the left and Republicans to the right. These data corroborate the assertion that it is parties, not what colleagues say, that really shape congressional votes. Party leaders have many powers, both formal and informal, that allow them to influence member behavior. They include the manipulation of procedures and effective control of the committee assignment process. Leaders also have resources they can trade with colleagues. They have grown adept at helping rank-and-file members secure pork-barrel projects for their constituents—a contract for a nearby defense company, a grant for a local nonprofit, a tax break for one of the district's largest employers (Carroll and Kim 2010). Loyalty to the party agenda can be used as a metric by which assignments to popular committees are made (Frisch and Kelly 2006; Leighton and Lopez 2002). The congressional campaign committees and the PACs of party leaders can provide critical money for general election campaigns. The party can also work to secure a member's renomination. We saw this to mixed effect in Senate primaries during 2010 and 2012—the national parties were unable to save incumbents in Alaska (Republican Lisa Murkowski), Indiana (Republican Richard Lugar), Pennsylvania (Democrat Arlen Specter), and Utah (Republican Bob Bennett).[2]

These powers and resources furnish leaders with the capacity to mobilize floor votes, often viewed by scholars as the "twisting of arms" or "vote buying" (Snyder and Groseclose 2000; Wiseman 2004).[3] Evidence that party pressure influences members' voting decisions comes in many forms. Procedural votes tend to be partisan, not least because the public does not seem to hold legislators accountable for them (Crespin, Finocchiaro, and Wilk 2006). Votes on special rules in the House, for example, divide the parties much more neatly than do the votes on underlying bills (Theriault 2009). This is particularly the case for closed rules. Scholars have argued majority parties apply pressure so as to get a floor majority to accept the restriction or complete prohibition of amendments. With legislation immune from change and individual preferences quite transparent, chamber leaders can present a bill both they and a floor majority like and consequently leave members free to vote their true preferences (Jenkins, Crespin, and Carson 2005).

Similarly, majority party leaders will reduce pressure when they are certain they have enough votes to pass a measure. David King and Richard Zeckhauser (2003) argue the party leadership exercises options on members' votes, and "pay"—in the sense they provide favors—for the votes of those needed to ensure the bill passes. Leaders release those from supporting the party if the bill can be approved without their vote. This produces many narrow victories on significant and controversial legislation. For instance, in the House of the 111th Congress health care reform and the cap-and-trade energy-environment bill passed by a combined twelve votes on original passage. There was talk in the media the Democratic leadership had "allowed" some members to vote against the bills if they were under considerable constituent pressure to do so.[4] In September 2011, the Republican leadership found these options to be largely worthless. During a vote on a continuing resolution, or stopgap appropriations bill designed to keep the government running until a permanent budget could be put in place, many conservative and junior members, chafing at the prospect of supporting legislation they believed spent too much, switched their votes from yes to no when they could see Democrats were practically unanimous in their opposition and the bill was unlikely to pass. The measure was altered and, a few days later, passed.

There has been some interesting quasi-experimental work demonstrating the presence of these party effects on members' behavior. Scheduling a party conference meeting prior to a vote has been shown to bring about greater unity on the floor (Forgette 2004). The reason is presumably the recent application of pressure from leadership. When members defect from a party and join the other—as Rep. Parker Griffith (D-AL) and Sen. Arlen Specter (R-PA) did in 2009, the first in apparent disgust at the Obama administration's health care proposal and the latter after suspecting he would lose the Republican primary for his office the following year—their voting behavior changes dramatically (Nokken and Poole 2004). Given that constituency is unaltered, party pressure is an obvious cause. Studies of whip counts found in the archives of prominent members confirm presence of party influence (Burden and Frisby 2004; Meinke 2008). The counts tend to show a large majority of members who switch positions on a bill—changing course between their stated position to the whip and their actual vote—move toward the party.

Lame-duck Congresses can also provide a useful test of the potency of party pressures. When members meet after the November election but before the new Congress comes to town in January, constituency pressures are minimized. The public does not get to decide on members' futures for at least another two years. If the member is retiring or has been defeated, the influence of constituents is particularly low. Scholars have indeed found evidence of party pressures using such data (Jenkins and Nokken 2008). President Clinton was impeached on party-line votes in a lame-duck session in December 1998. After the 2006 elections, House Republicans unified to block appropriations from passing and to force the succeeding Democratic majority to deal with them. Still lame-duck sessions need not be so partisan. Take the productive and apparently cooperative December 2010 meeting, for example. In the space of a couple of weeks in December, the 111th Congress approved a big tax bill that included an extension of the Bush tax cuts passed a decade earlier, a repeal of DADT, an arms treaty with Russia, medical care for 9/11 first responders, and a continuing resolution to fund the government through to the following March. At the end of 2012, the 111th Congress reconvened in an effort to agree on legislation to prevent significant tax increases and spending cuts from stifling a weak economic recovery.

Constituents

Party is not the only source of pressure as members consider legislation, of course. As we have already seen, lawmakers are extremely sensitive to the policy preferences of their constituents. Interest groups can also be important. They mobilize voters by endorsing candidates and asking supporters to assist with campaigns (Skinner 2007, 101–122). Groups like the US Chamber of Commerce, AFL-CIO, National Rifle Association, and National Abortion Rights Action League have hundreds of thousands of members and chapters, or regional and state associations, across the country. They furnish information to lawmakers that can be helpful during the legislative process (Carpenter, Esterling, and Lazer 2004; Boehmke, Gailmard, and Patty 2006). They lobby energetically for their legislative interests—the Chamber of Commerce alone spends about $130 million annually on the practice. Groups rate legislators and give points to those who vote with their agenda, hence providing a cognitive shortcut to citizens attempting to assess how close an elected official's values are to their own. Interest groups will also tell legislators in advance which measures will be scored in hopes of influencing their decision (Roberts and Bell 2008). And, of course, organized interests give money to campaigns. Because the vast majority of groups' PAC contributions go to incumbents, about 79 percent of them in the 2010 cycle according to Center for Responsive Politics, and because incumbents generally win reelection, in 2010 at rates of 87 percent in the House and 84 percent in the Senate, financial donations seem more a strategy to shape the policy process than an effort to affect election results. This theory is confirmed by research suggesting that PAC contributions to a member are a reward for votes previously taken and an appeal for access to her in the future (Gordon and Hafer 2007; McCarty and Rothenberg 1996).

The President

Of course, presidents have the motivation and capacity to structure votes. They can throw their weight behind or in front of bills that are important to legislators. They can use their authority to help guide federal spending to members' constituents (Berry, Burden, and Howell 2010). They have an Office of Legislative Affairs and other White House staff who can lobby on their behalf. Like congressional leaders, presidents can assist with members' re-election campaigns, by joining them on the stump or directing contributions their way (Herrnson, Morris, and McTague 2011; Hoddie and Routh 2004). In just one night in late October 2010, Barack Obama raised about $1.8 million for local Democraticcongressional candidates at private-home fundraisers in the San Francisco area.[5] During years when sitting presidents are unpopular, however, members of their party may ask them to keep away from their districts and states. Obama was a walking ATM, but he allowed his wife Michelle to do much of the family's on-the-stump campaigning in 2010. George W. Bush, with approval ratings near 30 percent, stuck to fundraising and motivating the conservative base in safe Republican districts during 2006.

Patronage is an important resource for presidents. Members of Congress can land desirable positions within an administration if a president likes them. Barack Obama nominated six sitting federal lawmakers to cabinet-level positions for his first term—

Sen. Joe Biden (D-DE) as vice president, Sen. Hillary Clinton (D-NY) as secretary of state, Sen. Ken Salazar (D-CO) as secretary of the interior, Rep. Rahm Emanuel (D-IL) as chief of staff, Rep. Hilda Solis (D-CA) as secretary of labor and, in an effort to demonstrate his bipartisanship, Rep. Ray LaHood (R-IL) as secretary of transportation. Another Republican, Rep. John McHugh (R-NY) became secretary of the army in the fall of 2009. Short of that, legislators can request supporters and constituents be put up for the more than seven thousand lower-level positions—in agencies such as the International Boundary and Water Commission and Nuclear Waste Technical Review Board—found in the "Plum Book," a thick compendium describing jobs presidents can fill (Rottinghaus and Bergen 2011).

Presidents can "go public" and reach out directly to Americans in an effort to leverage congressional votes for their agenda (Cohen 2005; Edwards 2003).[6] Research demonstrates that popular presidents enjoy greater success on foreign policy (Canes-Wrone, Howell, and Lewis 2008) and are more capable of getting the important parts of their domestic agenda through Congress (Canes-Wrone and De Marchi 2002). The opposite is true of presidents with relatively low approval ratings. In the late summer and fall of 2011, following a speech to a joint session of Congress laying out his proposals, Barack Obama travelled the country promoting his American Jobs Act, designed to boost the economy and reduce unemployment. In a variety of venues from high school gymnasiums to factory floors, he repeatedly asked people to contact their congressional representation to ask them to pass the bill. Everywhere the president went, he attracted attention, securing column space and airtime in dozens of local media outlets. There was initially little movement in Washington. For all Obama's work, the percentage of people who approved of the job he was doing as president remained around forty. So, he resorted to implementing small pieces of the plan unilaterally by executive action; in one week in late October alone, he announced mortgage relief for troubled homeowners, minor regulatory relief for small businesses, and tax credit for those who employ veterans. With a stagnant economy, an election looming, and a president still solidly supported by a sizeable number of Americans, Congress did then relent somewhat and passed a short-term extension of a payroll tax holiday for workers and minor legislation aimed to help small businesses attract investment income.

Alternatively, presidents can work on important individual legislators using direct appeals and their personal powers of persuasion (Beckmann 2008). George W. Bush quite frequently invited senators and representatives to functions at the White House for the principal purpose of chatting about impending legislation. Super Bowl parties were a favorite forum.

With these tremendous resources, presidents quite clearly influence members' votes on occasion. Their success is conditional, however. Figure 6.1 reveals the average of House and Senate presidential support scores from 1953 to 2011. The figures are calculated by *Congressional Quarterly*, which takes the proportion of

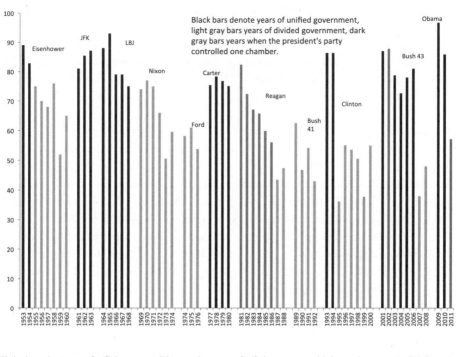

Black columns denote years of unified government, light gray columns years of unified government, and dark gray columns years in which the parties split their control of Congress.

FIGURE 6.1 Presidential support scores, 1953–2010

measures that pass which the president has made a position known. In an absolute sense the numbers are pretty high and suggest that when the president wants something approved it happens. But presidents do seem to have a honeymoon with Congress: presidential support is generally lower in the second Congress of a president's term (Marshall and Prins 2007). What is more, support for the president's legislation is much lower under divided than under unified government, particularly as the parties have polarized. Notice how George W. Bush's scores dropped off precipitously after the Democrats won back Congress in the 2006 elections. Even though the Democrats lost only the House in 2010, Obama's success ratings fell off markedly after that year too.

In these polarized and partisan times, presidents seem to do as good a job of persuading members to oppose their positions as to support them. Indeed, during recent divided governments, congressional majorities appear to believe generating a roll-call record in direct opposition to the president is the best way to weaken him. Immediately after the 2010 election, Senate Minority Leader Mitch McConnell announced his prime objective in the upcoming 112th Congress would be to make sure President Obama was not re-elected in 2012. This involved blocking the president's agenda to make him look ineffective and promoting legislation he clearly opposed. In January 2011, the House's first item of business was a repeal of the health care reform legislation passed the previous year, even though there was no possibility the bill would even be perfunctorily considered by the Senate, let alone muster the necessary two-thirds of both chambers to override the president's inevitable veto. For good measure, it passed a further repeal in July 2012, just after the Supreme Court had upheld the law.

Colleagues

Even when members are influenced by their congressional colleagues, it does not often seem to be the result of debate or deliberation within formal proceedings. Across Capitol Hill hundreds of caucuses—groups of likeminded lawmakers formally called congressional member organizations—meet and frequently share information, formulate policy proposals, and strategize about legislation(Ainsworth and Akins 1997). Some caucuses are ideological factions of parties. Perhaps the most famous of these are the liberal Democratic Study Group established after the 1958 elections and Newt Gingrich's Republican Conservative Opportunity Society that essentially served as the incubator for his party's takeover of the House in the 1994 elections. Today liberal and conservative groups, like the Congressional Progressive Caucus and the newly formed Tea Party caucus, grab the headlines, but there are party groups of moderates as well, such as the Blue Dog Democrats and the Republican Main Street Partnership. There are caucuses that represent demographic groups such as the Congressional Black Caucus (CBC). The CBC has a good track record for concerted action, but, because its policy positions are generally quite far to the left of the median member of Congress, its success in affecting legislative outcomes has been minimal (Singh 1997). There are state and regional caucuses like the Northeast-Midwest Congressional Coalition that is interested in issues like low-income home energy assistance, incentives to weatherize homes, and help for communities adversely affected by trade deals. There are also hundreds of single policy caucuses on issues as diverse as Parkinson's disease, coal, freedom of the press, Serbia, wine, shellfish, soccer, refugees, and intellectual property. Members generally join groups that reflect their constituents' interests—representatives from more heterogeneous districts tend to belong to more caucuses, for example (McCormick and Mitchell 2007; Miler 2011). But there is some evidence these groups influence legislative proceedings, member behavior, and, therefore, the decisions made on Capitol Hill (Ainsworth and Akins 1997; Hammond 2001).

Some individual senior members, particularly committee leaders and renowned policy experts, find their views respected, bills cosponsored, and votes followed (Cox and Terry 2008; Krutz 2005; Wawro 2000). This is undeniably influence. On many issues that defy ideological categorization and draw little media attention, members are affected by colleagues in their state's delegation. Local and state problems are often felt across district lines, and coordinated responses lead to better solutions, and better politics, regardless of the party affiliation of the members involved (Schiller 2000). Across the Hill there are thousands of unobserved, informal, and overlapping networks of members and staff. The conversations that take place within them can have significant effects on important action in committee and on the floor. They might sometimes be deliberative but lack the transparency of formal proceedings.

Ideology and Strategy

Despite, or perhaps because of, these competing pressures, members do not change their macrolevel policy preferences much over time—whether the unit of analysis be the Congress or career. In the words of Keith Poole (2007, 435) members "die in their ideological boots." Some scholars have found senators' policy preferences shift a little within a term, a finding attributed to its significant length (Ahuja 1994). Shawn Treier (2011) uses a new method to suggest there is actually more movement than has been previously revealed. But, generally speaking, even over protracted time series and presumably many committee proceedings and floor debates, members' voting records are pretty stable (Lott and Bronars 1993; Stratmann 2000).

Moreover, when legislators do alter their behavior, it is often for strategic reasons, matters quite different from the content of legislation and arguments made for its approval or rejection. Examples of this abound. Particularly in the more permissive Senate, members frequently litter floor time with questions of procedure and motions to delay proceedings—quorum calls are a popular way of doing this, although the "time out" needed to corral members to the floor can be used by leaders to find ways to remove obstacles and get on with debate. Substantive proceedings are sometimes obfuscated by the disposition of superfluous, dilatory, or "killer" amendments designed strategically to defeat the underlying measure by parliamentary maneuver rather than to revise its content or defeat it on its merits in a straight vote (Finocchiaro and Jenkins 2008; Jenkins and Munger 2003).[7]

A particularly dramatic example of the strategic manipulation of the legislative process occurred in the summer of 1996. In May of that year, Republican presidential nominee, Sen. Bob Dole (R-KS), stepped down as majority leader so that he could focus his attention on his presidential campaign against incumbent Bill Clinton. No sooner than Dole's office was vacated, the Clinton White House and congressional Republicans pivoted from a strategy of blocking each other's proposals to cooperating with one another. A whole host of legislation that had found itself stuck in the process somehow broke free. Among the laws passed after Dole left the Senate were a minimum wage and small business job creation package, health insurance portability for those changing jobs, food safety legislation, gun control, the Defense of Marriage Act, and the historic overhaul of welfare that replaced the Aid to Families with Dependent Children (AFDC) program with a block grant and "workfare" program called Temporary Assistance for Needy Families (TANF). The effect was to make both President Clinton and the congressional majorities look capable and productive. Clinton waited until the summer so Dole could not share the credit and, more damningly, appear as the singular obstacle in Washington. Presumably, Republicans on the Hill played along because they thought doing so would enhance their chances of retaining control in the 1996 elections. Dole's interests were secondary to theirs.

For the most part, therefore, members come to committee meetings and floor proceedings with fixed preferences and a general unwillingness to change their minds. Parties, constituents, interest groups, colleagues, and presidents place decisive pressure on them before measures are fully considered. Ideological convictions can be strong as well. Legislators might debate and deliberate but it does not seem to have a great effect. What they say in committee and on the floor to colleagues does little to influence outcomes. If preferences and actions are changed, it is frequently for strategic reasons. Indeed, Steiner and others (2004) demonstrate that, compared to British and German legislators, members of Congress are more likely to have entrenched positions undisturbed by counterarguments and efforts to generate broad agreement.

As a result, members have little incentive to invest time and effort into formal proceedings. Mucciaroni and Quirk's (2006) study of congressional debates on welfare reform, estate tax repeal, and telecommunications deregulation bills from the 1990s leads them to conclude that "congressional debate is typically no better than moderately informed" and floor proceedings are "a roughly even balance of fact and fiction" (197). Steiner and colleagues (2004) show members present positions with little justification and based upon faulty reasoning and incorrect assertions.

BENCHMARK #27
Formal congressional proceedings should
consist of broad and equal participation.

Justification

Broad and equal participation by legislators is central to debate and deliberation (Fishkin 1995; Lascher 1996). A significant proportion of the membership needs to be engaged in proceedings. Matters should not be dominated by a privileged or assertive few. These are also characteristics essential to the vigorous representation of a broad array of societal interests.

It is not surprising scholars shy away from systematic analysis of participation rates in legislative proceedings; collecting data on these matters is difficult and time consuming. There have, however, been some exciting breakthroughs using special software designed to categorize parliamentary speeches (Mikhaylov and Herzog 2010; Quinn et al. 2010; Slapin and Proksch 2008). Much of the work is intended to link talk with policy preferences, but scholars are beginning to analyze participation rates. Jonathan Slapin and Sven-Oliver Proksch (2010) demonstrate that a disproportionate number of plenary speeches in the European Parliament of 1999–2004 were made by members of smaller fringe parliamentary parties from northern European countries. Ross Young et al. (2003) note the number of times each member of the British House of Commons participated in debate in the 2001–2002 session of parliament. The coefficient of variation for the data—that is, the standard deviation divided by the mean—was 0.8. Much of the unevenness in both the European Parliament and Commons data might be attributable to rules on speeches that allow party leaders to dish out plenary time and reward loyal members and punish dissidents. I think we should expect a little more breadth and equality in congressional floor proceedings than what is on display in Europe.

Appraisal

Andrew Taylor's (2012a, 142–180) work on the House and Senate floors is helpful in our evaluation of this benchmark. He analyzes aggregate proceedings in every fifth Congress from the Thirty-Second (1851–1853) and those of important trade bills and decisions to go to war since the early 1800s. Taylor demonstrates that, whereas during the nineteenth century floor proceedings were effectively monopolized by better-educated members with substantial interests in the legislation under consideration, these days most members get to participate in the debates on contentious bills, and, when measured across an entire Congress, there is a remarkable lack of variation in the number of contributions made by individuals. With the exception of those who manage debate for a side and have expertise in the bill's policy area—usually chairs and ranking members of committees and subcommittees with jurisdiction over the legislation—lawmakers tend to come to the floor, speak about the bill, and then leave to allow others to take a turn.

So, unlike the past, congressional floor proceedings are not dominated by a relatively small number of members. Emerging norms and formal procedures have created a process that gives recognition to members who wish to speak. They are the product of increasing representational demands and the careerism that pervades Capitol Hill. Members must participate on the floor, particularly on the important issues of the day, because they need to demonstrate competence, concern, and a particular policy position to the outside world. The benchmark is largely met.

BENCHMARK #28
Formal congressional proceedings should reveal frequent interaction among members.

Justification

Interaction is quite clearly a central tenet of deliberation. Give-and-take among members as they formulate policy proposals, discuss their likely implications, and decide whether to approve them is critical to a deliberative legislative process. Lawmaking is an inherently collaborative exercise. It needs to be if potential laws and their likely effects are to be properly evaluated, the talent of a body's membership fully exploited, and policy outcomes deemed legitimate.

Appraisal

The quality and quantity of interaction in today's congressional proceedings are not so good. In a comparative study that includes analyses of the British, German, and Swiss legislatures, Steiner and his colleagues analyze bills on issues like crime prevention, rights for the disabled, the minimum wage, and partial birth abortion (Steiner et al. 2004). Members of Congress show greater respect for opponents and their arguments than do colleagues in parliamentary bodies, but they do not directly engage others as much.

In fact, American legislators talk past each other and enjoy making speeches more than their European counterparts. On the House floor, where time is limited and demand for it is high, the result is a series of short, sharp statements that often have little connection to one another. Members are each granted a minute or two to make their remarks before handing off to a colleague. As House Majority Leader Dick Gephardt (D-MO) put it in the early 1990s, floor proceedings are now divided into "small units of time in which statements are read and no real debate or dialogue occurs" (US Congress Joint Committee on the Organization of Congress 1993, 2:36).

Of course, members of Congress can debate and deliberate in committees as well as on the floor. In fact, if anything, there is greater opportunity for legislators to engage in detailed and extensive discussions in this forum. Observers tend to agree, however, that what ails the floor has also afflicted committees. Intense partisanship and greater transparency seem to have reduced deliberation within them as well (Connor and Oppenheimer 1993).

Congress used to be different. Although studies of nineteenth-century proceedings tend to be anecdotal and impressionistic, they make quite laudatory conclusions. The early-to-mid-nineteenth century was generally acclaimed to be "The Golden Age of American Oratory" (Parker 1857), not least because Congress was populated by skilled speakers and revered statesmen like Sens. John C. Calhoun (Dem./Nullifier-SC), Henry Clay (Rep./Whig-KY), and Daniel Webster (Fed./Rep./Whig-MA)—the so-called Great Triumvirate. According to one historian, "Men and women flocked to the Capitol" to hear Clay, Calhoun, and Webster, and "all across the country their speeches were read as if the fate of the nation hung on them" (Peterson 1987, 234). The Congresses of the early twentieth century were similarly praised. George Rothwell Brown (1922, 282) remarked that "one finds nothing in the great discussions over slavery and secession exceeding in power and majesty the debates of the Senate at the close of the [First World] war."

More systematic studies confirm this. Wirls (2007) examines floor proceedings on four crucial pieces of legislation in the forty years prior to the Civil War—the Missouri

Compromise, the gag rule governing antislavery petitions, the declaration of war with Mexico, and the Kansas-Nebraska Act. Although the findings more clearly demonstrate that the House's consideration at the time was as deliberative as the Senate, they also suggest a level of discussion that is rarely even reached today. Taylor's (2012a, 121–180) more comprehensive study of entire Congresses and floor proceedings on trade and war declaration measures reveals there was significantly more interaction among members in the past than there is today.

A good way to determine the quantity of interaction is to examine the number of colloquies that take place on the floor and the percentage of times members yield to their colleagues when asked. These practices force members to support their arguments, and they expose them to direct questioning, making proceedings a little like cross-examination in a courtroom. Taylor's (2012a, 142–180) analysis of trade and war declaration measures demonstrates that over the past twenty years or so both House members and senators frequently ignore colleagues' requests to yield and are generally uninterested in entering into colloquies. Whereas there was give-and-take and often cut and thrust in the past, today the practice of floor debate is rather dull and antiseptic. Assertions do not meet with rebuttal. Instead, in a rather disjointed way, members state their positions with little reference to those made by their colleagues. In Taylor's (2012a, 173) words, the situation is one of "members coming to the floor, delivering prepared speeches, largely respecting each other's desires not to be interrupted, and leaving after their remarks with the effect that they are not around to engage colleagues when it is time for others to participate." The House has only encouraged this by setting aside portions of the day for members to make one minute or "special order" speeches on any topic of their choosing (Harris 2005; Maltzman and Sigelman 1996; Morris 2001; and Rocca 2007). It seems fair to conclude the benchmark is largely unmet.

It is interesting to speculate why interaction has diminished so dramatically, though. I think four quite compelling explanations quickly present themselves. The first is partisanship and polarization. Mucciaroni and Quick (2006, 187–189) argue that the debates in their dataset that are of the highest quality occur on issues with a sizeable number of moderates who do not have entrenched positions. Without moderates to win over, extreme members overstate their claims and are unwilling to engage opposing ideas. Second, procedures probably have an important effect on the quality of debate. Both Mucciaroni and Quick (2006) and Taylor (2012a) conclude that deliberation, particularly, is better and more frequent in the Senate, where rules are less constraining and members have greater freedom to offer amendments and engage in discourse.

Third, the representational demands placed on members make deliberation unappealing. With large constituencies, members have little time to inform themselves on issues sufficiently to participate effectively in proceedings. Media coverage of Congress has also discouraged debate and deliberation. Although there are those who believe live television coverage of the House and Senate floors has improved their quality

(Frantzich and Sullivan 1996), many observers contend the cameras encourage show-boating, the use of emotive, as opposed to intellectual, appeals, and simple rather than complex arguments (Smith 1989, 62–69; Zelizer 2004, 206–232).

Finally, the issues placed in front of legislators are considerably more numerous and complicated than they were just fifty years ago. Although Mucciaroni and Quick (2006) demonstrate that members do not exploit policy complexity to make false or exaggerated claims, legislatures probably pass on the opportunity to study an issue because they have a hard time understanding it themselves. Taylor's (2012a, 142–180) detailed analysis of debates on trade bills across congressional history shows that before World War II members had a stronger grasp of the legislation's intricacies than their successors do today. This is not because they were any smarter. He suggests it is probably a function of a policy agenda populated by fewer and simpler issues.

An Example of Today's Congressional Proceedings: The Dodd-Frank Bill

A good, if not necessarily authoritative, way to demonstrate the quality of debate and deliberation in today's Congress is to look at how both the House and Senate have disposed with an important and highly publicized piece of legislation. As the dust was settling on the partial collapse of the American financial system in the early months of 2009, a number of political leaders on both sides of the aisle called for changes in federal policy to minimize the possibility of similar—or worse—calamities in the future.[8] In June 2009, President Obama proposed a bill to increase the regulation of financial markets and the firms that operate within them, with particular emphasis on exotic and complex instruments; to provide greater protections for investors and individuals seeking credit, particularly through the establishment of a consumer protection agency; to grant the government more tools to manage crises; and to bring greater coordination to international financial policy. Congressional leaders on banking and financial issues then set to work crafting legislation that reflected these general principles.

As chairs of their bodies' respective committees of jurisdiction—Banking, Housing, and Urban Affairs in the Senate and Financial Services in the House—Rep. Barney Frank (D-MA) and Sen. Chris Dodd (D-CT) took the lead for the Democrats, who then controlled both chambers of Congress and the White House. With the controversial Troubled Assets Relief Program (TARP) in place and government money propping up weak banks, Dodd and Frank mobilized a sizeable group of mostly Democratic members who agreed with the president that the financial industry was ripe for reform. Getting a bill passed would not be easy, however. The banking industry vehemently opposed many of the proposed regulations, particularly the consumer credit agency. Most Republicans joined the industry, and several, particularly Alabamans Sen.

Richard Shelby and Rep. Spencer Bachus, who were ranking minority members of the Dodd and Frank committees, orchestrated a concerted effort to stop the legislation, appearing frequently in the media to further the cause. Republicans referred repeatedly to Democrats' plans as a government "takeover" of the banks. It did not help reformers that Dodd was dogged by scandal. In 2008, at the height of the financial crisis, he had received mortgage loans at below market prices as a product of this relationship with Angelo Mozilo, the CEO of Countrywide Financial, a troubled company that had been a principal player in the subprime market.

Initially, Frank made the decision to break the Obama legislation into bits and undertake a piecemeal strategy to pass financial reform. A bill requiring minimum standards for mortgages and attempting to prevent predatory lending practices, HR 1728, was introduced by Rep. Brad Miller (D-NC) back in March. The full House passed it in May. Another piece, HR 3126, was just over two hundred pages long and focused largely on the creation of a government agency to protect and advocate for the consumer in the credit markets. Introduced a month after Obama's announcement, it was referred to both Frank's Financial Services and the Energy and Commerce Committees. Both approved the bill on largely party-line votes in late October. During committee markup members stuck to their partisan talking points, the Democrats' perhaps supplied by groups like the Center for Responsible Lending, the Republicans by those such as the American Financial Services Association.

A third bill, HR 3817, the Investor Protection Act sponsored by Rep. Paul Kanjorski (D-PA), was considered at the committee level over three days in the fall of 2009. Members of Financial Services offered forty-three amendments, and the discussion was lively, although again the bill, which reorganized the SEC, was passed on a strict party-line vote. Kanjorski's Accountability and Transparency in Ratings Agencies Act, HR 3890, was quickly approved by Financial Services in a relatively consensual manner by a 49–14 vote.

HR 3269, the Corporate and Financial Institution Compensation Fairness Act of 2009, was designed to give shareholders greater control over executives' compensation. It took ten days to pass the full House after it was introduced in July 2009. Considered on the floor under a special rule that provided one hour for general debate, fewer than twenty members participated. The vote was quite partisan, with only sixteen Democrats voting against the bill and just two Republicans voting for it.

On December 2, 2009, Frank's committee approved the sixth and final major component of the Democrats' financial regulatory overhaul agenda. The panel passed HR 3996, the Financial Stability Improvement Act, on a strict party-line vote with most black members absent as part of a protest that the legislation did not address the needs of minority communities adequately. The bill was designed to solve the "too big to fail" problem: it would minimize systemic risk in markets should large financial institutions go under by creating a pool of resources to help distressed companies unwind in an orderly manner. The bill's consideration was quite deliberative, as demonstrated by the more than sixty amendments that were discussed. All told, there were more than fifty hours devoted to markup of financial reform legislation in the Financial Services Committee in 2009. In that time 258 total amendments were considered.

With pressure mounting for coordinated policy reform and legislative strategy, Frank immediately fused the various parts and rolled out HR 4173, initially known as the Wall Street Reform and Consumer Protection Act of 2009. This bill contained all the principal elements of the previous bills. It was 1,279 pages long and similar in breadth and content to the president's proposal. In an extremely complicated parliamentary maneuver, Speaker Nancy Pelosi (D-CA) referred it to eight committees. Then, in what Rep. Pete Sessions (R-TX) labeled a "martial law" process that circumvented regular procedure and allowed the new "mega" bill to essentially go unreported by any of them, she brought HR 4173 to the floor using a self-executing special rule on December 9.[9] The rule provided for three hours of debate controlled largely by Frank and Bachus. Consideration of the bill was soon interrupted by postponements and motions to accommodate disgruntled Democrats who were threatening to vote against the measure if they could not revise it. Two amendments were particularly popular. Rep. Melissa Bean (D-IL) won support from moderate Democrats for a uniform standards provision that would effectively prohibit states with more liberal inclinations from strengthening consumer credit rules beyond those set by federal statute. Rep. Walt Minnick's (D-ID) amendment, supported by a similar group of wavering Democrats, cut out the new consumer credit agency completely, replacing it with a council of existing regulators. A new special rule was hastily reported from the Rules Committee, which also waived the requirement that there be three days between the bill's reporting and its disposition by the floor. The new rule provided for the consideration of thirty-six amendments, including twenty minutes of debate each on the Bean and Minnick proposals. Twenty-three went to a vote and twelve of them passed.

In the end the bill was approved on December 11 at 2:28 p.m. The vote was 223–202 with no Republicans voting for and 27 Democrats voting against. Less than 10 percent of members spoke during the debate on the bill and the two rules. Many members, however, took advantage of the privilege, nearly always granted to them by unanimous consent, to provide written remarks for the *Congressional Record*. Because these remarks are submitted after debate, they have no impact on floor deliberations.[10] The debate was characterized by a series of sometimes lengthy speeches. The chairs and ranking members of committees with jurisdiction over the bill were particularly prominent—including Frank, Bachus, Rep. Joe Barton (R-TX) of Energy and Commerce, and Rep. Collin Peterson (D-MN) of Agriculture. Some participants demonstrated a degree of mastery of the bill's technical details, but others focused on its predicted impact on the macroeconomy and the partisan politics of financial reform. In the aggregate, members' contributions did not constitute deliberation in any real sense of the word. Few claims were rebutted and proceedings were largely devoid of colloquies. There was little direct interaction. Frank and Rep. Scott Garrett (R-NJ) were the only two members who really involved themselves in meaningful exchange. On one or two occasions, their discussion could conceivably be considered of high quality. But most of it was not. A short dispute between the two over whether the bill contained a provision that effectively gave a bailout to failed institutions ended abruptly with a disagreement over which side's time it had consumed.[11]

Sen. Dodd's initial effort, S3217, a 1,400-page bill called the Restoring American Financial Stability Act, called for, among other things, the reorganization of government regulatory agencies, enhanced oversight of the mortgage industry and the trading of complicated financial instruments, invigorated consumer protection, and increased capital holding requirements for banks. It was similar, although not identical, to Frank's legislation. The principal differences were that the Senate bill included the Volcker Rule—a regulation preventing depository banks from conducting proprietary lending—but excluded the House's $150 billion reserve to manage the too-big-to-fail problem. Dodd's committee held thirteen hearings on related matters prior to its disposition of the bill in March 2009—in all it conducted seventy-nine hearings on topics related to the financial crisis between January 2007 and March 2010. It heard from more than thirty witnesses, including heads of important executive, congressional, and independent agencies like Timothy Geithner at Treasury, Sheila Bair at the Federal Deposit Insurance Corporation (FDIC), Donald Kohn at the Federal Reserve, and Elizabeth Warren at Congress's oversight panel for the TARP program; individuals largely retired from perches atop the industry, such as former Fed chair Paul Volcker and Securities and Exchange (SEC) head Arthur Levitt; distinguished academics; representatives from think tanks like the American Enterprise Institute and the Brookings Institution; and industry leaders from trade associations like the American Bankers Association and the National Association of Mutual Insurance Companies. These individuals provided committee members with a library of information. Senators engaged them in some valuable conversations. The committee's internal discussions about the bill itself were not particularly deliberative, however. It was quite clear positions were entrenched and had not been altered particularly by witness testimony. Members seemed to talk past rather than to one another. On March 22, the bill was approved on a strict party-line vote.

One other Senate committee wrote a meaningful part of the body's legislation. After a turf battle with Dodd's committee, an important component was separated from the omnibus bill and given to Sen. Blanche Lincoln's (D-AR) Agriculture, Nutrition, and Forestry Committee. The stated reason was that it dealt with derivatives, an issue regulated by the Commodities Futures Trading Commission (CFTC), and therefore was within the committee's jurisdiction. Agriculture passed Lincoln's stand-alone bill before Dodd's committee could act, with Sen. Charles Grassley (R-IA) the only Republican supporting it. The bill, which forced financial institutions to spin off their derivatives businesses into separate companies, created an important substantive difference between the two chambers' legislation.

When it reached the floor in April 2010, Dodd's bill was initially stuck, blocked by a Republican filibuster on the motion to proceed. At most only fifty-seven senators—and not a single Republican—voted to invoke cloture in the three attempts made. But by early May, Majority Leader Reid brought the bill to the floor fortified by the notion that four members of the minority, Scott Brown, Susan Collins (R-ME), Grassley, and Olympia Snowe (R-ME) might support it. A significant amount of behind-the-scenes negotiating had diluted some of its more liberal aspects. A barrage of amendments was also likely to come, and many Republicans, resigned to having some kind of legislation, took solace in the fact that Dodd's bill would be altered somewhat.

Republican obstacles began to disintegrate. On May 19, a cloture motion to bring to an end consideration of the bill also received only fifty-seven votes, but, by the very next day, and on a second cloture attempt, the Democrats got the sixty they needed— Brown, Collins, and Snowe supporting the motion. Collins and Snowe had been accommodated by promised minor changes in the legislation, and Brown persuaded by some lobbying from Frank, his Massachusetts colleague in the House. Senators then agreed to largely forego the usual thirty hours of debate that are allowed after cloture is invoked and limited their speeches to ten minutes. At 8:25 p.m. on May 20, they voted 59–39 for Dodd's bill. All four Republicans the Democrats thought might vote for the bill did. Maria Cantwell (D-WA) and Russ Feingold (D-WI) opposed the measure because they believed it did not go far enough.

All told, the bill was debated for about two weeks on the Senate floor. Many amendments were offered, the most successful by Democrats who wanted to make the bill even tougher, including one presented by Sen. Dick Durbin (D-IL), the assistant senate majority leader, that restricted fees credit card companies could charge. Proceedings were "unusually civil" according to some press accounts, although Majority Leader Reid was exasperated by Republican obstructionism and particularly with many of the amendments the minority party's senators offered after the motion to proceed had passed. He let them have it on some occasions. For the most part the proceedings consisted of lengthy speeches by members who frequently exhibited tremendous knowledge of the complex issues, but there was little interaction. What give-and-take there was generally amounted to little more than obsequiousness, as senators yielded to colleagues of their own party for a kind of self-congratulatory discussion about their position on the legislation.[12] The majority of senators participated at some stage, many quite extensively.

Unlike health care reform earlier in the year, financial regulatory overhaul went to a conference committee. Before the committee met, however, the Senate approved two

Republican motions that effectively called on its conferees to stick to their guns during the negotiations with the House. The House rejected a "motion to instruct" from Bachus that implored its delegation to prevent a "too big to fail" provision from being included in the measure and ensured that members would have at least three days to examine the final bill before having to vote. There were thirty-one House conferees, mainly members of Financial Services, and thirteen Senate conferees. The extent to which House conferees could involve themselves was limited to matters in the bill that were within the jurisdiction of the standing committee on which they sat. Both parties were represented. The conference was held on eight separate days between June 10 and June 29. There were sixteen matters the conference agreed needed to be reconciled. The differences were bridged with a series of offer-counteroffer bargaining sessions that are quite usual for conference proceedings. In an unprecedented move designed to improve transparency and increase confidence in the process, the entire formal proceedings were televised live on C-SPAN. This did little to excite the public, however, and conferees, particularly the principals like Dodd, Frank, Shelby, and Bachus, realized that much of the difficult negotiating would have to be done by them and their staff behind closed doors. The House passed the conference report 237–192 on June 30, the Senate 60–39 fifteen days later.

The passage of the Dodd-Frank bill provides a nice illustration of debate and deliberation in today's Congress—or at least what there is of it. Most members had clearly taken positions on the issue of reform of the financial industry prior to legislation reaching them in committee or on the floor. When they could be influenced—for example by an amendment about which they were unsure—they tended to fall in line with the position of their party, a position determined by the floor and committee leaders and, in the case of the Democrats, the Obama administration. Still, amendments from both parties were considered, and some important Republican concerns, such as Rep. Ron Paul's (R-TX) suggestion the Fed be audited by the GAO, were incorporated into the final product.

Some members demonstrated an impressive command of complicated material, particularly those on committees with jurisdictional authority over the legislation, many of whom had spent years studying the issue. The proceedings were clearly transparent, and the conference committee made an important decision to open its consideration of the bill to television cameras. But, perhaps because of procedural constraints in the House, floor debate was not as broadly participated in as we might have hoped. Like deliberation on health care reform, the process was extremely complex and difficult for members and their staff to follow, let alone the public. There was also a disappointing lack of interaction, which is necessary for deliberation. There were few colloquies, and members more often than not refused to yield any of their floor time when asked to do so by colleagues, probably because such time is precious in the House and conversing with opponents would undermine their capacity to convey an

BENCHMARK FOR CONGRESSIONAL PERFORMANCE	APPRAISAL
26. Formal congressional proceedings should have significant influence on members' preferences and actions.	Not met
27. Formal congressional proceedings should consist of broad and equal participation.	Largely met
28. Formal congressional proceedings should reveal frequent interaction among members.	Largely not met

TABLE 6.1   Appraising congressional performance on benchmarks related to a healthy legislative process

unambiguous position to constituents. As is too often the case these days, the result was numerous short and repetitive speeches consisting of selective evidence and unsubstantiated and disregarded claims.

CONCLUSION

The public does not seem to care much about the lack of debate and deliberation in congressional proceedings (Hibbing and Theiss-Morse 2002). It seems to care much more about outcomes. Evidence suggests that when individuals do hold Congress and its members accountable for their performance, it is for policy, not process. As we saw earlier, this is true for members as individuals as well as the majority party collectively. It is the case for single pieces of legislation like health care reform in 2010 and the aggregate record of accomplishment.

But Americans should want a particular kind of legislative process, one characterized by significant amounts of debate and deliberation. Although Congress today meets an important benchmark that demonstrates this, fairly broad and equal participation by its members in committee and on the floor, there is still significant room for improvement. There is little interaction among lawmakers as they discuss bills, and positions are not directly challenged. What is more, a great deal of data suggest preferences do not change very much as a result of committee or floor proceedings and that when they do it is not the result of a persuasive and well-argued claim by a colleague but political considerations and pressure exerted by party leaders, presidents, and other actors. As Table 6.1 reveals, committee and floor proceedings provide some of the best evidence we have so far uncovered that congressional performance is not all that it should be.

7

DOES CONGRESS MAKE EFFECTIVE POLICY?

A need for effective policy generates the benchmarks in this chapter. Congress must be productive or at least have the capacity to be productive so that it can solve societal problems as they arise. It must create legislation that makes the daily lives of millions of people better than they were before its intervention. It must look after the country's interests, of which peace and prosperity are surely the most important.

Policy must also be effective in the aggregate. It should be made with an eye on the future and with internal consistency so that legislation enacted in one issue area does not undercut efforts to further the public interest in another.

BENCHMARK #29
Congress should be productive when it needs to be—
demonstrating this by making around four hundred total
and twelve important laws per Congress.

Justification
Congress's principal product is laws. Federal laws regulate social, political, and economic behavior by individuals, groups, corporations, and governments, including the national one. They create, expand, reduce, or abolish programs that serve many, or just a few, Americans. They govern our relationships with other countries and can send us into armed conflict. In other words, when Congress legislates, its actions have profound consequences.

Congress should be capable of generating new laws whenever the public feels a need for it to do so, even as it remains mindful of the potential damage bad legislation can do. This is the case when it is confronted by an obstructionist president or other political conditions that render action difficult. Any public institution that cannot meet its central responsibility is demonstrably not a good one.

Measuring a body's capacity to make laws is difficult. There will be occasions when it is appropriately inactive and occasions when its lack of productivity is symptomatic of a problem. What is more, although scholars have looked a little at legislative productivity across the democratic world, international results cannot often be compared with congressional performance. Amie Kreppel's (1997) study of the Italian parliament is not helpful because the body passes different types of laws and much important policy is produced by government decree. Dimiter Toshkov (2011) examines the quantity of directives passed by the European Union. Directives are quite like legislation in the American sense—they are offered by the European Commission for approval or rejection by the European Parliament—but they also need ascent from the Council of Ministers and their effect on member countries is somewhat ambiguous, a state of affairs that frequently makes their issuance rather meaningless.

Useful comparative data do exist, however. Richard Conley (2011) calculates that the Fifth Republic in France—a presidential system rather like that of the United States—enacted an average of 101 laws a year from 1959 to 2007. At the state level in this country, legislatures have approved somewhere between 100 to upwards of 1,000 laws on a yearly basis over the past decade. Even though many of these laws have no real impact on the vast majority of people who live within the jurisdiction, they are indicators of the capacity of the legislature to get at least something done. The roughly 400 laws enacted by individual states on average each year over the past couple of decades may provide a fair goal for Congress.

The laws that affect citizens' lives deeply are most important, however. A second target takes account of these. Richard Conley and Marija Bekafigo (2010) look through statute books and major newspaper reports to count what they consider to be the significant bills passed by the Irish parliament between 1949 and 2000. They come up with a data set that ranges from four to nineteen a year.[1] Unfortunately, there is no real analysis of the production of important laws at the American state level. Still, the study on Ireland, particularly because it uses Mayhew's (2005) methods (more on which later), provides us with some kind of comparison. A target of about twelve significant laws per Congress seems fair.

Appraisal

The amount of laws passed by Congress fluctuates considerably over time. Figure 7.1 shows the number of public laws and the total pages of statute they consume for each Congress from the 82nd (1951–1953) through the 111th (2009–2011).[2] The data are from the *United States Statutes At Large*, a publication distinct from the widely known *Federal Register*, which includes proposed rules and regulations made by executive agen-

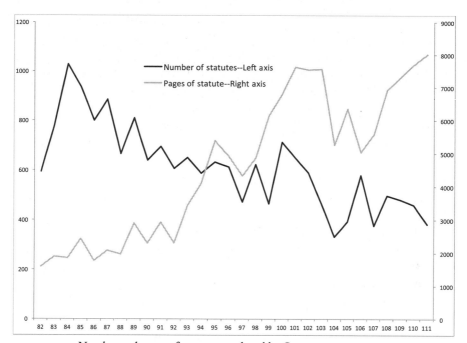

FIGURE 7.1 **Number and pages of statutes produced by Congresses, 1951–2011**

cies and executive orders from the president. The number of laws generated tends to decrease over time—prior to its lame-duck session, at least, the 112th Congress (2011–2013) had only enacted 178—although it still regularly exceeds the benchmark of around four hundred. In fact, Congress passes laws at a rate quicker than one every two days and only failed to meet the standard set for it in four Congresses, all since the mid-1990s. As for statute length, it tends to move in the opposite direction. This means, of course, that the average law is getting longer. In the 84th Congress (1955–1957) it was just 1.8 pages; in the 111th on average each law took up 20.9 pages.

Laws are becoming fewer and longer because Congress has a growing penchant for what are frequently called omnibus bills, single legislative packages that contain many parts that in the past may have been approved separately.[3] The 1974 Budget and Impoundment Control Act created a new process within which Congress found it procedurally advantageous to group changes to tax law and entitlement programs like Social Security into one large reconciliation bill.[4] In the early 2000s, the omnibus also became the preferred way to pass many of the twelve appropriations bills that must be enacted every year so the federal government can operate.[5] Faced with deadlines—either because the fiscal year is coming to a close or, as is more likely the case these days, a continuing resolution providing temporary funding for the government is about to expire—the leadership often finds consolidating appropriations bills a useful strategy. Since 2010, however, Congresshas essentially done away with the individual and consolidated appropriation approaches and funded the government using a series of simple continuing resolutions that determine spending levels for departments and programs based upon the previous year's amounts.

Omnibus bills can contain "sweeteners," or provisions important to many members and added in an effort to garner their support for the larger underlying legislation that might not be quite so palatable. These can be narrowly targeted, such as the exemption from Medicaid funding obligations exclusively for the state of Nebraska, part of a deal made by the Democratic leadership to acquire Sen. Ben Nelson's (D-NE) support for health care reform in 2010. Or the inducements might have broad appeal. In the fall of 2008 after TARP had initially been rejected by the House, the Bush administration and congressional Democratic leaders were forced to add items to the legislation extending deposit insurance and some tax breaks in order to get the federal bailout program through Congress.

Legislative add-ons like these are particularly useful during divided government. Rather than present the president with a bill he does not like and will probably veto, congressional majorities can offer a broader legislative proposal that includes components that appeal to him (Krutz 2001). This is an effective strategy because the president does not have the line-item veto, a device that allows executives to block portions of a bill and accept the rest as law.[6]

Many of the laws approved during a Congress are commemorative and symbolic. They have little meaningful effect. Examples from the 112th Congress (2011–2013) include laws to designate a post office in Cary, Mississippi, as the Spencer Byrd Powers Jr. Post Office and to provide a two-year extension to the term of FBI director Robert S. Mueller III. Although analysis of raw productivity is useful, we ought to dig deeper to discern more important legislation. Have the Congresses of recent years been able to pass laws of significance, laws that affect the daily lives of millions of Americans?

Unsurprisingly, this question has been addressed by a number of political scientists. They have used a variety of data sets in their work. Paul Light (2002) looks at broader accomplishments rather than specific pieces of legislation. In a survey of political scientists and historians, he comes up with a catalog of the federal government's fifty "greatest endeavors" from 1944 to 1999. The list seems impressive, although it is interesting to note that scholars do not think the policies have been particularly effective. On only six challenges to the nation did at least one-third of participants believe Congress's and the broader federal government's response was "very successful." Most of these occurred before 1980—including rebuilding Europe after World War II, containing communism, and expanding the right to vote.

Others use different measures. Sarah Binder (1999) defines legislative productivity as the proportion of items on the agenda that passed, although she prefers to talk about gridlock and the proportion of these items that failed. According to her data, of the Congresses between the end of World War II and 2000, output was clearly lowest in the 1980s and 1990s.

The most popular method is just to count pieces of legislation. By this metric the Congresses of today do a bit better, although the results are mixed. The Policy Agendas Project reports 576 important laws passed by Congress from 1948 to 1994. Because 93 of them are from the 1990s, congressional performance in the period is slightly above average.[7] Stephen Stathis (2003) identifies landmark legislation from the beginning of the republic through 2002. Post–World War II he counts about 18.1 per Congress. Productivity for Congresses since 1980 is about 1.5 laws above that amount.

William Howell and colleagues (2000) split public laws into groups based upon their importance. If the top three categories are used, productivity in the last few Congresses of the data series—the authors start their study in 1945 and end it in 1994—is relatively meager. Whereas from the 1960s through to the mid-1970s just about every Congress generated more than one hundred of these laws, those in the 1980s and 1990s were typically in the seventy to eighty range. J. Tobin Grant and Nathan Kelly's (2008) findings show a similar decline in that their "major legislation index" is typically around nineteen or twenty in the 1960s but more often around seventeen or eighteen since then. Joshua Clinton and John Lapinski (2006) discover something similar. Using existing data sets of significant legislative accomplishments, they score all enactments from 1877 to 1993 for their effectiveness. Summed significance scores for each Congress suggest those of the 1980s and 1990s were less productive than those of the 1960s, 1970s, the New Deal, and the Progressive Era but as productive, and perhaps slightly more productive, than the Congresses of the 1950s, 1920s, and the Gilded Age of the 1880s and 1890s.

The best known of these studies is Mayhew's (2005) *Divided We Govern*. Written to test the hypothesis that the federal government produces fewer laws at times when the president's party is in the minority in Congress, it presents a data set of important legislation from the period since 1947 using contemporaneous and retrospective academic and journalistic discussions of Congress's policy outputs. Through to the end of the 110th Congress in 2008, Mayhew identified 369 important laws over the thirty-one Congresses for an average of 11.8 each. The group contains all the usual suspects, including thirty-three bills deemed historically important (Mayhew 2005, 74). Among these particularly weighty laws are the Marshall Plan, the Civil Rights Act of 1964, the Tax Reform Act of 1986, the approval of the North American Free Trade Agreement (NAFTA) in 1993, the Bush tax cut in 2001, and the $750 billion TARP bailout in 2008.

Figure 7.2 shows the distribution of all of the laws identified by Mayhew across Congresses through 2008. To a large extent they are consistent with the analyses examined earlier. The fifteen years that followed 1960 are especially productive. This is

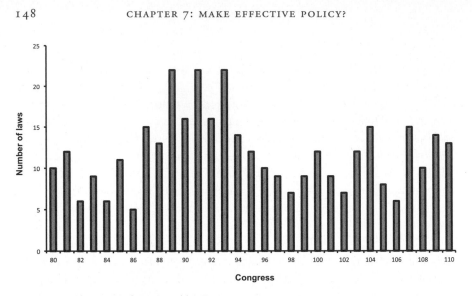

FIGURE 7.2 Important laws passed by Congress, 1947–2008

the period of the Great Society and the significant extension of existing social welfare programs like Social Security and food stamps as well as the creation of new ones like Medicare, Medicaid, and Supplemental Security Income (SSI).[8] It is also a period of tremendous expansion in the reach of the federal government in the areas of civil rights, workplace regulation, housing, food safety, the environment, and the economy more generally. But the past decade or so does not fare too badly either. Five of the eight Congresses since 1993 generated more than the average number of laws. It is true the 112th Congress (2011–2013) was viewed, at least until a lame-duck session, as extremely unproductive. The legislature was unable to pass traditionally uncontroversial matters like the farm bill and assistance to the postal system. Sen. Susan Collins (R-ME) called it "a very disappointing session with few accomplishments" (Steinhauer 2012b). The previous 111th Congress (2009–2011), however, is generally believed to have enacted many important and even historic laws including the American Recovery Act (or stimulus, the largest government expenditure outside the budget process in history), the PPACA, or Obamacare, Dodd-Frank, the extension of the Bush tax cuts of 2001, and the DADT repeal. The benchmark for the quantity of important policy output is probably met.

Mayhew's (2005) central argument is that party control of the branches of the federal government has, at most, negligible effect on how productive it is. Intuitively, ideological and partisan differences should render lawmaking difficult, given the president's veto and that Congress writes laws. This seemed to be the case in the 112th Congress when the president clashed repeatedly with the House Republican majority. American national politics are replete with pressures and incentives that mitigate the effect of divided government, however. For example, Taylor (1998) shows that, at least until the 1990s, policy productivity was driven by deficits because it was frequently necessary to attach extraneous spending items to persuade members to support bills. This occurred regardless of the partisan makeup in Washington. Krehbiel (1998) emphasizes the importance of the distance between status quo policy and the preferences of pivotal actors like the president and House median. The further away they are from one another, the more productive a Congress is because presidents and congressional majorities are likely to find legislative change and the bills that bring it about appealing. Because status quo policies are the product of the positions of previous presidents and Congresses, Krehbiel's argument is that large numbers of laws are passed when there are significant alterations to the personnel and policy attitudes of government.

In a slightly different vein, incentives for presidents and members of Congress to demonstrate action and policy making to the electorate are continuous, and internal hurdles to legislation—such as bicameralism and the filibuster in the Senate—are permanent fixtures of American political life. As we saw earlier, when the public desires policy change, as it did during the liberal era of the 1960s, it tends to get it. What party controls what institution is largely immaterial. Moreover, skilled presidential leadership, important for the passage of laws (Chiou and Rothenberg 2003), is distributed across occupants of the White House with little regard to party politics. And, of course, random and external events are critical to productivity. If you include the resolution permitting military action against Iraq that passed in late 2002, nine of the fifteen important laws passed by the 107th Congress were directly related to the terrorist attacks of 9/11 (Mayhew 2005, 217–218).

It should be noted scholars have taken issue with Mayhew's assessment that unified government is no more productive than divided government. Binder (1999) puts the blame for gridlock quite squarely on ideological polarization and the decline of bipartisanship. Divided government obviously exacerbates the problems they cause. John Coleman (1999) and Howell and colleagues. (2000) produce robust findings consistent with the claim that divided government reduces output. Regardless, there is no clear evidence the Congresses of today are markedly less productive than their predecessors.

BENCHMARK #30
The United States should enter military conflict under strict conditions that, among other things, minimize costs and maximize the probability of success.

Justification

Quantity is not everything. Americans should want Congress to generate certain types of policy. Of course, there will always be ideological and partisan squabbles over what is the best course of action for the country. But peace and economic health are surely goals that can be broadly agreed upon.[9] Few, if any other, aims of public policy generate as much consensus—we saw earlier that both are mentioned explicitly in the Constitution's preamble and Article I, Section 8. Congress should, therefore, be keeping Americans relatively safe and prosperous.

It is clear Congress does not do this alone. Although the Constitution extended power to conduct foreign affairs to both the executive and legislative branches, the president has dominated much of the policy making on the issue. This is particularly the case for national security. In 1973 Congress did pass the War Powers Resolution that, among other things, permits the president to send troops into action abroad only with their explicit authorization and, in the case of a direct attack on US territory or forces, requires him to come to them periodically with requests to extend the operation.[10] But the president maintains near complete control of the armed forces. Through the State Department and intelligence agencies, he also commands the information required to direct effective military campaigns. America's international relations are also shaped greatly by the attitudes and actions of other states and institutions that are obviously free of direct congressional influence. Still, I think it is fair to say that, as a fundamental goal of the broader government, the nation's security is to some great extent strengthened or weakened by congressional action or inaction.

It may seem quite simple to recognize the existence of a state of war, but there is no reasonable expectation for how often a country might find itself in one. Moreover, war is often unavoidable, and, if fought skillfully, victory can save and appreciably improve thousands, if not millions, of lives. Perhaps a reasonable benchmark for congressional performance on matters of war and peace is that the modern United States should be involved in as few military confrontations as possible but that, when it goes into conflict, its efforts should clearly promote American interests, yield minimal American casualties, and ultimately be successful.[11]

Appraisal

America has generally been a tranquil place, at least relative to Europe and Asia, continents that have repeatedly found themselves as theaters of war. No wide-scale conflagration has been fought on United States soil for nearly one hundred and fifty years. But the country has not necessarily been at peace. Just since 1950 and the end of the American occupation of the powers defeated in World War II, US armed forces have been used abroad on many different occasions in many different roles. These have cost about a hundred thousand American lives and about $2.3 trillion. The conflicts in Korea, Vietnam, Afghanistan, and the two with Iraq's Saddam Hussein have been particularly expensive (Daggett 2010). It is important to ask whether this immense sacrifice was worthwhile and to what extent we should hold Congress accountable for it.

Clearly direct, deadly, and unprovoked attack is a legitimate reason for military response. On September 11, 2001, nineteen terrorists trained and financed by Al Qaeda executed an operation in the United States that claimed the lives of nearly three thousand people. Over the previous few years, Al Qaeda and its leader Osama Bin Laden had found a home in Afghanistan and were made welcome by its militant Islamist government called the Taliban. Exactly a week after the attack, President George W. Bush signed a joint resolution of Congress authorizing him to "use all necessary and appropriate force against those nations, organizations, or persons he determines planned, authorized, committed, or aided the terrorist attacks that occurred on September 11, 2001."[12] The resolution was approved by votes of 98–0 in the Senate and 420–1 in the House, with Rep. Barbara Lee (D-CA) the only member voting against. Considered over about twelve hours in total, it has provided the basis for action that has lasted more than a decade, cost about $325 billion and more than two thousand American lives, and removed the Taliban, greatly weakened Al Qaeda, and killed Bin Laden. Congress may have essentially been ratifying action the president would have taken anyway, but its behavior was nevertheless crucial for the purposes of constitutional legitimacy and national unity.[13]

Other recent occasions when the United States has used military force do not lend themselves to such easy analysis. This country has claimed direct and legitimate interests in Western Hemisphere affairs since the proclamation of the Monroe Doctrine in 1823, but that does not mean the interventions in Grenada in 1983 and Panama in 1989–1990 constituted good policy. Both actions were condemned as violations of international law by important American allies and the United Nations.[14] Yet both achieved their stated limited goals at minimal cost. The Grenada operation quickly secured law and order on the island and reversed a leftist countercoup at the cost of nineteen American casualties. Forty Americans lost their lives in Panama, but the government was overthrown, and its leader Manuel Noriega captured in what was arguably a successful effort to reduce drug trafficking, protect the Panama Canal, and bring democracy to the isthmus.

A strong, although far from irrefutable, argument can be made the United States should protect allies that have been attacked. The doctrine of collective security states the international system will remain stable if countries threaten to respond to military aggression, regardless of the victim (Morgenthau 1948; Organski 1958). As the world's most powerful country, the maintenance of international peace and existing institutions and arrangements are also presumably in American interests. So, during the fall of 1990, President George H. W. Bush set about coordinating a broad international effort to evict Iraqi forces that had invaded Kuwait. Ultimately a coalition of thirty-four countries committing financial resources, supplies, and about one million personnel dealt a quick and devastating defeat to Saddam Hussein's military. About three hundred Americans died, and the effort cost about $100 billion in today's money. Bush was criticized for not toppling Hussein, and, of course, if he had, the second war against Iraq begun in 2003 may well not have happened.[15] The operation was, however, almost universally acclaimed a success. It was one Congress could reasonably share in.

The debates that took place in January 1991 over whether to authorize the president's use of force were widely considered to be thoughtful, thorough, and deliberative. Nearly everyone who wanted to participate did (Taylor 2012a, 164–166). Congress was torn between support for Bush's proposed military action and a continuation of economic sanctions, as the House and Senate votes illustrated.[16] Once it had made a decision, though, the legislative branch offered the president the support he needed to win the war.

Protecting people who face suppression and elimination from authoritarian regimes is perhaps more tenuously linked to core American interests. But there are many who believe this kind of operation should be undertaken.[17] In 2011, the Obama administration supported a British- and French-led NATO effort to support rebels and remove Libyan leader Muammar Gaddafi. The president defended the action by stating regime change in Libya was in the national interest but that in cases of genocide, humanitarian relief, and regional instability such as this one, the United States should not act alone. Congress was mixed in its support for the administration. In June, the Senate approved but the House rejected a resolution authorizing US involvement. As such, Congress essentially deferred to the White House and effectively distanced itself from whatever course the civil war might take.[18]

The crisis generated additional questions about when, exactly, the United States should intervene militarily. There have been other civil wars in which one of the parties appears to have had as legitimate a claim on American support as the Libyan rebels. In 1994, President Bill Clinton ordered US troops to Haiti to support an uprising led by Jean-Bertrand Aristide, the democratically elected leader who had been deposed by a coup in 1991, against the country's military rulers. The operation was a significant success because the government stepped down before US troops could even land on the island. Clinton also ordered American forces into action in the Balkans during the wars that raged as the old Yugoslavia ripped apart. In Bosnia, the United States participated in the NATO-led Implementation Force to protect the new country's sovereignty and help execute the Dayton Peace Accords. Later, in 1999, the United States participated in NATO bombing attacks on Serbia as evidence emerged of its brutal suppression of ethnic Albanians in Kosovo. Clinton also sent troops there after the Serbian leadership had accepted peace terms. The public generally approved of these efforts (Lyon and Malone 2009; Sobel 1998), and Congressional votes were bipartisan and overwhelmingly supportive. There were few American casualties—thirty-two US deaths in all—and the two operations cost about $25 billion (Serafino 2007).

The United States has also been absent on these occasions, however. In 1994, again on Clinton's watch, ethnic Hutus massacred more than five hundred thousand Tutsis in the east African country of Rwanda. The politics were complex, accurate information elusive, and the genocide rapid, but many, including members of Congress, faulted the United States for not intervening until it sent a moderate peacekeeping effort later in the year. The criticism from Capitol Hill was not loud enough to affect the administration's policy. As of late 2012, the same could be said of efforts by prominent Senators—such as John McCain (R-AZ) and Joseph Liberman (D-CT)—to have the United States assist in the overthrow of the Syrian regime.

Of all the conflicts in which the United States has been involved since Vietnam, the Iraq War begun in 2003 is probably the most controversial. The justification President George W. Bush gave for sending US forces to overthrow Saddam Hussein had many components: most notably that the Iraqi regime had access to weapons of mass destruction, it had close links to Al Qaeda, it had violated its ceasefire agreement imposed after the Gulf War, and it brutally suppressed its own people. In retrospect, there is only really strong evidence for the last two statements, the two that likely motivated the administration the least. Saddam Hussein was captured nine months after the invasion began and was hanged in December 2006. Today, Iraq has something that resembles a democracy and a government that is officially friendly to the United States. However, it is still unstable and torn by ethnic strife and religious disputes that often turn violent. The war was also expensive: about 4,400 Americans lost their lives and the federal government spent approximately $790 billion. Prior to the withdrawal of American troops in December 2011, the public tended to be more supportive of the conflict going on simultaneously in Afghanistan.[19]

The congressional debate on the resolution to authorize the president to do whatever he felt "necessary and appropriate" to "defend the national security of the United States against the continuing threat posed by Iraq" as well as "enforce all relevant United Nations Security Council Resolutions regarding Iraq" was lengthy and generated broad participation.[20] More than 70 percent of House members and ninety-two senators contributed to it. Many stated they believed this would be the most important vote of their careers. The proceedings were sober and judicious, although not as deliberative as those on similar resolutions considered earlier in American history (Taylor 2102a, 162–167). Support for the action was significant and bipartisan, although a majority of Democrats in the House did vote against it.[21] In many ways, this was Congress at its best.

But it was also Congress at close to its worst. One reason it is difficult to judge congressional performance on war is that talk is cheap, congressional action is not particularly meaningful, and legislators, unlike the president, have the luxury of shifting their positions rapidly and repeatedly as events change.[22] In their defense, many members who voted for the war did so after attending classified meetings with administration officials in which Saddam Hussein's menace was obviously exaggerated.[23] Still, the numerous subsequent debates and votes on the Iraq operation—measures concerning spending levels and expressions of discontent about how things were going— allowed them to craft a nuanced public position to fit the mood of the day.[24] For some, like the conservative representative Walter Jones Jr. (R-NC), the conversion made them a principled hero. For others, like Sen. John Kerry (D-MA), who famously remarked during the 2004 presidential campaign that "I actually did vote for the $87 billion [appropriation for Iraq and Afghanistan] before I voted against it," it helped brand them as "flip-floppers."

How do we judge the full record of recent congressional performance on military action and armed conflict? The headline is that, despite the cumulative cost in lives and money, most operations have been successful or, where the term is appropriate, "won." There has been no repeat of the Vietnam disaster. These conflicts have been relatively few in number, although we have essentially been at war for the entire past decade. To some great extent, then, the benchmark has been met. Whether the United States is safer because of these conflicts is difficult to say. Certainly there is no clear evidence that, absent these actions, we would be more secure. Yet many argue the costs, particularly of the recent Iraq and Afghanistan wars, are still really to be felt. Some claim, for instance, they have contributed greatly to the country's recent economic decline.[25]

How much of the success is directly attributable to Congress, though? The institution can take its role seriously, as the debates prior to the two wars with Iraq demonstrate. It might sometimes have tangible influence when it exerts behind-the-scenes pressure on administration personnel (Hersman 2000). However, for the most part Congress really sits back, offering advice from the sanctuary of the bleachers as the president grapples with the very difficult issues of war and peace (Hinckley 1994). In Grenada and Panama, for example, congressional participation was limited to some cheerleading and after-the-fact justification for the administrations' actions (Burgin 1992). The government's Afghanistan policy has scarcely a legislator's fingerprint on it. Even when it attempts to get involved, Congress's actions seem halfhearted and have little substantive effect. They tend to be advisory, as floor debates and votes during the conflicts in the Balkans, Iraq, and Libya demonstrate. This, of course, means that when things go well Congress cannot really claim credit. It also means that when things go poorly Congress might legitimately be blamed for not standing in the president's way.

BENCHMARK #31
The US economy should be among the strongest in the world.

Justification

Analyzing Congress's performance on economic policy is easier. The institution's actions are more determinative of the country's economic health than America's foreign policy successes or failures. Presidential influence is not quite so overbearing in the domestic realm—the differences between executive power on foreign and domestic policy matters distinguish what are often called the two presidencies (Canes-Wrone,

Howell, and Lewis 2008)—and citizens expect Congress to be more assertive on these issues.[26] Still the president has the veto and frequently an agenda, a sizeable staff, control over policy implementation, and a political interest in how the country is doing. Economic outcomes are also shaped by the Federal Reserve, multinational corporations, foreign governments, and millions of firms and consumers. We know public prosperity should be a goal of Congress's economic policy making, but how should this be transformed into a more specific benchmark?

I suggest that on critical economic indicators we should expect the United States to be a top performer among advanced industrialized countries. Given the nation's size and other natural advantages, Congress should be capable of making the United States wealthier than most of the world.

Appraisal

An examination of the basic indicators of American prosperity reveals Congress to be doing quite well. Compared to those of similar advanced industrialized countries, the American economy has generally been in good shape. The financial crisis and resultant deep recession that began in 2008 hurt the United States just as it did others. But excluding that slump, the country has suffered only five recessions since 1971.[27] Over the course of recent American history, only the 2008–2009 downturn was particularly large in terms of the change in GDP peak-to-trough. Average annual GDP growth in recent years is not what it was from World War II until the 1980s, but over the past thirty years it has held steady at around 2.5 percent, and since the 1990s it has been more robust than that of established industrialized nations like Germany and Japan. The United States ranks about seventh in GDP per capita; only small and sometimes oil-rich countries best it. Although higher today than in countries like Canada, Japan, Mexico, and the United Kingdom, the unemployment rate hovered around the relatively low 5 percent range for the twenty years before the financial crisis. With the exception of a spell in the late 1970s and early 1980s, the country's inflation rate has been lower than most as well. Prices tend to rise a benign 2.5 percent a year on average. The benchmark, at least for widely used macroeconomic indicators, is met.

This all suggests that congressional stewardship of the American economy has been reasonably sound. There certainly has been a lot of federal legislation passed in the effort. Whereas the early 1970s witnessed a significant amount of regulation on issues like workplace safety, the environment, and minimum wage, the late 1970s and 1980s saw a wave of deregulation in industries such as trucking, airlines, and railroads. Deregulation continued in the 1990s as Congress weakened federal rules governing financial institutions and telecommunications and greatly reduced farm subsidies, but it was meanwhile attenuated by invigorated environmental standards, health insurance portability protection, the Americans with Disabilities Act (ADA), and family and medical leave legislation.[28] Despite being an era of Republican control, the early twenty-first century saw some regulation too, perhaps most dramatically in the form of corporate responsibility in the aftermath of the Enron scandal.[29] Enhanced regulation of health care and financial services was a central component of Obama's and congressional Democrats' record in 2009–2010.

Congress has frequently changed tax law as well. In 1981, with help from the more conservative Democrats in Congress, Republicans led by President Ronald Reagan enacted large cuts in income tax rates.[30] Republicans did something similar under President George W. Bush in 2001.[31] In between, the tax code was simplified in 1986, and taxes incrementally increased, in 1982, 1990, and 1993, largely to alleviate federal budget problems.[32] Both parties have periodically invested in social welfare programs like housing and education. Overhauls of welfare programs occurred in 1988 and, more significantly, in 1996.[33] A massive new prescription drug benefit was added to Medicare by Republicans in 2003. Legislation in the 1980s and 1990s facilitated a boom in immigration.[34] A large number of trade deals and treaties have been passed. For the most part, these have liberalized trade with other countries, either directly as a stated goal of the measure, such as the creation of NAFTA in 1993 and the establishment of permanent normal trade relations with China in 2000, or indirectly by granting the president authority to make deals alone, as illustrated by congressional approval of trade promotion authority in 2002.[35]

Of course, Congress has little direct control over the industriousness and ingenuity of the American manager, entrepreneur, and worker. It does not dictate the behavior of the American consumer. The country has benefitted from copious natural resources and from operating the world's reserve currency. Largely because of its power and size, the country's bonds have nearly always been considered a safe haven for the world's investors, and, therefore, somewhat regardless of the government's policies it can borrow at low rates. Throughout much of 2012, the ten-year US Treasury note had a yield of around 1.5 percent, the lowest it had ever been and about the same as its German equivalent. On the economy, then, an argument can be made that Congress has been lucky as well as good.

BENCHMARK #32
The federal budget deficit should be less than 5 percent of GDP.

Justification

Fiscal discipline and a tidy government balance sheet are desirable economic goals as well. As the recent problems of many European countries attest, an imbalance between spending and liabilities on one side and revenues and assets on the other raises borrowing costs and forces austerity measures that deter economic growth and generate political division. We should want a fiscal policy that recognizes the need to balance expenditures with revenues and that reflects the underlying state of the country's finances. Complete budgetary balance and zero debt are probably unreasonable targets, even if, as President Andrew Jackson's efforts demonstrated, there is an American tradition of strict fiscal rectitude.[36] In the American states, which, with the exception of Vermont, are legally obligated to balance their budgets, debts are still incurred through bonds, pension liabilities, and other borrowing. According to State Budget Solutions, the total debt of the fifty states amounted to about $13,700 per American in 2011.[37] But peer advanced industrialized countries provide an even better guide. The mean budget deficit as measured as a percentage of GDP for OECD (Organization for Economic Cooperation and Development) countries in recent years is around 5 percent. Besting that ought to be a goal of Congress.

Appraisal

Fiscal policy, however, is no longer what it should be. With the exception of a couple of years in the mid-1980s, the deficit had always been below 5 percent of GDP since World War II. Indeed, as recently as fiscal year 2001 the federal government was producing a modest surplus. In 2009, the federal deficit reached 10 percent of GDP—or $1.4 trillion—and has stayed close to that mark since. Much can be attributed to efforts, misguided or not, to stave off economic catastrophe in the wake of financial crisis. The bailouts of major banks like Citigroup and Bank of America, car giants General Motors and Chrysler, and the mortgage financiers Fannie Mae and Freddie Mac cost about $550 billion. The TARP payments to private companies have been largely repaid, and some estimate the program might now end up costing taxpayers only about $50 billion and quite possibly less. The American Recovery and Reinvestment Act of 2009—often called the stimulus—provided tax cuts and spending for health care, education, state governments, and infrastructure. Its tab was nearly $800 billion. The costs of social welfare programs have escalated considerably. Medicaid expenditures increased by nearly 25 percent between 2008 and 2009 and are projected to increase by near double-digit percentages in the immediate future. They are now over $250 billion a year. Unemployment compensation more than tripled between 2008 and 2010 and currently costs the federal government about $150 billion annually. The government has also cut taxes recently, specifically with a holiday on about a third of workers' payroll taxes and a two-year extension of individual income tax reductions initially passed in 2001.[38]

Recalcitrant economic forces aside, Congress's track record on the budget is subject to legitimate criticism. It has generally responded to, rather than resisted, political pressures to increase spending and reduce revenues. At the aggregate level, fiscal prudence might help a party's reputation, but core constituencies of the Republican Party expect Congress to cut, or at least hold the line on, taxes, and many Democrats expect their party to withstand reductions in core programs like Medicare, Medicaid, and Social

Security, which together make up about 43 percent of annual federal government spending. At the individual level, members see the benefit in "pork-barrel politics," discretionary spending or tax breaks narrowly targeted at a particular district or state. They provide obvious electoral benefits and—although some, such as members of the majority (Balla et al. 2002), senior legislators (Lee 2003), and those from districts where demand for federal spending is high (Bickers and Stein 1996; Lazarus 2010) are better at collecting pork than others—most members make concerted efforts to secure federal largess. The Cato Institute estimates the federal government spends about $95 billion on subsidies, grants, and loan guarantees to American businesses annually—"corporate welfare," as some call it. The budgets of federal departments most obviously connected to domestic programs have grown spectacularly over the past decade. Between 2001 and 2010, spending at the Department of Commerce grew by 164 percent, at the Department of Housing and Urban Development by 79 percent, and at the Department of Education by 161 percent.

To its credit, Congress has tried hard to create budget procedures to ameliorate this pressure and improve the country's fiscal situation. But these have largely failed. In 1985, it passed what came to be known as the Gramm-Rudman-Hollings Act—after its three sponsors, Rep. Phil Gramm (R-TX) and Sens. Warren Rudman (R-NH) and Ernest Hollings (D-SC). The legislation established targets for deficit reduction that, if not met, would lead to the automatic sequestering of funds. Five years later, and with the budget situation worse, it approved the Budget Enforcement Act (BEA).[39] BEA put caps on discretionary spending—the spending that needs approval every year in the appropriations process, excluding Medicare, Medicaid, and Social Security—and instituted a pay-as-you-go, or PAYGO, procedure that mandated any tax cuts or increases in entitlement programs had to be offset with savings from other programs or revenue sources. In 1993 and 1997, Congress joined the Clinton administration to approve budget deals that first reduced deficits and then brought about surpluses. However, a $236 billion surplus in 2000 was turned into a $413 billion deficit by 2004 as PAYGO provisions were at first waived or ignored and then, when BEA expired in 2002, no longer in effect. The financial crisis and the government's reaction to it brought about a staggering $1.63 trillion deficit in 2009. The House has resuscitated PAYGO rules, but in the wave of red ink and lacking statutory authority they have not, despite President Obama's exhortations, had any meaningful effect. Opposed by the White House and Senate, neither has the House Republicans' legislation, passed in 2011, to "cut, cap, and balance" government spending and the budget.

The deal struck by Obama and congressional Republicans to raise the debt ceiling in the summer of 2011 gave birth to the latest effort to improve the country's fiscal health. A bicameral and bipartisan supercommittee was charged with generating $1.5 trillion in deficit reduction over ten years. By Thanksgiving 2011 it was clear the panel would fail and automatic cuts of $1.2 trillion, drawn equally from domestic and de-fense programs, would be scheduled to take effect in January 2013. Together with a series of tax increases scheduled to kick in at the same time—essentially the reversal of reductions signed into law by President Bush in 2001 and 2003 and renewed by President Obama in 2010—the deep spending cuts constitute the so-called fiscal cliff off of which many economists predict we will fall into recession. The concerted effort to avoid the cliff clearly demonstrates the difficulties of balancing deficit reduction with economic health. But it also reveals that to act, Congress must sometimes make inaction highly unpalatable.

It is not surprising many Americans now see the federal budget as a critical issue. Opinion polls consistently show a majority wishes Congress would reduce the deficit rather than cut taxes and maintain spending levels.[40] As unemployment continued at worryingly high levels during 2011 and 2012, Americans repeatedly cited the economy and jobs as the biggest challenges facing the federal government. But between 15 and 25 percent of respondents regularly offered the debt and deficits as the most important issue in surveys—nearly always besting topics like health care, education, and foreign policy by quite some distance.[41] Given Americans' feelings about fiscal policy and the elevated attention paid to the issue by politicians and the media, it is likely congressional efforts at deficit reduction will shape public views of institutional performance a great deal in the coming years.

BENCHMARK #33
Congress should use sound principles when
managing the country's financial liabilities.

Justification

Legislators should aim not just to solve current problems but to assist their successors in meeting the economic challenges of the future. In addition to tangible debt—of which we are sure the government has a great deal—public pension and health care liabilities provide an opportunity to evaluate congressional performance on this score. Existing policies promise public assistance in old age. From what we know about a country's demographics, we can make predictions about the costs of these promises. Ambitious pledges to large numbers of retirees will place huge strains on other government programs and likely constitute an intergenerational transfer of wealth. Obtaining comparable and accurate measures of these liabilities across countries is difficult. Although it is widely recognized that, of advanced industrialized nations, Italy's and Japan's are among the very worst—a mixture of generous retirement benefits and a shrinking workforce.[42] Still, we should see evidence that Congress is using sound principles as it manages this matter.

Appraisal

The country's current fiscal health suggests Congress is failing to meet this benchmark. Nowhere is this admonition more important than in the commitment of resources that effectively bind future generations. For centuries, Americans have argued restraining the liberty of our children and those yet to be born has moral implications—Jefferson argued each generation should reconstitute society as it desired (Matthews 1984, 19–21), and many members of Congress today believe saddling our successors with debt is reprehensible.[43] The accumulation of budget deficits creates significant constraints on policy makers down the road, restricting policy options and diverting resources from social investments to debt servicing.

Statutory pledges to classes of citizens have similar effects. By far and away the largest of what are called "entitlement programs" are Social Security and Medicare. The Social Security program, enacted in 1935, provides public pensions and disability benefits to Americans. Medicare, established in 1965 as an expansion of Social Security, furnishes these individuals with health insurance and prescription drug plans. Both are funded automatically and do not require congressional action in the form of an annual appropriation to distribute benefits. So long as individuals meet eligibility requirements, they are entitled to the services and payments these programs provide.

Demographic and economic changes, as well as periodic statutory increases in benefits and relaxation of eligibility rules, mean the programs' future obligations are huge. Because workers pay into the programs through payroll taxes, both Medicare and Social Security currently have more than enough funding to meet their obligations. However, as large cohorts retire and live longer than their predecessors, these reserves will quickly run dry. Officials estimate that, at today's levels, the Social Security trust fund will be depleted by 2033 and covered workers will only be paying enough in taxes to provide about 75 percent of scheduled benefits. Medicare's actuarial situation is worse. Its reserves will be exhausted by 2024, and rapidly escalating health care costs mean revenues will be unable to cover a significant percentage of expenditures for very long after that.[44]

Congress has yet to come to grips with this situation. With so many other challenges and demands, the future demise of entitlement programs seems unimportant and hypothetical to many Americans. As part of the renewal of tax cuts at the end of 2010, for example, the Obama administration and Congress agreed to give workers a payroll tax holiday, which effectively cut their share of Social Security taxes—the employer's match was left untouched—by 32 percent. The holiday was extended at the end of 2011. This action, theoretically at least, put the program on weaker footing. There was hardly any sign of concern in Washington.

Those genuinely interested in reform face large and well-organized groups mobilized to protect the status quo. In 2005, President Bush expended considerable time and energy pushing a proposal to allow current workers to invest a portion of their payments in personal accounts over which they would have control. Despite Republican congressional majorities, the effort did not go particularly far. Rep. Paul Ryan (R-WI) proposed Medicare be transformed into a "voucher" program in which beneficiaries could shop for their own insurance when he presented his budget to the House during the spring of 2011. It was panned by Democrats and possibly cost Republicans a House seat; they lost a special election in a conservative-leaning New York district in May when the Democrat campaigned heavily on Ryan's plans. In April 2012, a bipartisan budget written by Reps. Steven C. LaTourette (R-OH) and Jim Cooper (D-TN) and modeled on the report published by the President's National Commission on Fiscal Responsibility and Reform headed by Erskine Bowles and Alan Simpson received just thirty-eight votes on the House floor. Bowles and Simpson had recommended deep cuts to Social Security and Medicare and increases in payroll deductions and the retirement age. During the early stages of the 2012 campaign for the Republican presidential nomination, opponents of Governor Rick Perry of Texas pointed to a book he wrote in which he implied quite strongly that Social Security was unconstitutional.[45] Perry's candidacy took a nosedive after the issue came up. With the public so supportive of Social Security, it is not surprising that those who dare touch the "third rail of American politics" get such an adverse reaction. A September 2011 CNN/ORC poll reported that 79 percent of respondents felt the program was a good thing for the country. In response to a Pew Research Center June 2011 poll, 41 percent of those surveyed believed Social Security "works pretty well and requires only minor changes," 34 percent that it required "major changes," and only 18 percent that it should be "completely rebuilt." Quite clearly Congress's sensitivity to public opinion can conflict with its capacity to solve policy problems.

But that does not mean Congress is ignoring the challenges generated by Medicare and Social Security entirely. In the summer of 2011, accounts of a summit meeting between President Obama and House Speaker John Boehner over the debt ceiling suggested both were close to agreeing to a legislative package containing significant cuts to entitlements (Mann and Ornstein 2012, 15–25). During 2012, Sen. Ron Wyden (D-OR) expressly supported Paul Ryan's efforts to subsidize Medicare beneficiaries who buy private insurance. It became clear from discussions about the fiscal cliff later that year that entitlement reform needed to be part of a comprehensive solution to the country's fiscal problems. The health care reform legislation passed in 2010 supports Medicare's long-term financing by expanding the proportion of wealthy Americans' earnings that are subject to Medicare tax and cutting the drug reimbursement rate and spending to doctors and hospitals.

Congress has also previously had success shoring up Social Security. Faced with a trust fund that was borrowing billions of dollars and the prospect of benefit checks being delayed after July 1983, it teamed with the Reagan administration to create a lasting fix to the program. A mixture of increased payroll taxes, taxes on benefits, delays to cost-of-living adjustments, and raising the retirement age bolstered Social Security's finances. Democrats and Republicans were provided political cover for the compromise and its somewhat painful policy changes by the National Commission on Social Security Reform, a bipartisan panel of prominent legislators and the business community selected by President Reagan and the congressional leadership and headed by Alan Greenspan. The commission's report, issued in early 1983, had the support of House and Senate leaders, who were committed to pushing it through the legislative process intact. Although a few changes were made, the agreement held together (Light 1995, 185–203). Members from both parties knew they would share any blame the public attached to the reform with their colleagues across the aisle.

Nevertheless, I think it is fair to say the preponderance of evidence suggests Congress fails to meet this benchmark. The achievement of 1983 is an isolated case. Perhaps because members' terms are short and careers finite or perhaps because there are other more pressing issues and the public cares only about the present, Congress does not seem particularly adept at casting an eye beyond the immediate future. Its legislative action—and inaction for that matter—is rarely taken with consideration for long-term effects.

BENCHMARK #34
Congress should pass laws that are short and general.

Justification

As noted in Chapter 2, we should want laws to be concise and render themselves as generally applicable as possible.[46] Laws should enunciate broad principles, exceptions to which should be avoided. Uneven policy is costly to administer and is frequently seen as illegitimate in societies that value fairness and equity. We should want an important feature of what Lowi termed "juridical democracy."

Creating measures of policy simplicity and uniformity capable of supporting comparative analysis is essentially impossible. I will therefore retreat to absolutes and suggest Congress should create short laws that are applied in general fashion—that is, exceptions to them, if they exist at all, should be minimal.

Appraisal

Some of the data on laws enacted by Congress offer encouragement. I discussed the recent precipitous decline of private bills and earmarks in Chapter 3. But other data disappoint to the extent that I think it is fair to say this benchmark is not met. Take federal tax law, for example. It constitutes, according to Congress's Joint Economic Committee (2003, 1), "an extraordinarily complex code that is frequently at cross-purposes with itself." In 2002 then–Treasury Secretary Paul O'Neill—the head of the department charged with enforcement—called the byzantine character of the tax code "an abomination" (Crenshaw 2002). Although there is no property or sales tax at the federal level, Americans pay income, estate, excise, capital gains, and payroll taxes to Washington. Corporations pay income tax and customs duties.[47] Individual income taxes are paid at different rates, and there are scores of deductions and exemptions—for anything from child care, to uniforms for work, to energy-saving home improvements. The code reflects all of these exceptions.

Unfortunately, recent reforms have added to, and not reduced, the general complexity. Congress is moving policy in the wrong direction. In 1939, after important legislation, the tax code was about 500 pages long, even though it already contained deductions for charitable giving and mortgage interest payments. By the time Congress passed a serious simplification in 1986, the number of pages devoted to federal tax laws and regulations had reached around 27,000. Although the goal of the Tax Reform Act was to reduce the number of brackets and deductions in individual income tax rules, the code soon got more complicated again. Credits and deductions were given and then expanded for children, medical expenses, and retirement savings. Between just 1995 and 2000, 6,400 pages were added to federal tax laws and regulations, increasing their length by 16 percent to 47,000 pages. This extended the time the average American spent filing tax forms by five hours. The Bush years did little to change things. A variety of tax laws cut rates and estate taxes, lowered dividends and capital gains liabilities, and expanded certain credits and exemptions (Steuerle 2008, 199–220). But, although the aggregate burden was lessened, the code became more complex. As of 2011, federal tax laws and regulations filled about 72,500 pages.[48]

There are ongoing efforts to reverse this. Tax reform has been a central part of the debate over fiscal policy and deficit reduction. Chaired by former Sen. Pete Domenici (R-NM) and Clinton budget director Alice Rivlin, the Bipartisan Policy Center's Debt Reduction Task Force recommended eliminating itemized deductions when it reported in November 2010. It proposed turning the charitable and mortgage interest deductions into refundable credits, for example. The Simpson-Bowles Commission likewise suggested deductions for health care insurance premiums be capped or done away with.[49] Reducing or eliminating the mortgage interest deduction was apparently a central part of the aborted Obama-Boehner "Grand Bargain" deal to lift the debt ceiling in the summer of 2011. Many Republican members are wriggling free of the straitjacket in which they placed themselves when they signed pledges not to increase taxes at all—such as the one Grover Norquist's Americans for Tax Reform asks candidates to commit themselves to. These legislators report a desire to support the removal of loopholes and other exceptions in the code. To date, however, there has been no breakthrough on comprehensive tax reform. And proponents of simplification face an extremely difficult fight. Although provisions like the mortgage interest deduction might make little economic sense, they have powerful champions—in this case the homebuilders and realtors.

BENCHMARK #35
Congress should make policy that is consistent across issue areas.

Justification

The final benchmark in this chapter calls for programmatic public policy. As we saw in Chapter 2, for the purposes of accountability and consistency, the aggregate legislation produced by Congress at any one period of time should have a great deal of ideological coherence. Political scientists have not looked at this concept comprehensively, but history reveals numerous periods of programmatic policy making across the Western world. In the United Kingdom, for example, the 1980s were a time when policy moved palpably in a conservative direction. Under Prime Minister Margaret Thatcher, numerous industries were privatized, top income tax rates were slashed, and the power of labor unions curtailed (Jenkins 1987; Kavanagh 1990). Meanwhile, France, under Socialist President François Mitterrand, nationalized industries, increased the minimum wage, shortened the work week, instituted a wealth tax, extended union rights, and abolished the death penalty (Tiersky 2000). Mitterrand was forced into a dramatic U-turn on economic policy in 1983, but there is no doubting the leftward direction of the initial move (Hall 1987). In both cases, the leaders were clearly assisted by their countries' forms of parliamentary democracy, where the majority party in the legislature is elected by a partisan and ideological electorate and has significant freedom to enact its agenda. Congress does not quite work this way. Still, it seems reasonable to expect periodic episodes of policy coherence across recent American history.

Appraisal

Interestingly, the federal government in the United States has, despite its design, also been capable of making policy programmatically. There have been periods of unified government, particularly under Democrats, when policy across a broad array of issue areas moved discernibly in one direction in coordinated fashion. The creation and expansion of social programs and extensive regulatory policy characterized the liberal direction taken in the 1960s under Kennedy and Johnson. The first Obama Congress, that of 2009–2011, produced historic health care reform, Keynesian-inspired stimulus legislation, new regulations for the financial services industry in Dodd-Frank, a repeal of DADT, and invigorated regulation of tobacco. But divided governments have produced legislative records of ideological coherence as well. Presidents Nixon and Ford worked with Democratic Congresses to augment Social Security with added programs and benefits, promote the environment, protect consumers, improve working conditions and pay, and invest in infrastructure.[50] The 101st Congress during George H. W. Bush's residency in the White House produced a surprisingly liberal record. There was a minimum wage hike, tax increases (admittedly coupled with spending cuts for the purposes of deficit reduction), and the ADA. The Clinton years, six of which were spent with Republican Congresses, saw aggressive deficit reduction; a revolutionary overhaul of welfare policy; and deregulation in agriculture, banking, and telecommunications.[51] This was not a uniform and decisive move in a rightward direction, but in the aggregate the policies of the 1990s do have a perceptibly conservative hue.

It is true that separation of powers, bicameralism, and political necessity force policy compromises at times. Characterized by deregulation, tax cuts, and neoconservative foreign policy, the George W. Bush years also saw tremendous increases in spending on domestic policy and the creation of a new entitlement program, Part D of Medicare, which provides a prescription drug benefit to recipients at the cost of about $40 billion to $70 billion a year. Ideological inconsistency is sometimes evident within individual pieces of legislation. Large budget bills—like those of 1990 and 1997—tend to contain items that please both Democrats and Republicans. The historic education reform known formally as No Child Left Behind (NCLB) that passed in 2001 was a real mishmash of principles. Liberals like Sen. Edward Kennedy (D-MA) and Rep. George Miller (D-CA) were able to increase federal spending on elementary and secondary education quite considerably. The president and congressional Republicans like John Boehner forced performance standards on schools and gave some children the option to transfer. By doing so, they held public schools and their teachers accountable and provided students with choice. They also greatly extended federal power into a policy area that had traditionally been reserved to the states.

I think it is fair to say then, that Congress approaches this benchmark. It can, and very often does, generate a legislative record of some ideological homogeneity.

CONCLUSION

Congress's efforts to produce effective policy are summarized in Table 7.1. To many in Washington and around the country, Congress is gridlocked, incapable of making public policy with any meaningful effect. We have seen, however, it can be productive and generate laws that have profound effects on the everyday lives of millions of Americans. In just the past decade, it has, among many other things, passed large tax cuts, created a huge new homeland security apparatus, overhauled federal policy toward elementary and secondary education, added a massive new program to Medicare, injected enormous amounts of capital into banks and large corporations so as to protect the broader economy, revamped the financial services industry, and revolutionized the way health care is provided. Individual pieces of legislation are not without their critics. But it cannot be denied these laws are far reaching and historically important.

The quality of the policy produced by Congress might reasonably be considered spotty. The institution's role in creating the world's pre-eminent military and economic power should not be overlooked. Congress is also capable of producing comprehensive programs of legislation that are reminiscent of governments in parliamentary systems.

BENCHMARK FOR CONGRESSIONAL PERFORMANCE	APPRAISAL
29. Congress should be productive when it needs to be—demonstrating this by making around four hundred total and twelve important laws per Congress.	Met
30. The United States should enter military conflict under strict conditions that, among other things, minimize costs and maximize the probability of success.	Largely met
31. The US economy should be among the strongest in the world.	Met
32. The federal budget deficit should be less than about 5 percent of GDP.	Largely not met
33. Congress should use sound principles when managing the country's financial liabilities.	Not met
34. Congress should pass laws that are short and general.	Not met
35. Congress should make policy that is consistent across issue areas.	Largely met

TABLE 7.1 Appraising congressional performance on benchmarks related to effective policy

Yet members seem to have a penchant for carving out exceptions to broad bodies of policy that complicate them and generate the impression, problematic in a democracy, that some groups of citizens receive favorable treatment at the expense of others. Congress has also demonstrated an inability to tackle societal problems that will get progressively worse and pose significant challenges in the future. Political incentives encourage members to deal with more immediate policy concerns.

8

DOES CONGRESS CARRY OUT VIGOROUS CHECKING AND BALANCING?

The benchmarks in this chapter are crafted with the assumption Congress should maintain its independence and protect its prerogatives in the system of separation of powers. At the very least the Framers believed Congress had a clear responsibility to check and balance the other branches. Because power naturally concentrates and individuals are intrinsically self-interested, James Madison argued in *Federalist 48* the Constitution should "provide some practical security for the branches, against the invasion of the others" (Hamilton, Madison, and Jay 1982, 301) or, as he put it a little later in *Federalist 51*, "the necessary constitutional means and personal motives to resist encroachments of the others" (Hamilton, Madison, and Jay 1982, 315–316). Protecting congressional interests and prerogatives in the branch's relationships with the executive and judiciary would require concerted effort. The Founders had given it "provision for defense" that was "commensurate to the danger of attack" (Hamilton, Madison, and Jay 1982, 316). They understood the intensity with which personal ambition burned. They exhorted the institutions of government to work assiduously to fend off rivals. But then it was up to all of them, including Congress, to look out for themselves.

BENCHMARK #36
Congress should maintain a balance of power with the executive branch.

Justification
Using the experiences of peer bodies to understand what precisely constitutes the appropriate exercise of legislative power in a system like that of the United States is very

difficult. Our presidential government is distinctly different from the Westminster Model replicated in much of western Europe and the British Commonwealth (Lijphart 1999). A version related to the American system is on display in France, but for the most part it is the relatively new democracies of Latin America that separate governmental powers in the way we do.

Most executives in Latin America are considered more powerful than our president. Their authority derives from what Shugart and Mainwaring (1997) call constitutional and partisan sources. Presidents with strong constitutional powers include those in Brazil and Colombia, who have a formal capacity to set the policy agenda and issue decrees. Those with partisan powers can routinely rely on legislative majorities to support them because party politics are strong—as, for example, in Uruguay. Some have argued Latin American countries have a penchant for authoritarianism that is both reflected and facilitated by political systems which provide presidents with such significant power (Linz 1994). Further evidence, then, that legislative-executive balance is desirable.

The American states have, of course, separated their executives from their legislatures. Governors cannot serve in the legislative branch and are popularly elected. Beyond that, however, there is tremendous variance in the authority of the country's governors. Some have considerable power to write the budget and get to appoint their cabinet as opposed to having voters select it for them. Some experience no limits on the number of terms they can serve and have significant veto powers, enjoying the line-item veto and requiring relatively small proportions of the legislature, normally one-third of each body, to sustain their effort to block a bill from becoming law. The governors of Massachusetts, New Jersey, and New York are among the strongest on these counts.[1]

The powers the Framers gave the American presidency places the office somewhere in the middle of a ranking of current Western Hemisphere political executives. Apart from a short time in the mid-1990s, the American president has never had the line-item veto—more on which later. The president does not have formal powers to set the legislative agenda. When they approved the Twenty-Second Amendment in 1951, Congress and the states saw fit to make a tradition dating back to the beginning of the republic that presidents serve only two four-year terms part of the Constitution.[2]

The Framers wished, therefore, to temper presidential power. Alexander Hamilton (Hamilton, Madison, and Jay 1982, 426) argues in *Federalist 70* that the American presidency displayed "energy" in that it was a single-person executive with meaningful powers, a relatively lengthy term, and guaranteed resources. But Congress was thought to consist of a healthy blend of national, state, and local interests. It was to make laws, and without the president's assent if more than two-thirds of the membership of both bodies wanted to. It was given important and explicit powers in Article I, Section 8, to, among other matters, declare war, lay and collect taxes, regulate commerce, and borrow money. Article II, Section 4, states it could remove the president and other executive branch officials. The government the Founders designed had infused within it an elaborate system of checks to prevent either branch from becoming too powerful and encroaching on the rights of the other. Something approaching balance was a principal goal. Maintaining it ought to be one of Congress's.

Appraisal
The Rise of Executive Power

In the late 1880s Woodrow Wilson, at the time a newly minted PhD and Bryn Mawr professor, published a work that put Congress at the center of the country's federal government.[3] It was hard to argue with him. After Lincoln's assassination and the end of the Civil War, the United States was ostensibly led by a series of weak presidents, who seemed either to head corrupt administrations or obtain office in controversial or accidental circumstances. President Ulysses S. Grant left office in disgrace after two terms in 1877, debilitated by scandals involving members of his administration of which Crédit Mobilier was probably the most famous.[4] His successor, Rutherford B. Hayes, was inaugurated only after a special electoral commission appointed by Congress affirmed disputed returns in Florida, Louisiana, and South Carolina that gave him a one-vote victory in the Electoral College. Hayes's Democratic opponent, Samuel Tilden, won a majority of the popular vote and had significant claims to victory in all three contested states, but he was sacrificed to a deal, often called the Compromise of 1877, in which Republicans pledged to end Reconstruction and withdraw federal troops from the South. In 1880, James Garfield won the presidency, even though he secured fewer than ten thousand popular votes more than his Democratic rival Winfield Scott Hancock. Garfield was assassinated just six months into his term and was replaced by Chester A. Arthur, a relative unknown whose political career to that point had largely been as a cog in the New York Republican Party machine. The 1884 election was also tight, with Democrat Grover Cleveland winning the first of his two nonsequential terms—Benjamin Harrison would defeat him in 1888, even though Cleveland won a plurality of the popular vote.

In 1789, Thomas Jefferson wrote to James Madison, observing that "the tyranny of the legislature is really the danger most to be feared and will continue to be so for many years to come." He added, however, that "the tyranny of executive power will come in its turn, but at a more distant period."[5] By 1900, that time had arrived. Theodore Roosevelt's energetic and combative seven-and-a-half-year tenure saw American public policy move in a more progressive direction as the president clashed with, and then in many cases won over, his more conservative Republican brethren in charge of Congress. Leaders like Speaker Joseph Cannon (R-IL) and Sen. Nelson W. Aldrich (R-RI) could not prevent the president from forging progressive coalitions to strictly regulate the railroads, control the supply of food and drugs, and lay the foundation for a new and powerful central bank.[6] They were often worn down, and some like Aldrich and Sen. William B. Allison (R-IA) ultimately allied themselves with the president on several issues. Roosevelt exploited his office to galvanize public support for his agenda, calling it a "bully pulpit." He understood acutely the potential of presidential power. As he noted in a letter to historian George Otto Trevelyan, "I believe in a strong executive; I believe in power," adding, "while President, I have been President, emphatically; I have used every ounce of power there was in the office" (Abrams 2002, 327).

When he became president, Wilson expanded presidential power too, but in a different way. Like Roosevelt, he saw the presidency as a place to inspire public action, and he understood the importance of communication—Wilson held the first real presidential press conference. But Wilson spoke in loftier tones and of more abstract principles than TR (Kraig 2004; Stid 1998). His "rhetorical presidency" was intended to inspire Americans to a course of action rooted in morality (Tulis 1988). He certainly had legislative failures, including, quite spectacularly, the Senate's refusal to ratify the Treaty of Versailles at the end of World War I. He experienced success as well, however, and his domestic agenda during his first term included important antitrust, trade, regulatory, and banking laws.[7]

It would take the Great Depression and World War II for presidential power to take a real leap forward, though. Franklin D. Roosevelt's presidency, begun in March 1933, marked the beginning of what scholars have called the modern presidency.[8] To deal with an unprecedented economic crisis, FDR had a broad and ambitious agenda. Arguing that it was "the duty of the president to propose and it is the privilege of the Congress to dispose," he sent to the Hill an avalanche of legislation calling for banking reform, public works projects, unemployment relief, public pensions, labor protection, and controls on production, prices, and wages.[9] Nearly all of it passed, although some important components like the Agricultural Adjustment Act and National Industrial Recovery Act ran afoul of the Supreme Court. In 1939, Congress approved the Reorganization Act that provided for the Executive Office of the President, an institution designed to generate policy advice and political support the bureaucracy could not. Indeed, the federal government in general grew as spending escalated from about 11 percent of GDP when FDR entered office to about 20 percent just prior to the country's entry into World War II. The president exploited the new medium of radio with his near-monthly "fireside chats" that each reached an astounding sixty million Americans, about 40 percent of the total population—roughly the same proportion as today's Super Bowl television broadcast. World War II, of course, made the United States a superpower. With Britain and France exhausted by victory, the stage was set for a showdown with the Soviet Union that would motivate American presidents to project their nation's immense power all over the globe.

The presidency has not looked back. By the early 1970s, as the country found itself in the midst of a spellbinding scandal brought about by presidential hubris and wound down a war initiated and led by presidents at the cost of fifty-eight thousand American lives, there was talk of an "imperial presidency" (Schlesinger 1973)—one that worked to elevate the executive to a position of clear supremacy in the constitutional order. Congress has tried to push back. It seemed resolved that Watergate and Vietnam should be the zenith of presidential power. The War Powers Resolution of 1973 called on presidents to provide Congress with information and obtain from it permission when military force is used abroad. In 1974 the legislature moved to prevent presidents from impounding appropriated funds—a tactic regularly used by President Nixon.[10] Watergate inspired the Ethics in Government Act of 1978, a statute providing for an autonomous outside investigation of executive malfeasance. In 1998 it was an independent counsel, Kenneth Starr, whose report on the conduct of President Clinton led directly to the first impeachment of a president in 130 years. The 104th Congress that began in 1995 was the first under complete Republican control in forty years. It is a particularly good example of congressional assertiveness. Led mainly from the office of Speaker Newt Gingrich (R-GA), conservative lawmakers legislated with little regard for President Clinton's opinions.

Periods of congressional resurgence over the past forty years have generally been short lived, however. The War Powers legislation is largely irrelevant and presidents recognize it only nominally.[11] There was no appetite to renew the independent counsel statute after the Clinton impeachment battle in 1998–1999. Following a shutdown of the federal government during the Christmas holidays of 1995, Gingrich's popularity sank, and the Clinton administration and congressional Democrats began to cast the Speaker and his allies as too extreme. The second year of the 104th Congress was one of bipartisan cooperation and significant legislative achievements. It ended with Clinton's comfortable re-election.

Today's Powerful Presidency

In fact, observers are reviving the imperial presidency argument (Rudalevige 2005; Savage 2007). President George W. Bush's actions have probably done most to assist them. Bush aggressively fought the War on Terror, bristled at judicial and congressional efforts to influence his administration's policy on the detention of suspected terrorists at Guantanamo Bay, oversaw an interrogation policy that opponents believed constituted torture, initiated an electronic surveillance program that caught within it many American citizens and corporations, and shrugged off widespread criticism of the conduct of the Iraq and Afghanistan wars. Despite close electoral victories and slim Republican majorities in Congress, Bush was also able to push much of his legislative program into law—including a series of big tax cuts, reform to elementary and secondary education, and a new prescription drug benefit as part of Medicare.[12]

President Barack Obama has done nothing to suggest this state of affairs is about to change. Obama's first-term agenda was hugely ambitious and, thanks to cohesive and centralized Democratic majorities, pretty successful—perhaps the only important measure not to become law was the so-called cap-and-trade policy on energy and the environment. The health care and financial services laws created regulatory apparatuses housed in the executive branch to ultimately exercise significant policy-making powers.[13] Obama also appointed about twenty policy czars to White House positions, individuals independent of Congress who oversee broad issue areas such as health care and the auto industry, as well as narrow ones like the Great Lakes and California water (Sollenberger and Rozell 2012, 146–161). Czars often have policy-making authority but do not receive Senate confirmation. The conflict with Libya and the assassinations of terrorists in southwest Asia—most spectacularly Osama Bin Laden in May 2011— demonstrated the president's desire to conduct security policy alone.

The Executive Branch's Size and Resources

There are four pillars to the contemporary and tremendously powerful presidency. The first is its significant size and resources. Although massive organizations can be difficult to manage, the sheer number of personnel under the president's direction means he has access to considerable information and labor. Today, about 1.8 million civilians work in the executive branch. A further 2.2 million Americans are on active duty or in reserve for the armed forces. Scientists, intelligence officers, and other specialists give the fifteen executive departments and the hundreds of agencies within and outside them considerable informational advantages over Congress in the evaluation and making of policy. The personnel and the programs they run are supported by a roughly $3.5 trillion budget.

These assets are all the more imposing when considered in light of the theory of the unitary executive. This argument is based upon "departmentalism," or the idea that the three branches of government are distinctly separated and that they should each perform their duties unfettered. For the executive branch, this means the president has complete control over the policy-making actions of its personnel and Congress has no legitimate right to interfere. The theory has three distinct components: "the president's power to remove subordinate policy-making officials at will, the president's power to direct the manner in which subordinate officials exercise discretionary executive power, and the president's power to veto or nullify such official's exercises of discretionary executive power" (Calabresi and Yoo 2003, 668). It found its most forceful advocate in President George W. Bush, who invoked the unitary executive eighty-two times to justify his actions during his first term (Savage 2007, 240). The theory is not without its critics in Congress and the academic community (Savage 2007; Shane 2009, 143–174). But it is likely to have tremendous appeal to presidents in the future.

The Executive Branch's Policy-Making Capabilities

The second pillar is policy-making or legislative power. The Constitution provides the president with a formal role in the lawmaking process by granting him a veto. Initially, presidents used the weapon sparingly and only when they believed laws approved by Congress were unconstitutional. Andrew Jackson was the first president to deploy the veto routinely on legislation he believed to be bad public policy (Watson 1987, 408–409).[14] It was not until after the Civil War that the veto was utilized at the kinds of rates seen regularly in the twentieth century. Despite enjoying large Democratic majorities, FDR brandished his veto pen on a record 372 occasions. These days it tends to be during divided government that the veto gets used, and overridden, the most. George W. Bush cast all eight of his vetoes after Republicans lost control of Congress in the 2006 elections. Four of them were quashed. Nixon and Ford together vetoed seventy-four bills, of which just over a quarter were overturned by Congress. The modern period is also one in which presidents utilize the veto strategically in a sort of bargaining game where threats of its deployment are designed to pressure Congress into altering legislation so that it is more acceptable to the White House (Cameron 2000). The veto can have profound effects on congressional action even when the president's pen stays in his desk drawer.

In addition, the Constitution grants the president a pocket veto, essentially the ability to ignore bills presented to him within ten days of congressional adjournment so as to kill them. Pocket vetoes are particularly effective because there is no constitutional obligation to transmit an accompanying veto message and they cannot be overridden. The DC Circuit Court of Appeals has ruled that presidents are only able to use them when the legislature is about to adjourn *sine die* at the end of a Congress, but in December 2007, at the culmination of the first session of the 110th Congress, President George W. Bush issued a pocket veto to block a defense authorization bill he felt would expose the new Iraqi government to lawsuits deriving from the Saddam Hussein era.[15] Because the Democratic-led Congress agreed with Bush on policy grounds, it did not challenge his authority to issue the veto. Whether Bush's decision to do so constituted an expansion of presidential power is not yet clear.

Today presidents have many other legislative powers. Congress frequently delegates the authority to make rules that have the force of law to executive agencies and bureaus, a practice begun during the New Deal. Overwhelmed by societal demands and recognizing a wealth of expertise in other parts of government, Congress passes laws that essentially permit the executive branch to formulate, revise, and finally promulgate legally enforceable rules. Congress regularly draws tight and clear parameters around this authority to guide and constrain political appointees and bureaucrats as they craft regulations. It is, however, not compelled to. Initially, "delegation" was supposed to adhere to an "intelligible principle," but more recently the Supreme

Court has confirmed "without deviation, Congress's ability to delegate power under broad standards."[16]

Congress has done a great deal of delegating since the 1940s, and the passage of the Administrative Procedures Act was important legislation that established general principles for executive rulemaking. The *Federal Register*, the compendium of all rules issued by federal agencies, consisted of about 152,000 pages in 2009 and 2010. At the same time, Congress passed laws that consumed just over 8,000 pages. The Volcker Rule that restricts the capital banks can use to make investments on their own behalf and that formed Section 619 of the Dodd-Frank financial services overhaul bill consumed 11 pages of statute but produced a rule 298 pages long that includes 383 explicit questions made up of 1,420 subquestions firms must answer (Patterson and Zibel 2011). The health care reform law passed in 2010 greatly extends coverage by relaxing Medicaid eligibility, creating health insurance exchanges in states, and penalizing those who do not get covered. It subjects higher income earners to more Medicare tax and levies those with expensive insurance policies. But it leaves many details for the executive branch to work out. CRS reported the legislation contains forty-one provisions that call upon the executive branch, specifically the secretary of health and human services, to make rules "filling in the details" of these broad directives (Copeland 2011).

Indeed, executive rule making has become such an important activity that the White House has sought tight control to ensure regulations are consistent with the administration's general policy outlook. Originally viewed as strictly technical and administrative, the process has become distinctly political. Since the 1980s, presidents have deployed the Office of Information and Regulatory Affairs (OIRA) within the Office of Management and Budget (OMB) to oversee and control rule making. President Reagan used OIRA to subject promulgated agency rules to a variety of tests, including a vigorous cost-benefit analysis. His administration amended or blocked hundreds of rules, particularly those from agencies like the Environmental Protection Agency (EPA) and Occupational Safety and Health Administration (OSHA). In an effort to ensure that rules were strictly consistent with presidential policy objectives, Bill Clinton extended Reagan's approach by inserting the White House into the rule writing process itself. His successor, George W. Bush, did likewise.[17]

Presidents themselves make unilateral decisions that have the force of law. The executive order is perhaps the best known way this is done. Since the first recorded one was issued in 1862, there had been 13,623 documented orders through September 2012. It is estimated, however, that for reasons of poor record keeping and secrecy, there may be as many as three times more than this excluded from the official count (Mayer 2001, 67). Executive orders cannot contradict existing statute or the Constitution, and they must be found within the president's existing and legitimate constitutional or congressionally delegated powers (Mayer 2001, 34–65). The directives are also necessarily narrower in scope than statute, but like agency rules they can have profound effects on the lives of millions of Americans. Many deal with matters such as executive branch organization, but others deal with controversial and important issues. In November 2001, for example, President George W. Bush signed an order establishing special military tribunals to try suspected foreign terrorists. Executive orders were used by Franklin Roosevelt to end racially discriminatory practices in the federal government's hiring policies and Harry Truman to desegregate the armed forces. In 1971, Nixon used the device to freeze prices and wages in an effort to combat rising inflation.

Presidential proclamations and executive agreements are similar to executive orders. Proclamations explicitly apply to people outside of government (Cooper 2002). Historically important proclamations include President Washington's assertion of US neutrality in a European conflict in 1793 and President Lincoln's Emancipation Proclamation in 1863. Presidents frequently proclaim areas hard hit by hurricanes and earthquakes disaster areas, and pardons granted American citizens are issued in the form of a proclamation. Executive agreements constitute accords made between a foreign country and the United States, for whom the president acts as the sole representative.[18] They have the same effect on domestic law as treaties, but they do not require Senate ratification. The practice began around 1900 and quickly became routine. With a two-thirds vote needed to ratify treaties and the increased regularity of divided government, presidents have found them particularly helpful in the conduct of foreign relations in the post–World War II period (Krutz and Peake 2009, 24–50). Since 1945, about 95 percent of all arrangements entered into with other countries have been executive agreements. Included in this number are the Paris Peace Accords that ended the Vietnam War in the early 1970s and the Algiers Accords that resolved the Iranian hostage crisis. Today trade deals are often a form of executive agreement. By granting trade promotion authority, Congress has repeatedly foregone the formal Senate ratification process and accepted one in which both bodies vote expeditiously on pacts in take-it-or-leave-it form. Approval of these measures require simple majority votes.

Although not strictly policy making, temporary appointments also allow presidents to bypass the Senate. Article II, Section 2, of the Constitution states, "The President shall have Power to fill up all Vacancies that may happen during the Recess of the Senate, by granting Commissions which shall expire at the End of their next Session." Despite this legal authority, such recess appointments are contentious and are frequently viewed by the Senate as an underhanded way of circumventing regular procedure. There are certainly a large number of them: there were 308 judicial recess appointments from 1789 to 2004 (Graves and Howard 2010). President Obama made 28 executive and judicial recess appointments in 2010 alone. Presidents tend to use the method to place individuals whose nominations have awaited Senate approval for some time, but they are also clearly a way of avoiding the likelihood of Senate rejection. President George W. Bush appointed controversial conservative judges Charles Pickering and William Pryor during Senate recesses; Democrats in the body had blocked them with filibusters. Recent publicized recess appointments in the executive branch include Bill Clinton's choice of Bill Lann Lee as assistant attorney general for civil rights and George W. Bush's pick of John Bolton to be ambassador to the United Nations. In January 2012, Barack Obama appointed Richard Cordray to head the Consumer Financial Protection Bureau created by Dodd-Frank. Cordray was originally nominated in May, but his selection was opposed by Senate Republicans on both its merits and because without a director the agency, disliked by conservatives because of its assumed antagonistic stance toward business, could not operate. Majority Leader Harry Reid kept the Senate in pro forma sessions that constituted the meeting of a handful of members for literally seconds every few days explicitly to prohibit the president from making recess appointments over the Christmas holidays. Reid had begun the practice in 2007 to prevent the Bush White House filling vacancies this way and, in an agreement with Republicans, continued it with Obama in office. Not surprisingly, the Cordray decision evoked howls of protest on Capitol Hill, even from some Democrats.[19]

Presidents have recently attempted to alter the meaning of statute after Congress has approved it. This is done with a statement released at the same time the president signs a bill into law. The action can have profound effects. Meaningful signing statements—excluding those that essentially express praise for the legislation—are a post hoc effort to alter the impact of a law by directing executive branch personnel to interpret it in a manner that seems to be inconsistent with its language. There have been hundreds of signing statements since President James Monroe issued the first one. Over time, presidents have become more aggressive in their use of the practice, and it has been quantitatively and qualitatively transformed (Ackerman 2010, 89–95; Kelley and Marshall 2010; Savage 2007, 228–249). George W. Bush issued signing statements affecting 161 statutes, including important ones essentially negating congressional directives on how suspected terrorists should be treated while in custody. Through the end of 2011, Barack Obama had penned 19, even though in 2008 he said he would avoid using them. These directives amount to a formal executive policy of ignoring hundreds of provisions in the law. Signing statements are likely to remain popular, not least because the courts have yet to limit their use.

From January 1997 to May 1998, when it was declared an unconstitutional violation of the principle of the separation of powers by the Supreme Court, the president, like forty-four governors, had the line-item veto—the power to block parts of bills and sign the remainder into law.[20] Introduced ostensibly to reduce the amount of pork-barrel spending in the federal budget, it was restricted to appropriations and some tax bills.[21] President Clinton used it eighty-two times on eleven pieces of legislation between August and December of 1997, and when established it was believed to be an important addition to presidential power.

The executive is not alone in having a significant weapon to block the actions of another branch negated by the courts, however. In 1983, the Supreme Court declared, in *INS v. Chadha*, the one-house legislative veto to be an unconstitutional violation of the principles of separation of powers and bicameralism.[22] Legislative vetoes are written into statutes and provide ways for Congress to influence the execution of a law after it has been passed. The technique survives and, according to a 2005 CRS report, Congress has enacted more than 400 of them, generally asking for an executive agency to get approval from a House or Senate committee as it exercises discretion in the implementation of law (Fisher 2005). Quite naturally, presidents have worked to mitigate their effects by pointing out their illegitimacy in signing statements that accompany the enabling legislation. In any case, post-*Chadha* legislative vetoes are hardly a robust check on presidential power.

Finally, two additional and recent examples of unilateral policy making by the executive are worth touching on briefly. In 2011, President Obama aggressively deployed his authority to issue states waivers from some of the reading and math proficiency requirements of NCLB. In June 2012 he extended the Department of Justice's existing prosecutorial power so that it could permit hundreds of thousands of people who came to the United States illegally as children to remain in the country. In both cases, Obama's directives meaningfully altered the practical effects of legislation passed by Congress.

The Popular Presidency

The third pillar of contemporary executive authority is the result of a confluence of factors. The president is the only elected official in Washington with the entire nation as his constituency. Over time, the many loyalties of Americans have attenuated to the point that today, and indeed for the past half century or so, their psychological ties to nation are significantly tighter than those to their place of work, race, religion, region, or state (Theiss-Morse 2009, 33–62). At the same time, the federal government's power has increased dramatically, and Washington has garnered the resources necessary to meet policy challenges that no state can. It is therefore only natural that Americans would look to the president to solve their problems.

Presidents have encouraged this. They work assiduously to communicate with the masses. As noted earlier, Obama spent several weeks during the fall of 2011 traveling the country "selling" his American Jobs Act. Obama had announced the bill in a televised address in early September, and he and aides had made themselves accessible to journalists wishing to cover it. Some research shows this strategy of "going public" can be a potent mobilizing device that places significant public pressure on legislators (Heith 2004; Kernell 2007), even if the impact of the president's message is sometimes mitigated by an increasingly fragmented media, public inattentiveness, and partisanship (Cohen 2008; Edwards 2003) and is most effective when the public is predisposed to agree with him (Canes-Wrone 2006). The strategy did not work particularly well on the jobs legislation, but it is even less easily used by Congress, a heterogeneous and more decentralized institution that does not enjoy the same kind of access to the media and admiration from the public.

Scholars believe presidents sometimes feel so emboldened by public support that they embrace the notion of a "plebiscitary presidency." This is essentially the idea of president as sovereign, the presidency as a very personal office expected to serve the public interest and ignore interference from mediating institutions like Congress and political parties (Lowi 1985). It is not unrelated to President George W. Bush's idea of the president as "decider"; the notion that once elected, presidents legitimately and unilaterally make the real decisions that shape American public life.[23]

The Executive Branch's Control of Foreign Policy

The fourth and final pillar is foreign policy. Hamilton argued that the Constitution granted the president and Congress joint possession over foreign policy (Hamilton, Madison, and Jay 1982, 457–8). More recently, the Constitution's words on the issue have been characterized as an "invitation to struggle" (Corwin 1957, 171). It is clear, however, that the executive has come to dominate foreign policy. Tocqueville noted on his visits to the United States that "it is chiefly in its foreign relations that the executive power of a nation finds occasion to exert its skill and its strength" (Tocqueville 1945, 1:126). Jefferson realized this even earlier. "The transaction of business with foreign nations," he wrote, "is executive altogether" (Ford 2010, 50).

The discussions of foreign policy throughout this book reveal this quite dramatically. The executive branch is uniquely capable of acquiring critical information and then making decisions quickly and secretly. As a practical matter, Congress has accepted its secondary role. For example, it has not formally declared war for nearly seventy years. In 1947, it permitted the White House to exercise greater power by drawing the executive branch's disparate foreign policy units together into the National Security Council.[24]

The Congressional Response

Executive aggrandizement has been met with apathy, even complicity, from Congress. There have, however, been some rather spectacular episodes when Congress has fought back and asserted its rights and interests. In the post–World War II period, this combativeness has taken several forms. Perhaps the most obvious is the investigation. When Congress believes the president or other executive branch officials have acted in an unethical or illegal manner, it sometimes works diligently in an appraisal of events, an action that asserts congressional authority and prerogatives in the institution's relationship with the other elected branch. Ultimately these investigations might have little meaningful impact on executive behavior. The Senate Permanent Select Committee on Intelligence ruffled few feathers when it analyzed the Bush administration's use of information prior to the war with Iraq in 2003. Its report was released in three stages between 2004 and 2008 and came too late to make much of a difference to American policy.[25]

Often congressional inquiries do have impact, however. In late 1986, press accounts, subsequently confirmed by individuals involved, revealed that the National Security

Council had secretly traded arms to Iran in return for the release of hostages held in Lebanon and that the proceeds had been funneled to Contra rebels in Nicaragua. These actions were unlawful and contradicted the stated policy of the Reagan administration. National Security Adviser John Poindexter resigned immediately, and the president fired an aide implicated by the revelations, Oliver North. Reagan also set up a commission, headed by former senator John Tower, to look into the events that quickly became known as Iran-Contra. Congress created a parallel joint House and Senate committee, chaired by Rep. Lee Hamilton (D-IN) and Sen. Daniel Inouye (D-HI). Although the Tower Commission reported first and did blame President Reagan for his role in the affair, the congressional report was more thorough, deemed more credible, and markedly more scathing in its criticism of the president. Its release in November 1987 essentially killed any remaining influence Reagan had in Congress and assisted in several high-profile successful criminal investigations undertaken by independent counsel Lawrence Walsh. Congress acted deliberately, judiciously, and quite effectively.

The Clinton presidency had its reputation damaged irreparably by the investigation that first focused on Whitewater, a real estate development in the Ozark Mountains in which the Clintons had invested. The money was lost in a complex series of movements orchestrated by the first couple's partner in the deal, Jim McDougal.[26] Examinations of the matter, initially led by independent counsels Robert Fiske and Kenneth Starr, soon expanded into a whole host of controversies surrounding the Clinton administration—such as Travelgate, Filegate, and the suicide of Vince Foster.[27] The congressional investigation accelerated after Republicans took control of the House and Senate in January 1995. Sen. Alfonse D'Amato (R-NY) led a special Whitewater committee that issued an eight-hundred-page report in June 1996. Democrats issued a minority report excoriating it as a partisan witch hunt and insisted its credibility was undermined by the lack of clear evidence demonstrating wrongdoing on the president's part. Republicans thought otherwise. D'Amato argued the investigation provided "revealing insight into the workings of an American Presidency that misused its power, circumvented the limits on its authority, and attempted to manipulate the truth" (Labaton 1996).

That was just the beginning. In January 1998, at Starr's request, Attorney General Janet Reno expanded the scope of the investigation that had begun nearly four years earlier. The independent counsel was permitted to examine accusations that the president had impeded a sexual harassment suit brought against him by former Arkansas state employee Paula Jones by misleading investigators as to the nature of his relationship with a White House intern, Monica Lewinsky. After several months in which Lewinsky and presidential aides like Vernon Jordan and Sidney Blumenthal testified to a grand jury, President Clinton, on the evening of his own testimony in August, admitted publicly to an inappropriate relationship. Three weeks later, Starr released his report to the

House, recommending it begin impeachment proceedings. After dramatic hearings in the Judiciary Committee and a historic floor debate, the House ultimately impeached Clinton on two counts—one each of perjury and obstruction of justice—in December 1998. Two months later, the Senate voted to acquit him.[28]

More recently, the Obama administration sustained some damage from a series of investigations by House Republicans. In April 2012 the General Services Administration's head was forced to resign after a series of congressional hearings publicized excessive and wasteful spending at the agency. A $535 million loan guarantee made by the administration to a solar energy company, Solyndra, that went bankrupt came under scrutiny. The most dramatic example of Republicans' legislative assertiveness, however, came when the House voted 255–67—with many Democrats boycotting—to hold Attorney General Eric Holder in contempt of Congress for failing to hand over documents related to the investigation into the "Fast and Furious" gun-walking operation in Mexico. Many of the firearms were lost to government officials and ended up in the hands of drug traffickers; one was traced to the killing of a US border control agent. A report issued by the Department of Justice's inspector general in September 2012 admonished senior staff and stated twelve others should be reviewed for possible sanctions.

However, the most consequential congressional investigation of the past half century was indubitably Watergate. After a June 1972 break-in at the Democratic National Committee headquarters, a series of inquiries ultimately led to the resignation of President Richard Nixon just over two years later. The full extent of Nixon's involvement in the crime will never be known, but evidence that he was part of a cover-up of the White House's role became undeniable. The burglars were supported financially by the Campaign to Reelect the President (CREEP), which had many members, including Attorney General John Mitchell, G. Gordon Liddy, E. Howard Hunt, and Charles Colson, who worked in the administration. Prominent Nixon aides like John Dean, John Ehrlichman, and Chief of Staff H. R. Haldeman were forced to resign and were later convicted on charges of perjury and obstruction of justice as they worked to protect themselves and the president from inquisitors. Although much of the information in the matter was made public by the Department of Justice and journalists—notably Carl Bernstein and Bob Woodward of the *Washington Post*—the congressional investigations, led by Judiciary Committee Chair Peter Rodino (D-NJ) in the House and special Watergate committee chair Sam Ervin (D-NC) in the Senate, were critical in the collective effort to hold executive branch officials and the president to account. In fact, the congressional Watergate inquiry represented a pivotal moment. Just as the exploits of Bernstein and Woodward influenced a new generation of aggressive journalists (Feldstein 2004), the congressional investigations greatly emboldened the institution in its relationship with the executive. A new and younger group of House members—many, like Tom Harkin (D-IA), Henry Waxman (D-CA), and Tim Wirth

(D-CO), elected in 1974 and called the Watergate Babies—saw oversight of presidential behavior as an important part of their responsibilities.[29]

During these recent episodes, congressional assertiveness has been as robust as it was in the past. Rep. Thomas Fitzsimons (Fed-PA) conducted probably the first important congressional investigation of the executive when he looked into Gen. Arthur Saint Clair's defeat at the hands of Ohio Indians in 1792.[30] In 1868, the Senate came one vote shy of removing President Andrew Johnson from office, ostensibly for his violation of the Tenure of Office Act. Johnson was accused of illegally removing his Secretary of War Edwin Stanton but had become a target of Radical Republicans in Congress who doubted his commitment to Reconstruction. In 1872–1873, the Crédit Mobilier investigation into the defrauding of the federal government by Union Pacific brought down a vice president, Schuyler Colfax. The Teapot Dome investigation of 1922–1924 toppled Secretary of the Interior Albert B. Fall, who had traded government oil field leases for his own personal gain. The episode was also important because the Supreme Court upheld Congress's right to compel testimony.[31] In 1958, a House investigation led to the resignation of White House Chief of Staff Sherman Adams.[32] But if anything the frequency of investigations has actually increased a bit over time (Bruns, Hostetter, and Smock 2011). If investigations indicate power, then the Congress of today is clearly not especially weak.

Congress sometimes enacts legislation that expands its authority or at least undermines executive power. Spectacular examples from the past include the Pendleton Act of 1883 that instituted the merit system in the federal bureaucracy and greatly curbed presidential patronage powers, the Legislative Reorganization Act of 1946 that stipulated "careful watchfulness" by congressional committees as they monitored executive behavior, and the proposal of the Twenty-Second Amendment limiting presidential terms to two in 1947. As a response to perceived aggrandizement on the part of the Johnson and Nixon administrations, we have already noted Congress passed the War Powers Resolution in 1973 and the Budget and Impoundment Control Act in 1974. More recently, in 1996 to be exact, Congress passed the Congressional Review Act. This legislation allows the legislature to review rules passed by executive agencies and, by joint resolution, negate them. Although there have been several high-profile efforts to reverse regulations—on issues like union elections, health care reform, air pollution, and the mitigation of mad cow disease—only one has actually succeeded and passed both chambers, that preventing ergonomics policy from the Department of Labor in 2001.[33] Still, the Congressional Review Act remains available and, if used to its fullest potential, could have significant consequences for legislative-executive relations (Harvard Law Review 2009).

Congress has other similar tools. By "sunsetting," or limiting the length of time a law is operational, it effectively brings to a close implementation of a policy or program and allows itself the discretion over whether the responsible agency should continue in its execution. Forcing continual reauthorization of laws is therefore a form of oversight (Hall 2004). The limitation rider is a provision added to appropriations bills that prevents executive agencies from spending money for particular purposes. According to Jason MacDonald (2010), about three hundred of them are established annually. The riders provide Congress with additional capability to influence agencies' implementation of policy after it has been originally enacted.

Sometimes Congress goes to court to check executive power. This, however, has not proven to be a particularly successful strategy. Most of the time, the federal courts determine interbranch squabbles are a political question or the congressional plaintiff does not have standing. It will, as a result, refuse to rule on them. In 1979, the Supreme Court declined to intervene when members of Congress, led by Sen. Barry Goldwater (R-AZ), brought a case challenging President Jimmy Carter's unilateral nullification of a treaty made with China. Legislators have also sued unsuccessfully to prevent presidents' conducting military action in Grenada, the Persian Gulf, and the former Yugoslavia. Sometimes congressional power is furthered, as Supreme Court rulings against the line-item veto and for the independent counsel statute illustrate.[34] But it seems that when the courts do explicitly take sides, the executive's interests tend to win out. In addition to the diminishment of the legislative veto in the *Chadha* case, for example, the court ruled in 1986 that, because Congress cannot control how laws are executed, it could not delegate this particular authority to one of its agents. In the Gramm-Rudman-Hollings deficit reduction legislation, Congress had therefore unlawfully authorized the comptroller general to make recommendations to the president on how to reduce spending to meet budget targets.[35] More recently, the Supreme Court ruled that Congress's creation of the Public Company Accounting Oversight Board violated the separation of powers. The panel's members, supervised by the SEC, could only be removed for cause. This stipulation, according to Chief Justice John Roberts, unconstitutionally restricted the president's capacity to ensure the laws are faithfully executed.[36]

I think it would be fair to say Congress's efforts to maintain a balance of power with the executive have been mixed at best and the general belief that the executive branch continues to dominate—and frequently exhibit unchallenged imperialistic traits—is confirmed. Members often seem unwilling to stand up for their institution. Research demonstrates that oversight—whether measured by reports, hearings, or legislation designed to clip the executive's wings—increases during divided government, particularly in an era like the present when the parties are polarized ideologically (Kriner and Schwartz 2008; Parker and Dull 2009; Smith 2003; Walling 2006). The opposite occurs under unified government. As a result, there are times, such as 2003–2006 under George W. Bush and 2009–2010 under Barack Obama, when supervision of the administration and the promotion of congressional interests are neglected and deemed unnecessary because of partisan ties to the White House. Throughout 2005 and 2006, the Republican majority was criticized repeatedly by Democrats for not scrutinizing the conduct of the Iraq War sufficiently. In 2010 the Republican minority attempted unsuccessfully to get the ruling Democrats to investigate wasteful spending on the stimulus and Fannie Mae and Freddie Mac.

Still, regardless of Washington's partisan makeup, oversight happens, even if it is reactive and not terribly systematic. The public continues to be cynical of government, including the executive branch, and the country's fiscal challenges ought to provide Congress with an incentive to monitor the federal government's efficiency. There are now public interest groups—like Taxpayers for Common Sense and Common Cause—that scrutinize agency behavior and policy making. The new media, increasingly assertive and ubiquitous, also shines light on executive branch operations. Together, they are apt to draw public and congressional attention to unethical and malfeasant executive behavior. When this happens, legislators can issue subpoenas, write reports, and chastise officials in the name of the public interest without having to undertake the thankless and time-consuming preparatory work. So as to harness the full positive effect, they make sure much of this happens in transparent committee proceedings.[37]

Congressional oversight, therefore, seems to be done primarily for the electoral benefit of members. Promoting the power of Congress in its relationship with the administration is really of secondary concern, particularly because, as a 2006 Indiana University poll conducted by the Center on Congress revealed, only a very small number of Americans believe restraining executive power is Congress's principal responsibility—just 14 percent of respondents said "checking the power of the president" was "the most important" task for "individual members of Congress," whereas 46 percent said "making decisions on national policy issues," and 28 percent replied "bringing federal dollars back to their districts." When there are no obvious opportunities to place an unpopular president of the opposition party in a difficult position, pushback is undertaken sporadically and halfheartedly. Congress falls short of meeting this particular benchmark.

BENCHMARK #37
Congress should interfere with the courts only
when its prerogatives are threatened.

Justification

As for the courts, Congress is probably better advised to watch from afar and engage only when necessary. Judicial independence is critical to modern democracy (Russell and O'Brien 2001). As Montesquieu (1914, Book 6, Chapter 6), another French Enlightenment thinker who greatly influenced the Founders, wrote in his *Spirit of the Laws*, "There is no liberty, if the judiciary power be not separated from the legislative and executive."[38] However, although courts should do their work with minimal outside interference, the Constitution clearly provides Congress with the power to establish tribunals below the Supreme Court, shape court jurisdictions and the number of judges who serve, and confirm presidential appointments to the federal bench. Moreover, the federal courts have significant powers of their own and left completely unchecked might deploy them in a harmful manner, a threat made more worrisome, and perhaps more likely, because judges are unelected and life tenured. The most important of these is judicial review, or the authority to declare acts of Congress unconstitutional and therefore void, that the Supreme Court established with its decision in the 1803 case of *Marbury v. Madison*. Beyond its routine responsibilities, Congress should push against the courts when, and probably only when, legislative prerogatives are clearly threatened.

Appraisal

Congress's relationship with the federal courts has been far less combative than its experience with the executive branch. There have certainly been times in the country's history when the legislature has taken meaningful action to expand its power over the judicial branch, however. In the very first Congress, it passed the Judiciary Act establishing a federal bench with explicit limits on its power. Since then, scholars suggest there have been four eras of congressional assertiveness toward the courts (Geyh 2006, 51–108). The first, during the early years of Jefferson's presidency, constituted an angry response to the Supreme Court's proposition that it could exercise judicial review and rule acts of Congress unconstitutional. The one and only impeachment of a Supreme Court justice, that of Samuel Chase, took place in 1804. Jeffersonians also reversed some egregious Federalist court packing with the repeal of the 1801 Judiciary Act and worked assiduously to limit the terms of federal judges and make it easier to remove them (Ellis 1971). The second period occurred when Jackson was president. It was characterized by his congressional allies' efforts to make judges more accountable to the public and the legislature less accountable to their rulings. There were serious efforts to have the federal judiciary elected and to strip it of its ability to review appeals from state courts (Geyh 2006, 55–56). The third came just after the Civil War as Radical Republican members of Congress exacted retribution for the courts' role in protecting slavery and worked to limit its influence over Reconstruction. They effectively reduced the Supreme Court to seven members in 1866, and the following year, so as to protect the legal foundations of Reconstruction, Congress passed the Habeas Corpus Act to prevent the court from adjudicating on the constitutionality of military commissions used to try civilians in the South (Wert 2006, 73–106). The final period constituted a liberal backlash to a Supreme Court that became increasingly more conservative through the first third of the twentieth century. The highlight is probably the court-packing plan of President Franklin Roosevelt and many of his Democratic supporters in Congress. Although the proposal was never realized, the pressure exerted may well have been the decisive factor in persuading the Supreme Court to stop negating New Deal legislation.[39]

Today much of Congress's forcefulness is witnessed during the Senate's judicial confirmation process. Since the late 1980s, Supreme Court nominees have faced intense scrutiny by senators, largely because the public and organized interests on both the left and right have expressed great interest in the outcomes.[40] In 1987, Robert Bork was picked for the court by President Reagan. Bork's conservative record ignited a firestorm, and liberal groups assailed the selection with energy never before seen in the process (Bronner 2007). The Democratic-led Senate ultimately rejected him by a vote of 42–58. After sensational and riveting hearings in which he was accused of sexual harassment, Justice Clarence Thomas was only narrowly confirmed by the Senate in 1991. This time the conservative groups supporting the nominee seemed a bit more prepared to do battle.

It is becoming even more difficult for lower court appointments to win approval, particularly during a divided government or if they lack significant experience (Binder and Maltzman 2002; Hendershot 2010; Martinek, Kemper, and Van Winkle 2002). Ideological polarization and heightened partisanship have meant home-state senators are frequently unwilling to support lower court nominees nominated by a president of the other party's—under a principle known as senatorial courtesy, these judges need the assent of both senators from their own state to have their names forwarded (Binder 2007). Opponents have other means to block appointments. The majority can refuse to send the nominee's name to the floor by preventing the Judiciary Committee from holding hearings. The minority can filibuster once the nomination reaches the floor—during George W. Bush's presidency Democrats obstructed many high-profile appointments, including those of Miguel Estrada, Janice Rogers Brown, Priscilla Owen, William Pryor, and Charles Pickering. Even after the famous bipartisan Gang of Fourteen of largely moderate senators agreed in 2005 to reserve the filibuster only for extraordinary circumstances, Senate confirmation can be challenging.[41] President Obama saw most of his lower court appointments approved in frequently lopsided votes, but there have been delays—perhaps the best example is Goodwin Liu's nomination to the Ninth Circuit that was ultimately withdrawn in 2011 after a lengthy Republican filibuster. Whereas Obama's Supreme Court nominees Sonia Sotomayor and Elena Kagan made it through relatively unscathed, George W. Bush's pick of Samuel Alito only passed the Republican-controlled Senate 58–42 in early 2006. Bush's legal counsel, Harriet Miers, was swiftly withdrawn after she attracted opposition from conservatives for her policy positions and consternation over her lack of judicial experience.

It is probably the case that congressional assertiveness in the confirmation process is aimed as much at the president as it is the courts. This cannot be said of judicial impeachments. These do not happen particularly frequently, however. Only fifteen federal judges have ever been impeached by the House, of these eight were removed by the Senate and three resigned before the upper body could dispose of their cases. Although two of them were very recent—District Court Judge Samuel B. Kent was impeached and resigned in 2009 and District Court Judge Thomas Porteous was impeached and removed in 2010—trends do not suggest a newly aggressive Congress. The judges' actions were so egregious—Kent was already serving prison time for lying in a sex-abuse case, and Porteous was demonstrably corrupt—that they were both impeached on several counts by the House in unanimous votes.

Legislative efforts are also often suggestive of a Congress that desires to be on friendly terms with the judiciary. Congress certainly responds to Supreme Court decisions, but with as much legislation codifying court rulings as efforts to override them (Staudt, Lindstaedt, and O'Connor 2007). For its part, the Supreme Court is acutely aware of the policy preferences of presidents and members of Congress and acts in a constrained way so as not to antagonize its overseers (Bailey and Maltzman 2011; Segal, Westerland, and Lindquist 2011). Scholars have shown the conservative Rehnquist court increased the frequency by which it voided liberal laws after Republicans took control of Congress in 1995 (Harvey and Friedman 2006).[42] This can be construed as a form of indirect congressional influence.

Still the courts clearly irritate Congress on occasions. Conservatives, particularly, have taken umbrage. Between 1937 and the late 1960s, the Supreme Court moved decidedly leftward, especially under the leadership of Chief Justice Earl Warren. It repeatedly handed down liberal decisions in cases on segregation, voting rights, criminal procedure, and the First Amendment. Although not pursued seriously by Congress, there was even a fairly energetic public effort, led by the John Birch Society, to impeach Warren (Kyvig 2008, 35–60). Richard Nixon made criticism of the Warren court a part of his 1968 campaign (Keck 2004, 107–111). Despite successive Republican presidencies and the appointment of conservative jurists at the federal level, these attacks on the judiciary as an essentially liberal and inappropriately activist institution have become more frequent and forceful.[43] In 1996, the Republican Party platform noted the Supreme Court had "overstepped its authority" and "usurped the right of citizen legislators." More recent platforms have used similar language (Siegel 2010). The congressional criticism possibly reached a crescendo around 2004 (Miller 2009, 17–19). That year, the House voted to strip federal courts of jurisdiction over cases involving same-sex marriage and the Pledge of Allegiance. In the spring of 2005, and in a frenzy of judge-bashing, House Majority Leader Tom DeLay (R-TX) led a successful effort to have the case of Terri Schiavo removed from state to federal court. Schiavo was in a vegetative condition, and her husband had asked for her to be taken off life support and allowed to die. Florida courts generally supported his decision, but legal and political efforts by Schiavo's parents prevented it from happening. After these efforts were exhausted, conservative congressional Republicans immediately took up the cause and passed the bill providing for federal court jurisdiction in an unusual Sunday session. Their efforts were fruitless, and a series of federal court decisions confirmed earlier state verdicts that Schiavo's husband was perfectly within his rights.[44]

Cumulatively, recent congressional action does not amount to much. It is largely saber rattling and political posturing. In reality, Congress does not aggressively use the legislative, impeachment, and appointment processes to shape judicial policy making. Members are much more interested in employing the courts as a punching bag. Conservatives, particularly, see opposition to the judiciary as a way of activating base supporters—indeed, the issue quickly became an important part of the campaign for the party's 2012 presidential nomination and assumed even greater prominence after the Supreme Court upheld most of the Obama health care reform legislation in the summer of 2012. It is hard to disagree with assessments of Congress's current posture toward the federal judiciary as "constitutionally casual" (Baker 2007, 119–124) or part of a "tradition of congressional restraint" (Geyh 2006). Congress will seek to limit judicial independence when it feels the public supports such action (Clark 2011; Ura and Wohlfarth 2010). The Supreme Court will be more leery of challenging Congress when legislative positions are the same as the public's (Casillas, Enns, and Wohlfarth 2011; Giles, Blackstone, and Vining 2008). But, as a general matter, the court is popular. At nearly every point in time over the past couple of decades, a majority of Americans have stated they approve of the job the Supreme Court is doing. Even after *Bush v. Gore*, the controversial decision that effectively made George W. Bush the winner of the 2000 presidential election, public support for the court did not fall much (Gibson, Caldeira, and Spence 2003). The only time this number had dipped below 50 percent was in the summer of 2012 when the court's disposition of the health care case split the country deeply along partisan lines. Americans largely remain enamored by what has been called the Cult of the Robe (Murphy 1964, 16–17), holding a pervasive and powerful reverence for the Supreme Court.

Meaningful congressional action in the legislative-judicial relationship is therefore infrequent. As the benchmark suggests, this is appropriate. All other things being equal, Congress should provide the courts with greater autonomy than it does the president.

CONCLUSION

Effective oversight of the executive and judicial branches is challenging. It requires vigilance and a concerted and collective effort to respond if legislative interests are seriously threatened. These interests are not easily discerned and vary depending on which branch Congress is relating to. Much oversight is unrewarding. Citizens are more likely to notice lawmaking and constituency service because these have palpable effects on their lives. Interbranch tussles seem esoteric and, when societal problems are in urgent need of solutions, distracting. But Congress still monitors and attempts

BENCHMARK FOR CONGRESSIONAL PERFORMANCE	APPRAISAL
36. Congress should maintain a balance of power with the executive.	Largely not met
37. Congress should interfere with the courts only when its prerogatives are threatened.	Largely met

TABLE 8.1 Appraising congressional performance on benchmarks related to vigorous checking and balancing

to supervise the other parts of government. Members are probably not motivated by collective and distant institutional concerns when they do this. It is policy and elections that drive much of this behavior (Kriner and Schwartz 2008; Parker and Dull 2009). These are members' personal and immediate interests. Court bashing and revelatory investigations into the executive branch can result in front-page stories. Much oversight might not have meaningful or lasting effects on legislative power, but some of it garners attention and shows legislators to be acting in the public interest.

The motives might not be what we want. For some, Congress is not fighting back against executive and judicial power energetically enough. The legislature has not, however, surrendered completely. When directly attacked, or when entrepreneurial members see an opportunity to advance their interests, Congress frequently stands up for itself and sometimes even throws a few punches of its own. I think its mixed performance on the two benchmarks in this chapter, shown in Table 8.1, is a reasonable reflection of this.

9

Appraising Congress

Congress's performance ought to be appraised thoughtfully and comprehensively. It is our national legislature. It makes public policy that directly affects the daily lives of 310 million people and the welfare of not just this nation but, because of American might, the world. This book constitutes an effort to offer appraisal in an objective fashion. I created a series of benchmarks for Congress to meet. These benchmarks were built from a number of basic aspirations for congressional performance found in normative political theory and the thinking of Americans, particularly influential ones like the Founders. The benchmarks are then given precision by an evaluation of congressional history and the performance of national parliaments and American state legislative bodies. The benchmarks are desirable and reasonable.

As Table 9.1 reveals, Congress approximates much of this desired behavior and meets or exceeds most of the specific benchmarks. In other words, it tends to do the right thing in a manner matching or even surpassing best practices in peer bodies, including Congresses of the past. To be sure, of the six aspirations, its performance can be reasonably criticized on four. But even on these the assessment is at worst mixed. Of the thirty-seven benchmarks I set for it, it meets or largely meets twenty-three; two additional benchmarks are reached by the House but not the Senate. Congress therefore clearly does some things well. On many dimensions, its membership is pretty diverse. In the aggregate, at least, members' policy preferences closely track public opinion. It has transparent proceedings and procedures that balance broad and equal participation with necessary centralization to maintain efficiency. It can be very productive when it needs to be and has helped steer the United States to the pinnacle of world economic and military power. It would not be inaccurate to claim that, in both the absolute and relative senses, it is a pretty good legislature.

This raises a question: If Congress is performing at a reasonably high standard, why is it so maligned? The public, it is fair to say, loathes it. Unfair though this assessment may be, it is not entirely inexplicable.

ASPIRATION FOR CONGRESSIONAL PERFORMANCE	BENCHMARK FOR CONGRESSIONAL PERFORMANCE	APPRAISAL
A robust representative democracy	1. To reflect the will of the American people, Congress should track alterations in the policy preferences of the general public quite closely.	Largely met
	2. About half of members' time and resources should be committed to local issues and concerns.	Met
	3. At least 25% of members should be women.	Not met
	4. At least 9% of members should be African-American and 3% Hispanic.	House met, Senate not met
	5. Membership should reflect patterns of military service in the general population.	Met
	6. Membership should reflect patterns of religious affiliation in the general population.	Met
	7. Membership should reflect patterns of occupational diversity in the general population.	Met
A transparent, accessible, and trustworthy legislature	8. Congress's daily business should be visible to the public.	Met
	9. Congress should have many formally recorded plenary votes.	Met
	10. Congress should have open committee proceedings.	Met
	11. Congress should have rules that are simple, clear, and few in number.	Not met
	12. Congress should have member disclosure requirements that exceed those of most of the American states.	Met
	13. Members should have adequate staff—about ten to fifteen for each.	Met
	14. Members should spend about half of their time in the district or state.	Met
	15. Congress should have meaningful turnover: approximately 20 percent of the House should turn over each Congress, about 50 percent of the Senate each six years.	Not met
	16. Congress should have sizeable proportions of members who take at least several distinct paths to office.	Largely not met
	17. Congressional membership should not just be for the rich; the mean wealth of members should put them somewhere close to halfway between the average and richest Americans.	Not met
	18. Members of Congress should generally be educated and a large majority of them have college degrees.	Met
	19. To maintain the public's trust, unethical and illegal behavior of members of Congress should be very rare.	Not met

Category	Statement	Status
Desirable principles of organization	20. The floor agenda should be set by entities that constitute a representative and fairly large but manageable subgroup of the membership — perhaps 10 to 20 percent of the body.	Met
	21. A majority should be able to bring floor debate on a bill to a close.	House met, Senate unmet
	22. All members should have approximately the same number of committee assignments.	Met
	23. The House and Senate should have an appropriate number of committees — perhaps around fifteen to twenty.	Met
	24. Bill introduction procedures should be open.	Met
	25. Restrictions on members' floor amendments should be minimal.	Met
A healthy legislative process	26. Formal congressional proceedings should have significant influence on members' preferences and actions.	Not met
	27. Formal congressional proceedings should consist of broad and equal participation.	Largely met
	28. Formal congressional proceedings should reveal frequent interaction among members.	Largely not met
	29. Congress should be productive when it needs to be — demonstrating this by making around four hundred total and twelve important laws per Congress.	Met
	30. The United States should enter military conflict under strict conditions that, among other things, minimize costs and maximize the probability of success.	Largely met
Effective policy	31. The US economy should be among the strongest in the world.	Met
	32. The federal budget deficit should be less than about 5 percent of GDP.	Largely not met
	33. Congress should use sound principles when managing the country's financial liabilities.	Not met
	34. Congress should pass laws that are short and general.	Not met
	35. Congress should make policy that is consistent across issue areas.	Largely met
Vigorous checking and balancing	36. Congress should maintain a balance of power with the executive.	Largely not met
	37. Congress should interfere with the courts only when its prerogatives are threatened.	Largely met

TABLE 9.1 **Appraising congressional performance**

First, Congress does not provide the type of governance Americans want. Americans are "stealth democrats" and believe government should be more like a business (Hibbing and Theiss-Morse 2002). It should be organized hierarchically and operate efficiently by coming to decisions swiftly and in consensus. In doing so, it should not bother citizens with details or constant requests for validation. The executive branch might be capable of making policy in this manner, but Congress is decidedly not. It seems polarized and partisan and hopelessly gridlocked. Members intrude into people's lives—generally via media like television—discussing complicated issues that do not ever seem to get resolved.

But Congress should not change in this way. As we have noted, debate and deliberation are healthy. Legislators should disagree with one another. They need to ask for guidance from constituents occasionally because they are democratically elected officials and the public would soon get upset if they did not. It is likely, therefore, improved performance would only intensify public disparagement of the institution. Americans will only be really satisfied if Congress is remade and its mission dramatically altered. As Hibbing and Larimer (2008) note, "it may well be the case that it is difficult for any large, collegial, transparent, lawmaking body in an incredibly diverse country facing serious challenges to endear itself to the people."

Second, Congress sometimes passes legislation opposed by a sizeable proportion of the American public—as the Obama health care legislation revealed. But the people seem to blame Congress more often for matters over which the institution does not have significant control. We might criticize Congress because the economy is particularly bad or the world an increasingly threatening place—indeed, studies have shown congressional approval is related to the strength of macroeconomic indicators (Rudolph 2003; Stimson 2004). But these are facts of life that, as we have noted, congressional action is sometimes capable of affecting minimally.

Third, Congress is the victim of the general cynicism Americans have about public institutions. It is very difficult for it to be viewed as successful in this environment. It is true Congress is held in lower esteem than state governments and the executive and judicial branches, but public support for all has been dropping precipitously over the past forty years. The process began in the immediate aftermath of Watergate and the Vietnam War and continues unabated—with perhaps the exception of several months after the 9/11 attacks—through to today. In September 2011, the proportion of respondents to a Gallup poll who had a "great deal" or a "fair amount" of confidence in the "men and women in political life in this country" had dropped by twenty-five percentage points from its high water mark of 68 percent in 1974.[1]

The fourth reason is that Congress is a decentralized institution and, as such, has difficulty responding to criticism. At any one time, the presidency is the president, and he is clearly motivated to protect and promote the interests of the office he occupies. Congress is made up of 535 individuals in two distinct bodies whose prime interests are getting re-elected and enacting public policy consistent with their preferences and the wishes of their constituents. Members frequently find attacking their own institution helps with re-election, especially because they are considerably more popular as individuals than they are collectively (Davidson, Oleszek, and Lee 2012, 488–490; Durr, Gilmour, and Wolbrecht 1997). The strategy was prevalent in 2010 when candidates ran on platforms that included drastic cuts in member pay and such proposals as forcing legislators to live in army barracks or spend three-quarters of their time in state capitols. When the media report on issues like partisan conflict, gridlock, the influence of special interests, and wasteful spending, members find it more profitable to confirm these impressions with their public comments, press releases, and floor speeches than to stand up for Congress and prove them inaccurate. Some legislators are interested in defending the institution's reputation, but, because such behavior has little electoral payoff and is not rewarded on the Hill, they are few in number (Adler, Ensley, and Wilkerson 2008; Lipinski, Bianco, and Work 2003).

Finally, as this analysis reveals, Congress's performance is not unambiguously strong. Although the United States has a vigorous representative democracy, congressional elections rarely bring great change in membership, even when the public seems to want it. In 2010, a historic election in which the majority party lost more seats than in any other since 1938, 85 percent of incumbents were still re-elected to the House. The House and Senate are not particularly diverse with regards race, ethnicity, and gender. Both bodies' fundamental procedures are desirable, but each has added, and probably unnecessarily, layers of complexity that undermine transparency and the public's comprehension of how they work. When Congress wants to be productive it can, but it does not always produce policy of the greatest quality. Proceedings are accessible and broadly participated in, but the substance of members' contributions is not what we might like. Instead of debate and deliberation, the public witnesses a series of speeches from the House and Senate floors. Members are not always very interested in promoting legislative interests, and the executive branch, as a result, often has the upper hand in its relationship with Congress. There are still too many examples of unethical and illegal behavior.

Congress does better than many give it credit for. But it is far from perfect. With the shortcomings discussed earlier in mind, we can identify some reforms that might improve congressional performance. These reforms are modest and attainable and would bring positive effects.

ENHANCING CONGRESSIONAL PERFORMANCE

Membership of both the House and Senate changes at a very low rate. Meaningful turnover is critical for an accessible and accountable legislature, and it is one of the benchmarks clearly left unmet. One obvious way to rectify the situation is to establish term limits for members. During the early 1990s, there was a vigorous effort to do just this. US Term Limits, a grassroots organization, pushed particularly hard. Between 1990 and 1995, twenty-three states acted unilaterally to restrict the number of congressional terms members of their delegations could serve. When in 1995 the Supreme Court declared these rules unconstitutional, congressional Republicans took up the cause.[2] Term limits were a central element of House Republicans' Contract with America. The party focused on a proposal that would allow members of both bodies to complete twelve years—six House terms and two in the Senate. It never reached anywhere close to the two-thirds vote necessary to be sent on its way to the states as a constitutional amendment.[3]

Although term limits would force turnover, they would be harmful in other ways, as demonstrated by studies of the fifteen states that have the policy for their legislative bodies. Understanding that their time in the House or Senate is finite, members have fewer incentives to invest in necessary periodic institutional maintenance and in forging the kinds of relationships with colleagues that foster an institutional identity. They feel less of a need to attend to public opinion (Carey et al. 2006). They seem less capable of maintaining their states' fiscal health (Lewis 2012). They focus on their careers beyond the body and "go for a big, short-term splash and leave the long-term mess to the next wave of their successors" (Mann and Ornstein 2012, 127). As a result, the legislature's standing relative to the other branches is reduced (Bowser and Moncrief 2007; Powell 2007).

Making elections more competitive could increase turnover. One way to do this would be to change campaign finance laws. The goal, presumably, would be to greatly reduce the disparity in the amount of money raised and spent by incumbents and challengers. Public financing could do this, and capping contributions to and expenditures from candidates in the current privately financed system would at least put candidates' treasuries on a more equal footing. However, the most important recent effort to overhaul federal campaign finance rules, the Bipartisan Campaign Reform Act (BCRA) of 2002, clearly did little to influence the competitiveness of congressional races.[4] Moreover, the current federal judiciary, citing the First Amendment, has little tolerance for impediments to campaign spending. In *Citizens United*, the Supreme Court declared BCRA's regulation of expenditures external to campaigns by corporations and unions unconstitutional.[5] Even if they were desirable, policies forcing citizens, parties, interest groups, and candidates to abide by rules that effectively give all campaigns the same or nearly the same resources are unlikely to generate much support in Washington.

That does not mean the campaign finance regime cannot be improved. I noted earlier transparency was critical to accountability in a representative democracy. To that end, Congress might try to pass something like the DISCLOSE Act which, would make large contributions from individuals to the independent groups unleashed by the *Citizens United* ruling fully visible. This would allow the public to more easily form connections between these donations and the legislators who benefit from them.[6]

Perhaps a better way to bring about competition and turnover is to change congressional districts. Senate races have proven themselves more competitive than those for House seats. One reason is that states are considerably more heterogeneous than House members' constituencies. Over time, residential patterns and the work of state legislatures have created congressional districts that are quite monolithic (Carson et al. 2011; Stonecash, Brewer, and Mariani 2003).[7] Public policy cannot be used to force certain types of people to live in certain places, but the redistricting process used in most of the country can be changed. A considerable majority of states currently allow their legislatures to draw district lines after each census. Iowa, however, has an independent bipartisan redistricting commission that proposes computer-generated plans to the legislature. Input data are devoid of any political information. Legislators must either accept or reject the plan in its entirety. The result is a generally less contentious process that creates diverse districts that approximate conventional shapes and are quite competitive. Iowa congressional districts turn over at disproportionately high rates, and its delegations, befitting such a purple state, frequently consist of members of both parties, many of whom are ideologically moderate (Carson and Crespin 2004; Goedert 2011). Now that seniority is no longer inextricably linked to advancement within the House, states have greater incentive to expose entrenched members to political competition. Unfortunately, state legislators are not really interested in relinquishing control of redistricting, and Congress has little direct power to force changes in the way it is done. It might try, however, and could at least propose and push a national model similar to Iowa's bipartisan and mechanistic process. Making general elections for House seats more competitive would encourage a larger number of talented people to run and, of course, increase turnover.

Several House and Senate procedures could be made less complicated. A number of changes come immediately to mind. The House could alter standing rules to greatly restrict the types and intricacy of the special rules given to bills by the Rules Committee. As we have seen, some of these rules are quite byzantine and, among other things, allow members to avoid accountability for their actions (Oleszek 2011a, 155–162). Perhaps restricting the Rules Committee to the promulgation of only open, closed, or modified rules would be a good idea—that is, permitting only special rules that render all, most, some, or none of a bill susceptible to germane amendments on the floor. Amendments offered would simply be rejected if a majority voted against them, accepted if a majority voted in favor. Structured rules that permit specific precleared amendments aid transparency as well.

The Senate could get rid of holds. As noted earlier, the mysterious practice allows senators to prevent a bill from coming to the floor by communicating their concerns with the legislation to the leadership. Until recently, holds were anonymous. This made it difficult for a bill's supporters to identify the source and reason for the obstruction and work to remove it. Recent changes discussed earlier have weakened the procedure—holds must now be quickly attributed to members—but it survives as an extremely useful way to slow the lawmaking process to a crawl and extract meaningful concessions from colleagues.

Transparency would be enhanced if the bodies made sure the precise language of bills was available to members well before they were asked to consider and vote on them. This is particularly important given the greater use of omnibus legislation and increased policy complexity in Washington. At the beginning of the 112th Congress in 2011, the new Republican House majority instituted a seventy-two-hour rule requiring a bill be published on the Internet at least three days before it goes to the floor (Taylor 2012a, 187). Unfortunately, the regulation is not being enforced adequately. A massive 596-page transportation and student aid bill passed by the House in late June 2012 was made available less than twenty-four hours before it went before the full body.

The Senate failed to meet one of the benchmarks because it frequently requires a supermajority of members to end debate—a filibuster is killed by sixty votes. Over the past couple of decades, the congressional literature has discussed filibuster reform extensively. Senators themselves have recently begun to consider the idea seriously. In early 2010, for example, Sens. Tom Harkin (D-IA) and Jeanne Shaheen (D-NH) proposed, over time, permitting the invocation of cloture with fewer than sixty votes, in increments of three down to fifty-one.[8] In May 2012, frustrated at the lack of progress on a post office bill, Sens. Carl Levin (D-MI) and Lamar Alexander (R-TN) suggested doing away with the filibuster on motions to proceed in return for a guarantee a bill would be open to all germane amendments.

Others have recommended all procedural motions be made nondebatable or at least immune from filibuster.[9] There is also support for the reinstitution of "real" filibusters by requiring members to "go to the mattresses" in old-fashioned Mr. Smith style (Koger 2010, 197–199; Smith 2010). This might be achieved by eliminating the track system. Both reforms have been touted by the nonpartisan group No Labels and were part of a much-discussed rules package introduced at the beginning of the 112th Congress in 2011 by Harkin and Sens. Tom Udall (D-NM) and Jeff Merkley (D-OR).[10] Merkley, moreover, has suggested the Senate approve a change doing away with the filibuster altogether at some arbitrary point in the future, a time when no one today can be sure which party will be in the majority. Any one of these would make it easier for a floor majority to ensure a more timely disposition of legislation. Fortunately, significant discussion of the filibuster continues at the commencement of the 113th Congress.

Congress can improve the quality of its policy outputs. It has worked hard to minimize private bills and greatly reduce earmarks. Both of these help mitigate the unhealthy impact of particularism. But more could be done to wipe it out. In the summer of 2012 it was clear narrow but important exceptions to tariff rates were being engineered by House members for industries in their districts. These breaks are merely earmarks in a different guise.

The American public can also encourage and pressure Congress to make better laws. Consistent with Lowi's (1979) suggestions, Congress should write legislation clearly so that administrators have unambiguous guidelines and the public understands exactly what has been done. Congress should make laws general so specific classes of Americans are neither advantaged nor disadvantaged. The implementation of policy should be guided by reasonable and lucid formulas based upon broad principles. There will be winners and losers, but they should not be distinguishable by anything as specific as, say, residency in a particular congressional district or membership in a particular organization. Local concerns can still be met, even if legislation no longer targets discrete beneficiaries. Government contracts, for example, are already granted based upon competitive bid, Davis-Bacon wage, and "buy American" principles.[11] There is no reason similarly discriminating and broad maxims with public support cannot be used to shape other kinds of policy outputs, especially taxing and spending.

Congress should move aggressively to put the country on sound fiscal footing. Any reforms ought to provide the additional benefit of ensuring a healthy economy in the future. As I have noted at various points in the book, plenty of ideas on how to do this are currently circulating. A legislative package of comprehensive tax simplification and meaningful entitlement reform might generate enough bipartisan support to be realized. If accompanied by intelligent cuts to discretionary domestic and defense spending, Congress can do much to solve the federal government's profound budget problems.

Congressional debate and deliberation need improvement. Elsewhere, I have suggested a variety of different procedures designed to do this (Taylor 2012a, 190–193). They include Oxford Union– and Lincoln-Douglas-style debates—in both, a policy issue would be the subject and, presumably, the proceedings would help guide the formation, in addition to the disposal of, legislative measures. Congress has dabbled in these before.[12] The House, particularly, could encourage greater interaction among members on the floor if it set aside time in communal accounts from which legislators could draw for the purpose of engaging in colloquies with colleagues. With time short and members eager to demonstrate positions on legislation, the House currently displays much less deliberation than the Senate.

Oversight, particularly of the executive branch, should be increased. One way to do this would be to mandate, through statute and chamber rules, more hearings with and reports from departments and agencies. Still without motivated and energetic members willing to conduct it, additional oversight is unlikely to constrain executive behavior much. It is a greater sense of the collective and the importance of Congress as an institution that is really needed. Promoting this appreciation will be difficult. Bringing members together periodically in informal settings might be a useful start, though. Leaders in both bodies could organize off-the-record meetings of all or a bipartisan cross-section of their memberships to nurture relationships and instill a sensibility for congressional interests. The substance of discussions would be secondary but might center on points of consensus so as to build trust and recognition of common needs and concerns. It is not much. But it is something, and the pure symbolism of these get-togethers is likely to please the public.[13]

Finally, it is worth mentioning the ethics problems that periodically afflict Congress. Throughout history House members and senators have violated congressional rules governing personal conduct and crossed ethical and legal lines. The appearance of more instances of such behavior today may be a function of invigorated surveillance and enforcement mechanisms. We live with a large and assertive media, hungry for scandal. The House and Senate adopted their codes of official conduct in the late 1960s and passed important ethics reforms in the late 1980s and mid-1990s. The House has demonstrated a concerted effort to deal with this lasting problem as recently as 2007 when it set up the Office of Congressional Ethics (OCE); its six members, all outsiders picked by the Speaker and the minority leader, have the authority to initiate preliminary reviews of allegations against House members, conduct investigations, refer their findings to the House Ethics Committee, and submit public reports. When it comes to ethics issues, it is hard to imagine a procedure much better equipped to balance the interests of the institution with that of its members. At the very least, OCE and the new procedure should be given an opportunity to work.

CONCLUSION

These reforms would likely elevate congressional performance and address many of the weaknesses discussed earlier in the book. There are significant obstacles to their adoption, however. Several will be unpopular with the legislature's leaders and much of the rank and file. Many cannot be mandated by policy and constitute efforts to educate and alter the behavior of members—individuals with significant demands on their time and with interests in many matters other than advancing the institution to which they belong.

Even if members were willing to adopt them, there is some doubt these reforms would have significant impact. This is because Congress is essentially a reflection of this country and its values, habits, and faults. The most effective way to achieve meaningful change in Congress is to generate meaningful change in American society. This is, naturally, a very difficult thing to do. Still, recognizing the principal cause of Congress's failings should at least make Americans a little more forgiving of their national legislature.

Congress's most important flaws—or at least several of the characteristics of which the public is most critical—have roots in contemporary American life. A large number of citizens still think of themselves as politically independent. The proportion of Americans who do not identify with either of the major parties has, since it rose perceptibly in the mid-1970s, remained roughly the same in American National Election Studies (ANES) surveys, at about 35–40 percent. Other indicators suggest, however, that many of these people are moving into one or the other of two polarized ideological camps. Over the past few years, Gallup has reported a steady increase in the proportion of Americans who consider themselves conservative. This has been at the expense of moderates because the proportion of liberals has risen by about a quarter since the mid-1990s.[14]

This development is even more pronounced if we think of those who are most engaged in the political process and vote regularly, volunteer for campaigns, and donate money to candidates and parties. These individuals are polarizing at rates similar to office holders (Abramowitz 2010; Hetherington and Weiler 2009). Political activists watch different cable news stations—Republicans tend to like Fox, Democrats CNN.[15] We do not have much systematic information about the electorate for congressional primaries, but, if it is anything like that of presidential contests, it is dominated by partisans more extreme than other voters who regularly support candidates of the same party in general elections (Norrander 2010, 67–68). Delegates to national conventions are quite ideological; Republican delegates are further to the right than all registered Republicans, and Democratic delegates further to the left than their party's supporters within the populace (Fiorina, Abrams, and Pope 2011, 16–18; Layman et al. 2010). Ideological candidates receive more money from individual contributors than do moderates, suggesting that donors themselves are more extreme than most other members of the public (Ensley 2009; Francia et al. 2003; Johnson 2010).[16] Raymond LaRaja and David Wiltse's (2012) study of giving by individuals verifies this assertion. Finally on this point, the Tea Party and Occupy Wall Street movements are hardly representative of the American people, but they dominated much political debate and media coverage of mass politics during the 2010–2012 period. If Congress is listening for public direction on policy matters, the loudest voices are quite clearly coming from the ideological wings.

Those members of the general public who participate most in politics are therefore polarizing along with Congress. It has been suggested politicians in Washington are driving this process. They force voters to choose between two starkly different policy options when, without their leadership, citizens would choose more nuanced, and moderate, outcomes (Levendusky 2009). The "culture war" the media believe deeply divides Americans on issues like abortion, homosexual rights, and the role of religion in public life takes place largely at the elite level (Fiorina, Abrams, and Pope 2011, 167–182). Yet in many ways the sequence of events is immaterial. Americans, or at least those who are active in politics, are now increasingly pressuring members of Congress to move to the ideological extremes. Legislators might have initiated the process, but they also respond to cues from the public because it is their job to do so. The middle is still a place where a good number of citizens reside. These people are, however, shrinking in number and, at least relative to ideologues, increasingly silent.

Congressional parties therefore often take very clear and delineated positions on issues. The public recognizes this—in the 2008 ANES poll, 78 percent of respondents saw an "important difference" in what the parties stood for; in 1992 only 60 percent did. Many individuals run for Congress on these positions (Crespin, Gold, and Rohde 2006): they are committed to a particular view of the world. But this view is distant from that of opponents, and aspiring members are immediately primed in a kind of tribal mindset.

Beyond ideology and commitment to particular policies, the fundamental motivations of candidates are unclear.[17] It is probably fair to say, however, that a good proportion of them pursue congressional office because they are attracted to politics as a vocation. They are ambitious and competitive.[18] They have to be to succeed because, although parties actively recruit candidates, capturing a seat in Congress means winning a primary and raising significant amounts of money on one's own. Candidates consequently often view politics as much as a contest between personalities as between policies. To win, they must defeat an opponent; if they lose, someone beats them. It is unsurprising that congressional life should reflect this combative spirit and that the conflicts within the institution seem frequently to be about political maneuvering and personal animosities, not substantive ideas.

Congressional performance is diminished by the tendency of wider society to celebrate individuals and vilify institutions. We idolize celebrities from all walks of life—sports, popular culture, public service, business, politics. Fairly or not, success is attributed to their unique abilities; it is not believed to be collective. Football teams win because of their quarterback, music groups are popular because of their lead singers, armies triumph because of their generals, and corporations are profitable because of their CEOs. The International Social Survey (ISS) has repeatedly found that Americans, much more than people of other nationalities across the world, attribute an individual's success in life to her own effort and talent, not the support of others (Isaacs 2008).[19]

To be sure, individuals are sometimes disparaged in this country, but institutions almost universally are. In the 2004 election, the ANES survey asked respondents to place Catholics and the Catholic Church on a scale of 0 to 100, with 100 meaning the individual felt very highly of the subject. The mean score for the church was 59.7; the score for its followers was 68.9. The same scores for labor unions and working-class people in 2008 were 50.9 and 75.2 respectively. In 2012, congressional leaders had pretty low favorability ratings. The polls suggested Speaker John Boehner was viewed favorably by about 35 percent of Americans, Minority Leader Nancy Pelosi between 30 and 35 percent, Senate Majority Leader Harry Reid by about 30 percent, and Senate Minority Leader Mitch McConnell by about 30–35 percent. But these were approximately ten percentage points higher than the congressional parties and twenty percentage points more than the parent bodies they led.

Congress must be intelligent; the challenges it faces and problems it must solve demand nothing less. But Americans exhibit a streak of anti-intellectualism, a quality comprehensively described by Richard Hofstadter (1966) in the 1960s and detected repeatedly since then.[20] They prioritize a variety of characteristics in their candidates to the same degree as—and sometimes above—mental ability. Surveys have demonstrated respondents believe a candidate's moral fortitude and a capacity to empathize with people like themselves are more important than intellectual ability. Two-thirds of voters in a 2011 Public Religion Research Institute poll stated it was "important" or "somewhat important" that a presidential candidate has "strong religious beliefs."[21] Over the past few elections, ANES has found that the public generally perceives presidential candidates to be of similar intellectual ability. In the only election of the past five when that has not been the case, the least intelligent candidate won. That was 2004, when 85 percent of respondents stated "intelligence" was a character trait that described John Kerry "extremely well" or "quite well" and 61 percent believed it accurately described President George W. Bush.[22]

This is intensified and exploited by pervasive media appeals to emotion rather than intellect. The news often frames political developments in threatening ways with profound effects on public attitudes, for example (Gadarian 2010; Nacos, Bloch-Elkon, and Shapiro 2011). Campaigns have naturally found emotional appeals an effective strategy (Ridout and Searles 2011). A number of influential studies suggest that Americans' political actions are motivated as much by passion as they are reason (Caplan 2007; Lakoff 2008; Westen 2007).

When we do use our brains, moreover, it seems we cannot focus them for more than a short period of time. In the political world this is demonstrated by the constant shrinking of the news sound bite—a chunk of television or radio time allotted to the coverage of a candidate explaining her policy positions (Bucy and Grabe 2007; Hallin 1992). We are less capable of making concerted and sustained efforts to engage in singular and complex mental tasks. We cannot or, perhaps because we find them tedious, will not do them. Mastering these tasks, however, requires precisely the same kind of skills lawmakers need to evaluate societal problems and fashion effective policy solutions within a participatory and deliberative legislative process.

Finally, all professions and communities have within them individuals who break the rules of appropriate behavior. There are teachers who help their students cheat on tests. There are doctors who prescribe their patients certain drugs to receive kickbacks from pharmaceutical companies. There are priests and prominent college football coaches who have molested children.[23] People in positions of authority throughout American public life are, needless to say, far from perfect.

That congressional behavior is similar to ours should come as no surprise—as Madison wrote in *Federalist 51*, "But what is government itself, but the greatest of all reflections on human nature?" Congress is made up of human beings. Members might be a little wealthier, whiter, and more likely to be male than the average American, but they are often our neighbors, our friends, and our colleagues.[24] Congress is also a transparent and responsive legislature in a media-saturated, robust, representative democracy that values vigorous competition, majority rule, individual liberty, and political and legal equality. This does not make it very easy for its members to conceal their human frailties. When we characterize Congress in derisive terms and call on it to improve, we should perhaps first look in the mirror. To be sure, Congress leads, and we should hold its members to high standards. But it follows, too, and that, I think most Americans would agree, is entirely appropriate.

NOTES

I: THE MUCH-MALIGNED LEGISLATIVE BRANCH

1. Other popular replies included "inept," "incompetent," "lazy," and "crooked." For more on the study, see http://pewresearch.org/pubs/1533/congress-in-a-word-cloud-dysfunctional-corrupt-selfish.

2. Only 13 percent of Americans approved of the job it was doing according to the Gallup poll. The previous low had been 14 percent in July 2008; before then it had not plumbed similar depths since the early 1990s.

3. The full poll results can be found at http://i2.cdn.turner.com/cnn/2011/images/08/02/rel12a.pdf.

4. A PAC is essentially the campaign finance arm of an organized interest group.

5. Congress's approval ratings rose to over 40 percent in 1986. The ascent in the 1990s was even more dramatic. Helped by a strong economy, the figure reached nearly 60 percent for a time in 1998.

6. The quote is from Pudd'nhead Wilson's calendar in *Following the Equator: A Journey Around the World*.

7. For more on Abramoff and his exploits, see Kaiser (2009).

8. Wright was the first Speaker to resign because of a scandal. The ethics charges were filed by then–Republican whip Newt Gingrich and helped deepen a partisan divide that was emerging on the Hill. For more on Wright's fall from grace, see Barry (1992).

9. The tables were then turned on Gingrich. Gingrich became the first Speaker to be disciplined by the House for wrongdoing. The committee's punishment was approved by a large and bipartisan majority of members. For more, see Yang (1997).

10. Only 21 percent of respondents believed members had "low" or "very low" "honesty and ethical standards" in Gallup's November 2000 poll.

11. The survey question was open ended. Fifteen percent of respondents said something along the lines that members were not working for the country's best interests, 13 percent that they were self-serving, and 6 percent that they were not listening to the public. The 29 percent who said they were doing a "bad job" might have had the same things in mind.

12. The members were John Campbell (R-CA), Joe Crowley (D-NY), Jeb Hensarling (R-TX), Christopher Lee (R-NY), Frank Lucas (R-OK), Tom Price (R-GA), and Mel Watt (D-NC). Another, Earl Pomeroy (D-ND), was also scrutinized by OCE.

13. The phrase is Blumenthal's (1980).

14. The one exception is January 2009, presumably because the public believed President-elect Barack Obama when he said he would reduce partisanship in Washington.

15. The precise wording was "bickering and opposing one another more than usual."

16. For more on this rather dramatic episode, see Draper (2012, 222–280) and Mann and Ornstein (2012, 10–30).

17. I use the first dimension scores throughout the book. These indicate members' positions along an ideological scale based largely upon views on economic matters.

18. See, for example, Eilperin (2006).

19. For more on this argument, see Schaffner (2011, 534–535) and Theriault (2008, 45–48).

20. McCarty, Poole, and Rosenthal (2006, 184–189) argue polarization leads to a disproportionally large amount of conservative policy. This, presumably, gives liberals greater reason to dislike Congress.

21. A July 2011 Pew Research Center for the People and the Press poll found that 68 percent of respondents wanted members whose position they supported to compromise to get a debt ceiling agreement passed even if it meant getting a deal they personally did not like. The full poll results can be found at http://pewresearch.org/pubs/2071/debt-limit-ceiling-tea-party-compromise-deficit-reduction.

22. In every other instance, a majority believed the Congress of the time had accomplished the same amount or more than recent Congresses. Until 2003, less than 30 percent of respondents were arguing the current Congress had accomplished less.

23. Foley (2012) argues the principles at the heart of Tea Party members' views are limited government, American sovereignty, and constitutional originalism. "Tea" is actually an acronym for "Taxed Enough Already."

24. This was the average for all respondents. Interestingly, liberals felt that forty-four cents was wasted. For the full results, see http://www.gallup.com/poll/149543/americans-say-federal-gov-wastes-half-every-dollar.aspx.

25. The Associated Press's exit poll showed that 31 percent wanted the law expanded and 16 percent wanted it left as it is.

26. The term's origin is not completely clear. The writings of historians and political scientists such as Greenstein (1978) and Leuchtenburg (1963) have pushed it into the scholarly vernacular, however.

27. *Boston University Law Review* 89, no. 2.

28. See, for instance, thirty-thousand.org and Conley and Stevens (2011).

2: WHAT WE SHOULD WANT OF CONGRESS

1. For more on the survey, see http://www.harrisinteractive.com/NewsRoom/HarrisPolls/tabid/447/mid/1508/articleId/693/ctl/ReadCustomDefault/Default.aspx.

2. Snyder and Stromberg (2010) show that citizens who live in districts with minimal press coverage of Congress know less about their representatives.

3. Only 40 percent of respondents reported getting their news from a newspaper, 46 percent said they received it from online sources.

4. Cap and trade is an effort to outlaw further increases in carbon emissions and allow corporations to trade emissions allowances with one another.

5. For more on Pew's political knowledge surveys see http://pewresearch.org/politicalquiz/.

6. Alan Rosenthal (1999) has written about what makes a good state legislature. He focuses on issues discussed throughout this book—matters like quality representation, pushing back against executive power, and deliberation and broad participation in the lawmaking process.

7. Nineteenth-century English philosopher Jeremy Bentham (2007) is known as the father of utilitarian thought. Although Bentham promoted majority rule, he did also believe

policy makers should take account of what proposals would generate the greatest aggregate "happiness."

8. The line is often quoted but there is no evidence that the conversation it is reportedly part of actually took place.

9. Hetherington's (2005) work on trust defines it quite specifically as the belief that policy outcomes should match public will—that is, it is quite similar to substantive representation.

10. The seniority system, particularly, has undergone some significant changes over the past forty years. Whereas the principle was considered inviolable and the most senior member of a committee was automatically made its chair before the mid-1970s, today the House parties respect it but ultimately appoint chairs based upon other factors—including party loyalty.

11. Krehbiel's (1991) model of the legislative process is often called the informational model.

12. When he was running for president in 2011, Gingrich talked about his policy goals in more traditionally conservative terms. On NBC's *Meet the Press*, he dismissed a House Republican plan to overhaul Medicare and announced that he did not think "imposing radical change from the right or left is a very good way for a free society to operate" (Hernandez 2011).

13. Not everyone agrees such consistency is needed. Political scientists who embraced the pluralist model of policy making in the 1950s and 1960s, for example, felt that interest group struggles for influence in individual policy areas had many important virtues and were not particularly injurious to the operation of American government and the broad economy (Lindblom 1965; Truman 1959).

14. Lowi (1979) believed using the courts was the best way to ensure these kinds of policy outcomes. I think the view of Congress taken in this book suggests he was wrong on that point.

15. Locke argues in the *Two Treatises* that legislative power is supreme, noting in the second that it is "how the force for the commonwealth shall be employed" (Locke 1988, 2:143). He does suggest, however, that an enlightened executive could dissolve a legislature that is no longer serving the public interest (Faulkner 2001).

16. Executive orders are promulgated by presidents. They have the force of law but must not be precluded by statute or the Constitution and need to find authority in either of those two sources as well. Some executive orders can have profound effects on public policy; most deal with the organization and policies of the executive branch of government (Howell 2003; Mayer 2001).

17. Examples from the Civil War era include the Joint Committee on the Conduct of the War and the Johnson impeachment and trial, from the Grant years the Fisk-Gould gold standard and the Crédit Mobilier investigations, from the 1920s Teapot Dome and the investigation into corruption at the Veterans' Bureau, from FDR's time the Smith committee's investigation into the National Labor Relations Board and the Truman committee's investigation into World War II contracting, and during the Cold War the investigation into the MacArthur dismissal and the Fulbright committee (Taylor 2012b).

18. Watergate was essentially about the White House's involvement in a burglary of Democratic National Committee headquarters and the president's strategy to cover up his knowledge of it. Iran-Contra was an illegal policy of the National Security Council to trade arms with Iran and direct the proceeds to Nicaraguan Contra rebels. The investigations into the Clinton administration were numerous, the most debilitating, of course, was that into his efforts to keep his relationship with a White House intern, Monica Lewinsky, secret.

19. Today the EOP houses numerous agencies and several thousand staff in entities like the White House staff (a catchall term for senior policy advisers, the press office, clerical staff,

etc.), the Office of the Vice President, the Council of Economic Advisers, the National Security Council, and the Office of Management and Budget.

20. Congress did try to exert some control over the policy. In 2005 it passed the Detainee Treatment Act to regulate the management of prisoners at Guantanamo Bay. It used the Military Commissions Act of 2006 and its 2009 amendments to regulate how the federal government would dispose of cases involving "enemy combatants."

21. May 20, 1977.

22. For more on the survey, see Quirk and Binder (2005, 551–553).

23. It might be argued that the US House and Senate will look like state legislatures because the latter attempt to emulate Congress. As a result, any benchmarks constructed from observations of state legislatures are more likely to be met than not. However, if this is the case we might consider imitation to be the most sincere form of flattery and suggest such evidence places Congress in a favorable light.

3: DO WE HAVE A ROBUST REPRESENTATIVE DEMOCRACY?

1. Throughout 2010, most polls showed that between 40 and 50 percent of Americans had an "unfavorable" view of the health care bill passed by Congress or felt that it was a "bad idea."

2. The same poll showed that 80 percent of Americans felt their country was run "by a few big interests looking out for themselves." The average score on the "will of the people" scale for the entire survey was 4.6. Scores in Europe were much higher than those in the United States. The full details of the poll can be found at http://www.worldpublicopinion.org /pipa/pdf/may08/WPO_Governance_May08_countries.pdf.

3. The Commons does not have a fixed term, but the government must call a general election within five years of the previous one. Terms in the Lords are for life.

4. Some research demonstrates measurable interelection accommodation of changing public views in the policy preferences of cohesive majority parties. Calvo's (2007) work on Argentina is a good example.

5. The legislation passed in the thirty years between 1890 and 1920 constituted an impressive package of reform. Among the highlights were the Pure Food and Drug Act of 1906, the Seventeenth Amendment that brought about the direct election of senators in 1913, the Sherman Antitrust Act of 1890, the Hepburn Act of 1906 that regulated railroad rates, and the Clayton Antitrust Act of 1914.

6. As scholars of comparative politics are acutely aware, proportional representation, a system widely deployed in Europe, is designed to transform the percentage of the aggregate vote won by a party's candidates into a roughly equivalent percentage of the legislative body's seats (Lijphart 1999, 143–70).

7. In eleven states (Alaska, Arizona, California, Colorado, Hawaii, Idaho, Iowa, Missouri, Montana, New Jersey, and Washington), the legislature has delegated the responsibility to special bipartisan or nonpartisan commissions.

8. In reality, however, House members have significant influence over how their colleagues in state legislatures draw the boundaries of congressional districts (Bullock 2010). This is generally exerted through the party's organization and is perhaps best demonstrated by Majority Leader Tom Delay's (R-TX) orchestration of the Texas redistricting after the 2000 census (Bickerstaff 2007).

9. As of July 2011, thirty states required voter identification—of which fourteen required a photo ID. Thirty-two states permitted "no-excuse" early voting in person at government offices or satellite facilities prior to the traditional election day.

10. The agreement called for at least $1 trillion in cuts over ten years, regardless of how a bicameral and bipartisan supercommittee convened to recommend a plan to reduce the deficit fared (it ultimately failed).

11. More specifically, the contract called for legislation to, among other things, reduce crime, give the president a line-item veto, reduce the burden of federal mandates on states, reform product liability and tort law, limit congressional terms, and add a balanced budget amendment to the Constitution.

12. According to Mike Allen of Politico, she said it twice in one Sunday talk show alone—on CNN's Late Edition, February 10, 2008. For more, see http://www.politico.com/news/stories/0208/8422.html.

13. The two major pieces of legislation were the Economic Recovery Tax Act (ERTA) of 1981 that cut tax rates and linked them to inflation and the Omnibus Reconciliation Act of 1981 that made quite dramatic cuts in domestic spending.

14. It is not clear that the Thomas hearings led directly to any of these women deciding to run. It seems to have helped them campaign energetically, however (Boxer and Boxer 1993).

15. These proposals had mixed success. Although most became law, the Clinton health care plan did not even get a vote in the House or Senate.

16. The House had passed a version of this in 1994. However, it became law in 1995 and was a part of the Republicans' Contract with America.

17. Of the seven, six had won their seats in 1980: Jeremiah Denton (R-AL), Hawkins, Mack Mattingly (R-GA), Mark Andrews (R-ND), James Abdnor (R-SD), and Slade Gorton (R-WA). James Broyhill (R-NC) lost the seat John East (R-NC) had won. He was appointed to it upon East's death in June 1986.

18. Daschle was actually majority leader for the seventeen days between the swearing in of the 107th Congress and Cheney's swearing in as vice president on January 20, 2001. Although the body was split 50–50, Democrat Al Gore was still vice president and therefore made the Democrats the de jure majority.

19. For the most part, throughout the 1990s about 40 percent of Americans considered themselves moderate.

20. Bovitz and Carson (2006) show that votes given greater treatment by the media are more likely to affect an incumbent's electoral performance.

21. Under the general ticket system, all of a state's members were elected at large in what constituted a single multimember district. Some states used a single ballot, others separate ballots for each seat. Although the 1842 Apportionment Act stated that representatives "should be elected by districts composed of contiguous territory equal in number to the number of representatives to which said state may be entitled, no one district electing more than one representative," states continued to use the general ticket, and the House continued to seat members elected this way. The single-member district language of the 1842 legislation was expunged in 1850, but successive apportionment acts in the last thirty years of the nineteenth century and first decade of the twentieth, Congress iterated the belief that members should be elected from districts of contiguous territory and roughly equal population. The 1929 Apportionment Act was conspicuously silent on the complexion of congressional districts. This meant that when in 1932 the Supreme Court ruled the provisions of each apportionment act lasted only until a new one was passed, states were clearly not compelled to elect their United States representatives in single-member districts. Legislation approved in 1967 explicitly mandated single-member districts—although by then it really affected only two states, Hawaii and New Mexico.

22. The project has been undertaken by Scott Adler and John Wilkerson. For more, see http://www.congressionalbills.org/.

23. Data can be found at the Inter-Parliamentary Union website: http://www.ipu.org /wmn-e/world.htm.

24. Data can be found at the NCSL website: http://www.ncsl.org/legislatures-elections /wln/women-in-state-legislatures-2009.aspx.

25. Latin American countries with strong Catholic cultures have been particularly aggressive in establishing quotas, possibly because their traditional values make it more difficult for women to get elected.

26. For example Hughes (2011) shows that gender quotas largely benefit majority, not minority, women.

27. Caraway was appointed to replace her deceased husband in 1931, won a special election in January 1932, and secured a full term by winning another election in November 1932.

28. Caraway was actually the first to chair a Senate standing committee. She led the panel on enrolled bills between 1933 and 1945.

29. In *Shaw v. Reno* (1993), the Supreme Court ruled that redistricting for racial purposes was, although plausibly permissible, subject to strict scrutiny. In *Miller v. Johnson* (1995), the court declared unconstitutional any maps drawn where race was the "predominant factor."

4: IS CONGRESS A TRANSPARENT, ACCESSIBLE, AND TRUSTWORTHY LEGISLATURE?

1. The maxim does not seem to work in the American case. The United States is quite transparent but, according to Transparency International's widely used indicators, only the twenty-second least corrupt in 2010 (see http://www.transparency.org/cpi2010).

2. The *House Journal* and *Senate Journal* have recorded votes, the history of bills, procedural matters, and presidential messages since 1789. They include no verbatim or summary remarks of debates. The *Register of Debates in Congress* that covered the period from 1824 to 1837 was the first contemporaneous attempt to accurately report the leading debates and incidents in Congress but was not a verbatim account.

Initially, the *Congressional Globe*, started in 1833, provided what its early subtitle called only "sketches of the debates and proceedings" of Congress. By 1851, however, the *Globe* was using corps of reporters trained in the latest stenographic techniques and began publishing close to a verbatim record. It was replaced in 1873 by the *Congressional Record*.

3. A September 2010 Pew Research Center for the People and Press study found that 21 percent of Fox News viewers considered themselves Democrats. MSNBC's viewership was 53 percent Democratic. For more on the study see http://www.people-press.org/2010/09/12 /section-4-who-is-listening-watching-reading-and-why/.

4. There are six nonvoting delegates in the House of Representatives, one each from American Samoa, the District of Columbia, Guam, the Northern Marinara Islands, Puerto Rico (the resident commissioner), and the US Virgin Islands. They can be members of committees and participate in floor debate, but they do not have a plenary vote. The delegates have been able to vote on the floor under Democratic majorities since 1993—mainly because most, if not all, have generally been Democrats—but only in the Committee of the Whole and when their votes have not been decisive.

5. This was the assessment of a survey done by the South Carolina Policy Council published in November 2008. The council also reported that the vast majority of bills in the state's legislature are passed by voice vote—approximately 75 percent in 2009 alone.

6. Article I, Section 7, of the Constitution mandates that veto override attempts be recorded votes.

7. In teller votes members walk past counters, but votes are not formally attributed to individuals.

8. The green button means "aye," the red button "no," and the yellow button "present."

9. We do know that voice voting has been used extensively though. Clinton (2006) shows many pieces of historically important legislation have passed by voice.

10. The report can be found at http://www.ncsl.org/documents/legismgt/ILP/04Tab4Pt5 .pdf.

11. Articles of state constitutions that govern legislatures are nearly always much longer than Article I of the United States Constitution.

12. By contrast, the United States Constitution has just under 4,500 words.

13. Most bills treated this way are, however, because committee approval helps win support for them.

14. In recent years, when in the majority, House Republicans have placed a $100 million spending limit on bills eligible to be treated under suspension. They have also suggested that proposers demonstrate some support in the minority party for the bill before the Speaker moves to suspend the rules (Carr 2005).

15. For more on holds, see Oleszek (2011a, 230–232; 2011b).

16. Bunning technically did this by refusing to consent to the bill's advancement.

17. This was a principle first enunciated by the Supreme Court in *Field v. Clark* (1892) and iterated more recently by Justice John Paul Stevens in his opinion in *Clinton v. City of New York* (1998), the case that invalidated the line-item veto.

18. Probably the most contentious of these was the "Cornhusker kickback," a provision that gave Nebraska, and only Nebraska, a permanent exemption from its share of Medicaid funding.

19. Rep. Jim Cooper (D-TN) voted for the Senate bill but not the "fix." Reps. Dan Lipinski (D-IL) and Stephen Lynch (D-MA) voted for the "fix" but not the Senate bill.

20. Sinclair (2012, 186–232) provides a more detailed description of the events surrounding the passage of health care reform. My goal has been to focus upon procedural complexity.

Of course, Obama's signature may have only been the beginning. Several state attorneys general took the federal government to court, arguing the law was unconstitutional. The Supreme Court upheld the legislation in a June 2012 decision.

21. The studies can be found at http://www.publicintegrity.org.

22. The Campaign Finance Institute provides a great deal of research on campaign finance law and how it pertains to Congress. Much can be found at its website: http://www.cfinst.org.

23. Today's disclosure rules are largely a product of the Ethics in Government Act passed in 1978. Detailed descriptions of the rules can be found at the ethics committees' websites (the House at http://ethics.house.gov/; the Senate at http://ethics.senate.gov/).

24. For more on Abramoff, see Kaiser (2009).

25. See, for example, Daniel J. Mitchell of the Cato Institute's argument at http://www.cato-at-liberty.org/the-number-of-congressional-staff-is-the-real-problem/.

26. The franking privilege was suspended in 1873 and only fully restored in 1895.

27. There are now fifteen states with term limits. Most rules limit legislators to eight years of service.

28. This number was provided to Rasmussen Reports by the NCSL's Tim Story. See http://www.rasmussenreports.com/public_content/political_commentary/commentary_by_tim _storey/gop_makes_historic_state_legislative_gains_in_2010.

29. For an interesting overview of turnover through House history, see Swain et al. (2000).

30. Research investigating the motivations for member retirement reveals that legislators often decide to step down when they believe there is a significant possibility they will be defeated

in the next election (Stone et al. 2010; Wolak 2007). This suggests incumbency re-election rates exaggerate the lack of turnover somewhat.

31. The Australian ballot was a state-produced document on which all qualified candidates and parties appeared. Voters were given it and they marked their choices in secret. The United States moved to use the procedure in the late 1880s. Prior to its establishment, party members could provide ballots for voters to submit.

32. For more on the study, see http://www.opensecrets.org/news/2010/11/congressional-members-personal-weal.html.

33. Interestingly, Milyo and Groseclose (1999) have found that wealthy incumbents are not necessarily more difficult to defeat.

34. They were Horatio William Bottomley (1922 for fraud), Garry Allighan (1947 for breach of privilege), and Peter Arthur David Baker (1954 for forgery). Interestingly, nine members were expelled in the 1800s and thirty-one in the 1700s.

35. Electoral systems that allow party leaders to place candidates on the ballot are believed to encourage corrupt activities (Gingerich 2009).

36. A June 2011 Public Religion Research Institute poll found that 91 percent of respondents believed a "very" or "extremely" serious moral problem occurs when an elected official takes a bribe, 81 percent when she does not report all of her income on her tax return. The same study found that 61 percent of those surveyed believe elected officials should be held to higher moral standards than people in other professions. For more on the survey, see http://publicreligion.org/newsroom/2011/06/more-americans-say-financial-misconduct-by-elected-officials-is-a-very-serious-moral-problem-than-say-sexual-misconduct/.

37. Perhaps Ralph Waldo Emerson (1883, 287) best linked civility and ethics when he remarked, "There can be no high civility, without a deep morality."

38. For a taste of some of the survey work done on civility in American life, see Allegheny College's Center for Political Participation (http://sites.allegheny.edu/civility/) and public relations firm Weber Shandwick's civility polls (http://www.webershandwick.com/resources/ws/flash/CivilityinAmerica2011.pdf).

39. By comity Uslaner (1993, 8) is basically referring to courtesy.

40. For the full report, see http://www.annenbergpublicpolicycenter.org/Downloads/Civility/Civility_9–27–2011_Final.pdf. Words are ruled out of order when a member complains about what a colleague has said on the floor and the chair agrees. The ruling prevents a member from speaking again on the same day, unless allowed to do so by motion or unanimous consent, and it may, if again approved by motion or unanimous consent, result in the violator's words being expunged from the *Congressional Record*.

41. For a basic overview of the media's role in American politics today, see Graber (2010).

42. Between January 2009 and June 2012, the OCE had initiated a preliminary review of 101 cases of which 32 were transmitted for review to the House Ethics Committee.

43. The term was coined, or at least popularized, by White (1957).

5: DOES CONGRESS HAVE DESIRABLE PRINCIPLES OF ORGANIZATION?

1. An ABC News/Washington Post poll conducted after the 2006 elections revealed that 58 percent of respondents believed the new Democratic congressional majorities should "compromise" with President Bush rather than "carry out their agenda"; 58 percent believed Bush should use the same strategy.

2. Much of the congressional literature describes the period between World War II and the early 1970s as decentralized because committee chairs had great power. But the House and Senate were only decentralized relative to earlier periods—particularly around 1900—when the majority party leadership controlled the bodies.

3. Article I calls on the House to appoint a Speaker and on the Senate to make the vice president of the United States its president and appoint a stand-in for him known as the president pro tempore. The bodies must keep journals of their proceedings and Article I, Section 7, states that revenue bills must first be passed by the House. A quorum is a majority of the bodies and certain votes must be recorded

4. House Democrats approved the "subcommittee bill of rights" in 1973. Among other things, it guaranteed referral of legislation to subcommittees and gave them fixed jurisdictions. Minority rights to staff and budgets were recognized in 1974.

5. Rule XIV is invoked when a senator objects to further consideration of a bill at second reading. The majority leader is then in a position to call it up for floor consideration when he wishes.

6. In the House, both parties have a steering committee that makes assignments. Some members of these committees are elected by the rank and file, but they are dominated by party leaders. For the Republican majority in the 112th Congress, for instance, nine leaders sat on the twenty-member panel—including the majority leader, whip, and chairs of important standing committees. Speaker John Boehner chaired the committee and had five of the twenty-six votes. In the Senate, the Democratic leader selects members of the Democratic Steering and Outreach Committee that makes appointments. On the Republican side, the leader works with the party's Committee on Committees to make appointments. All Senate committee appointments must be formally ratified by the body.

7. Republicans established the limit when they took control of the House in 1995. Under pressure from rank and file, the Democratic leadership adopted the policy for its party on its return to the majority in 2007, but Speaker Nancy Pelosi repealed it in 2009 at the beginning of the 111th Congress. Republicans reinstated it when they again took control in 2011.

8. Members can call up bills by motion under unanimous consent. The germaneness provision and Rule XIV are discussed elsewhere in the chapter.

9. Interestingly, little research has been done on how supportive Americans are of pure majority rule. Smith, Gibson, and Park (2011) show the public is about evenly split on the legitimacy of the filibuster in the Senate, and those who identify with the minority party in the body tend to favor it more than those who support the majority party.

10. The Committee of the Whole House on the State of the Union, to use its formal title, is where most legislation is debated—and where tax and spending bills must be debated. It was established in the early Congresses to allow the House to expedite legislative matters. In addition to the smaller quorum, amendments are debated under the five-minute rule in the Committee of the Whole, while they are subject to the hour rule in the House (the times refer to the length of debate permitted) (Oleszek 2011a, 180–182). Certain motions, including the previous question, are not permitted in the Committee of the Whole, however.

11. The motion to recommit was placed into House rules in 1909. In 1932, Speaker John Nance Garner (D-TX) ruled the right belonged to a member of the minority party who opposed the bill. Democratic majorities in the 1970s and 1980s eroded this right. In 1995 Republicans enumerated Garner's ruling into House rules. For more on the procedure's history, see Wolfensberger (2003).

In recent years, minorities have tried to use it to embarrass the majority. Rather than consider it a viable tool to block the passage of legislation, for instance, the Republican minority in the 110th and 111th Congresses deployed the motion to force Democrats to take public positions against popular issues.

12. The figures on the number of motions filed are about 40 per Congress in the 1980s and early 1990s, about 80 per Congress from about 1993 to about 2007, and, in the two Congresses since then, approximately 130. For more, see Mann and Ornstein (2012, 88–89).

13. Because the vice president can break a tie, the president's party needs only fifty seats to take control. This was illustrated dramatically in the 107th Congress. When Congress convened at the beginning of January 2001 with fifty Democrats and fifty Republicans, the Democrats effectively had control because Al Gore was still vice president. When Vice President Dick Cheney was sworn in on January 20, the Republicans took command of the chamber's leadership and committees.

14. The fifty-nine included two independents who effectively caucused with the Democrats, Sen. Joseph Lieberman (Ind-CT) and Sen. Bernie Sanders (Ind-VT).

15. For more on filling the amendment tree, see Beth et al. (2009); Rybicki (2010); and Oleszek (2011a, 264–266).

16. Senators can also kill amendments by making a point of order against them if they believe they violate procedures determined by the Constitution or law (Den Hartog and Monroe 2011, 139–141); however, this motion is debatable.

17. There were three rounds initially, in 1991, 1993, and 1995. Ninety-seven bases were closed. Later Congress passed amendments to the law to enable an additional round in 2005. Over one hundred facilities were affected. The 2005 commission recommended another round occur in 2015.

18. These are mainly senates in western and small states.

19. There are a number of ways this could play out. For more detail, see Beth (2005); and Binder, Madonna, and Smith (2007).

20. The fourteen were mainly moderates and included prominent senators such as Robert Byrd (D-WV) and John McCain (R-AZ). The extraordinary circumstances were to be defined by each member of the gang.

21. The Rules Committee tends not to receive bills directly, instead reporting resolutions generally in the form of special rules.

22. House rules call for the Speaker to appoint conferees who were "primarily responsible for the legislation" and "principal proponents of the major provisions of the bill." A majority of conferees must have supported the bill. The Senate appointment process is guided by convention and agreements between the majority and minority.

23. There are formal restrictions designed to prevent conferees from straying too far from the two versions of the bill in front of them. Rule XXVIII of the Senate, for example, states that "conferees shall not insert in their report matter not committed to them by either House, nor shall they strike from the bill matter agreed to by both Houses." House members can raise points of order against conference reports that are deemed to have violated limits placed on their scope (Oleszek 2011a, 317–318). As a practical matter, however, these rules are not enforced.

24. With Republicans the majority in the House and Democrats in control of the Senate, several important bills died at the conference stage in the 107th Congress of 2001–2003, including bankruptcy reform and comprehensive energy legislation.

25. But, as Lazarus and Monroe (2007) note, conferees tend to have a clear bias for the majority party position on the bill.

26. For more on the personalities of recent speakers, see Strahan (2007, 127–180) on Gingrich and Peters and Rosenthal (2010) on Pelosi.

27. No one really knows much about the genesis of the House's germaneness rule. A germaneness requirement was in the original standing rules of the First Congress. The current language was adopted in 1822. For more on this rule, see Taylor (2012a, 82–85).

6: DOES CONGRESS HAVE A HEALTHY LEGISLATIVE PROCESS?

1. There has been some, however, and I discuss it periodically throughout the chapter. Bessette (1994) qualitatively analyzes twenty-nine case studies of bills dealt with between

1946 and 1970. Connor and Oppenheimer (1993) examine deliberation in just three Congresses. Wirls (2007) looks at four debates in the House and Senate of the nineteenth century. Taylor (2012a) provides a much more systematic analysis of congressional floor proceedings across American history. There is a project that uses computer programs to analyze the frequency and use of words in the *Congressional Record* (see, for example, Monroe, Colaresi, and Quinn 2008). It will have many applications.

2. All but Lugar ran in 2010. Although she lost her primary, Murkowski went on to win the general election as a write-in candidate. This was the first time since 1954 when Strom Thurmond won in South Carolina that a write-in candidate had won a Senate seat.

3. The language is informative, but not entirely accurate. Votes are, of course, not literally bought. It is illegal to offer money for a legislator's vote. During the House's roll call on passage of the Medicare prescription drug legislation in November 2003, Reps. Tom DeLay (R-TX) and Candice S. Miller (R-MI) were accused of asking Rep. Nick Smith (R-MI) to vote for the bill in exchange for contributions to Smith's son's upcoming campaign to succeed the father. DeLay and Miller ultimately received rebukes from the ethics committee.

4. For example, on cap and trade, see Kane, Pershing, and Fahrenthold (2009).

5. That was nothing compared to what Obama could raise for himself. His record one-night haul was $15 million at a May 2012 Hollywood event hosted by the actor George Clooney.

6. The term is Samuel Kernell's (1986).

7. Scholars are skeptical about how frequently members vote in a sophisticated manner on these "poisoned pills"—that is, how often they vote insincerely on the amendment to increase the likelihood the body will dispose of the bill in the way they would like it to (Groseclose and Milyo 2010).

8. The financial crisis of 2008 really began with the demise of the global investment banks Bear Stearns and Lehman Brothers. The Federal Reserve essentially rescued Bear Stearns in March by orchestrating its takeover by JP Morgan Chase. Many observers complained that the bailout would encourage more reckless behavior by banks. Rather controversially, and perhaps sensitive to its handling of Bear Stearns, the Fed decided not to save Lehman when it was struggling the following September. Lehman was forced to declare bankruptcy.

9. Sessions is quoted from the *Congressional Record*, December 10, 2010, H 14481.

10. They are also rarely read by anyone except extremely interested constituents, energetic reporters, and congressional scholars.

11. This is at H 14426–14427 of the *Congressional Record*, December 9, 2009.

12. Two good examples of this are the colloquies between Scott Brown and Ted Kaufman (D-DE) in the *Congressional Record* of May 6, 2010, on S3309 and Durbin and Jeff Merkley (D-OR) on S3320.

7: DOES CONGRESS MAKE EFFECTIVE POLICY?

1. There have been other comparative studies focused on legislation produced in a particular policy area. Probably the most influential is Tsebelis's (1999) analysis of the number of important labor laws passed by fifteen Western European parliaments in the 1980s.

2. Public laws differ from private laws. Public laws are applied generally, private laws to a specific individual.

3. It should be noted, however, that omnibus bills are as old as the country. The first national budget bill of 1789 was considered an omnibus.

4. As we saw in Chapter 5, one advantage of reconciliation bills is that they cannot be filibustered in the Senate. Recent and important legislation Congress has approved using the

reconciliation process includes the big domestic spending cuts in 1981, the important deficit reduction bill of 1984, welfare reform in 1996, and the Bush tax cuts of 2001.

5. Congress has split the federal government's operations into twelve parts for the purposes of funding it. The twelve appropriations bills are: Agriculture, Commerce/Justice/Science, Defense, Energy and Water, Financial Services, Homeland Security, Interior and Environment, Labor/HHS/Education, Legislative Branch, Military/Veterans, State/Foreign Operations, Transportation/HUD. Before 2008, there were thirteen.

6. The line-item veto existed at the federal level for about eighteen months in the1990s. It will be discussed in more detail in the next chapter.

7. The Policy Agendas Project can be found at http://www.policyagendas.org/.

8. Medicaid is a program jointly funded and administered by the federal government and the states. It provides financial support for the health care of those who qualify after a means test. Medicare provides health care of most types to Social Security recipients. Both were created by the same act in 1965. SSI provides stipends for those of little means who are aged, blind, or disabled. It was established in 1974.

9. For instance, when economists talk of public goods, they frequently think of things like national defense and economic institutions, like a healthy financial system.

10. If the president uses force legitimately without first obtaining congressional approval, he must report his actions to the legislature within forty-eight hours and then, after sixty days, receive explicit permission to continue the operation.

11. Ethicists have another, although not unrelated, benchmark they call just war (see, for example, Walzer 1977).

12. The resolution was known as HJRes 64 in the House and SJRes 23 in the Senate.

13. Of course, the Afghanistan policy has not been free of controversy. The US presence in that country is now opposed by about two-thirds of Americans, according to recent polls.

14. Because the island nation was a member of its Commonwealth, Britain was particularly critical of the American invasion of Grenada. The Organization of American States formally condemned the US operation in Panama.

15. Bush was criticized for not assisting revolts against Hussein in both the Kurdish north and Shiite south of the country in the spring of 1991. The revolts ultimately failed at the cost of more than one hundred thousand lives. American inaction during the cease-fire that effectively ended its role in the conflict was viewed by many as encouraging the revolts.

16. The Senate approved the resolution to authorize the president to use force 52–47; the House by a 250–183 vote.

17. For a strong argument that such actions are just, see Evans (2008).

18. The Obama administration seemed to care little for Congress's views anyway. It ignored several War Powers Act requirements in the conduct of the operation. When the US ambassador to Libya was killed by militants in September 2012, the risidual discord escalated into intense Republican criticism of the administration's policy.

19. From 2006 to 2011, about one-third of Americans favored the US war in Iraq according to the CNN/ORC poll. Although support for the war in Afghanistan declined in the same five-year period, it was always greater than that for the operation in Iraq. For much of 2006–2009, a slim majority of respondents in the CNN/ORC poll favored what the United States was doing in Afghanistan.

20. The resolution was HJRes 114.

21. The Senate vote was 77–23. The House vote was 297–133, with 82 Democrats voting for and 126 voting against.

22. It is even easier to be critical of others' decisions from the safe confines of state government. That is essentially what happened during the 2008 primary when Barack Obama excoriated Sens. Joe Biden (D-DE), Chris Dodd (D-CT), and Hillary Clinton (D-NY) for their votes in favor of the Iraq resolution. He took his costless position in 2002 as an Illinois state senator.

23. Several members who had received the briefings, particularly Democrats, later explained they had been told Iraq possessed chemical and biological weapons of mass destruction and was actively developing nuclear arms.

24. In addition to the votes authorizing force, a December 2005 House Republican resolution, ostensibly offered as a parliamentary maneuver to ease pressure on Democrats, called for the immediate cessation of US operations in Iraq. It received only three votes. There were also resolutions in early 2007 disapproving of the Bush administration's "troop surge" policy (one passed 246–182 in the House but failed to get the needed sixty votes to invoke cloture in the Senate).

25. Stiglitz and Bilmes (2008) argue the war in Iraq alone had, by 2008, effectively cost the United States $3 trillion.

26. The "two presidencies" thesis was first explained by Aaron Wildavsky (1966). He argued presidents have greater influence over foreign policy outcomes than domestic policy outcomes and, as a result, prefer to focus on international affairs.

27. A recession is usually considered to be at least two consecutive quarters of decline in the country's GDP as calculated by the National Bureau of Economic Research (NBER).

28. Gramm-Leach-Bliley, or the Financial Services Modernization Act of 1999, repealed much of Glass-Steagall, a centerpiece of the early New Deal. The new law allowed companies to consolidate investment, commercial banking, and insurance services into a single operational unit. The health insurance portability legislation (sometimes known as Kennedy-Kassebaum) was important, but it passed as a kind of consolation prize for those who had sought more comprehensive health care reform. It allowed individuals to take insurance with them when they left a job. The ADA and Family and Medical Leave Act (FMLA) were truly landmarks. The ADA was the first civil rights law of any consequence that focused on disability. FMLA guaranteed workers unpaid leave to be at home to deal with personal or family illnesses or other issues.

29. Enron was a Houston energy corporation that used complicated accounting procedures to mask extensive fraud. Its bankruptcy and the subsequent exposure of its executives' crimes led to the Sarbanes-Oxley Act of 2002. The legislation forced greater transparency on public companies and increased federal regulation of their accounting practices.

30. The 1981 ERTA decreased marginal individual income tax rates by about a quarter and indexed brackets to inflation.

31. Among other things, the Economic Growth and Tax Relief Reconciliation Act (EGTRRA) of 2001 reduced all individual income tax brackets and the capital gains tax.

32. The 1986 Tax Reform Act is discussed in Chapter 2. The 1982 Tax Equity and Fiscal Responsibility Act (TEFRA) mainly raised excise taxes and those on dividends. It increased revenues by about $35 billion a year. Ultimately working together, President Bush and congressional Democratic leaders agreed to limit exemptions and deductions and increase Medicare and some income taxes when they passed the 1990 Omnibus Budget and Reconciliation Act (OBRA). The legislation is famous for breaking Bush's "no new taxes" pledge. Without a single Republican vote in Congress, President Clinton pushed through the OBRA of 1993 that reduced deductions, increased the gas tax, and raised the top rate of the individual income tax.

33. The 1988 legislation, the Family Support Act, required parents of children over three who were on welfare to enroll in education, training, and job search programs. It constituted the first major revision to the AFDC program since its creation in 1935. The 1996 Personal Responsibility and Work Opportunity Act had greater effects. It turned AFDC into a block grant program, TANF, and established work requirements and lifetime eligibility limits on recipients.

34. The number of immigrants obtaining permanent resident status in the United States rose from just over half a million in 1980 to 1.8 million in 1991. With some ups and downs—the number was low immediately after the 9/11 attacks, for example—it remains over one million per year today.

35. Without trade promotion authority, Congress could amend agreements, effectively sending the administration back to its partner to renegotiate. By granting this authority, Congress binds itself to a simple up-or-down vote. A formal treaty is often difficult to obtain because it requires the support of two-thirds of senators.

36. There is also an American tradition of debt, however, and the country was born into it. For more on that and Jackson's views about budgets, see Gordon (2010, 11–61).

37. For more, see http://www.statebudgetsolutions.org/.

38. In a 2010 lame-duck session of Congress, President Obama and congressional Democrats extended the EGTRRA cuts initially passed by President George W. Bush and Republican majorities in 2001. The two-year extension was necessary because the original legislation was due to expire at the end of 2010. The payroll tax holiday was a 2 percentage reduction in workers' Social Security and Medicare tax.

39. Deficits were very high in the late 1980s and early 1990s, reaching $290 billion or 4.7 percent of GDP in 1992. As a proportion of the size of the economy, however, the deficit was twice as big in 2009.

40. In a May 2011 Ipsos poll, for example, 27 percent of respondents said cut existing programs, 9 percent said raise taxes, 52 percent said do both, and 10 percent said do neither.

41. In a March 2011 Bloomberg poll, for instance, "unemployment and jobs" was considered the country's number one priority by 43 percent of respondents, but the budget deficit came in second, with 29 percent saying it should be the top priority.

42. Japan, for example, has a debt that is about 200 percent of GDP, by 2025 it will have only two workers for each retiree, and it provides generous pension and health care programs to its older citizens.

43. Rep. Scott Garrett (R-NJ) nicely summarized this view in an argument for passage of a balanced budget amendment to the Constitution made on the House floor on November 17, 2011 (H 7723–7724 of the *Congressional Record*).

44. The estimates for both Social Security and Medicare are from the 2010 report of the Board of Trustees of the Federal Old-Age and Survivors Insurance and Federal Disability Insurance Trust Funds. It can be found at http://www.ssa.gov/oact/tr/2010/tr2010.pdf.

45. Perry's book is called *Fed Up!* In it, he calls Social Security a "Ponzi scheme" and questions whether Congress had the taxing authority to establish the program.

46. Note that we are talking about policy collectively. As a result, the single-subject rule expressed in seven state constitutions (and in statute in other states) is not particularly useful as a potential solution. This requirement compels state legislatures to dispose of individual bills that are short and focused on one topic. For more, see Gilbert (2006).

47. Interestingly, customs duties, the source of most of the federal government's revenue until the ratification of the Sixteenth Amendment establishing a direct income tax in 1913, are in Title 19 and not part of Title 26, the tax section of the US Code.

48. The 72,500 pages approximation comes from Chris Edwards at Cato. See http://www.cato-at-liberty.org/federal-tax-rules-72536-pages. For more on the recent history of federal tax law, see Brownlee (2004) and Steuerle (2008).

49. The Bipartisan Policy Center's Debt Reduction Task Force document can be found at http://www.bipartisanpolicy.org/projects/debt-initiative/about. The Simpson-Bowles report can be found at http://www.fiscalcommission.gov/sites/fiscalcommission.gov/files/documents /TheMomentofTruth12_1_2010.pdf.

50. Among Nixon and Ford's biggest domestic accomplishments were the creation of the EPA and OSHA, the Clean Air Act, and several large increases in Social Security benefits.

51. We have noted several of these before. The 1996 farm bill was intended to phase-out subsidies, although it had mixed success. The telecommunications bill of the same year broke up local monopolies.

8: DOES CONGRESS CARRY OUT VIGOROUS CHECKING AND BALANCING?

1. Thad Beyle has tracked gubernatorial power for a long time. He provides a wealth of data and a ranking system at http://www.unc.edu/~beyle/gubnewpwr.html.

2. Congress passed the amendment in March 1947. It was not approved by the necessary three-fourths of states until the winter of 1951, however. The amendment restricts some presidents to fewer than two full four-year terms if that person was president "for more than two years of a term to which some other person was elected President."

3. The book was *Congressional Government*, published in 1885.

4. Crédit Mobilier was the vehicle by which Rep. Oakes Adams (R-MA) offered colleagues shares of Union Pacific at a discount in return for their support of government spending on railroads. The investigation led by Rep. Luke Poland (R-VT) and Sen. Lot M. Morrill (R-ME) forced Grant to replace Vice President Schuyler Colfax on the Republican ticket. Other Grant administration scandals included the Treasury Department's assistance in the effort of James Fisk and Jay Gould to corner the gold market in 1869 and the Whiskey Ring episode in 1875 in which government officials, including the president's private secretary Orville Babcock, conspired with producers to redirect tax revenues.

5. The quote is from a letter from Jefferson to Madison, dated March 15, 1789.

6. Important legislation passed in the Roosevelt years includes the Elkins and Hepburn Acts that regulated the railroads, the Pure Food and Drug Act of 1906, and the Aldrich-Vreeland Act of 1907 creating the National Monetary Commission that, in turn, recommended the establishment of the Federal Reserve.

7. These include the creation of the Federal Reserve in 1913 and the Clayton Antitrust Act of 1914. His administration took especially aggressive control of economic life when the country entered World War I in 1917.

8. Gould (2003) believes the modern presidency starts with William McKinley and Theodore Roosevelt. Most scholars use 1933 as the starting date, however (Greenstein 1988; Neustadt 1990).

9. The quote is from a July 23, 1937, press conference given by FDR.

10. To address escalating inflation during 1973 and 1974, Nixon refused to spend nearly $12 billion in congressionally appropriated funds.

11. Presidents do conform to the letter of the reporting requirement. As of June 2011, they have submitted 130 reports to Congress under the law (Grimmett 2011).

12. For the most part, these actions have been discussed earlier. For more, see Foreman (2007).

13. Congressional Republicans claimed health care reform would lead to the creation of over 150 new executive agencies. This was disputed. Experts agree, however, that Dodd-Frank

created five new ones—including the Consumer Financial Protection Bureau and the Financial Stability Oversight Council.

14. Washington's second veto, used in February 1787 on legislation to help establish the military, was ostensibly issued for policy reasons (Spitzer 1988, 27–28).

15. The case was *Barnes v. Kline* (1985).

16. Delegation was first permitted by the Supreme Court in *J. W. Hampton, Jr. and Co. v. United States* (1928) when it approved a law giving the president the power to adjust tariff rates because he was guided by an "intelligible principle." In *Mistretta v. United States* (1988), the court upheld Congress's creation of the US Sentencing Commission, essentially claiming that it should be given the benefit of the doubt when delegating legislative power. For more, see Bressman (2000).

17. For much more on presidents' use of regulatory review, see Crenson and Ginsberg (2008, 205–211).

18. When executive agreements are made pursuant to statutory authority, they are generally called congressional-executive agreements. When their basis is to be found in the president's plenary powers in foreign policy, they are termed sole executive agreements (Krutz and Peake 2009, 30).

19. Despite this, the Senate passed a bill in April 2011 designed to reduce the number of presidential appointments requiring Senate approval by about 250 relatively low-level positions. The House did not approve such legislation.

20. The case was *Clinton v. City of New York* and involved the president's veto of provisions in the Balanced Budget and Taxpayer Relief Acts of 1997. Justice John Paul Stevens's majority opinion stated that the procedure violated the presentment clause of the Constitution because it essentially gave the president the capacity to write law.

21. The line-item veto could be used only on appropriations and limited tax-benefit provisions. The president had five days to block parts he did not like in the bill he was signing. Those that he prevented from becoming law then had to be passed as stand-alone bills. If taken up within the thirty days immediately following the president's action, they could be considered under expedited procedures. For more, see Joyce and Reischauer (1997).

22. Chadha was a foreign exchange student facing a deportation order. He sought a suspension that was granted by the INS. The House of Representatives then vetoed a number of these suspensions, including Chadha's. The Supreme Court ruled the House's decision was unconstitutional because, as a legislative institution, its actions necessarily had to conform to the constitutionally described legislative process and the bicameralism and presentment that guarantee roles for the Senate and president.

23. Rep. Barney Frank (D-MA) was one of the first to term Bush's presidency plebiscitary. Frank took to the House floor in July 2006 to give a nearly hour-long and widely publicized speech making the case (*Congressional Record*, July 13, 2006, H 5212–5216).

24. This was done with the National Security Act. The National Security Council is chaired by the president. Its meetings are also regularly attended by the vice president, the secretary of defense, the secretary of state, the secretary of treasury, the chairman of the joint chiefs of staff, the director of national intelligence, and the national security adviser.

25. The first iteration of the report was critical, although, because it was written when the Senate was under Republican control, was not as assertive as the two released—one each in 2007 and 2008—when the Democrats were in the majority. However, it took the Senate four years to conclude Saddam Hussein had neither viable weapons of mass destruction nor close links to Al Qaeda.

26. The story is complex. Ultimately fifteen people were convicted of crimes like fraud and conspiracy, including Jim McDougal on eighteen counts. For more on Whitewater, see Stewart (1997).

27. Travelgate was the unprecedented and wholesale firing of the White House travel office staff in order, it was claimed, to direct business to acquaintances. Filegate was the administration's improper request for FBI files on hundreds of individuals, including those who worked in previous Republican administrations. Vince Foster was a Clinton friend and White House counsel who, various investigations determined, committed suicide in 1993. For more on these episodes, see Stewart (1997).

28. The House's votes on the counts of perjury to the grand jury and obstruction of justice were 228–206 and 221–212 respectively. The Senate's votes on these two counts were 45–55 and 50–50, well short of the two-thirds needed to convict.

29. The story of Watergate is complicated, but has been told many times. For more, see Bernstein and Woodward (2005); Emery (1995).

30. St. Clair led a rather personal and punitive expedition against the Miami and Shawnee Indians at the battle of Wabash. The outcome was the costliest ever defeat for the US Army at the hands of Native Americans.

31. Mally Daugherty, former Harding Attorney General Harry Daugherty's brother, appealed his contempt conviction given for failing to appear before a Senate committee investigating the Teapot Dome scandal. The court confirmed the original determination in *McGrain v. Daugherty* (1927).

32. Adams resigned in 1958 after it was discovered he had accepted gifts—including a vicuna coat—from Bernard Goldfine, an industrialist who was under investigation from the Federal Trade Commission.

33. Perhaps the most high profile of the failures was Sen. Rand Paul's (R-KY) effort to override the EPA's power plant pollution rules in October 2011.

34. The independent counsel case was *Morrison v. Olson* (1988).

35. This is *Bowsher v. Synar* (1986).

36. The case is *Free Enterprise Fund v. Public Company Accounting Oversight Board* (2010).

37. This is often called the "fire alarm" approach to oversight. For more, see McCubbins and Schwartz (1984).

38. Madison uses this quote from Montesquieu's famous *Spirit of the Laws* in *Federalist 47*. Hamilton employs it in *Federalist 78*.

39. Frustrated the Supreme Court was repeatedly voiding parts of the New Deal, Roosevelt proposed he appoint one new justice for all sitting members of the court who were more than seventy-and-a-half years old, up to a maximum of six. The potential effects were obvious. Congress was ultimately unconvinced, but observers often point to the "switch in time that saved nine" as evidence of the plan's indirect effect. In *West Coast Hotel v. Parrish* (1937), as Congress and the country debated Roosevelt's suggestion, Justice Owen Roberts switched from his general opposition to New Deal legislation and voted to uphold a minimum wage law. From that point on, the court was much more supportive of FDR's agenda.

40. For example, data show that during Samuel Alito's confirmation in 2005–2006, ideological interest groups spent about $2.5 million on advertising trying to persuade the public that the judge should or should not be confirmed (Gibson and Caldeira 2009, 63).

41. Estrada and Pickering withdrew before the Gang of Fourteen's agreement in May 2005 when it became clear their nominations were stuck in the Senate. Brown, Owen, and Pryor were confirmed to circuit court positions on narrow votes after the agreement was announced.

42. Owens (2010), however, demonstrates the preferences of presidents and Congresses have minimal effects on Supreme Court decisions.

43. As of the end of 2011, there were slightly more judges appointed by Republican presidents than appointed by Democratic presidents at all three levels of the federal courts—the Supreme Court, the circuit courts of appeal, and the district courts.

44. The Schiavo episode is therefore also an example of bad lawmaking since the legislation was specific to one person, not general.

9: APPRAISING CONGRESS

1. Details of the poll can be found at http://www.gallup.com/poll/149678/americans-express-historic-negativity-toward-government.aspx.

2. The case was *U.S. Term Limits v. Thornton* (1995). In its decision, the court ruled an Arkansas law precluding members who had served three terms in the House and two in the Senate from the ballot.

3. It won 227 votes in 1995 and 217 in 1997.

4. BCRA did two things that, theoretically at least, weakened incumbents. Individual contribution limits were doubled in 2002 to $2,000 per candidate per election and indexed to inflation. For the 2012 cycle the figure was $2,500. Individual contributors do not seem to care particularly whether a candidate holds office or not. The Millionaires Amendment allows the opponents of self-financiers to raise up to six times the normal limit from individual donors (Steen 2006b, 147–160).

5. BCRA prohibited corporations and unions from broadcasting the names of federal candidates in the sixty days before a general election and thirty days prior to a primary. By declaring this unconstitutional, *Citizens United* has facilitated the rise of Super PACs.

6. DISCLOSE stands for Democracy Is Strengthened by Casting Light on Spending in Elections Act. An effort to get it through the Senate failed in the summer of 2012.

7. There is evidence, however, that district complexity aids incumbents (Ensley, Tobias, and de Marchi 2009).

8. Binder and Smith (1997, 210–212) support this proposal. As they report, in 1957 Sen. Paul Douglas (D-IL) suggested a fifteen-day advanced notice requirement for cloture within a proposed fifty-one-vote rule (Binder and Smith 1997, 212).

9. Sen. Majority Leader Harry Reid (D-NV) began seriously talking about this in May 2012.

10. For more on No Labels and its fixes for Congress, see http://www.nolabels.org/work.

11. The Davis-Bacon rules state that federal government construction projects should pay prevailing local wages. There are also minority business ownership rules, which seem a little more problematic from the perspective taken here.

12. In 1994, the House engaged in three Oxford-style debates, one each on health, welfare, and trade. In 1993, it had a Lincoln-Douglas-style debate on the resolution "Shall the United States adopt a single-payer Canadian-style health care system?"

13. There is no need to reinvent the wheel here. The congressional parties already hold such retreats on an annual basis. My proposal is to establish a bipartisan version—a little like House Republicans did when they invited President Obama to their meeting in 2010.

No Labels, moreover, suggests both chambers should institute monthly bipartisan gatherings and create a bipartisan leadership committee.

14. In its 2010 survey, Gallup found 42 percent considered themselves conservative, 35 percent moderate, and 20 percent liberal. In 1996, these figures were 38, 40, and 16 respectively.

15. According to a September 2010 poll by the Pew Research Center for the People and the Press, 40 percent of Republicans regularly watch Fox News; only 15 percent of Democrats do. Twenty-five percent of Democrats regularly watch CNN; only 12 percent of Republicans do.

16. Reps. Michele Bachmann (R-MN), Allen West (R-FL), Alan Grayson (D-FL), and Joe Wilson (R-SC) were in the top seven in total contributions from individual donors in 2010. Bachmann and Grayson—the former a conservative, the latter a liberal—were arguably the two most colorful ideologues of the 111th Congress. West was a challenger but had proven himself a respected member of the Tea Party group and, as an African American, an obvious draw for the media. Wilson's claim to fame is having shouted "you lie!" to Barack Obama during the president's address to Congress on health care in September 2009.

17. Boatright (2004) suggests many "no hopers" run to bring attention to an issue or cause. He calls their candidates "expressive".

18. Certainly the preponderance of the literature perceives them as ambitious and seeking advancement to higher office (Fox and Lawless 2005; Victor 2011).

19. In the ISS surveys of the past decade, more Americans agree with the terms "people get rewarded for their effort" and "people get rewarded for their intelligence and skills" than any other nationality. See http://www.issp.org/.

20. Hofstadter is not alone. Jacoby (2008) and Lim (2008) agreed recently with this general proposition. There are also adherents on the right, perhaps most notably Bloom (1988).

21. For more on the survey, see http://publicreligion.org/site/wp-content/uploads/2011/11/PRRI-2011-American-Values-Survey-Web.pdf.

22. Of course there are many qualities an effective president needs in addition to basic intelligence. It is plausibly the case that high levels of intelligence detract from presidential performance, and that perceived intelligence is not the same as actual intelligence. My point here is merely that the public seems to vote for presidential candidates on the basis of qualities other than intelligence.

23. There are recent examples of all of this behavior. In the summer of 2011, 178 Atlanta Public Schools teachers and principals were found to have cheated by raising their students' scores on standardized tests. A variety of books demonstrate the nefarious link between drug companies and doctors (see, for example, Angell 2005). In 2004, a report by the John Jay College commissioned by the US Conference of Catholic Bishops documented child sex-abuse charges against 4,392 priests in the United States. Jerry Sandusky, an assistant of famed head coach Joe Paterno at Penn State, was convicted of forty-eight counts of sexual abuse of young boys in 2012.

24. My personal experience is instructive. I have gotten to know many members over time. These include two I went to graduate school with, Rep. Charlie Dent (R-PA), who was elected in 2004, and Rep. Rob Simmons (R-CT), who served in the House from 2001 to 2007. I taught Rep. Patrick McHenry (R-NC), elected 2004, and Rep. Ric Keller (R-FL), who served from 2001–2009, is the brother of a woman who used to cut my hair. Reps. David Price (D-NC), first elected in 1986, and Dan Lipinski (D-IL), 2004, are both colleagues in political science. I worked as an American Political Science Association Congressional Fellow for Rep. Christopher Shays (R-CT) who served from 1987 to 2008.

REFERENCES

Abramoff, Jack. 2011. *Capitol Punishment: The Hard Truth About Washington Corruption from America's Most Notorious Lobbyist.* Los Angeles: WND Books.

Abramowitz, Alan I. 1985. "Economic Conditions, Presidential Popularity, and Voting Behavior in Midterm Congressional Elections." *Journal of Politics* 47: 31–43.

———. 2010. *The Disappearing Center: Engaged Citizens, Polarization, and American Democracy.* New Haven, CT: Yale University Press.

Abramowitz, Alan I., and Jeffrey A. Segal. 1992. *Senate Elections.* Ann Arbor: University of Michigan Press.

Abrams, Richard M. 2002. "Theodore Roosevelt." In *The Presidents: A Reference History*, edited by Henry F. Graff, 325–346. New York: Charles Scribner.

Ackerman, Bruce. 2010. *The Decline and Fall of the American Republic.* Cambridge, MA: Belknap Press of Harvard University Press.

Adams, John. 1776. *Thoughts on Government: Applicable to the Present State.* Boston: Gill.

Adler, E. Scott, Michael Ensley, and John Wilkerson. 2008. "Are Congressional Incumbents Accountable?" Paper presented at the annual meeting of the Midwest Political Science Association, Chicago.

Adler, E. Scott, Chariti E. Gent, and Cary B. Overmeyer. 1998. "The Home Style Homepage: Legislator Use of the World Wide Web for Constituency Contact." *Legislative Studies Quarterly* 23: 585–595.

Adsera, Alicia, Carles Boix, and Mark Payne. 2003. "Are You Being Served? Political Accountability and Quality of Government." *Journal of Law, Economics and Organization* 19: 445–490.

Ahuja, Sunil. 1994. "Electoral Status and Representation in the United States Senate: Does Temporal Proximity to Election Matter?" *American Politics Quarterly* 22: 104–118.

Ainsworth, Scott H., and Frances Akins. 1997. "The Informational Roles of Caucuses in the U.S. Congress." *American Politics Quarterly* 25:407–430.

Aldrich, John H. 1995. *Why Parties? The Origin and Transformation of Political Parties in America.* Chicago: University of Chicago Press.

Aldrich, John H., Mark M. Berger, and David W. Rohde. 2002. "The Historical Variability of Conditional Party Government, 1877–1994." In *Party, Process, and Political Change in Congress: New Perspectives on the History of Congress* edited by David W. Brady and Mathew D. McCubbins, 17–35. Stanford, CA: Stanford University Press.

Aldrich, John H., and David W. Rohde. 2000. "The Republican Revolution and the House Appropriations Committee." *Journal of Politics* 62: 1–33.

———. 2001. "The Logic of Conditional Party Government: Revisiting the Electoral Connection." In *Congress Reconsidered*, edited by Lawrence C. Dodd and Bruce I. Oppenheimer, 269–292. 7th ed. Washington, DC: Congressional Quarterly Press.

Allen, Jonathan. 2012. "With Olympia Snowe's Retirement, the Center Crumbles." *Politico*, February 29, p. 1.

Amar, Akhil Reed. 2005. *America's Constitution: A Biography*. New York: Random House.

Ames, Barry. 1995. "Electoral Rules, Constituency Pressures, and Pork Barrel: Bases of Voting in the Brazilian Congress." *Journal of Politics* 57: 324–343.

Angell, Marcia. 2005. *The Truth About the Drug Companies: How They Deceive Us and What to Do About It*. New York: Random House.

Ansolabehere, Stephen, David Brady, and Morris Fiorina. 1992. "The Vanishing Marginals and Electoral Responsiveness." *British Journal of Political Science* 22: 21–38.

Ansolabehere, Stephen, and Phillip Edward Jones. 2010. "Constituents' Responses to Congressional Roll-Call Voting." *American Journal of Political Science* 54: 583–597.

———. 2011. "Dyadic Representation." In *The Oxford Handbook of the American Congress*, edited by Eric Schickler and Frances E. Lee, 293–314. New York: Oxford University Press.

Anzia, Sarah F., and Molly J. Cohn. 2011. "Legislative Organization and the Second Face of Power: Evidence from U.S. State Legislatures." Unpublished manuscript, Stanford University.

Aristotle. 1981. *The Politics*. With an introduction by T. A. Sinclair. New York: Penguin.

Asher, Herbert B. 1974. "Committees and the Norm of Specialization." *The Annals of the American Academy of Political and Social Science* 411: 63–74.

Atlas, Cary M., Robert J. Hendershott, and Mark A. Zupan. 1997. "Optimal Effort Allocation by U.S. Senators: The Role of Constituency Size." *Public Choice* 92: 221–229.

Avery, James M., and Jeffrey A. Fine. 2012. "Racial Composition, White Racial Attitudes, and Black Representation: Testing the Racial Threat Hypothesis in the United States Senate." *Political Behavior*, 34: 391–410.

Azari, Julia R., and Jennifer K. Smith. 2012. "Unwritten Rules: Informal Institutions in Established Democracies." *Perspectives on Politics* 10: 37–55.

Bader, John B. 1996. *Taking the Initiative: Leadership Agendas in Congress and the "Contract with America."* Washington, DC: Georgetown University Press.

Bafumi, Joseph, and Michael Herron. 2010. "Leapfrog Representation and Extremism: A Study of American Voters and Their Members of Congress." *American Political Science Review* 104: 519–542.

Bailey, Michael A., and Forrest Maltzman. 2011. *The Constrained Court: How the Law and Politics Shape the Decisions Justices Make*. Princeton, NJ: Princeton University Press.

Baker, Ross K. 2007. *Strangers on a Hill: Congress and the Court*. New York: W. W. Norton.

Balla, Steven J., Eric D. Lawrence, Forrest Maltzman, and Lee Sigelman. 2002. "Partisanship, Blame Avoidance, and the Distribution of Legislative Pork." *American Journal of Political Science* 46: 515–525.

Banducci, Susan A., Todd Donovan, and Jeffrey A. Karp. 2004. "Minority Representation, Empowerment, and Participation." *Journal of Politics* 66: 534–556.

Barry, John M. 1992. *The Ambition and the Power: The Fall of Jim Wright, a True Story of Washington*. New York: Viking.

Bartels, Larry M. 2000. "Partisanship and Voting Behavior, 1952–96." *American Journal of Political Science* 44: 35–50.

———. 2008. *Unequal Democracy: The Political Economy of the New Gilded Age*. Princeton, NJ: Princeton University Press.

Beckmann, Matthew N. 2008. "The President's Playbook: White House Strategies for Lobbying Congress." *Journal of Politics* 70: 407–419.

Bentham, Jeremy. 2007. *An Introduction to the Principles of Morals and Legislation.* Mineola, NY: Dover.

Berkman, Michael. 1994. "State Legislators in Congress: Strategic Politicians, Professional Legislatures, and the Party Nexus." *American Journal of Political Science.* 38: 1025–1055.

Berman, William C. 1994. *America's Right Turn: From Nixon to Bush.* Baltimore: Johns Hopkins University Press.

Bernstein, Carl, and Bob Woodward. 2005. *The Final Days.* New York: Simon and Schuster.

Berry, Christopher R., Barry C. Burden, and William G. Howell. 2010. "The President and the Distribution of Federal Spending." *American Political Science Review* 104: 783–799.

Bessette, Joseph M. 1982. "Is Congress a Deliberative Body?" In *The United States Congress,* edited by Dennis Hale, 3–11. Chestnut Hill, MA: Boston College Press.

———. 1994. *The Mild Voice of Reason: Deliberative Democracy and American National Government.* Chicago: University of Chicago Press.

Best, Heinrich, and Maurizio Cotta, eds. 2000. *Parliamentary Representatives in Europe, 1848–2000: Legislative Recruitment and Careers in Eleven European Countries.* New York: Oxford University Press.

Beth, Richard S. 2005. "'Entrenchment' of Senate Procedure and the 'Nuclear Option' for Change: Possible Proceedings and Their Implications." Congressional Research Service, RL32843.

Beth, Richard S., Valerie Heitshusen, Bill Heniff Jr., and Elizabeth Rybicki. 2009. "Leadership Tools for Managing the U.S. Senate." Paper prepared for delivery at the annual meeting of the American Political Science Association, Toronto, Canada.

Bianco, William T. 2005. "Last Post for the 'Greatest Generation': The Policy Implications for the Decline of Military Experience in the U.S. Congress." *Legislative Studies Quarterly* 30: 85–102.

Bickers, Kenneth N., and Robert M. Stein. 1996. "The Electoral Dynamics of the Federal Pork Barrel." *American Journal of Political Science* 40: 1300–1326.

———. 2000. "The Congressional Pork Barrel in a Republican Era." *Journal of Politics* 62: 1070–1086.

———. 2004. "Interlocal Cooperation and the Distribution of Federal Grant Awards." *Journal of Politics* 66: 800–822.

Bickerstaff, Steve. 2007. *Lines in the Sand: Congressional Redistricting in Texas and the Downfall of Tom DeLay.* Austin: University of Texas Press.

Binder, Sarah A. 1997. *Minority Rights, Majority Rule: Partisanship and the Development of Congress.* New York: Cambridge University Press.

———. 1999. "The Dynamics of Legislative Gridlock, 1947–1996." *American Political Science Review* 93: 519–533.

———. 2003. *Stalemate: Causes and Consequences of Legislative Gridlock.* Washington, DC: Brookings Institution Press.

———. 2007. "Where do Institutions Come From? Exploring the Origins of the Senate Blue Slip." *Studies in American Political Development* 21: 1–15.

Binder, Sarah A., Anthony J. Madonna, and Steven S. Smith. 2007. "Going Nuclear, Senate Style." *Perspectives on Politics* 4: 729–740.

Binder, Sarah, and Forrest Maltzman. 2002. "Senatorial Delay in Confirming Federal Judges, 1947–1998." *American Journal of Political Science* 46: 190–199.

Binder, Sarah A., and Steven S. Smith. 1997. *Politics or Principle? Filibustering in the United States Senate.* Washington, DC: Brookings Institution.

Birkhead, Nathaniel A., Gabriel Uriate, and William T. Bianco. 2010. "The Impact of State Legislative Term Limits on the Competitiveness of Congressional Elections." *American Politics Research* 38: 842–861.

Bishin, Benjamin G. 2000. "Constituency Influence in Congress: Does Subconstituency Matter?" *Legislative Studies Quarterly* 25: 389–415.

Bishop, Bill. 2008. *The Big Sort: Why the Clustering of Likeminded America Is Tearing Us Apart.* New York: Houghton Mifflin.

Black, Duncan. 1948. "On the Rationale of Group Decision-Making." *Journal of Political Economy* 56: 23–34.

Bloom, Alan. 1998. *The Closing of the American Mind.* New York: Simon and Schuster.

Blumenthal, Sidney. 1980. *The Permanent Campaign.* New York: Touchstone.

Boatright, Robert G. 2004. *Expressive Politics: The Issue Strategies of Congressional Challengers.* Columbus: Ohio State University Press.

Bobo, Lawrence, and Franklin D. Gilliam Jr. 1990. "Race, Sociopolitical Participation and Black Empowerment." *American Political Science Review* 84: 377–393.

Boehmke, Frederick J., Sean Gailmard, and John W. Patty. 2006. "Whose Ear to Bend? Information Sources and Venue Choice in Policy-Making." *Quarterly Journal of Political Science* 1: 139–169.

Bolling, Richard W. 1965. *House out of Order.* New York: Dutton.

Book of the States. 2010. Lexington, KY: Council of State Governments.

Bovitz, Gregory, and Jamie Carson. 2006. "Position Taking and Electoral Accountability in the U.S. House of Representatives." *Political Research Quarterly* 59: 297–312.

Bowser, Jennifer Drage, and Gary Moncrief. 2007. "Term Limits in State Legislatures." In *Institutional Change in American Politics: The Case of Term Limits,* edited by Bruce Cain, R. Niemi and K. Kurtz, 10–21. Ann Arbor: University of Michigan Press.

Boxer, Barbara, and Nicole Boxer. 1993. *Strangers in the Senate: Politics and the New Revolution of Women in America.* Washington, DC: National Press Books.

Boylan, Richard T. 2002. "Private Bills: A Theoretical and Empirical Study of Lobbying." *Public Choice* 111: 19–47.

Bressman, Lori Schultz. 2000. "Schechter Poultry at the Millennium: A Delegation Doctrine for the Administrative State." *Yale Law Journal* 109: 1399–1442.

Bronner, Ethan. 2007. *Battle for Justice: How the Bork Nomination Shook America.* New York: Union Square Press.

Brown, George Rothwell. 1922. *The Leadership of Congress.* Indianapolis: Bobbs-Merrill.

Brown, Robert D., and James A. Woods. 1991. "Toward a Model of Congressional Elections." *Journal of Politics* 53: 454–473.

Brownlee, W. Elliot. 2004. *Federal Taxation in America: A Short History.* New ed. New York: Cambridge University Press.

Bruns, Roger A., David L. Hostetter, and Raymond W. Smock. 2011. *Congress Investigates: A Critical and Documentary History.* Rev. ed. Shepherdstown, WV: Robert C. Byrd Center.

Bucy, Erik P., and Maria Elizabeth Grabe. 2007. "Taking Television Seriously: A Sound and Image Bite Analysis of Presidential Campaign Coverage, 1992–2004." *Journal of Communication* 57: 652–675.

Bullock, Charles S., III. 2010. *Redistricting: The Most Political Activity in America.* Lanham, MD: Rowman and Littlefield.

Burden, Barry C. 2002. "United States Senators as Presidential Candidates." *Political Science Quarterly* 117: 81–102.

————. 2003. "The Discharge Rule and Minority Rights in the U.S. House of Representatives." Paper presented to the annual meeting of the American Political Science Association, Chicago, IL.

————. 2007. *The Personal Roots of Representation*. Princeton, NJ: Princeton University Press.

Burden, Barry C., and Tammy M. Frisby. 2004. "Preferences, Partisanship, and Whip Activity in the House of Representatives." *Legislative Studies Quarterly* 29: 569–590.

Burgin, Eileen. 1992. "Congress, the War Powers Resolution and the Invasion of Panama." *Polity* 25: 217–242.

Burke, Edmund. 1997. *Edmund Burke: Selected Writings and Speeches*. Washington, DC: Gateway Editions.

Burnham, James. 1959. *Congress and the American Tradition*. Chicago: H. Regnery.

Cain, Bruce, John Ferejohn, and Morris Fiorina. 1987. *The Personal Vote: Constituency Service and Electoral Independence*. Cambridge, MA: Harvard University Press.

Cairney, Paul 2007. "The Professionalization of MPs: Refining the 'Politics-Facilitating' Explanation." *Parliamentary Affairs* 60 (2): 212–233.

Calabresi, Stephen, and John Yoo. 2003. "The Unitary Executive During the Second Half Century." *Harvard Journal of Law and Public Policy* 26: 668–802.

Calvo, Ernesto. 2007. "The Responsive Legislature: Public Opinion and Law Making in a Highly Disciplined Legislature." *British Journal of Political Science* 37: 263–280.

Cameron, Charles M. 2000. *Veto Bargaining: Presidents and the Politics of Negative Power*. New York: Cambridge University Press.

Campbell, James E. 1991. "The Presidential Surge and Its Midterm Decline in Congressional Elections, 1868–1988." *Journal of Politics* 53: 477–487.

Canes-Wrone, Brandice. 2006. *Who Leads Whom? Presidents, Policy, and the Public*. Chicago: University of Chicago Press.

Canes-Wrone, Brandice, David W. Brady, and John F. Cogan. 2002. "Out of Step, Out of Office: Electoral Accountability and House Members' Voting." *American Political Science Review* 96: 127–140.

Canes-Wrone, Brandice, and Scott De Marchi. 2002. "Presidential Approval and Legislative Success." *Journal of Politics* 64: 491–509.

Canes-Wrone, Brandice, William Howell, and David E. Lewis. 2008. "Toward a Broader Understanding of Presidential Power: A Reevaluation of the Two Presidencies Thesis." *Journal of Politics* 70: 1–16.

Canes-Wrone, Brandice, William Minozzi, and Jessica Bonney Reveley. 2011. "Issue Accountability and the Mass Public." *Legislative Studies Quarterly* 36: 5–35.

Canon, David T. 1990. *Actors, Athletes, and Astronauts: Political Amateurs in the United States Congress*. Chicago: University of Chicago Press.

————. 1999. *Race, Redistricting, and Representation: The Unintended Consequences of Black Majority Districts*. Chicago: University of Chicago Press.

Canon, David T., and Charles Stewart III. 2001. "The Evolution of the Committee System in Congress." In *Congress Reconsidered*, edited by Lawrence C. Dodd and Bruce I. Oppenheimer, 163–190. 7th ed. Washington, DC: Congressional Quarterly Press.

Caplan, Bryan. 2007. *The Myth of the Rational Voter: Why Democracies Choose Bad Policies*. Princeton, NJ: Princeton University Press.

Carey, John M., Richard G. Niemi, Lynda W. Powell, and Gary F. Moncrief. 2006. "The Effects of Term Limits on State Legislatures: A New Survey of the fifty States." *Legislative Studies Quarterly* 31: 105–34.

Carey, John M., and Matthew Soberg Shugart. 1995. "Incentives to Cultivate a Personal Vote: A Rank Ordering of Electoral Formulas." *Electoral Studies* 14: 417–439.

Carnes, Nicholas. 2012. "Does the Numerical Underrepresentation of the Working Class in Congress Matter?" *Legislative Studies Quarterly* 37: 5–34.

Carpenter, Daniel, Kevin Esterling, and David Lazer. 2004. "Friends, Brokers and Transitivity: Who Informs Whom in Washington Politics?" *Journal of Politics* 66: 224–246.

Carr, Thomas P. 2005. "Suspension of Rules in the House: Measure Sponsorship by Party." Congressional Research Service, 97–901.

Carroll, Royce, and Henry A. Kim. 2010. "Party Government and 'The Cohesive Power of Public Plunder.'" *American Journal of Political Science* 54: 34–44.

Carson, Jamie, and Michael Crespin. 2004. "The Effect of State Redistricting Methods on Electoral Competition in United States House Races." *State Politics and Policy Quarterly* 4: 455–469.

Carson, Jamie, Michael Crespin, Carrie Eaves, and Emily Wanless. 2011. "Constituency Congruency and Candidate Competition in U.S. House Elections." *Legislative Studies Quarterly* 36: 461–482.

Carson, Jamie, Gregory Koger, Matthew Lebo, and Everett Young. 2010. "The Electoral Costs of Party Loyalty in Congress." *American Journal of Political Science* 54: 598–616.

Casellas, Jason P. 2011. *Latino Representation in State Houses and Congress.* New York: Cambridge University Press.

Casillas, Christopher J., Peter K. Enns, and Patrick C. Wohlfarth. 2011. "How Public Opinion Constrains the U.S. Supreme Court." *American Journal of Political Science* 55: 74–88.

Chang, Eric C. C. 2005. "Electoral Incentives for Political Corruption Under Open-List Proportional Representation." *Journal of Politics* 67: 716–730.

Chang, Eric C. C., Miriam A. Golden, and Seth Hill. 2010. "Legislative Malfeasance and Political Accountability." *World Politics* 62: 177–220.

Chi, Feng, and Nathan Yang. 2010. "Twitter Adoption in Congress." *Review of Network Economics* 10: 52–95.

Chiou, Fang-Yi, and Lawrence S. Rothenberg. 2003. "When Pivotal Politics Meets Partisan Politics." *American Journal of Political Science* 47: 503–522.

Cho, Wendy K. Tam, James G. Gimpel, and Daron R. Shaw. 2011. "The Geography of Tea: Expressive Protest or Strategic Activism?" Presented at the annual meeting of the Midwest Political Science Association, Chicago.

Clark, Tom S. 2011. *The Limits of Judicial Independence.* New York: Cambridge University Press.

Clinton, Joshua D. 2006. "Representation in Congress: Constituents and Roll Calls in the 106th House." *Journal of Politics* 68: 397–409.

Clinton, Joshua D., and John S. Lapinski. 2006. "Measuring Legislative Accomplishment, 1877–1946." *American Journal of Political Science* 50: 232–249.

Cohen, Jeffrey E. 2005. "Presidential Going Public in an Age of New Media." Paper presented at the annual meeting of the American Political Science Association, Washington, DC.

———. 2008. *The Presidency in the Era of 24-Hour News.* Princeton, NJ: Princeton University Press.

Coleman, John C. 1999. "Unified Government, Divided Government, and Party Responsiveness." *American Political Science Review* 93: 821–835.

Conley, Dalton, and Jacqueline Stevens. 2011. "Build a Bigger House." *New York Times*, January 23, p. A27.

Conley, Richard S. 2011. "C'est en Forgeant Qu'On Devient Forgeron? Assessing Legislative Productivity in Fifth Republic France." *French Politics* 9: 158–181.

Conley, Richard S., and Marija Bekafigo. 2010. "'No Irish Need Apply?' Veto Players and Legislative Productivity in the Republic of Ireland, 1949–2000." *Comparative Political Studies* 43: 91–118.

Connor, George E., and Bruce I. Oppenheimer. 1993. "Deliberation: An Untimed Value in a Timed Game." In *Congress Reconsidered*, edited by Lawrence C. Dodd and Bruce I. Oppenheimer, 315–330. 5th ed. Washington, DC: Congressional Quarterly Press.

Cook, Timothy E. 1986. "House Members as Rational Newsmakers: Effects of Televising Congress." *Legislative Studies Quarterly* 11: 203–226.

———. 1989. *Making Laws and Making News: Media Strategies in the U.S. House of Representatives*. Washington, DC: Brookings Institution Press.

Cooper, Joseph, and Cheryl D. Young. 1989. "Bill Introduction in the Nineteenth Century: A Study of Institutional Change." *Legislative Studies Quarterly* 14: 67–105.

Cooper, Phillip J. 2002. *By Order of the President: The Use and Abuse of Executive Direct Action*. Lawrence: University of Kansas Press.

Copeland, Curtis W. 2011. "New Entities Created Pursuant to the Patient Protection and Affordable Care Act." Congressional Research Service, R41315.

Corwin, Edward S. 1957. *The President: Office and Powers*. New York: New York University Press.

Cox, Gary W. 2005. "The Organization of Democratic Legislatures." In *The Oxford Handbook of Political Economy*, edited by Donald Wittman and Barry R. Weingast, 141–161. New York: Oxford University Press.

Cox, Gary W., and Mathew D. McCubbins. 2005. *Setting the Agenda: Responsible Party Government in the U.S. House of Representatives*. New York: Cambridge University Press.

Cox, Gary, and William C. Terry. 2008. "Legislative Productivity in the 93d–105th Congresses." *Legislative Studies Quarterly* 33: 603–618.

Crenshaw, Albert B. 2002. "No Simple Explanation for Tax Code's Complexity." *Washington Post*, March 3, p. H5.

Crenson, Matthew, and Benjamin Ginsberg. 2008. *Presidential Power: Unchecked and Unbalanced*. New York: W. W. Norton.

Crespin, Michael, Charles Finochiaro, and Eric Wilk. 2006. "Different Votes for Different Folks: Rules, Procedure, and Electoral Accountability." Paper presented to the annual meeting of the Southern Political Science Association, Atlanta.

Crespin, Michael H., Charles Finocchiaro, and Emily Wanless. 2009. "Perception and Reality in Congressional Earmarks." *Forum* 7: Article 1.

Crespin, Michael H., Suzanne Gold, and David W. Rohde. 2006. "Ideology, Electoral Incentives, and Congressional Politics: The Republican House Class of 1994." *American Politics Research* 34: 135–158.

Crisp, Brian F., Kristin Kanthak, and Jenny Leijonhufvud. 2004. "The Reputations Legislators Build: With Whom Should Representatives Collaborate?" *American Political Science Review* 98: 703–716.

Daggett, Stephen. 2010. "Costs of Major U.S. Wars." Congressional Research Service, RS22926.

Dahl, Robert. 1956. *A Preface to Democratic Theory*. Chicago: University of Chicago Press.

Dallek, Robert. 1999. *Flawed Giant: Lyndon Johnson and His Times, 1961–73*. New York: Oxford University Press.

Davidson, Roger H., Walter J. Oleszek, and Frances E. Lee. 2012. *Congress and Its Members*. 13th ed. Washington, DC: Sage, Congressional Quarterly Press.

Deering, Christopher, and Steven S. Smith. 1997. *Committees in Congress*. 3rd ed. Washington, DC: Congressional Quarterly Press.

Den Hartog, Chris, and Nathan Monroe. 2008. "Agenda Influence and Tabling Motions in the U.S. Senate." In *Why Not Parties? Party Effects in the U.S. Senate*, edited by Nathan W. Monroe, Jason M. Roberts, and David W. Rohde, 142–158. Chicago: University of Chicago Press.

———. 2011. *Agenda Setting in the U.S. Senate*. New York: Cambridge University Press.

Desposato, Scott, and Ethan Scheiner. 2009. "Governmental Centralization and Party Affiliation: Legislator Strategies in Brazil and Japan." *American Political Science Review* 102: 509–524.

Dewar, Helen. 2003. "For Senators, Soul-Searching About the Rules." *Washington Post*, June 23, A19.

DioGuardi, Joseph A. 2010. *Unaccountable Congress: It Doesn't Add Up*. N.p.: Create Space.

Dion, Douglas. 1997. *Turning the Legislative Thumbscrew: Minority Rights and Procedural Change in Legislative Politics*. Ann Arbor: University of Michigan Press.

Dodd, Lawrence C., and Scot Schraufnagel. 2007. "A Conflict-Theory of Policy Productivity in Congress: Party Polarization, Member Incivility and Landmark Legislation, 1891–1993." Paper presented at the annual meeting of the American Political Science Association, Chicago, IL.

Döring, Herbert. 2001. "Parliamentary Agenda Control and Legislative Outcomes in Western Europe." *Legislative Studies Quarterly* 26: 145–165.

Dovi, Suzanne. 2002. "Preferable Descriptive Representatives: Or Will Just Any Woman, Black, or Latino Do?" *American Political Science Review* 96: 745–754.

Downs, Anthony. 1957. *An Economic Theory of Democracy*. New York: Harper.

Draper, Robert. 2012. *Do Not Ask What Good We Do: Inside the U.S. House of Representatives*. New York: Free Press.

Durkheim, Emile. 1947. *The Division of Labor in Society*. Glencoe, IL: Free Press.

Durr, Robert H., John B. Gilmour, and Christina Wolbrecht. 1997. "Explaining Congressional Approval." *American Journal of Political Science* 41: 175–207.

Eaton, Kent. 2002. "Fiscal Policy Making in the Argentine Congress." In *Legislative Politics in Latin America*, edited by Scott Morgenstern and Benito Nacif, 287–314. New York: Cambridge University Press, 2002.

Edsall, Thomas B. 1991. *Chain Reaction: The Impact of Race, Rights, and Taxes on American Politics*. New York: Norton.

Edwards, George C., III. 2003. *On Deaf Ears: The Limits of the Bully Pulpit*. New Haven, CT: Yale University Press.

Eggen, Dan, and T. W. Farnum. 2010. "'Super PACs' Alter Campaign." *Washington Post*, September 28, p. A1.

Eilperin, Juliet. 2006. *Fight Club Politics: How Partisanship Is Poisoning the House of Representatives*. Lanham, MD: Rowman and Littlefield.

Ellis, Richard E. 1971. *The Jeffersonian Crisis: Courts and Politics in the Young Republic*. New York: W. W. Norton.

Emerson, Ralph Waldo. 1883. *The Conduct of Life; and, Society and Solitude*. London: Macmillan.

Emery, Fred. 1995. *Watergate: The Corruption of American Politics and the Fall of Richard Nixon*. New York: Simon and Schuster.

Ensley, Michael J. 2009. "Individual Campaign Contributions and Candidate Ideology." *Public Choice* 138: 221–238.

Ensley, Michael J., Michael W. Tobias, and Scott de Marchi. 2009. "District Complexity as an Advantage in Congressional Elections." *American Journal of Political Science* 53: 990–1005.

Epstein, David, David Brady, Sadafumi Kawato, and Sharyn O'Halloran. 1997. "A Comparative Approach to Legislative Organization: Careerism and Seniority in the United States and Japan." *American Journal of Political Science* 41: 965–998.

Erikson, Robert S., Michael B. MacKuen, and James A. Stimson. 2002. *The Macro Polity*. New York: Cambridge University Press.

Etzioni, Amitai. 2004. *The Common Good*. New York: Polity.

Evans, Gareth. 2008. *The Responsibility to Protect: Ending Mass Atrocity Crimes Once and for All*. Washington, DC: Brookings Institution Press.

Farrand, Max. 1966. *The Records of the Federal Convention of 1787*. New Haven, CT: Yale University Press.

Faulkner, Robert. K. 2001. "The First Liberal Democrat: Locke's Popular Government." *Review of Politics* 63: 5–39.

Feldstein, Mark. 2004. "Watergate Revisited." *American Journalism Review* 26: 60–68.

Fenno, Richard F., Jr. 1973. *Congressmen in Committees*. Boston: Little, Brown.

———. 1978. *Home Style: House Members in Their Districts*. Boston: Little, Brown.

Ferejohn, John A., and Randall L. Calvert. 1984. "Presidential Coattails in Historical Perspective." *American Journal of Political Science* 28: 127–146.

Finocchiaro, Charles J., and Jeffery A. Jenkins. 2008. "In Search of Killer Amendments in the Modern U.S. House." *Legislative Studies Quarterly* 33: 263–294.

Fiorina, Morris P. 1977. *Congress: Keystone of the Washington Establishment*. New Haven, CT: Yale University Press.

Fiorina, Morris P., Samuel Abrams, and Jeremy C. Pope. 2010. *Culture War? The Myth of a Polarized America*. New York: Longman.

Fiorina, Morris P., and Matthew S. Levendusky. 2006. "Disconnected: The Political Class versus the People." In *Red and Blue Nation? Characteristics, Causes and Chronology of America's Polarized Politics*, edited by Pietro Nivola and David Brady, 49–118. Washington, DC: Brookings Institution Press and the Hoover Institution.

Fisher, Louis. 2005. "Legislative Vetoes After *Chadha*." Congressional Research Service, RS22132.

———. 2009. *On Appreciating Congress: The People's Branch*. Boulder, CO: Paradigm.

Fishkin, James S. 1995. *The Voice of the People: Public Opinion and Democracy*. New Haven, CT: Yale University Press.

Fogarty, Brian J. 2008. "The Strategy of the Story: Media Monitoring Legislative Activity." *Legislative Studies Quarterly* 33: 445–469.

Foley, Elizabeth Price. 2012. *The Tea Party: Three Principles*. New York: Cambridge University Press.

Ford, Paul L. 2010. *The Works of Thomas Jefferson*. Vol. 6. New York: Cosmo Classics.

Foreman, Christopher H., Jr. 2007. "The Braking of the President: Shifting Context and the Bush Domestic Agenda." In *The George W. Bush Legacy*, edited by Colin Campbell and Bert A. Rockman, 265–287 Washington, DC: Congressional Quarterly Press.

Forgette, Richard G. 2004. "Congressional Party Caucuses and Coordination: Assessing Caucus Activity and Party Effects." *Legislative Studies Quarterly* 29: 407–430.

Formisano, Ronald P. 1983. *The Transformation of Political Culture: Massachusetts Parties, 1790s–1840s*. New York: Oxford University Press.

Fox, Richard L., and Eric R. A. N. Smith. 1998. "The Role of Candidate Sex in Voter Decision-Making." *Political Psychology* 19: 405–419.

Fox, Richard L., and Jennifer L. Lawless. 2005. "To Run or Not to Run for Office: Explaining Nascent Political Ambitions." *American Journal of Political Science* 49: 642–659.

———. 2011. "Gains and Losses in Interest in Running for Office: The Concept of Dynamic Political Ambition." *Journal of Politics* 73: 443–462.

Francia, Peter L., Clyde Wilcox, Alexandra Cooper, John C. Green, Paul S. Herrnson, Lynda W. Powell, Jason Reifler, and Benjamin A. Webster. 2003. "With Limits Raised, Who Will Give More? The Impact of BCRA on Individual Donors." In *Life After Reform: When the Bipartisan Campaign Reform Act Meets Politics*, edited by Michael J. Malbin, 61–79. Lanham, MD: Rowman and Littlefield.

Frantzich, Stephen E., and John Sullivan. 1996. *The C-Span Revolution*. Norman: University of Oklahoma Press.

Frisch, Scott A., and Sean Q. Kelly. 2006. *Committee Assignment Politics in the U.S. House*. Norman: University of Oklahoma Press.

Fukuyama, Francis. 1995. *Trust: The Social Virtues and the Creation of Prosperity*. New York: Free Press.

Gadarian, Shana Kushner. 2010. "The Politics of Threat: How Terrorism News Shapes Foreign Policy Attitudes." *Journal of Politics* 72: 469–483.

Gaddie, Ronald Keith. 2004. *Born to Run: Origins of the Political Career*. Lanham, MD: Rowman and Littlefield.

Gailmard, Sean, and Jeffrey A. Jenkins. 2007. "Negative Agenda Control in the Senate and House: Fingerprints of Majority Party Power." *Journal of Politics* 69: 689–700.

Gaines, Brian J. 1998. "The Impersonal Vote? Constituency Service and Incumbency Advantage in British Elections, 1950–92." *Legislative Studies Quarterly* 23: 167–195.

Galloway, George B. 1953. *The Legislative Process in Congress*. New York: Thomas Y. Crowell.

Gamm, Gerald, and Kenneth Shepsle 1989. "Emergence of Legislative Institutions: Standing Committees in the House and Senate, 1810–1825." *Legislative Studies Quarterly* 14: 39–66.

Gamm, Gerald, and Steven S. Smith. 2002. "Policy Leadership and the Development of the Modern Senate." In *Party, Process, and Political Change in Congress: New Perspectives on the History of Congress*, edited by David W. Brady and Mathew D. McCubbins, 287–311. Stanford, CA: Stanford University Press.

Garand, James C., and Kelly M. Burke. 2006. "Legislative Activity and the 1994 Republican Takeover: Explaining Changing Patterns in Sponsorship and Co-Sponsorship in the U.S. House." *American Politics Research* 34: 159–188.

Geyh, Charles Gardner. 2006. *When Courts and Congress Collide: The Struggle for Control of America's Judicial System*. Ann Arbor: University of Michigan Press.

Gibson, James L., and Gregory A. Caldeira. 2009. *Citizens, Courts, and Confirmations: Positivity Theory and the Judgments of the American People*. Princeton, NJ: Princeton University Press.

Gibson, James L., Gregory A. Caldeira, and Lester Kenyatta Spence. 2003. "The Supreme Court and the US Presidential Election of 2000: Wounds, Self-Inflicted or Otherwise?" *British Journal of Political Science* 33: 553–556.

Gibson, Joseph. 2010. *A Better Congress: Change the Rules, Change the Results—A Modest Proposal*. Alexandria, VA: Two Seas.

Gilbert, Michael D. 2006. "Single Subject Rules and the Legislative Process." *University of Pittsburgh Law Review* 67: 803–870.

Giles, Micheal W., Bethany Blackstone, and Richard L. Vining. 2008. "The Supreme Court in American Democracy: Unravelling the Linkages Between Public Opinion and Judicial Decision Making." *Journal of Politics* 70: 293–306.

Gilmour, John B. 1995. *Strategic Disagreement: Stalemate in American Politics*. Pittsburgh: University of Pittsburgh Press.

Gilmour, John B., and Paul Rothstein. 1996. "A Dynamic Model of Loss, Retirement, and Tenure in the U.S. House of Representatives." *Journal of Politics* 58: 54–68.

Gimpel, James G. 1996. *Legislating the Revolution: The Contract with America in Its First 100 Days*. Needham Heights, MA: Allyn and Bacon.

Gingerich, Daniel. 2009. "Ballot Structure, Political Corruption, and the Performance of Proportional Representation." *Journal of Theoretical Politics* 21: 509–541.

Glassman, Matthew Eric. 2007. "Franking Privilege: Historical Development and Options for Change." Congressional Research Service, RL34274.

Glassman, Matthew Eric, Jacob R. Straus, and Colleen J. Shogan. 2010. "Social Networking and Constituent Communications: Member Use of Twitter During a Two-Month Period in the 111th Congress." Congressional Research Service, R41066.

Goedert, Nicholas M. 2011. "Redistricting Institutions, Partisan Tides, and Congressional Turnover." Paper presented at the annual conference of the Midwest Political Science Association, Chicago, IL.

Gold, Martin B., and Dimple Gupta. 2004. "The Constitutional Option to Change Senate Rules and Procedures: A Majoritarian Means to Overcome the Filibuster." *Harvard Journal of Law and Public Policy* 28: 206–266.

Goodwin, George, Jr. 1959. "The Seniority System in Congress." *American Political Science Review* 53: 412–436.

Gordon, James Steele. 2010. *Hamilton's Blessing: The Extraordinary Life and Times of Our National Debt*. New York: Walker.

Gordon, Sanford C., and Catherine Hafer. 2007. "Corporate Influence and the Regulatory Mandate." *Journal of Politics* 69: 300–319.

Gould, Lewis L. 2003. *The Modern American Presidency*. Lawrence: University Press of Kansas.

Graber, Doris A. 2010. *Mass Media and American Politics*. 6th ed. Washington, DC: Congressional Quarterly Press.

Grady, Robert C. 1984. "Juridical Democracy and Democratic Values: An Evaluation of Lowi's Alternative to Interest Group Liberalism." *Polity* 16: 404–422.

Grant, J. Tobin, and Nathan J. Kelly. 2008. "Legislative Productivity of the U.S. Congress, 1789–2004." *Political Analysis* 16: 303–323.

Grant, J. Tobin, and Thomas J. Rudolph. 2004. "The Job of Representation in Congress: Public Expectations and Representative Approval." *Legislative Studies Quarterly* 29: 431–445.

Graves, Scott E., and Robert M. Howard. 2010. *Justice Takes a Recess: Judicial Appointments from George Washington to George W. Bush*. Lanham, MD: Lexington Books.

Greene, John Robert. 1995. *The Presidency of Gerald R. Ford*. Lawrence: University Press of Kansas.

Greenstein, Fred I. 1978. "Change and Continuity in the Modern Presidency." In *The New American Political System*, edited by Anthony King, 45–86. Washington, DC: American Enterprise Institute.

————. 1988. "Nine Presidents in Search of a Modern Presidency." In *Leadership in the Modern Presidency*, edited by Fred I. Greenstein, 296–312. Cambridge, MA: Harvard University Press.

Griffin, John D. 2006. "Electoral Competition and Democratic Responsiveness: A Defense of the Marginality Hypothesis." *Journal of Politics* 68: 909–919.

————. 2010. "Public Evaluations of Congress." *Oxford Handbook of Congress*. New York: Oxford University Press.

Grimmer, Justin. 2010. "A Bayesian Hierarchical Topic Model for Political Texts: Measuring Expressed Agendas in Senate Press Releases." *Political Analysis* 18: 1–35.

Grimmett, Richard F. 2011. "War Powers Resolution: Presidential Compliance." Congressional Research Service, RL33532.

Grose, Christian R. 2011. *Congress in Black and White: Race and Representation in Washington and at Home*. New York: Cambridge University Press.

Groseclose, Tim, and Jeffrey Milyo. 2010. "Sincere Versus Sophisticated Voting in Congress: Theory and Evidence." *Journal of Politics* 72: 60–73.

Grossback, Lawrence J., and David A. M. Peterson. 2004. "Understanding Institutional Change: Legislative Staff Development and the State Policymaking Environment." *American Politics Research* 32: 26–51.

Gulati, Girish J. 2004. "Members of Congress and Presentation of Self on the World Wide Web." *Harvard International Journal of Press/Politics* 9: 22–40.

Haider-Markel, Donald P. 2007. "Representation and Backlash: The Positive and Negative Influence of Descriptive Representation." *Legislative Studies Quarterly* 32: 107–134.

Hall, Peter A. 1987. "The Evolution of Economic Policy Under Mitterand." In *The Mitterand Experiment: Continuity and Change in Modern France*, edited by George Ross, Stanley Hoffmann, and Sylvia Malzacher, 54–72. New York: Oxford University Press.

Hall, Thad. 2004. *Authorizing Policy*. Columbus: Ohio State University Press.

Hallin, Daniel C. 1992. "Sound Bite News: Television Coverage of Elections, 1968–1988." *Journal of Communication* 42: 5–24.

Hamilton, Alexander, James Madison, and John Jay. 1982. *The Federalist Papers*. With an introduction by Garry Wills. New York: Bantam.

Hammond, Susan Webb. 2001. *Congressional Caucuses in National Policymaking*. Baltimore, MD: Johns Hopkins University Press.

Harbridge, Laurel, and Neil Malhotra. 2011. "Electoral Incentives and Partisan Conflict in Congress: Evidence from Survey Experiments." *American Journal of Political Science* 55: 494–510.

Harfst, Philipp, and Kai-Uwe Schnapp. 2003. "Are Agents Able to Control Their Principal's Control Structures? An Empirical Investigation of Parliamentary Means to 'Keep an Eye' on the Executive." ECPR Joint Sessions of Workshops. Edinburgh.

Harris, Douglas B. 1998. "The Rise of the Public Speakership." *Political Science Quarterly* 113: 193–212.

————. 2005. "Orchestrating Party Talk: A Party-Based View of One-Minute Speeches in the House of Representatives." *Legislative Studies Quarterly* 30: 127–141.

Harvard Law Review. 2009. "The Mysteries of the CRA." *Harvard Law Review* 122: 2162–2183.

Harvey, Anna, and Barry Friedman. 2006 "Pulling Punches: Congressional Constraints on the Supreme Court's Constitutional Rulings, 1987–2000." *Legislative Studies Quarterly* 31: 533–562.

Hasecke, Edward B., and Jason D. Mycoff. 2007. "Party Loyalty and Legislative Success: Are Loyal Majority Party Members More Successful in the U.S. House of Representatives?" *Political Research Quarterly* 60 (4): 607–617.

Heith, Diane J. 2004. *Polling to Govern: Public Opinion and Presidential Leadership.* Stanford, CA: Stanford University Press.

Heitshusen, Valerie, Garry Young, and David Wood. 2005. "Electoral Context and MP Constituency Focus in Australia, Canada, Ireland, New Zealand, and the United Kingdom." *American Journal of Political Science* 49: 32–45.

Hendershot, Marcus E. 2010. "From Consent to Advise and Consent: Cyclical Constraints Within the District Court Appointment Process." *Political Research Quarterly* 63: 328–342.

Hernandez, Raymond. 2011. "Gingrich Calls GOP's Medicare Plan Too Radical." *New York Times,* May 16, p. 11.

Herrera, Richard, and Michael Yawn. 1999. "The Emergence of the Personal Vote." *Journal of Politics* 61: 136–150.

Herrnson, Paul S., Irwin L. Morris, and John McTague. 2011. "The Impact of Presidential Campaigning for Congress on Presidential Support in the U.S. House of Representatives." *Legislative Studies Quarterly* 36: 99–122.

Hersman, Rebecca K. C. 2000. *Friends and Foes: How Congress and the President Really Make Foreign Policy.* Washington, DC: Brookings Institution Press.

Hetherington, Marc J. 2005. *Why Trust Matters: Declining Political Trust and the Demise of American Liberalism.* Princeton: Princeton University Press.

Hetherington, Marc J., and Jonathan Weiler. 2009. *Authoritarianism and Polarization in America.* New York: Cambridge University Press.

Hibbing, John R., and Christopher W. Larimer. 2008. "The American Public's View of Congress." *Forum* 6: Article 6.

Hibbing, John R., and Elizabeth Theiss-Morse. 1995. *Congress as Public Enemy: Public Attitudes Towards American Political Institutions.* New York: Cambridge University Press.

———. 2002. *Stealth Democracy: Americans' Beliefs About How Government Should Work.* New York: Cambridge University Press.

Hill, Jeffrey S., and Kenneth C. Williams. 1993. "The Decline of Private Bills: Resources Allocation, Credit Claiming, and the Decision to Delegate." *American Journal of Political Science* 37: 1008–1031.

Hinckley, Barbara. 1994. *Less Than Meets the Eye: Foreign Policy Making and the Myth of the Assertive Congress.* Chicago: University of Chicago Press.

Hoddie, Matthew, and Stephen R. Routh. 2004. "Predicting Presidential Presence: Explaining Presidential Midterm Elections Campaign Behavior." *Political Research Quarterly* 57: 257–265.

Hofstadter, Richard. 1966. *Anti-Intellectualism in American Life.* New York: Vintage.

Howell, William G. 2003. *Power Without Persuasion: The Politics of Direct Presidential Action.* Princeton, NJ: Princeton University Press.

Howell, William G., E. Scott Adler, Charles Cameron, and Charles Riemann. 2000. "Divided Government and the Legislative Productivity of Congress, 1945–1994." *Legislative Studies Quarterly* 25: 285–312.

Hudson, William E. 2008. *The Libertarian Illusion: Ideology, Public Policy, and the Assault on the Common Good.* Washington: Congressional Quarterly Press.

Hughes, Melanie M. 2011. "Intersectionality, Quotas, and Minority Women's Political Representation Worldwide." *American Political Science Review* 105: 604–620.

Isaacs, Julia B. 2008. "International Comparisons of Economic Mobility." Washington, DC: Brookings Institution Press.

Jackson, Keith. 1994. "Stability, and Renewal: Incumbency and Parliamentary Composition." In *The Victorious Incumbent: A Threat to Democracy?* edited by Albert Somit, Rudolf Wildenmann, Bernhard Bell, and Andrea Rommel, 251–277. Aldershot, UK: Dartmouth.

Jacobson, Gary C. 1996. "The 1994 House Elections in Perspective." *Political Science Quarterly* 111: 203–223.

———. 2007. "Referendum: The 2006 Midterm Congressional Elections." *Political Science Quarterly* 122: 1–24.

———. 2011. "The Republican Resurgence in 2010." *Political Science Quarterly* 127: 27–52.

Jacoby, Susan. 2008. *The Age of American Unreason*. New York: Pantheon.

Jenkins, Jeffery A. 1998. "Property Rights and the Emergence of Standing Committee Dominance in the Nineteenth-Century House." *Legislative Studies Quarterly* 23: 493–519.

———. 2004. "Partisanship and Contested Election Cases in the House of Representatives, 1789–2002." *Studies in American Political Development* 18: 113–135.

Jenkins, Jeffery A., Michael A. Crespin, and Jamie L. Carson. 2005. "Parties as Procedural Coalitions in Congress: An Examination of Differing Career Tracks." *Legislative Studies Quarterly* 30: 365–389.

Jenkins, Jeffery A., and Michael C. Munger. 2003. "Investigating the Incidence of Killer Amendments in Congress." *Journal of Politics* 65: 498–517.

Jenkins, Jeffery A., and Timothy Nokken. 2008. "Legislative Shirking in the Pre-Twentieth Amendment Era: Presidential Influence, Party Power, and Lame-Duck Sessions of Congress, 1877–1933." *Studies in American Political Development* 22: 111–140.

Jenkins, Jeffery A., and Charles H. Stewart III. 2002. "Order from Chaos: The Transformation of the Committee System in the House, 1816–22." In *Party, Process, and Political Change in Congress: New Perspectives on the History of Congress*, edited by David W. Brady and Mathew D. McCubbins145–236. Stanford, CA: Stanford University Press.

Jenkins, Peter 1987. *Mrs Thatcher's Revolution: The Ending of the Socialist Era*. London: Cape.

Johnson, Bertram. 2010. "Individual Contributions: A Fundraising Advantage for the Ideologically Extreme?" *American Politics Research* 38: 890–908.

Johnson, Gbemende, Bruce I. Oppenheimer, and Jennifer L. Selin. 2012. "The House as a Stepping Stone to the Senate: Why Do So Few African-American House Members Run?" *American Journal of Political Science* 56: 387–399.

Joint Economic Committee of Congress. 2003. "Constant Change: A History of Federal Taxes." September 12.

Jones, David R. 2001. "Party Polarization and Legislative Gridlock." *Political Research Quarterly* 53: 125–141.

———. 2010. "Partisan Polarization and Congressional Accountability in House Elections." *American Journal of Political Science* 54: 323–337.

Jones, David R., and Monika L. McDermott. 2009. *Americans, Congress, and Democratic Responsiveness: Public Evaluations of Congress and Electoral Consequences*. Ann Arbor: University of Michigan Press.

Jones, Mark P. 2009. "Gender Quotas, Electoral Laws, and the Election of Women: Evidence from the Latin American Vanguard." *Comparative Political Studies* 42: 56–81.

Joyce, Philip G., and Robert D. Reischauer. 1997. "The Federal Line-Item Veto: What Is It and What Will It Do?" *Public Administration Review* 57: 95–104.

Kaiser, Robert G. 2009. *So Damn Much Money: The Triumph of Lobbying and the Corrosion of American Government.* New York: Knopf.

Kane, Paul, Ben Pershing, and David Fahrenthold. 2009. "Close Win Predicted for 'Cap-and-Trade' Bill: House Speaker Reports 'Progress.'" *Washington Post*, June 26, p. A4.

Kang, Shin-Goo, and G. Bingham Powell. 2010. "Representation and Policy Responsiveness: The Median Voter, Election Rules, and Redistributive Welfare Spending." *Journal of Politics* 72: 1014–1028.

Kanthak, Kristin. 2004. "Exclusive Committee Assignments in the U.S. House of Representatives." *Public Choice* 121: 391–412.

Karpowitz, Christopher, J. Quin Monson, Kelly D. Patterson, and Jeremy C. Pope. 2011. "Tea Time in America? The Impact of the Tea Party Movement on the 2010 Midterm Elections." *PS: Political Science and Politics* 44: 303–309.

Kavanagh, Dennis. 1990. *Thatcherism and British Politics: The End of Consensus?* New York: Oxford University Press.

Kazee, Thomas A. (ed.) 1994. *Who Runs for Congress: Ambition, Context, and Candidate Emergence.* Washington, DC: Congressional Quarterly Press.

Keck, Thomas M. 2004. *The Most Activist Supreme Court in History: The Road to Modern Judicial Conservatism.* Chicago: University of Chicago Press.

Kelley, Christopher S., and Bryan Marshall. 2010. "Going It Alone: The Politics of Signing Statements from Reagan to Bush II." *Social Science Quarterly* 91: 168–187.

Kendall, Willmoore. 1960. "The Two Majorities." *Midwest Journal of Political Science* 4: 317–345.

Kernell, Samuel. 1977a. "Presidential Popularity and Negative Voting: An Alternative Explanation of the Midterm Electoral Decline of the President's Party." *American Political Science Review* 71: 44–66.

———. 1977b. "Toward Understanding 19th Century Congressional Careers: Ambition, Competition, and Rotation." *American Journal of Political Science* 21: 669–693.

———. 1986. *Going Public: New Strategies of Presidential Leadership.* Washington, DC: Congressional Quarterly Press.

———. 2007. *Going Public: New Strategies of Presidential Leadership.* 4th ed. Washington, DC: Congressional Quarterly Press.

Kerr, Clara H. 1895. *The Origin and Development of the United States Senate.* Ithaca, NY: Andrus and Church.

Kimball, David C. 2005. "Priming Partisan Evaluations of Congress." *Legislative Studies Quarterly* 30: 63–84.

King, Anthony. 1997. *Running Scared: Why America's Politicians Campaign Too Much and Govern Too Little.* New York: Free Press.

King, David C., and Richard J. Zeckhauser. 2003. "Congressional Vote Options." *Legislative Studies Quarterly* 28: 387–411.

Kirk, Russell. 1953. *The Conservative Mind: From Burke to Santayana.* Chicago: H. Regnery.

Kittilson, Miki Caul. 2008. "Representing Women: The Adoption of Family Leave in Comparative Perspective." *Journal of Politics* 70: 323–334.

Koempel, Michael. 2005. "Routes to the Senate Floor: Rule XIV and Unanimous Consent." Congressional Research Service, RS22299.

Koger, Gregory. 2003. "Position-Taking and Co-Sponsorship in the U.S. House." *Legislative Studies Quarterly* 28: 225–246.

———. 2010. *Filibustering: A Political History of Obstruction in the House and Senate.* Chicago: University of Chicago Press.

Kopits, George, and Jon Craig. 1998. *Transparency in Government Operations*. Washington, DC: International Monetary Fund.

Kraig, Robert Alexander. 2004. *Woodrow Wilson and the Lost World of the Oratorical Statesman*. College Station: Texas A&M Press.

Krehbiel, Keith. 1991. *Information and Legislative Organization*. Ann Arbor: University of Michigan Press.

———. 1998. *Pivotal Politics: A Theory of U.S. Lawmaking*. Chicago: University of Chicago Press.

Kreppel, Amie. 1997. "The Impact of Parties in Government on Legislative Output in Italy." *European Journal of Political Research* 31: 327–350.

Kriner, Douglas, and Liam Schwartz. 2008. "Divided Government and Congressional Investigations." *Legislative Studies Quarterly* 33: 295–321.

Krutz, Glen S. 2001. *Hitching a Ride: Omnibus Legislating in the U.S. Congress*. Columbus: Ohio State University Press.

———. 2005. "Issues and Institutions: 'Winnowing' in the U.S. Congress." *American Journal of Political Science* 49: 313–326.

Krutz, Glen S., and Jeffrey S. Peake. 2009. *Treaty Politics and the Rise of Executive Agreements: International Commitments in a System of Shared Powers*. Ann Arbor: University of Michigan Press.

Kurtz, Donn M., II. 2010. "Veterans of Iraq and Afghanistan as Congressional Candidates." *Foreign Policy Journal*. November 9.

Kyvig, David E. 2008. *The Age of Impeachment: American Constitutional Culture Since 1960*. Lawrence: University Press of Kansas.

Labaton, Stephen. 1996. "Whitewater Hearing Cleared the Clintons, Democrats Say." *New York Times*, June 19, p. A1.

Ladewig, Jeffrey W. 2010. "Ideological Polarization and the Vanishing Marginals: Retrospective Roll-Call Voting in the U.S. Congress." *Journal of Politics* 72: 499–512.

Lakoff, George. 2008. *The Political Mind: Why You Can't Understand 21st-Century American Politics with an 18th-Century Brain*. New York: Viking Adult.

Langston, Joy. 2010. "Governors and 'Their' Deputies: New Legislative Principals in Mexico." *Legislative Studies Quarterly* 35: 234–258.

LaRaja, Raymond J., and David L. Wiltse. 2012. "Don't Blame Donors for Ideological Polarization of Political Parties: Ideological Change and Stability Among Political Contributors, 1972–2008." *American Politics Research* 40: 501–530.

Lascher, Edward L., Jr. 1996. "Assessing Legislative Deliberation: A Preface to Empirical Analysis." *Legislative Studies Quarterly* 21: 501–519.

Lau, Richard R., and David P. Redlawsk. 2006. *How Voters Decide: Information Processing During Election Campaigns*. New York: Cambridge University Press.

Lawless, Jennifer L. 2011. "Twitter and Facebook: New Ways to Send the Same Old Message." In *iPolitics*, edited by Richard L. Fox and Jennifer Ramos, 206–232. New York: Cambridge University Press.

Lawless, Jennifer L., and Richard L. Fox. 2005. *It Takes a Candidate: Why Women Don't Run for Office*. New York: Cambridge University Press.

Lawless, Jennifer L., and Kathryn Pearson. 2008. "The Primary Reason for Women's Under-Representation: Re-Evaluating the Conventional Wisdom." *Journal of Politics* 70: 67–82.

Lax, Jeffrey R., and Justin H. Phillips. 2012. "The Democratic Deficit in the States." *American Journal of Political Science* 56: 148–166.

Layman, Geoffery C., Thomas M. Carsey, John C. Green, Richard Herrera, and Rosalyn Cooperman. 2010. "Activists and Conflict Extension in American Party Politics." *American Political Science Review* 104: 324–346.

Lazarus, Jeffrey. 2010. "Giving the People What They Want? The Distribution of Earmarks in the U.S. House of Representatives." *American Journal of Political Science* 54: 338–353.

Lazarus, Jeffrey, and Nathan W. Monroe. 2007. "The Speaker's Discretion: Conference Committee Appointments from the 97th–106th Congress." *Political Research Quarterly* 60: 593–606.

Lebo, Matthew. 2008. "Divided Government, United Approval: Long Memory and the Dynamics of Congressional and Presidential Approval." *Congress and the Presidency* 35: 1–16.

Lee, Frances E. 2003. "Geographic Politics in the U.S. House of Representatives: Coalition Building and the Distribution of Benefits." *American Journal of Political Science* 47: 714–728.

Lee, Frances E., and Bruce I. Oppenheimer. 1999. *Sizing up the Senate: The Unequal Consequences of Equal Representation*. Chicago: University of Chicago Press.

Leighton, Wayne A., and Edward J. Lopez. 2002. "Committee Assignments and the Cost of Party Loyalty." *Political Research Quarterly* 55: 53–90.

Lepore, Jill. 2010. *The Whites of Their Eyes: The Tea Party Revolution and the Battle over American History*. New York: Public Square.

Leuchtenburg, William E. 1963. *Franklin D. Roosevelt and the New Deal*. New York: Harper Perennial.

Levendusky, Matthew. 2009. *The Partisan Sort: How Liberals Became Democrats and Conservatives Became Republicans*. Chicago: University of Chicago Press.

Lewis, Daniel C. 2012. "Legislative Term Limits and Fiscal Policy Performance." *Legislative Studies Quarterly* 37: 305–328.

Lichter, S. Robert, and Daniel R. Amundson. 1994. "Less News Is Worse News: Television News Coverage of Congress, 1972–92." In *Congress, the Press, and the Public*, edited by Thomas E. Mann and Norman J. Ornstein, 131–140. Washington, DC: American Enterprise Institute and Brookings Institution.

Light, Paul C. 1995. *Artful Work: The Politics of Social Security Reform*. New York: Random House.

———. 2002. *Government's Greatest Achievements: From Civil Rights to Homeland Security*. Washington, DC: Brookings Institution Press.

Lijphart, Arend. 1999. *Patterns of Democracy: Government Forms and Performance in Thirty-Six Countries*. New Haven, CT: Yale University Press.

Lim, Elvin T. 2008. *The Anti-Intellectual Presidency: The Decline of Presidential Rhetoric from George Washington to George W. Bush*. New York: Oxford University Press.

Lindblom, Charles. 1965. *The Intelligence of Democracy*. New York: Free Press.

Linz, Juan J. 1994. "Presidential or Parliamentary Democracy? Does It Make a Difference?" In *The Failure of Presidential Democracy: Comparative Perspectives*, edited by Juan J. Linz and Arturo Valenzuela, 3–90. Baltimore: Johns Hopkins University Press.

Lipinski, Daniel, William T. Bianco, and Ryan Work. 2003. "What Happens When House Members 'Run with Congress'? The Electoral Consequences of Institutional Loyalty." *Legislative Studies Quarterly* 28: 413–429.

Lisk, Kristen R. 2008. "The Resolution of Contested Elections in the U.S. House of Representatives: Why State Courts Should Not Help with the House Work." *New York University Law Review* 83: 1213–1247.

Locke, John. 1988. *Two Treatises of Government*. New York: Cambridge University Press.

Lockerbie, Brad. 1991. "Prospective Economic Voting in House Elections, 1956–1988." *Legislative Studies Quarterly* 16: 239–262.

Lott, John R., Jr., and Stephen G. Bronars. 1993. "Time Series Evidence on Shirking in the U.S. House of Representatives." *Public Choice* 76: 125–149.

Lowi, Theodore J. 1979. *The End of Liberalism: The Second Republic of the United States*. New York: Norton.

———. 1985. *The Personal President, Power Invested, Promise Unfulfilled*. Ithaca, NY: Cornell University Press.

Lowry, Robert C., and Matthew Potoski. 2004. "Organized Interests and the Politics of Federal Discretionary Grants." *Journal of Politics* 66: 513–533.

Lyon, Alynna J., and Mary Fran T. Malone. 2009. "Was Woodrow Wilson Right? Assessing American Attitudes Towards Humanitarian Intervention." *Journal of Peace, Conflict and Development* 13: 1–41.

MacDonald, Jason A. 2010. "Limitation Riders and Congressional Influence over Bureaucratic Policy Decisions." *American Political Science Review* 104: 766–782.

MacKenzie, Scott A. 2009. "Going Up, Getting Out, or Moving In? Congressional Career Paths and Their Effects on Reelection and Retirement." Paper presented to the annual meeting of the American Political Science Association, Toronto, Canada.

———. 2011. "From Political Pathways to Senate Folkways: Careerism in the U.S. Senate, 1868–1944." Unpublished manuscript, University of California, Davis.

Madonna, Anthony J., and Michael S. Lynch. Forthcoming. "Viva Voce: Implications from the Disappearing Voice Vote, 1807–1990." *Social Science Quarterly*.

Maestas, Cherie, Sarah A. Fulton, L. Sandy Maisel, Walter J. Stone. 2006. "When to Risk It? Institutions, Ambitions, and the Decision to Run for the U.S. House." *American Political Science Review* 100: 195–208.

Mainwaring, Scott. 1999. *Rethinking Party Systems in the Third Wave of Democratization: The Case of Brazil*. Stanford: Stanford University Press.

Malbin, Michael J., ed. 2006. *The Election After Reform: Money, Politics, and the Bipartisan Campaign Reform Act*. Lanham, MD: Rowman and Littlefield.

Malecha, Gary Lee, and Daniel J. Reagan. 2004. "News Coverage of the Postreform House Majority Party Leadership: An Expanding or a Shrinking Public Image?" *Congress and the Presidency* 31: 53–76.

Maltzman, Forrest, and Lee Sigelman. 1996. "The Politics of Talk: Unconstrained Floor Time in the U.S. House of Representatives." *Journal of Politics* 58: 819–830.

Mann, Thomas E., and Norman J. Ornstein. 2006. *The Broken Branch: How Congress Is Failing America and How to Get It Back on Track*. New York: Oxford University Press.

———. 2012. *It's Even Worse Than It Looks: How the American Constitutional System Collided with the New Politics of Extremism*. New York: Basic Books.

Manning, Jennifer E. 2011. "Membership of the 112th Congress: A Profile." Congressional Research Service, R41647.

Mansbridge, Jane. 1999. "Should Blacks Represent Blacks and Women Represent Women? A Contingent 'Yes.'" *Journal of Politics* 61: 628–657.

Marshall, Bryan W., and Brandon C. Prins. 2007. "Strategic Position Taking and Presidential Influence in Congress." *Legislative Studies Quarterly* 32: 257–284.

Martinek, Wendy L., Mark Kemper, and Steven R. Van Winkle. 2002. "To Advise and Consent: The Senate and Lower Federal Court Nominations, 1977–1998." *Journal of Politics* 64: 337–361.

Martorano, Nancy. 2006. "Balancing Power: Committee System Autonomy and Legislative Organization." *Legislative Studies Quarterly* 31: 205–234.

Matland, Richard E., and Donley T. Studlar. 2004. "The Determinants of Legislative Turnover: A Cross National Study." *British Journal of Political Science* 34: 87–108.

Matthews, Donald R. 1960. *U.S. Senators and Their World.* New York: Vintage Books.

Matthews, Richard K. 1984. *The Radical Politics of Thomas Jefferson.* Lawrence: University Press of Kansas.

Mattson, Ingvar. 1995. "Private Members' Initiatives and Amendments." In *Parliaments and Majority Rule in Western Europe,* edited by Herbert Döring. New York: Campus Verlag/St. Martin's.

Mayer, Kenneth R. 2001. *With the Stroke of a Pen: Executive Orders and Presidential Power.* Princeton, NJ: Princeton University Press.

Mayer, Kenneth R., and David T. Canon. 1999. *The Dysfunctional Congress? The Individual Roots of an Institutional Dilemma.* Boulder, CO: Westview Press.

Mayhew, David R. 1974a. *Congress: The Electoral Connection.* New Haven, CT: Yale University Press.

———. 1974b. "Congressional Elections: The Case of the Vanishing Marginals." *Polity* 6: 295–317.

———. 2005. *Divided We Govern: Party Control, Lawmaking and Investigations, 1946–2002.* 2nd ed. New Haven, CT: Yale University Press.

———. 2006. "Congress as Problem Solver." In *Promoting the General Welfare: New Perspectives on Government Performance,* edited by Alan S. Gerber and Eric M. Patashnik, 219–236. Washington, DC: Brookings Institution Press.

———. 2008. *Parties and Policies: How the American Government Works.* New Haven, CT: Yale University Press.

———. 2009. "Is Congress 'The Broken Branch'?" *Boston University Law Review* 89: 357–369.

McAdams, John C., and John R. Johannes. 1988. "Congressmen, Perquisites, and Elections." *Journal of Politics* 50: 412–439.

McCarty, Nolan, Keith T. Poole, and Howard Rosenthal. 2006. *Polarized America: The Dance of Ideology and Unequal Riches.* Cambridge, MA: MIT Press.

McCarty, Nolan, and Lawrence Rothenberg. 1996. "Commitment and the Campaign Contribution Contract." *American Journal of Political Science* 40: 872–904.

McCormick, James M., and Neil J. Mitchell. 2007. "Commitments, Transnational Interests, and Congress: Who Joins the Congressional Human Rights Caucus?" *Political Research Quarterly* 60: 579–592.

McCubbins, Mathew D., and Thomas Schwartz. 1984. "Congressional Oversight Overlooked: Police Patrols Versus Fire Alarms." *American Journal of Political Science* 28: 165–179.

McKelvey, Richard D. 1976. "Intransitives in Multidimensional Voting Models and Some Implications for Agenda Control." *Journal of Economic Theory* 12: 471–482.

———. 1986. "Covering Dominance and Institution Free Properties of Social Choice" *American Journal of Political Science* 30: 283–314.

Meinke, Scott R. 2008. "Who Whips? Party Government and the Expansion of House Whip Networks." *American Politics Research* 36: 639–668.

Michels, Robert. 1949. *Political Parties: A Sociological Study of the Oligarchical Tendencies of Modern Democracy.* Glencoe, IL: Free Press.

Mikhaylov, Slava, and Alexander Herzog. 2010. "A New Database of Parliamentary Debates in Ireland, 1922–2008." Unpublished manuscript, New York University.

alism. Amherst: University of Massachusetts Press.

Miler, Kris. 2011. "The Constituency Motivations of Caucus Membership." *American Politics Research* 39: 859–884.

Milkis, Sidney, and Jerome Mileur, eds. 2005. *The Great Society and the High Tide of Liber*Mill, John Stuart. 1982. *On Liberty.* New York: Penguin.

Miller, Mark C. 2009. *The View of the Courts from the Hill: Interactions Between Congress and the Federal Judiciary.* Charlottesville: University of Virginia Press.

Miller, Susan M., and L. Marvin Overby. 2010. "Parties, Preferences, and Petitions: Discharge Behavior in the Modern House." *Legislative Studies Quarterly* 35: 187–210.

Milyo, Jeffrey, and Tim Groseclose. 1999. "The Electoral Effects of Incumbent Wealth." *Journal of Law and Economics* 42: 699–722.

Milyo, Jeffrey, and Samantha Schosberg. 2000. "Gender Bias and Selection Bias in House Elections." *Public Choice* 105: 41–59.

Moncrief, Gary F. 1999. "Recruitment and Retention in U.S. Legislatures." *Legislative Studies Quarterly* 24: 173–208.

Moncrief, Gary F., Richard G. Niemi, and Lynda W. Powell. 2004. "Time, Term Limits, and Turnover: Trends in Membership Stability in State Legislatures." *Legislative Studies Quarterly* 29: 357–381.

Mondak, Jeffrey J., Edward G. Carmines, Robert Huckfeldt, Dona-Gene Mitchell, and Scot Schraufnagel. 2007. "Does Familiarity Breed Contempt? The Impact of Information on Mass Attitudes Toward Congress." *American Journal of Political Science* 51: 34–48.

Monroe, Burt L., Michael P. Colaresi, and Kevin M. Quinn. 2008. "Fightin' Words: Lexical Feature Selection and Evaluation for Identifying the Content of Political Conflict." *Political Analysis* 16: 372–403.

Monroe, Nathan W., and Gregory Robinson. 2008. "Do Restrictive Rules Produce Non-Median Outcomes? A Theory with Evidence from the 101st–108th Congresses." *Journal of Politics* 70: 217–231.

Montesquieu, Charles de Secondat, Baron de. 1914. *The Spirit of the Laws.* Translated by Thomas Nugent. London: Bell and Sons.

Morgenthau, Hans. 1948. *Politics Among Nations: The Struggle for Power and Peace.* New York: Alfred A. Knopf.

Morris, Jonathan S. 2001. "Reexamining the Politics of Talk: Partisan Rhetoric in the 104th House." *Legislative Studies Quarterly* 26: 101–121.

Mucciaroni, Gary, and Paul J. Quirk. 2006. *Deliberative Choices: Debating Public Policy in Congress.* Chicago: University of Chicago Press.

Murphy, Walter F. 1964. *Elements of Judicial Strategy.* Chicago: University of Chicago Press.

Nacos, Brigitte L., Yaeli Bloch-Elkon, and Robert Y. Shapiro. 2011. *Selling Fear: Counterterrorism, the Media and Public Opinion.* Chicago: University of Chicago Press.

National Conference of State Legislatures. 1996. *Legislative Organization and Procedures Overview.* Washington, DC: National Conference of State Legislatures.

Neustadt, Richard M. 1990. *Presidential Power and the Modern Presidents: The Politics of Leadership.* New York: Free Press.

Nicholson-Crotty, Sean, David Peterson, and Mark Ramirez. 2009. "Dynamic Representation(s): Federal Criminal Justice Policy and an Alternative Dimension of Public Mood." *Political Behavior* 31: 629–655.

Niven, David, and Jeremy Zilber. 2001. "Do Women and Men in Congress Cultivate Different Images? Evidence from Congressional Web Sites." *Political Communication* 18: 395–405.

Nokken, Timothy P., and Keith T. Poole. 2004. "Congressional Party Defection in American History." *Legislative Studies Quarterly* 29: 545–568.

Nokken, Timothy P., and Brian R. Sala. 2002. "Institutional Evolution and the Rise of the Tuesday-Thursday Club in the House of Representatives." In *Party, Process, and Political Change in Congress: New Perspectives on the History of Congress*, edited by David W. Brady and Mathew D. McCubbins, 270–286. Stanford, CA: Stanford University Press.

Norrander, Barbara. 2010. *The Imperfect Primary: Oddities, Biases and Strengths in U.S. Presidential Nomination Politics*. New York: Routledge.

Nyhan, Brendan, Eric McGhee, John Sides, Seth Masket, and Steven Greene. 2012. "One Vote out of Step? The Effects of Salient Roll Call Votes in the 2010 Election." *American Politics Research* 40: 844–879.

Oleszek, Walter J. 2007. *Congressional Procedures and the Policy Process*. 7th ed. Washington, DC: Congressional Quarterly Press.

———. 2011a. *Congressional Procedures and the Policy Process*. 8th ed. Washington, DC: Congressional Quarterly Press.

———. 2011b. "Proposals to Reform 'Holds' in the Senate." Congressional Research Service, RL 31685. August 31.

Organski, A. F. K. 1958. *World Politics*. New York: Alfred K. Knopf.

Owens, John, and J. Mark Wrighton. 2008. "Partisan Polarization, Procedural Control, and Partisan Emulation in the U.S. House: An Examination of Rules Restrictiveness over Time." Paper presented to the History of Congress conference, Washington, DC.

Owens, Ryan J. 2010. "The Separation of Powers, Judicial Independence, and Strategic Agenda Setting." *American Journal of Political Science* 54: 412–427.

Palazzolo, Daniel J. 1999. *Done Deal? The Politics of the 1997 Budget Agreement*. Chatham, NJ: Chatham House.

Pareto, Vilfredo. 1966. *Vilfredo Pareto: Sociological Writings*. With an introduction by S. E. Finer. New York: Praeger.

Parker, David C. W., and Matthew Dull, 2009. "Divided We Quarrel: The Politics of Congressional Investigations, 1947–2004." *Legislative Studies Quarterly* 34: 319–345.

Parker, David C. W., and Craig Goodman. 2009. "Making a Good Impression: Resource Allocation, Home Styles, and Washington Work." *Legislative Studies Quarterly* 34: 493–524.

Parker, Edward G. 1857. *The Golden Age of American Oratory*. Boston: Whittemore, Niles, and Hall.

Parker, Glenn R. 1980. "Sources of Change in Congressional District Attentiveness." *American Journal of Political Science* 24: 115–124.

Patzelt, Werner J. 1999. "Recruitment and Retention in Western European Parliament." *Legislative Studies Quarterly* 24: 239–279.

Peters, Ronald M., Jr., and Cindy Simon Rosenthal. 2010. *Speaker Nancy Pelosi and the New American Politics*. New York: Oxford University Press.

Petersoe, R. Eric, Parker H. Reynolds, and Amber Hope Wilhelm. 2010. "House of Representatives and Senate Staff Levels in Member, Committee, Leadership and Other Offices, 1977–2010." Congressional Research Service, R41366.

Peterson, Merrill D. 1987. *The Great Triumvirate: Webster, Clay, and Calhoun*. New York: Oxford University Press.

Phillips, Anne, 1995. *Politics of Presence*. New York: Clarendon.

Pitkin, Hannah Fenichel. 1967. *The Concept of Representation*. Berkeley: University of California Press.

Polsby, Nelson W. 1968. "Institutionalization of the United States House of Representatives." *American Political Science Review* 62: 144–168.

Polsby, Nelson W., Miriam Gallagher, and Barry Spencer Rundquist. 1969. "The Growth of the Seniority System in the U.S. House of Representatives." *American Political Science Review* 63: 787–807.

Poole, Keith T. 2007. "Changing Minds? Not in Congress!" *Public Choice* 131: 435–451.

Poole, Keith T., and Howard Rosenthal. 1997. *Congress: A Political Economic History of Roll-Call Voting*. New York: Oxford University Press.

Powell, Richard J. 2007. "Executive-Legislative Relations." In *Institutional Change in American Politics: The Case of Term Limits*, edited by Bruce Cain, R. Niemi and K. Kurtz, 134–147. Ann Arbor: University of Michigan Press.

Primo, David M., and James M. Snyder Jr. 2010. "Party Strength, the Personal Vote, and Government Spending." *American Journal of Political Science* 54: 354–370.

Prior, Markus. 2006. "The Incumbent in the Living Room: The Rise of Television and the Incumbency Advantage in U.S. House Elections." *Journal of Politics* 68: 657–673.

Quinn, Kevin M., Burt L. Monroe, Michael Colaresi, Michael H. Crespin, and Dragomir R. Radev. 2010. "How to Analyze Political Attention with Minimal Assumptions and Costs." *American Journal of Political Science* 54: 209–228.

Quirk, Paul J., and Sarah A. Binder, eds. 2005. *The Legislative Branch*. New York: Oxford University Press.

Ramirez, Mark D. 2009. "The Dynamics of Partisan Conflict on Congressional Approval." *American Journal of Political Science* 53: 681–694.

Rawls, John. 1997. "The Idea of Public Reason Revisited." *University of Chicago Law Review* 94: 765–807.

Rehfeld, Andrew. 2005. *The Concept of Constituency: Political Representation, Democratic Legitimacy, and Institutional Design*. New York: Cambridge University Press.

Ridout, Travis N., and Kathleen Searles. 2011. "It's My Campaign I'll Cry if I Want To: How and When Campaigns Use Emotional Appeals." *Political Psychology* 32: 439–458.

Rieselbach, Leroy N. 1994. *Congressional Reform: The Changing Modern Congress*. Washington, DC: Congressional Quarterly Press.

Roberts, Jason M. 2010. "The Development of Special Orders and Special Rules in the U.S. House, 1881–1937." *Legislative Studies Quarterly* 35: 307–326.

Roberts, Jason M., and Lauren Cohen Bell. 2008. "Scoring the Senate: Scorecards, Parties, and Roll-Call Votes." In *Why Not Parties? Party Effects in the United States Senate*, edited by Nathan W. Monroe, Jason M. Roberts, and David W. Rohde, 52–70. Chicago: University of Chicago Press.

Robinson, Michael J. 1981. "Three Faces of Congressional Media." In *The New Congress*, edited by Thomas Mann and Norman J. Ornstein, 55–98. Washington, DC: American Enterprise Institute.

Rocca, Michael S. 2007. "Nonlegislative Debate in the House of Representatives." *American Politics Research* 35: 489–505.

Rohde, David W. 1991. *Parties and Leaders in the Postreform House*. Chicago: University of Chicago Press.

Rosenthal, Alan. 1999. "The Good Legislature." *State Legislatures* July/August: 48–51.

Rottinghaus, Brandon, and Daniel E. Bergan. 2011. "The Politics of Requesting Appointments: Congressional Requests in the Appointment and Nomination Process." *Political Research Quarterly* 64: 31–44.

Rousseau, Jean-Jacques. 1968. *The Social Contract*. New York: Penguin.

Rudalevige, Andrew. 2005. *The New Imperial Presidency: Renewing Presidential Power After Watergate*. Ann Arbor: University of Michigan Press.

Rudolph, Thomas J. 2002. "The Economic Sources of Congressional Approval." *Legislative Studies Quarterly* 27: 577–599.

———. 2003. "Who's Responsible for the Economy? The Formation and Consequences of Responsibility Attributions." *American Journal of Political Science* 47: 697–712.

Rundquist, Barry S., and Thomas M. Carsey. 2002. *Congress and Defense Spending: The Distributive Politics of Military Procurement*. Norman: University of Oklahoma Press.

Russell, Peter H., and David M. O'Brien. 2001. *Judicial Independence in the Age of Democracy: Critical Perspectives from Around the World*. Charlottesville: University of Virginia Press.

Rybicki, Elizabeth. 2010. "Filling the Amendment Tree in the Senate." *Newsletter of the Legislative Studies Section of the American Political Science Association*, January.

Saalfeld, Thomas. 1995. "On Dogs and Whips: Recorded Votes." In *Parliaments and Majority Rule in Western Europe*, edited by Herbert Döring, 528–565. New York: St. Martin's Press.

Savage, Charlie. 2007. *Takeover: The Return of the Imperial Presidency and the Subversion of American Democracy*. Boston: Little, Brown.

Schaffner, Brian F. 2011. "Party Polarization." In *The Oxford Handbook of Congress*, edited by Eric Schickler and Frances E. Lee, 527–549. New York: Oxford University Press.

Schickler, Eric. 2000. "Institutional Change in the House of Representatives, 1867–1998: A Test of Partisan and Ideological Power Balance Models." *American Political Science Review* 94: 267–288.

———. 2001. *Disjointed Pluralism: Institutional Innovation and the Development of the U.S. Congress*. Princeton, NJ: Princeton University Press.

Schiller, Wendy. 2000. *Partners and Rivals: Representation in U.S. Senate Delegations*. Princeton, NJ: Princeton University Press.

Schlesinger, Arthur M., Jr. 1973. *The Imperial Presidency*. Boston: Houghton-Mifflin.

Schlesinger, Joseph A. 1966. *Ambition in Politics: Political Careers in the United States*. Chicago: Rand McNally.

Schweizer, Peter. 2011. *Throw Them All Out*. New York: Houghton Mifflin.

Segal, Jeffrey A., Chad Westerland, and Stephanie Lindquist. 2011. "Congress, the Supreme Court, and Judicial Review: Testing a Constitutional Separation of Powers Model." *American Journal of Political Science* 55: 89–104.

Serafino, Nina M. 2007. "Peacekeeping and Related Stability Operations: Issues of U.S. Military Involvement." Congressional Research Service, RL33557.

Serra, George, and David Moon. 1994. "Casework, Issue Positions, and Voting in Congressional Elections: A District Analysis." *Journal of Politics* 56: 200–213.

Shane, Peter M. 2009. *Madison's Nightmare: How Executive Power Threatens American Democracy*. Chicago: University of Chicago Press.

Shepsle, Kenneth A., and Barry R. Weingast. 1987. "The Institutional Foundations of Committee Power." *American Political Science Review* 81: 85–104.

Shor, Boris, and Nolan M. McCarty. 2011. "The Ideological Mapping of American Legislatures." *American Political Science Review* 105: 530–551.

Shugart, Matthew S., and Scott Mainwaring. 1997. "Presidentialism and Democracy in Latin America: Rethinking the Terms of the Debate." In *Presidentialism and Democracy in Latin*

America, edited by Scott Mainwaring and Matthew S. Shugart, 12–54. New York: Cambridge University Press.

Siegel, Neil. 2010. "Interring the Rhetoric of Judicial Activism." *DePaul Law Review* 59: 555–599.

Sinclair, Barbara. 2009. "Question: What's Wrong with Congress? Answer: It's a Democratic Legislature." *Boston University Law Review* 89: 387–397.

———. 2012. *Unorthodox Lawmaking*. 4th ed. Washington, DC: Congressional Quarterly Press.

Singh, Robert. 1997. *The Congressional Black Caucus: Racial Politics in the U.S. Congress*. Thousand Oaks, CA: Sage.

Skinner, Richard M. 2007. *More Than Money: Interest Group Action in Congressional Elections*. Lanham, MD: Rowman and Littlefield.

Skocpol, Theda, and Vanessa Williamson. 2012. *The Tea Party and the Remaking of American Conservatism*. New York: Oxford University Press.

Slapin, Jonathan B., and Sven-Oliver Proksch. 2008. "A Scaling Model for Estimating Time-Series Party Positions from Texts." *American Journal of Political Science* 52: 705–722.

———. 2010. "Look Who's Talking: Parliamentary Debate in the European Union." *European Union Politics* 11: 333–357.

Smith, Keith. 2003. "The Growth of Congressional Oversight." Paper presented at the annual meeting of the American Political Science Association, Philadelphia, PA.

Smith, Steven S. 1989. *Call to Order: Floor Politics in the House and Senate*. Washington, DC: Brookings Institution Press.

———. 2010. "The Procedural Senate, 1960–2010." Unpublished manuscript, Washington University, St. Louis, MO.

Smith, Steven S., and Marcus Flathman. 1989. "Managing the Senate Floor: Complex Unanimous Consent Agreements Since the 1950s." *Legislative Studies Quarterly* 14: 349–392.

Smith, Steven S., James L. Gibson, and Hong Min Park. 2011. "Party, Policy, and Procedure: Public Attitudes and the Senate Filibuster." Unpublished manuscript, Washington University, St. Louis, MO.

Snyder, James M., Jr., and Tim Groseclose. 2000. "Estimating Party Influence in Congressional Roll Call Voting." *American Journal of Political Science* 44: 193–211.

Snyder, James M., Jr., and David Stromberg. 2010. "Press Coverage and Political Accountability." *Journal of Political Economy* 118: 355–408.

Sobel, Richard. 1998. "Portraying American Public Opinion Toward the Bosnia Crisis." *International Journal of Press/Politics* 3: 16–33.

Sollenberger, Mitchel A., and Mark J. Rozell. 2012. *The President's Czars: Undermining Congress and the Constitution*. Lawrence: University Press of Kansas.

Spitzer, Robert J. 1988. *The Presidential Veto: Touchstone of the American Presidency*. Albany: SUNY Press.

Squire, Peverill. 2008. "The State Wealth–Legislative Compensation Effect." *Canadian Journal of Political Science* 41:1–18.

Squire, Peverill, and Keith E. Hamm. 2005. *101 Chambers: Congress, State Legislatures, and the Future of Legislative Studies*. Columbus: Ohio State University Press.

Stathis, Stephen W. 2003. *Landmark Legislation, 1774–2002*. Washington, DC: Congressional Quarterly Press.

Staudt, Nancy J., Rene Lindstaedt, and Jason O'Connor. 2007. "Judicial Decisions as Legislation: Congressional Oversight of Supreme Court Tax Cases, 1954–2005." *New York University Law Review* 82: 1340–1402.

Steen, Jennifer A. 2006a. "The Impact of State Legislative Term Limits on the Supply of Congressional Candidates." *State Politics and Policy Quarterly* 6: 430–447.

———. 2006b. *Self-Financed Candidates in Congressional Elections*. Ann Arbor: University of Michigan Press.

Stein, Robert M., and Kenneth N. Bickers. 1995. *Perpetuating the Pork Barrel: Policy Subsystems and American Democracy*. New York: Cambridge University Press.

Steiner, Jürg, André Bächtiger, Markus Spörndli, and Marco R. Steenbergen. 2004. *Deliberative Politics in Action: Analyzing Parliamentary Discourse*. New York: Cambridge University Press.

Steinhauer, Jennifer. 2011a. "In Siding with Leaders, a Freshman Finds Her Voice." *New York Times*, August 10, p. A14.

Steinhauer, Jennifer. 2011b. "Congress Nearing End of Session Where Partisan Input Impeded Output." *New York Times*, September 19, p. A21.

Steuerle, C. Eugene. 2008. *Contemporary U.S. Tax Policy*. 2nd ed. Washington, DC: Urban Institute Press.

Stevens Arthur G., Jr., Arthur H. Miller, and Thomas E. Mann. 1974. "Mobilization of Liberal Strength in the House, 1955–1970: The Democratic Study Group." *American Political Science Review* 68: 667–681.

Stewart, James B. 1997. *Blood Sport: The President and His Adversaries*. New York: Simon and Schuster.

Stid, Daniel D. 1998. *The President as Statesman: Woodrow Wilson and the Constitution*. Lawrence: University Press of Kansas.

Stiglitz, Joseph E., and Linda J. Bilmes. 2008. *The Three Trillion Dollar War: The True Cost of the Iraq Conflict*. New York: W. W. Norton.

Stimson, James A. 1991. *Public Opinion in America: Moods, Cycles, and Swings*. Boulder, CO: Westview Press.

———. 2004. *Tides of Consent: How Public Opinion Shapes American Politics*. New York: Cambridge University Press.

Stimson, James A., Michael B. MacKuen, and Robert S. Erikson. 1995. "Dynamic Representation." *American Political Science Review* 89:543–565.

Stone, Walter J., Sarah Fulton, Cherie Maestas, and L. Sandy Maisel. 2010. "Incumbency Reconsidered: Prospects, Strategic Retirement, and Incumbent Quality in U.S. House Elections." *Journal of Politics* 72: 178–190.

Stone, Walter J., and L. Sandy Maisel. 2003. "The Not-So-Simple Calculus of Winning: Potential U.S. House Candidates' Nomination and General Election Chances." *Journal of Politics* 65: 951–977.

Stonecash, Jeffrey M., and Mark D. Brewer, and Mack D. Mariani. 2003. *Diverging Parties: Social Change, Realignment, and Party Polarization*. New York: Westview Press.

Strahan, Randall W. 2007. *Leading Representatives: The Agency of Leaders in the Politics of the U.S. House*. Baltimore: Johns Hopkins University Press.

Stratmann, Thomas. 2000. "Congressional Voting over Legislative Careers: Shifting Positions and Changing Constraints." *American Political Science Review* 94: 665–676.

Struble, Robert, Jr. 1979. "House Turnover and the Principle of Rotation." *Political Science Quarterly* 94: 649–667.

Sulkin, Tracy. 2011. *The Legislative Legacy of Congressional Campaigns*. New York: Cambridge University Press.

Swain, John F., Stephen A. Borelli, Sean F. Evans, and Brian C. Reed. 2000. "A New Look at Turnover in the U.S. House of Representatives, 1789–1998." *American Politics Quarterly* 28: 435–457.

Swers, Michele L. 2002. *The Difference Women Make: The Policy Impact of Women in Congress.* Chicago: University of Chicago Press.

Swift, Elaine D. 1996. *The Making of the American Senate: Reconstitutive Changes in Congress, 1787–1841.* Ann Arbor: University of Michigan Press.

Taft, William Howard. 1895. "Criticisms of the Federal Judiciary." *American Law Review* 29: 641–674.

Taibbi, Matt. 2006. "The Worst Congress Ever: How Our National Legislature Has Become a Stable of Thieves and Perverts—in Five Easy Steps." *Rolling Stone*, November 2, 46–84.

Taylor, Andrew J. 1998. "Explaining Government Productivity." *American Politics Quarterly* 26: 439–458.

———. 2006. "Size, Power, and Electoral Systems: Exogenous Determinants of Legislative Procedural Choice." *Legislative Studies Quarterly* 31: 323–345.

———. 2012a. *The Floor in Congressional Life.* Ann Arbor: University of Michigan Press.

———. 2012b. "When Congress Asserts Itself: Examining Legislative Challenges to Executive Power." *The Forum*, forthcoming.

Taylor, Frederick Winslow. 1998. *The Principles of Scientific Management.* Norcross, GA: Institute of Industrial Engineers.

Theiss-Morse, Elizabeth. 2009. *Who Counts as an American? The Boundaries of National Identity.* New York: Cambridge University Press.

Theriault, Sean M. 2008. *Party Polarization in Congress.* New York: Cambridge University Press.

———. 2009. "Procedural Polarization in Congress." Paper presented to the annual meeting of the Midwest Political Science Association, Chicago.

Theriault, Sean M., and David W. Rohde. 2011. "The Gingrich Senators and Party Polarization in the U.S. Senate." *Journal of Politics* 73: 1011–1024.

Tiersky, Ronald. 2000. *François Mitterrand: The Last French President.* New York: Palgrave Macmillan.

Tocqueville, Alexis de. 1945. *Democracy in America.* With an introduction by Alan Ryan. New York: Alfred A. Knopf.

Tomasky, Michael. 2006. "Party in Search of a Nation." *The American Prospect* 17: 20–28.

Toshkov, Dimiter. 2011. "Public Opinion and Policy Output in the European Union: A Lost Relationship." *European Union Politics* 12: 169–191.

Treier, Shawn. 2011. "Comparing Ideal Points Across Institutions and Time." *American Politics Research* 39: 804–831.

Trilling, Lionel. 1950. *The Liberal Imagination: Essays on Literature and Society.* New York: Harcourt Brace Jovanovich.

Truman, David B. 1959. *The Governmental Process: Political Interests and Public Opinion.* New York: Knopf.

Tsebelis, George. 1999. "Veto Players and Law Production in Parliamentary Democracies: An Empirical Analysis." *American Political Science Review* 93: 591–608.

Tulis, Jeffrey K. 1988. *The Rhetorical Presidency.* Princeton, NJ: Princeton University Press.

Ura, Joseph Daniel, and Patrick C. Wohlfarth. 2010. "'An Appeal to the People': Public Opinion and Congressional Support for the Supreme Court." *Journal of Politics* 72: 939–956.

Urbinati, Nadia. 2006. *Representative Democracy: Principles and Genealogy.* Chicago: University of Chicago Press.

US Congress Joint Committee on the Organization of Congress. 1993. *Final Report on the Organization of Congress*, December. Washington, DC: Government Printing Office.

Uslaner, Eric M. 1993. *The Decline of Comity in Congress*. Ann Arbor: University of Michigan Press.

Vander Wielen, Ryan, and Steven S. Smith. 2011. "Majority Party Bias in U.S. Congressional Conference Committees." *Congress and the Presidency* 38: 271–300.

Victor, Jennifer Nicoll. 2011. "Legislating Versus Campaigning: The Legislative Behavior of Higher Office Seekers." *American Politics Research* 39: 3–31.

Waldron, Jeremy. 2009. "Representative Lawmaking." *Boston University Law Review* 89: 335–355.

Walling, J. D. 2006. "Divided Government and Oversight: Utilization of the Congressional Watchdog." Paper presented to the annual meeting of the Midwest Political Science Association, Chicago.

Walzer, Michael. 1977. *Just and Unjust Wars*. New York: Basic.

Warrick, Joby, and Walter Pincus. 2008. "Bush Inflated Threat from Iraq's Banned Weapons, Report Says." *Washington Post*, June 6, p. A3.

Watson, Richard A. 1987. "Origins and Early Development of the Veto Power." *Presidential Studies Quarterly* 17: 401–412.

Wawro, Gregory J. 2000. *Legislative Entrepreneurship in the U.S. House of Representatives*. Ann Arbor: University of Michigan Press.

Wawro, Gregory J., and Eric Schickler. 2006. *Filibuster: Obstruction and Lawmaking in the U.S. Senate*. Princeton, NJ: Princeton University Press.

Weber, Max. 1947. *The Theory of Social and Economic Organization*. New York: Oxford University Press.

Weingast, Barry W., and William J. Marshall. 1988. "The Industrial Organization of Congress, or, Why Legislatures, Like Firms, Are Not Organized as Markets." *Journal of Political Economy* 96: 132–163.

Wert, Justin J. 2006. *Habeas Corpus in America: The Politics of Individual Rights*. Lawrence: University Press of Kansas.

Westen, Drew. 2007. *The Political Brain: The Role of Emotion in Deciding the Fate of the Nation*. New York: PublicAffairs.

White, William S. 1957. *Citadel: The Story of the U.S. Senate*. New York: Harper Collins.

Wildavsky, Aaron. 1966. "The Two Presidencies." *Transaction* 4: 7–14.

Williams, Melissa, 1998. *Voice, Trust, and Memory: Marginalized Groups and the Failings of Liberal Representation*. Princeton, NJ: Princeton University.

Wills, Garry. 1999. *A Necessary Evil: A History of American Distrust of Government*. New York: Simon and Schuster.

Wilson, Woodrow. 1901. *Congressional Government*. Boston: Houghton Mifflin.

Wirls, Daniel. 2007. "The 'Golden Age' Senate and Floor Debate in the Antebellum Congress." *Legislative Studies Quarterly* 32: 193–222.

Wirls, Daniel, and Stephen Wirls. 2004. *The Invention of the United States Senate*. Baltimore: Johns Hopkins University Press.

Wiseman, Alan E. 2004. "Tests of Vote-Buyer Theories of Coalition Formation in Legislatures." *Political Research Quarterly* 57: 441–450.

Wlezien, Christopher. 2004. "Patterns of Representation: Dynamics of Public Preferences and Policy." *Journal of Politics* 66: 1–24.

Wolak, Jennifer. 2007. "Strategic Retirements: The Influence of Public Preferences on Voluntary Departures from Congress." *Legislative Studies Quarterly* 32: 285–308.

Wolf, Richard. 1994. "'Looks Like a Majority'—Gingrich." *USA Today*, November 9, p. 4A.

Wolfensberger, Donald. 2003. "The Motion to Recommit in the House: The Creation, Evisceration, and Restoration of a Minority Right." Paper presented to the History of Congress Conference, Cambridge, MA.

Yang, John E. 1997. "House Reprimands, Penalizes Speaker." *Washington Post*, January 22, p. A1.

Young, James Sterling. 1966. *The Washington Community, 1800–1828*. New York: Columbia University Press.

Young, Ross, Richard Cracknell, Edmund Tettah, Gini Griffin, and Dave Brown. 2003. "Parliamentary Questions, Debate Contributions and Participation in Commons Divisions: Statistics for Session 2001–02." UK House of Commons, Research Paper 03/32.

Zelizer, Julian E. 2004. *On Capitol Hill: The Struggle to Reform Congress and Its Consequences*. New York: Cambridge University Press.

Zernike, Kate. 2010. *Boiling Mad: Inside Tea Party America*. New York: Times Books.

Ziobrowski, Alan J., Ping Chen, James W. Boyd, and Brigitte J. Ziobrowski. 2004. "Abnormal Returns from the Common Stock Investments of the U.S. Senate." *Journal of Financial and Quantitative Analysis* 39: 660–676.

INDEX